HARRY MOON

Table of Contents

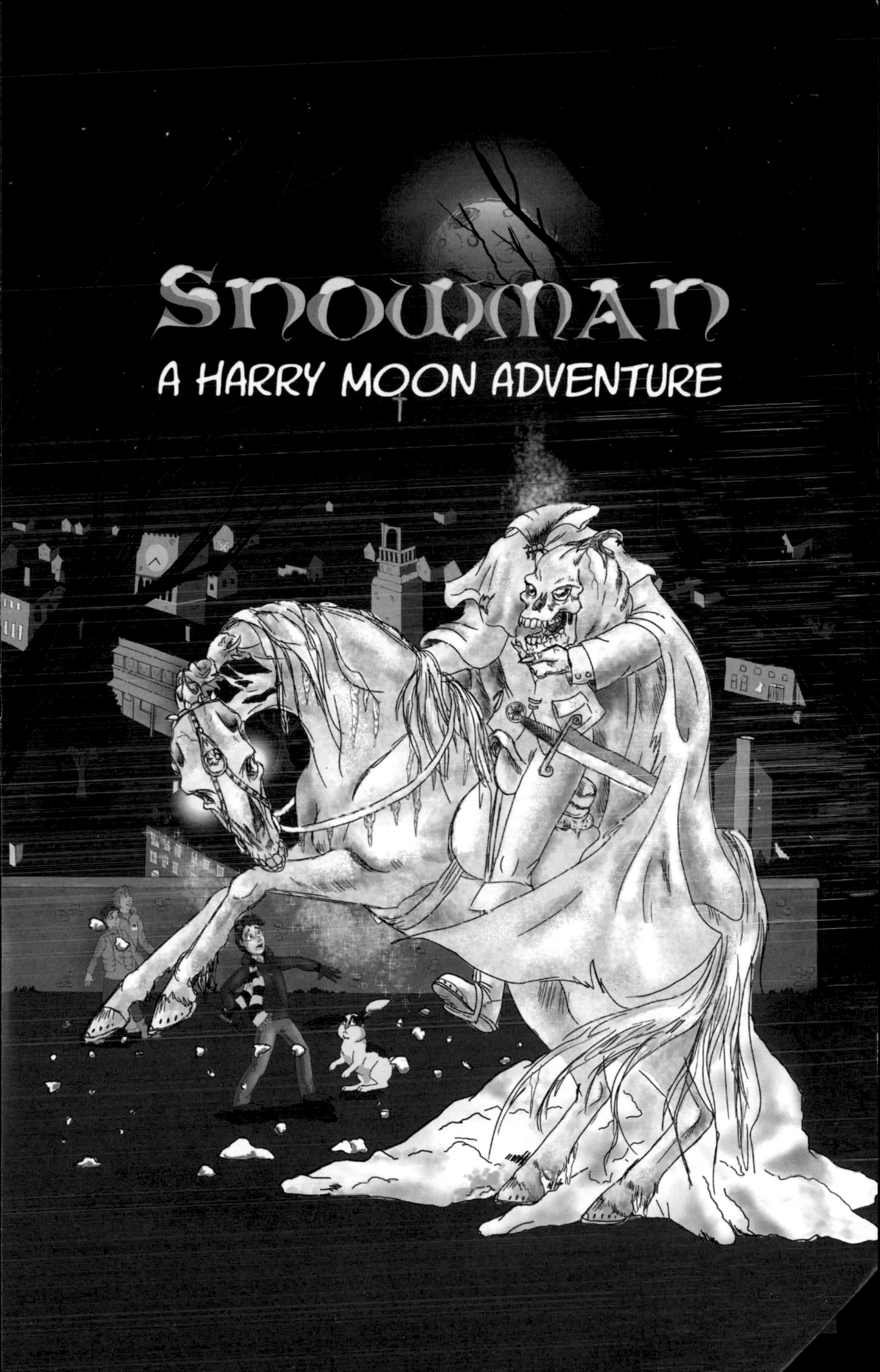
SNOWMAN
A HARRY MOON ADVENTURE

Based on the creation by
MARK ANDREW POE

Illustrated by
REBECCA P. MINOR

Written by
JOYCE MAGNIN

Storytellers
DAVID PAUL KIRKPATRICK
THOM BLACK

SNOWMAN (Harry Moon)
by Mark Andrew Poe
© Copyright 2017 by Mark Andrew Poe.
All rights reserved.

Creative consultant
MEGAN BOLEY

Rabbit Publishers
1624 W. Northwest Highway
Arlington Heights, IL 60004

Book Design by
PAUL LEWIS

ISBN: 978-1-943785-10-0

10 9 8 7 6 5 4 3 2 1

1. Fiction - Action and Adventure
2. Children's Fiction
First Edition
Printed in U.S.A.

Graphic consultant
SCOTT MINOR

Fan collaborators
CAIDEN RIECKS
DECLAN BLACK
BAILEY BLACK

Marketing Consultants
DIAMOND DISTRIBUTORS

Family, Friends & Foes
in Sleepy Hollow

HARRY MOON

Harry is the thirteen-year-old hero of Sleepy Hollow. He is a gifted magician who is learning to use his abilities and understand what it means to possess the real magic.

An unlikely hero, Harry is shorter than his classmates and has a shock of inky, black hair. He loves his family and his town. Along with his friend Rabbit, Harry is determined to bring Sleepy Hollow back to its true and wholesome glory.

RABBIT

Now you see him. Now you
don't. Rabbit is Harry Moon's
friend. Some see him.
Most can't.

Rabbit is a large, black-
and-white, lop-eared, Har-
lequin rabbit. As Harry has
discovered, having a friend
like Rabbit has its conse-
quences. Never stingy with
advice and counsel,
Rabbit always has Harry's
back as Harry battles the evil
that has overtaken
Sleepy Hollow.

HONEY MOON

She's a ten-year-old, sassy
spitfire. And she's Harry's
little sister. Honey likes to say
she goes where she is needed,
and sometimes this takes her
into the path of danger.

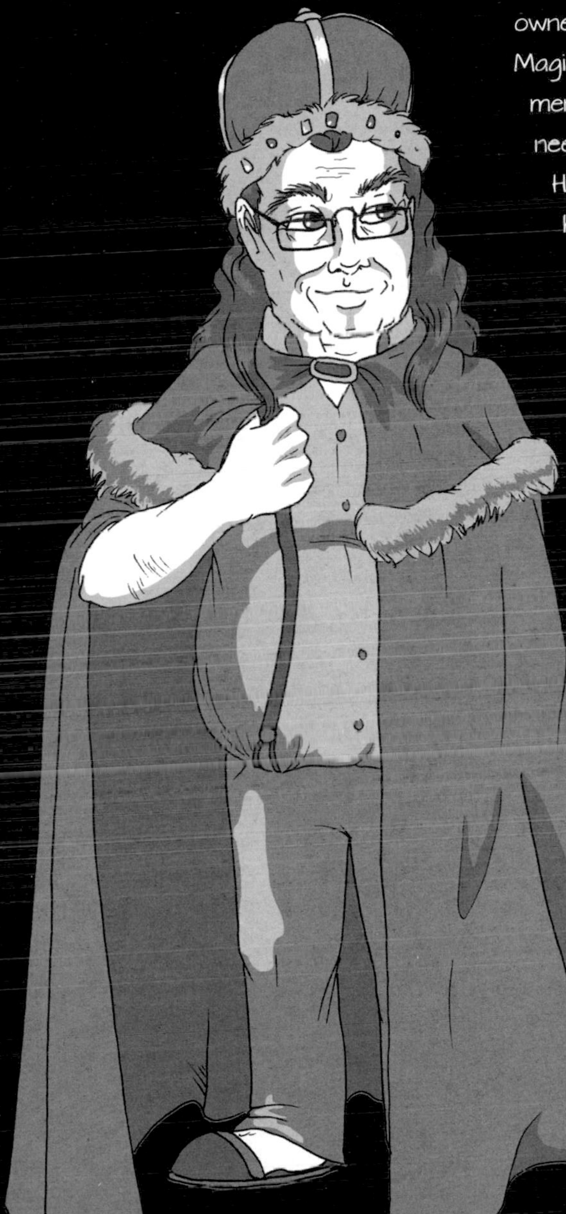

SAMSON DUPREE

Samson is the enigmatic owner of the Sleepy Hollow Magic Shoppe. He is Harry's mentor and friend. When needed, Samson teaches Harry new tricks and helps him understand his gift of magic.

Samson arranged for Rabbit to become Harry's sidekick and friend. Samson is a timeless, eccentric man who wears purple robes, red slippers, and a gold crown. Sometimes, Samson shows up in mysterious ways. He even appeared to Harry's mother shortly after Harry's birth.

MARY MOON

Strong, and fair, Mary Moon is Harry and Honey's mother. She is also mother to two-year-old Harvest. Mary is married to John Moon.

Mary is learning to understand Harry and his destiny. So far, she is doing a good job letting Harry fight life's battles. She's grateful that Rabbit has come alongside to support and counsel her. But like all moms, Mary often finds it difficult to let her children walk their own paths. Mary is a nurse at Sleepy Hollow Hospital.

JOHN MOON

John is the dad. He's a bit of a nerd. He works as an IT professional, and sometimes he thinks he would love it if his children followed in his footsteps. But he respects that Harry, Honey, and possibly Harvest will need to go their own way.

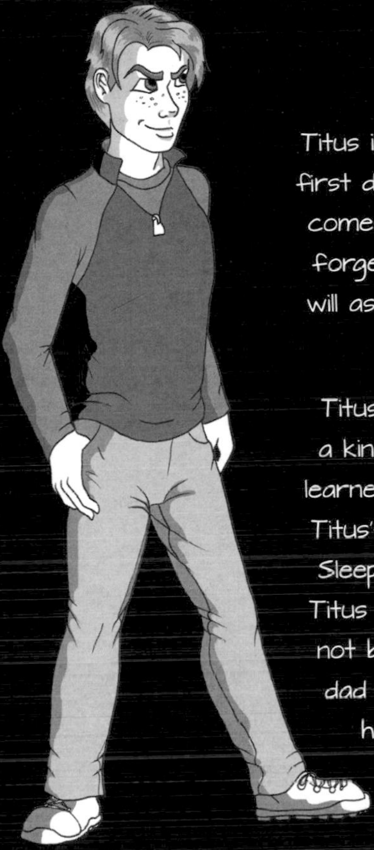

TITUS KLIGORE

Titus is the mayor's son. He is a bully of the first degree but also quite conflicted when it comes to Harry. The two have managed to forge a tentative friendship, although Titus will assert his bully strength on Harry from time to time.

Titus is big. He towers over Harry. But in a kind of David vs. Goliath way, Harry has learned which tools are best to counteract Titus's assaults while most of the Sleepy Hollow kids fear him. Titus would probably rather not be a bully, but with a dad like Maximus Kligore, he feels trapped in the role.

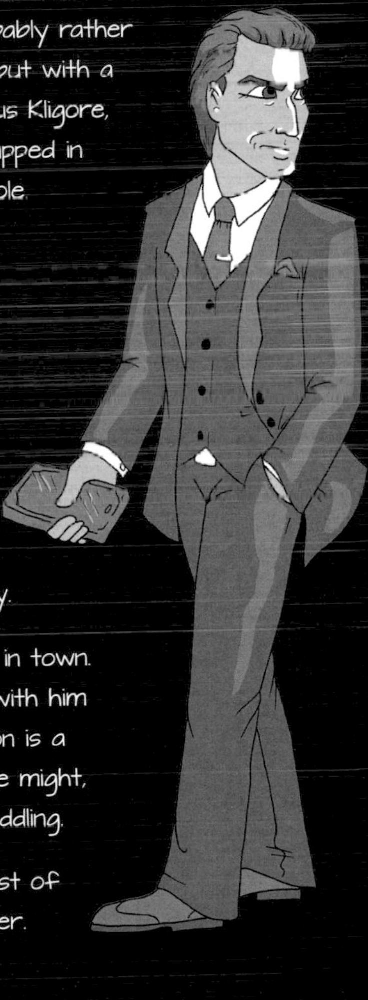

MAXIMUS KLIGORE

The epitome of evil, nastiness, and greed, Maximus Kligore is the mayor of Sleepy Hollow. To bring in the cash, Maximus turned the town into the nightmarish Halloween attraction it is today.

He commissions the evil-tinged celebrations in town. Maximus is planning to take Sleepy Hollow with him to Hell. But will he? He knows Harry Moon is a threat to his dastardly ways, but try as he might, he has yet to rid himself of Harry's meddling.

Kligore lives on Folly Farm and owns most of the town, including the town newspaper.

MANY MOONS AGO, A SLY AND EVIL MAYOR ENLISTED THE POWERS OF
DARKNESS AND TRANSFORMED THE ONCE QUIET, UNIMPORTANT TOWN
OF SLEEPY HOLLOW, MASSACHUSETTS INTO "SPOOKY TOWN."

IN SPOOKY TOWN, EVERY DAY IS HALLOWEEN NIGHT, AND NOW,
SLEEPY HOLLOW IS ONE OF THE NATION'S MOST CELEBRATED SCARY
DESTINATIONS. BUT IT ISN'T ENOUGH FOR THIS VILE MAYOR WHO
ALWAYS WANTS MORE. MORE PRESTIGE, MORE POWER.

MORE PRESS COVERAGE.

AS HIS THIRST FOR NATIONAL ATTENTION GROWS, THE MAYOR
AND HIS CONNIVING COHORTS MAKE YET ANOTHER MONSTROUS
ATTEMPT TO RULE THE DARKEST OF NIGHTS AS THE SNOW FALLS
IN SLEEPY HOLLOW!

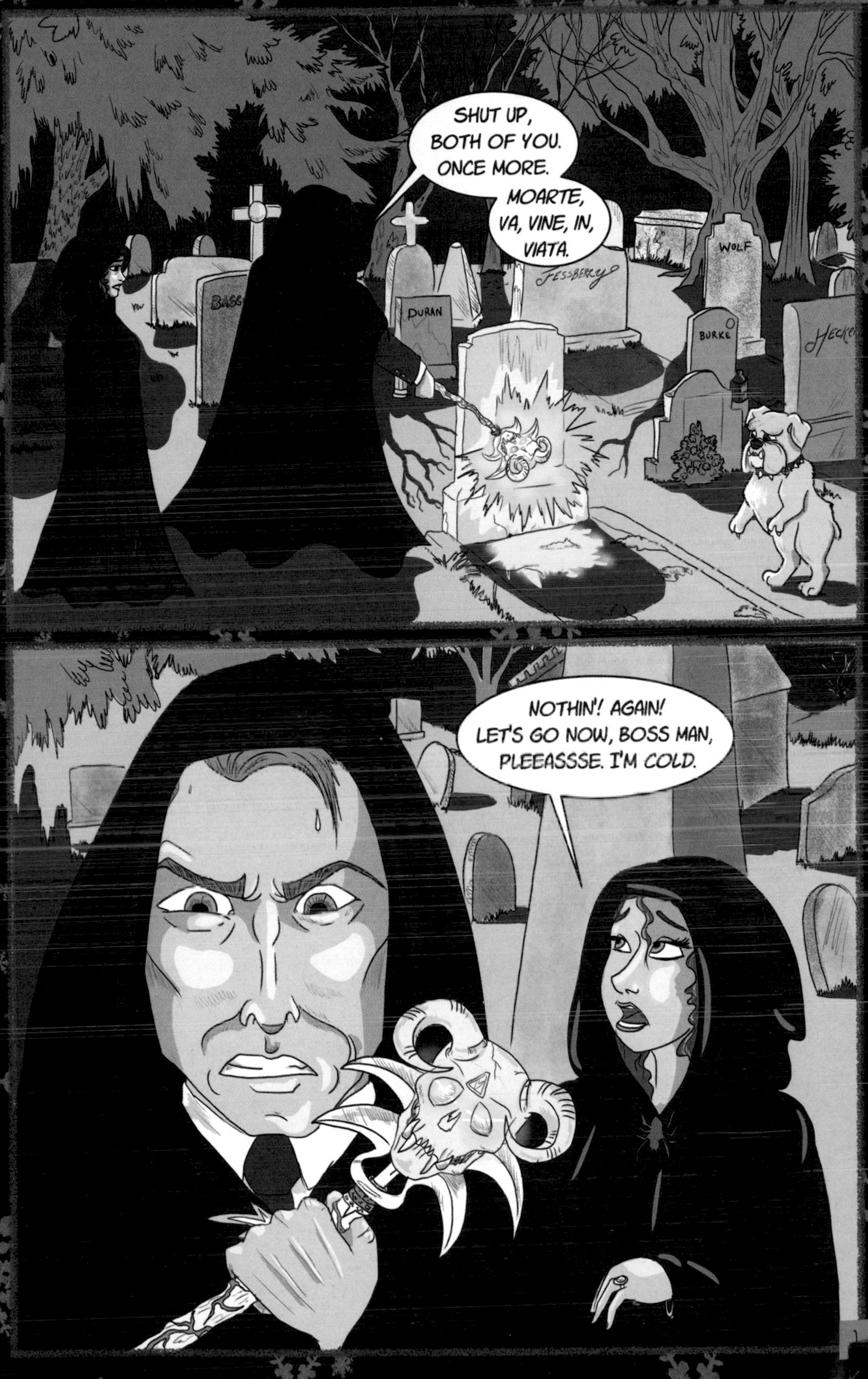
SHUT UP, BOTH OF YOU. ONCE MORE.
MOARTE, VA, VINE, IN, VIATA.
FESSBERRY
WOLF
DURAN
BURKE
NOTHIN'! AGAIN! LET'S GO NOW, BOSS MAN, PLEEASSSE. I'M COLD.

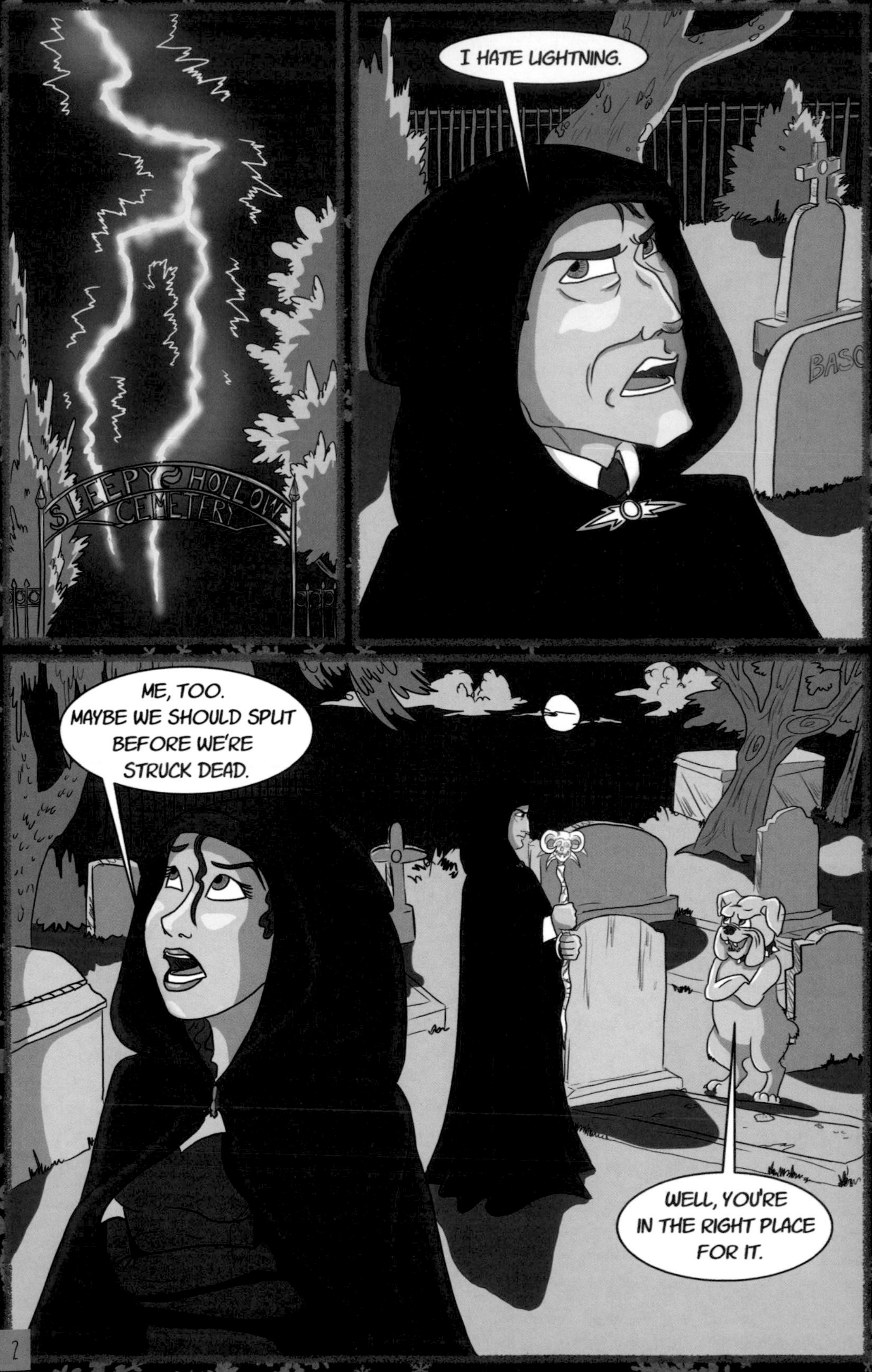
SLEEPY HOLLOW CEMETERY
I HATE LIGHTNING.
BASC
ME, TOO. MAYBE WE SHOULD SPLIT BEFORE WE'RE STRUCK DEAD.
WELL, YOU'RE IN THE RIGHT PLACE FOR IT.

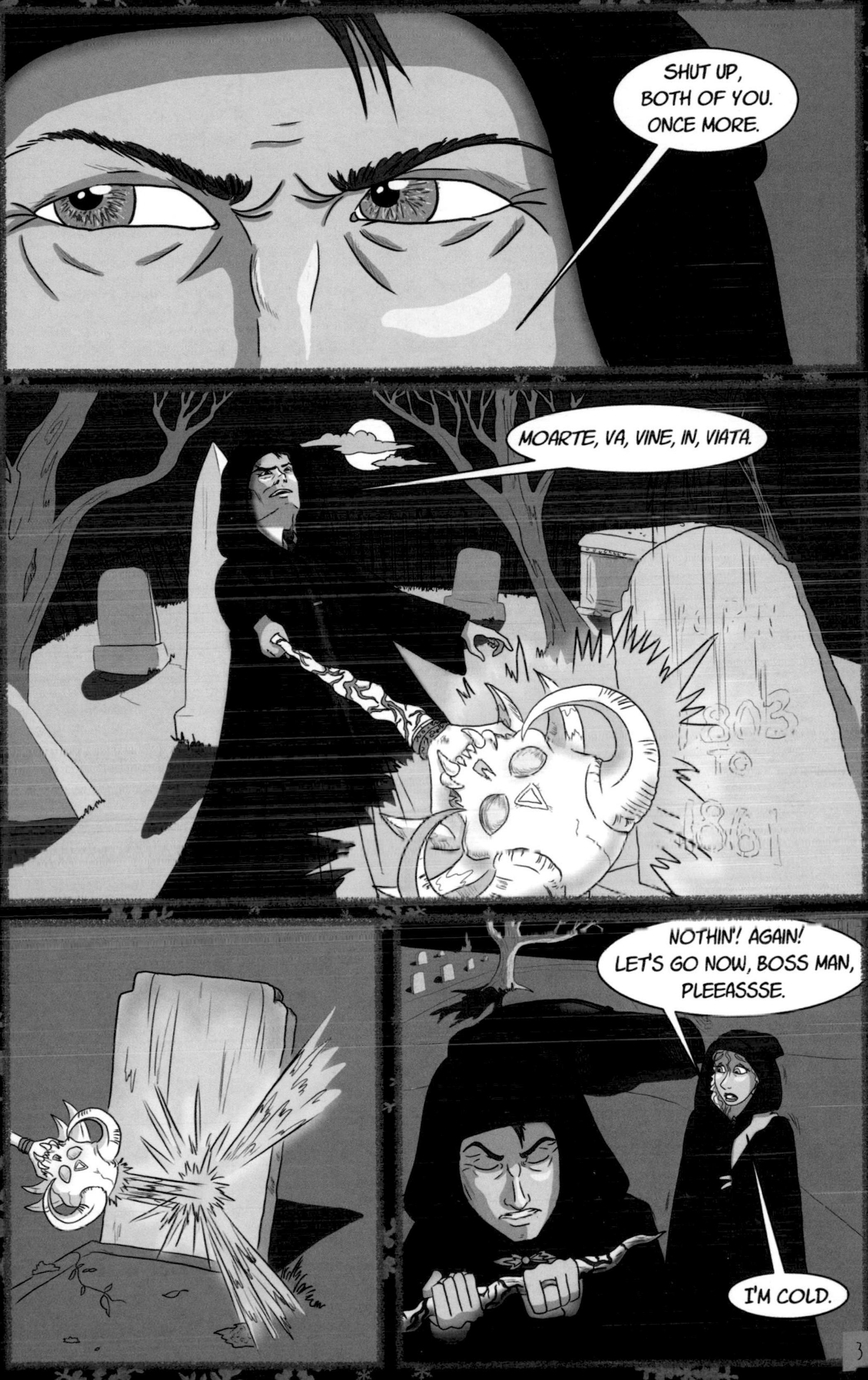
SHUT UP, BOTH OF YOU. ONCE MORE.
MOARTE, VA, VINE, IN, VIATA.
1803 TO 1861
NOTHIN'! AGAIN! LET'S GO NOW, BOSS MAN, PLEEASSSE.
I'M COLD.

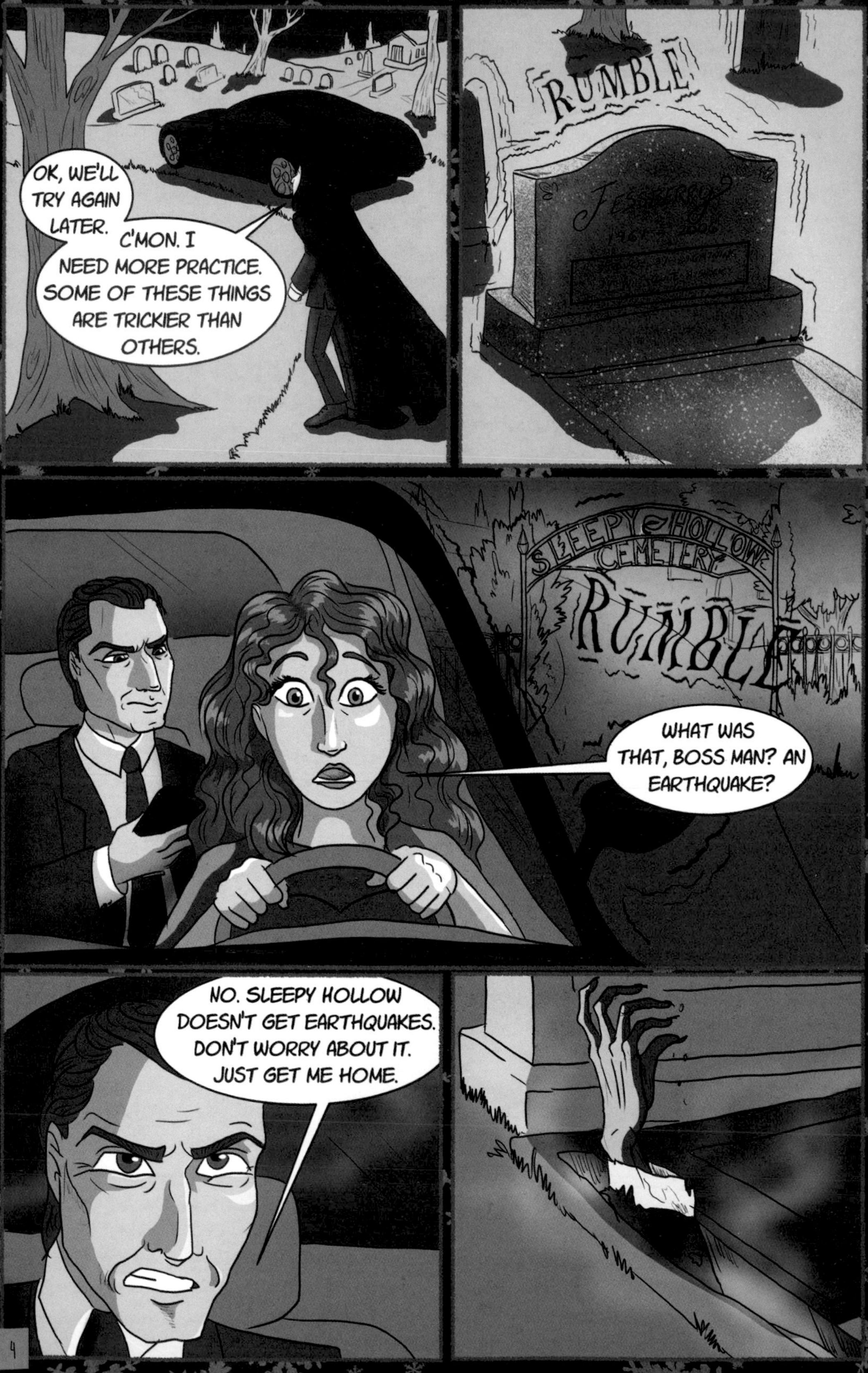
OK, WE'LL TRY AGAIN LATER.
C'MON. I NEED MORE PRACTICE. SOME OF THESE THINGS ARE TRICKIER THAN OTHERS.
RUMBLE
SLEEPY HOLLOW CEMETERY
RUMBLE
WHAT WAS THAT, BOSS MAN? AN EARTHQUAKE?
NO. SLEEPY HOLLOW DOESN'T GET EARTHQUAKES. DON'T WORRY ABOUT IT. JUST GET ME HOME.

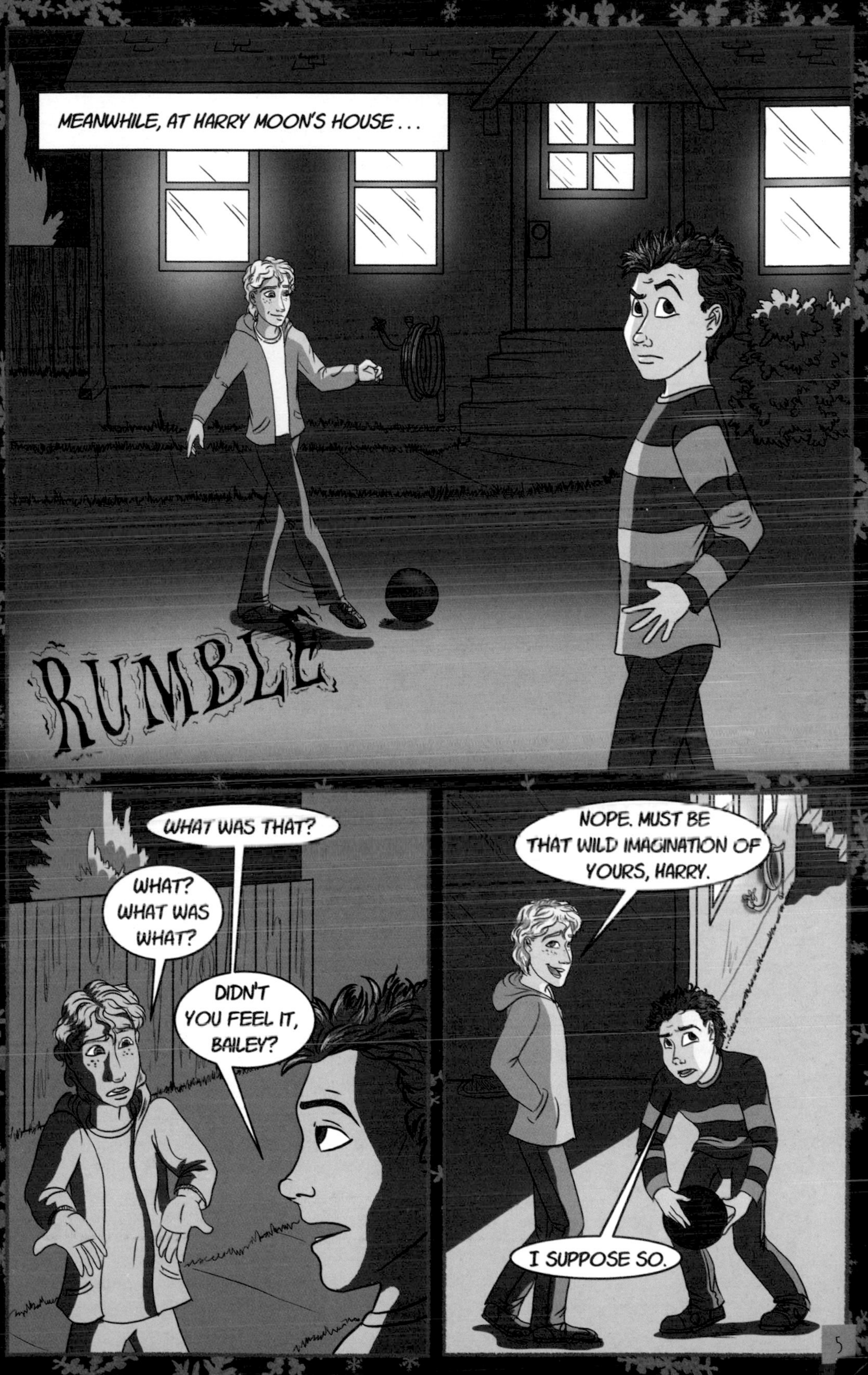

MEANWHILE, AT HARRY MOON'S HOUSE . . .
RUMBLE
WHAT WAS THAT?
WHAT? WHAT WAS WHAT?
DIDN'T YOU FEEL IT, BAILEY?
NOPE. MUST BE THAT WILD IMAGINATION OF YOURS, HARRY.
I SUPPOSE SO.

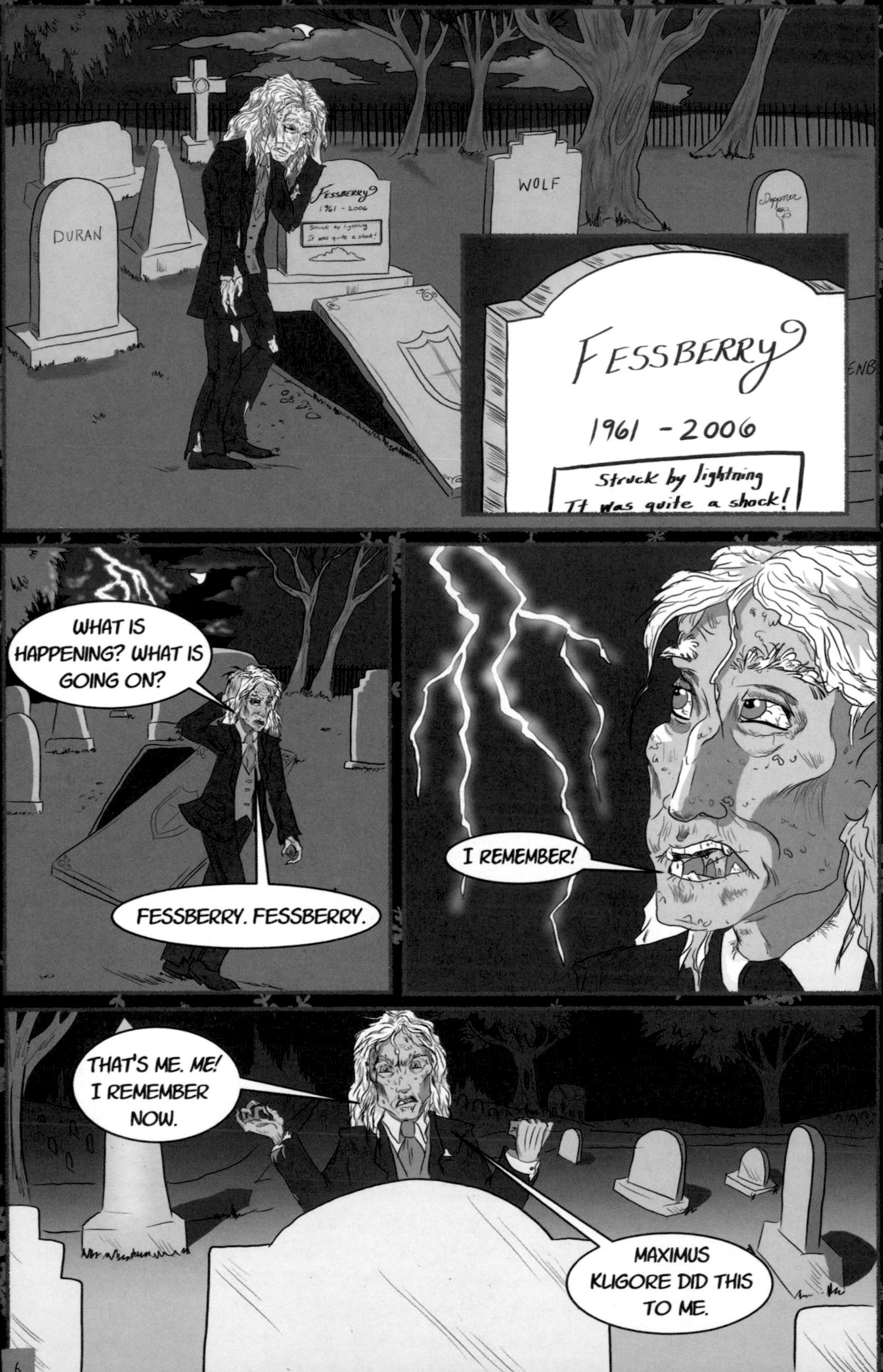
DURAN
FESSBERRY
1961 - 2006
Struck by lightning
It was quite a shock!
WOLF
WHAT IS HAPPENING? WHAT IS GOING ON?
FESSBERRY. FESSBERRY.
I REMEMBER!
THAT'S ME. ME! I REMEMBER NOW.
MAXIMUS KLIGORE DID THIS TO ME.

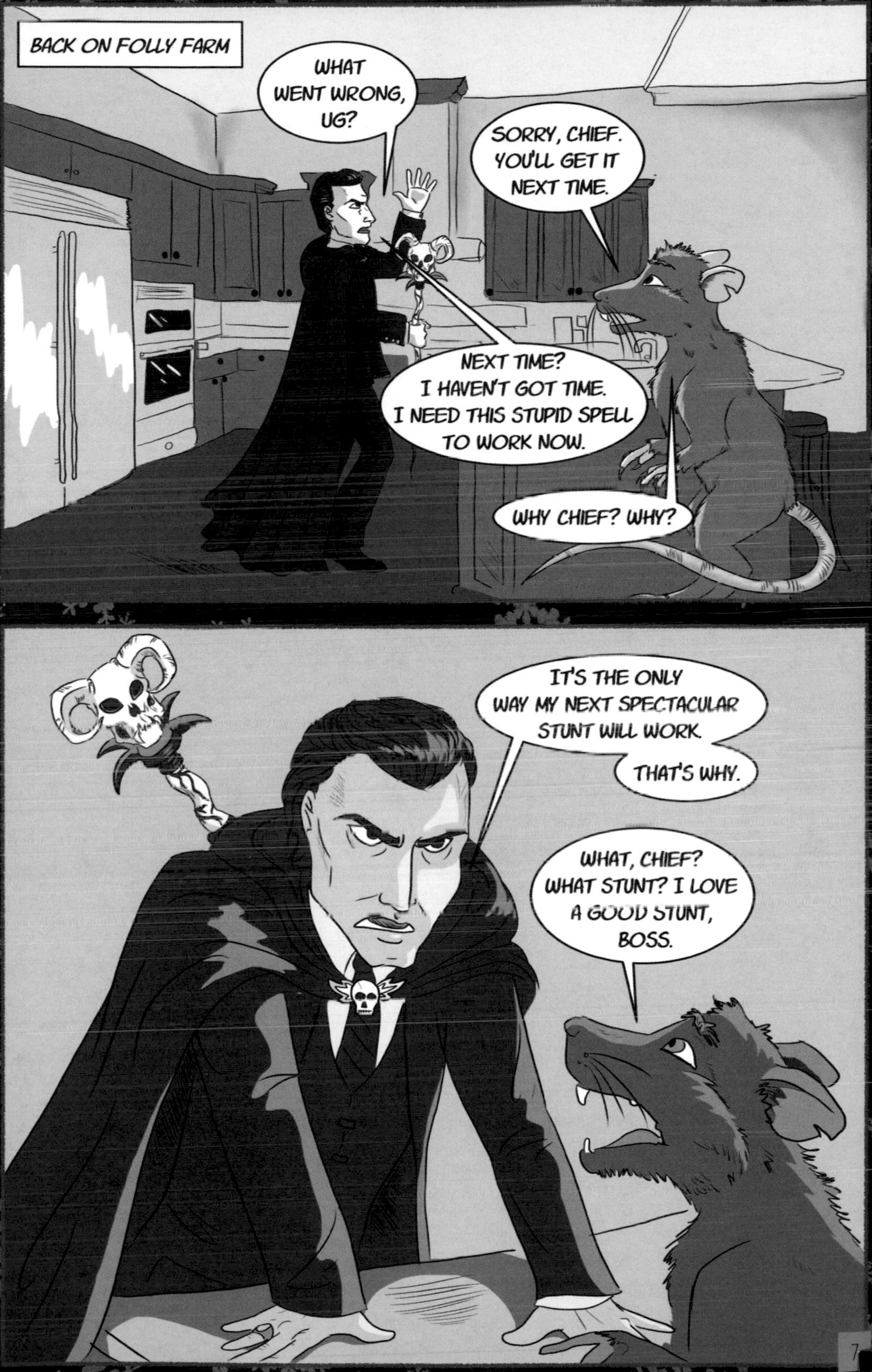
BACK ON FOLLY FARM
WHAT WENT WRONG, UG?
SORRY, CHIEF. YOU'LL GET IT NEXT TIME.
NEXT TIME? I HAVEN'T GOT TIME. I NEED THIS STUPID SPELL TO WORK NOW.
WHY CHIEF? WHY?
IT'S THE ONLY WAY MY NEXT SPECTACULAR STUNT WILL WORK.
THAT'S WHY.
WHAT, CHIEF? WHAT STUNT? I LOVE A GOOD STUNT, BOSS.

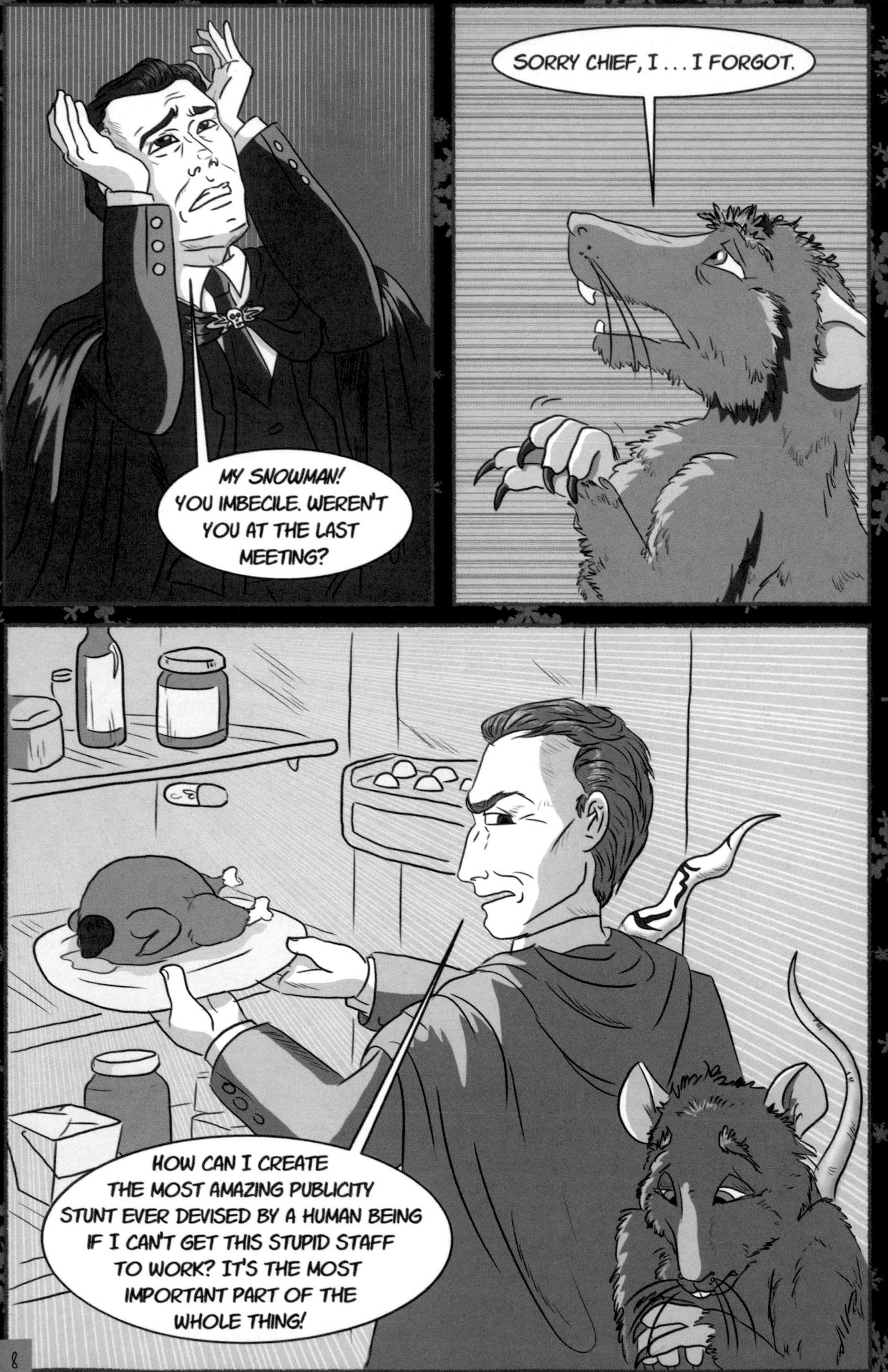
MY SNOWMAN! YOU IMBECILE. WEREN'T YOU AT THE LAST MEETING?
SORRY CHIEF, I . . . I FORGOT.
HOW CAN I CREATE THE MOST AMAZING PUBLICITY STUNT EVER DEVISED BY A HUMAN BEING IF I CAN'T GET THIS STUPID STAFF TO WORK? IT'S THE MOST IMPORTANT PART OF THE WHOLE THING!

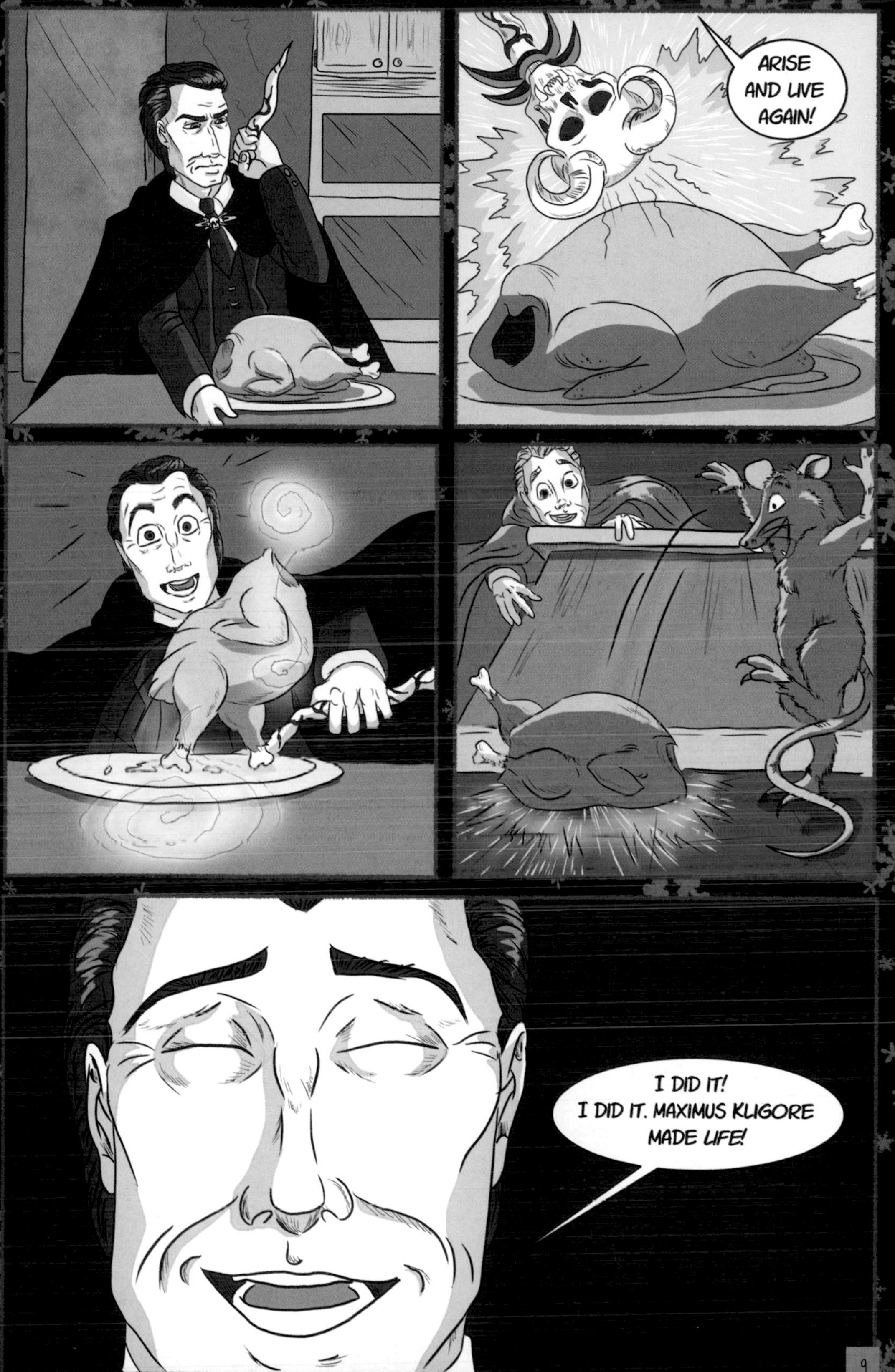
ARISE AND LIVE AGAIN!
I DID IT! I DID IT. MAXIMUS KLIGORE MADE LIFE!

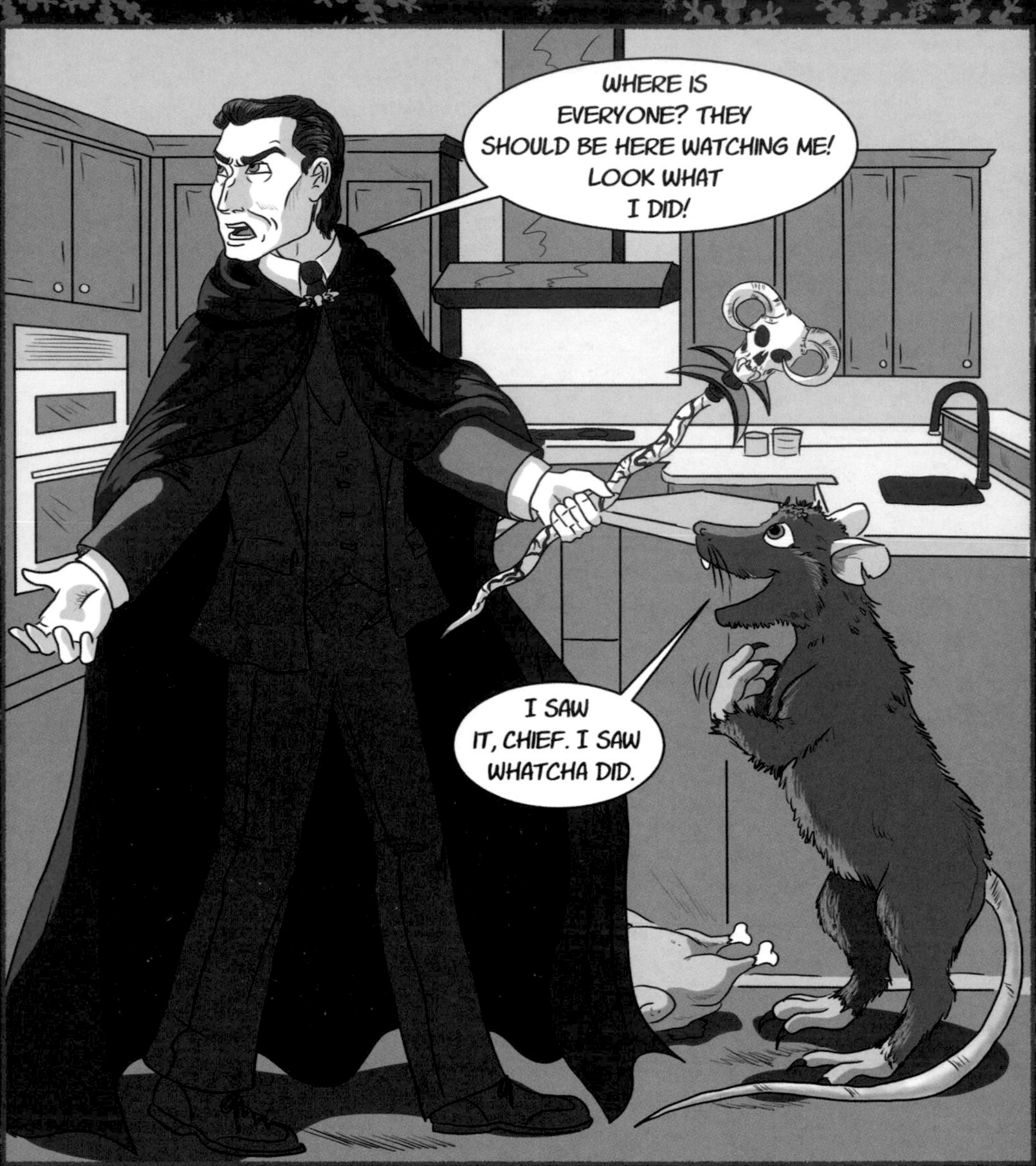
WHERE IS EVERYONE? THEY SHOULD BE HERE WATCHING ME! LOOK WHAT I DID!
I SAW IT, CHIEF. I SAW WHATCHA DID.

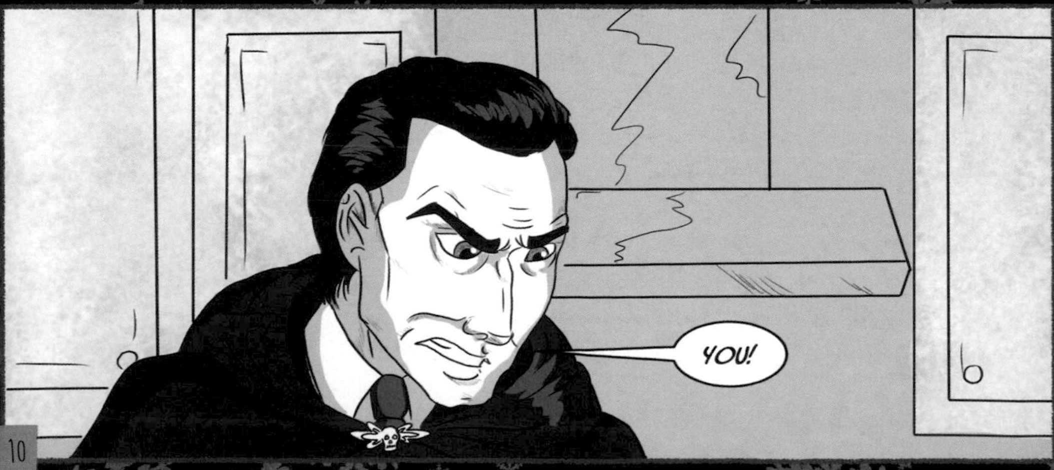
YOU!

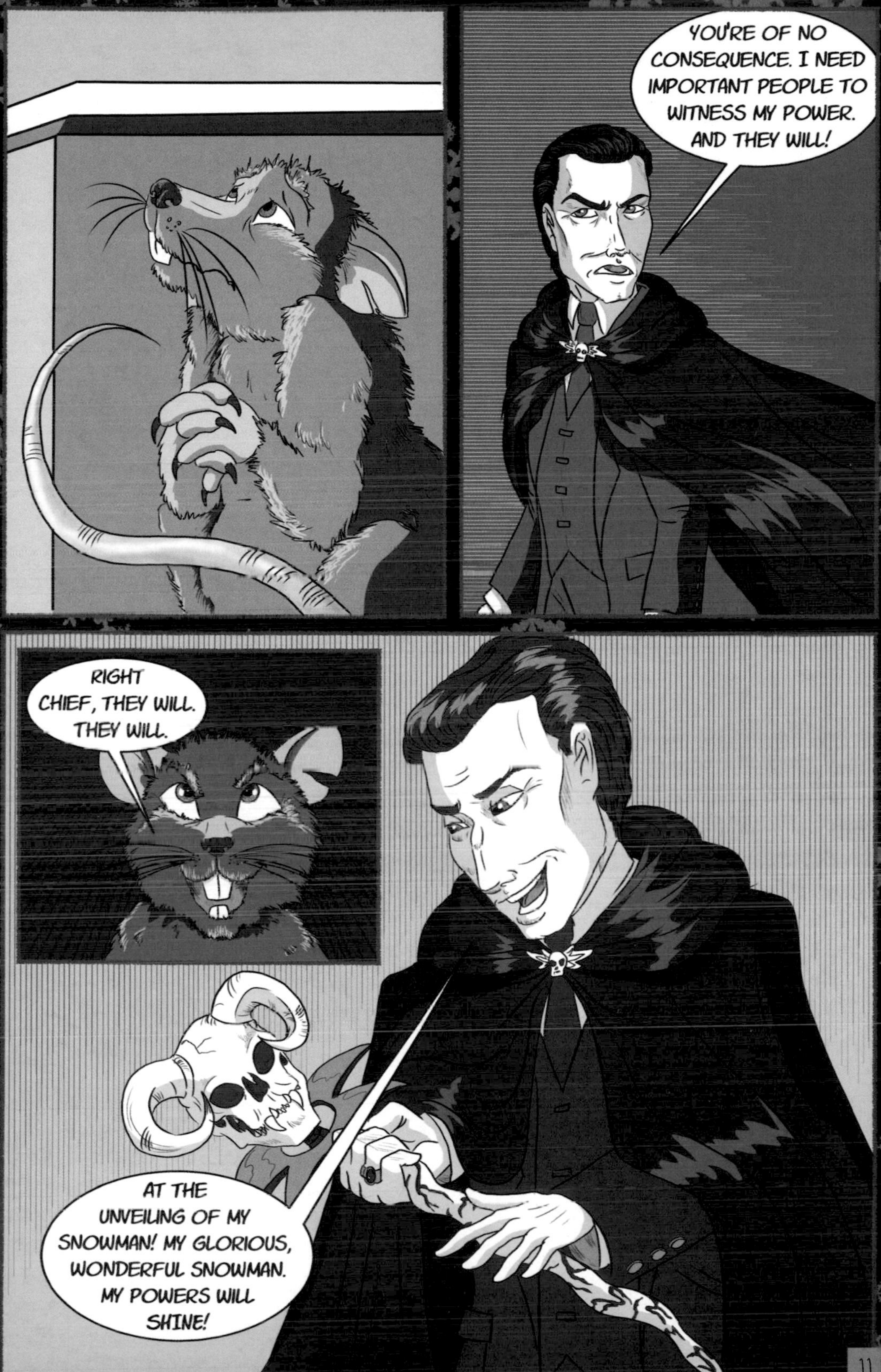
YOU'RE OF NO CONSEQUENCE. I NEED IMPORTANT PEOPLE TO WITNESS MY POWER. AND THEY WILL!
RIGHT CHIEF, THEY WILL. THEY WILL.
AT THE UNVEILING OF MY SNOWMAN! MY GLORIOUS, WONDERFUL SNOWMAN. MY POWERS WILL SHINE!

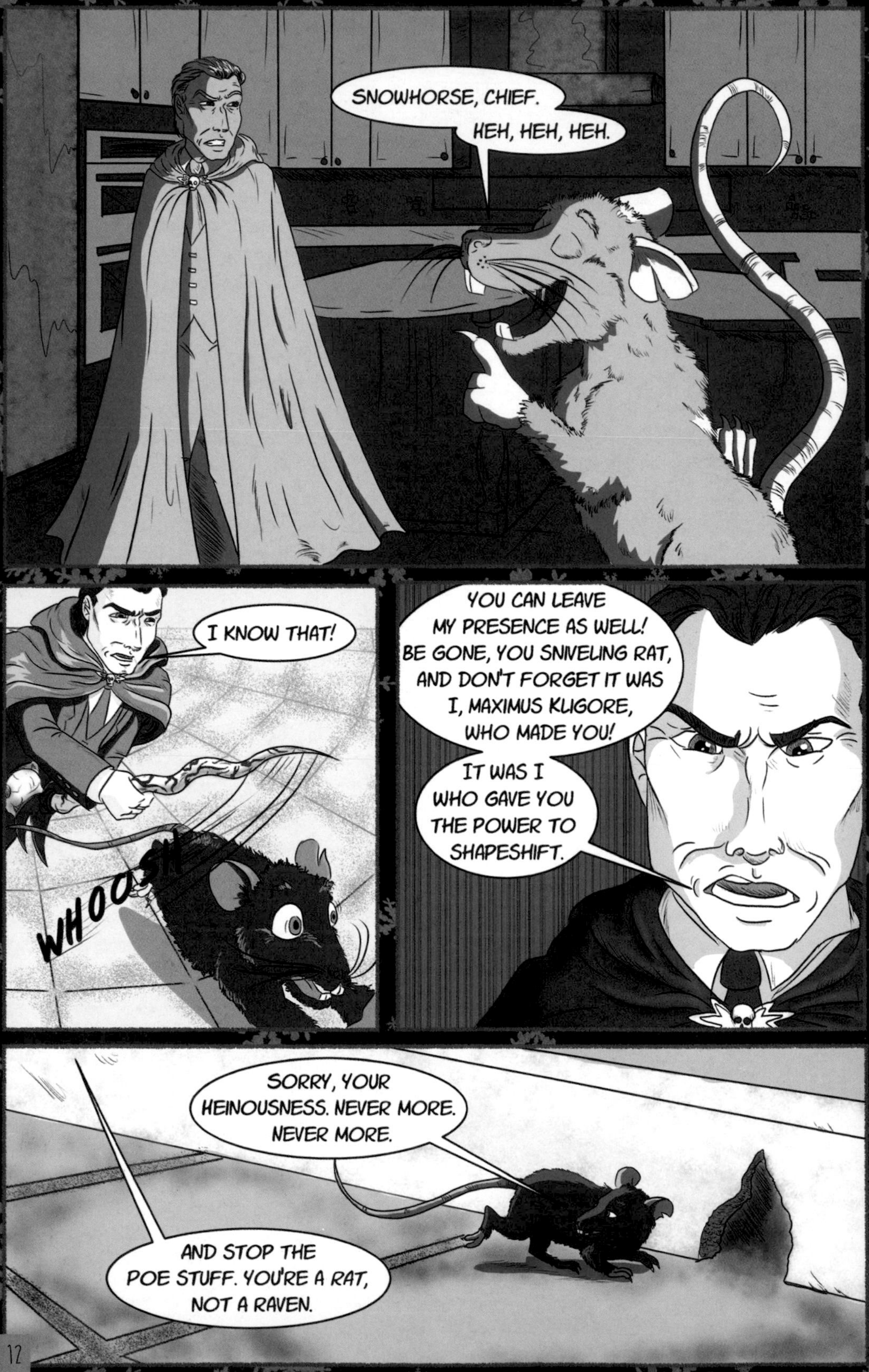

SNOWHORSE, CHIEF.
HEH, HEH, HEH.
I KNOW THAT!
WHOOSH
YOU CAN LEAVE MY PRESENCE AS WELL! BE GONE, YOU SNIVELING RAT, AND DON'T FORGET IT WAS I, MAXIMUS KLIGORE, WHO MADE YOU!
IT WAS I WHO GAVE YOU THE POWER TO SHAPESHIFT.
SORRY, YOUR HEINOUSNESS. NEVER MORE. NEVER MORE.
AND STOP THE POE STUFF. YOU'RE A RAT, NOT A RAVEN.

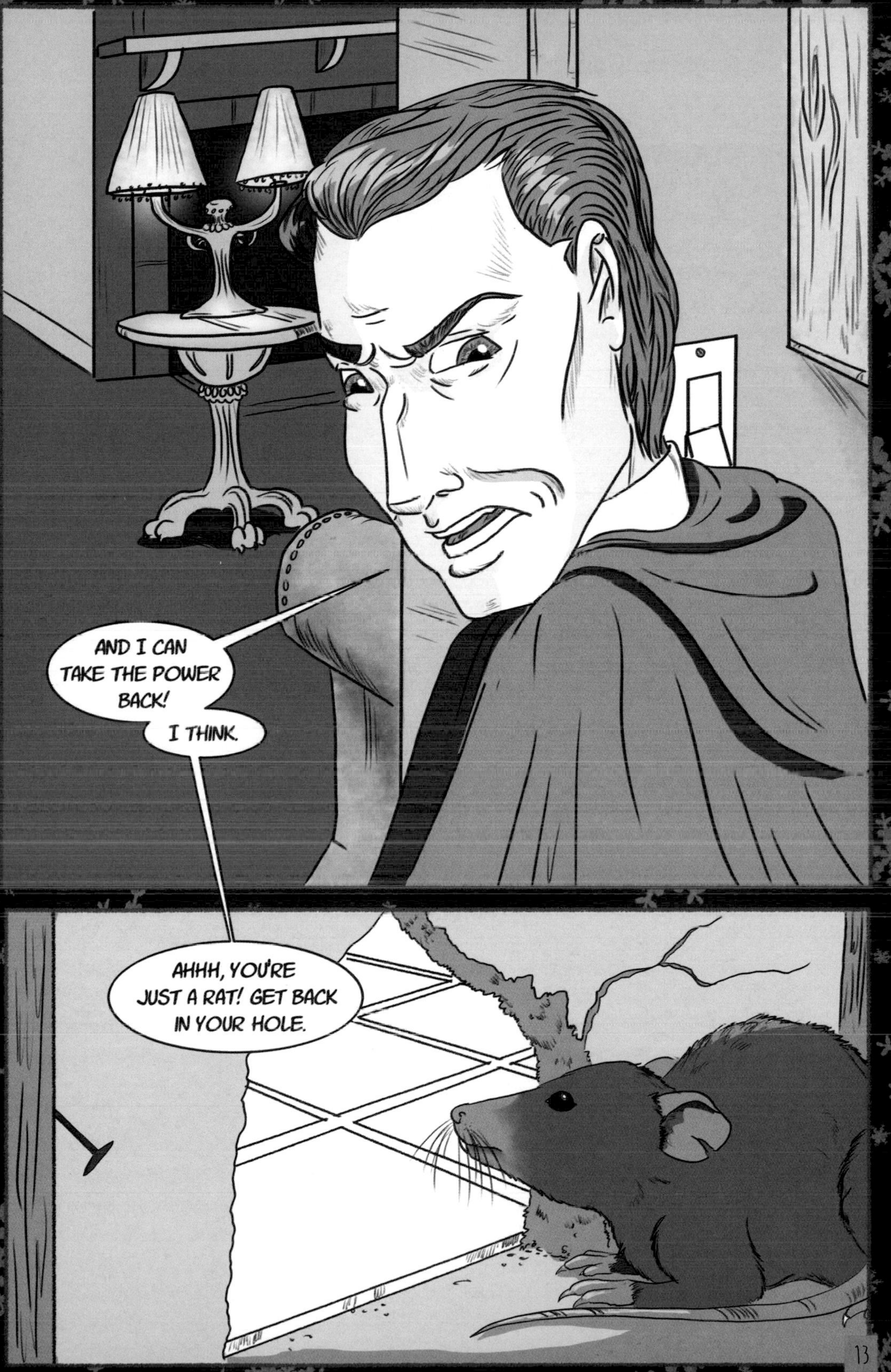
AND I CAN TAKE THE POWER BACK!
I THINK.
AHHH, YOU'RE JUST A RAT! GET BACK IN YOUR HOLE.

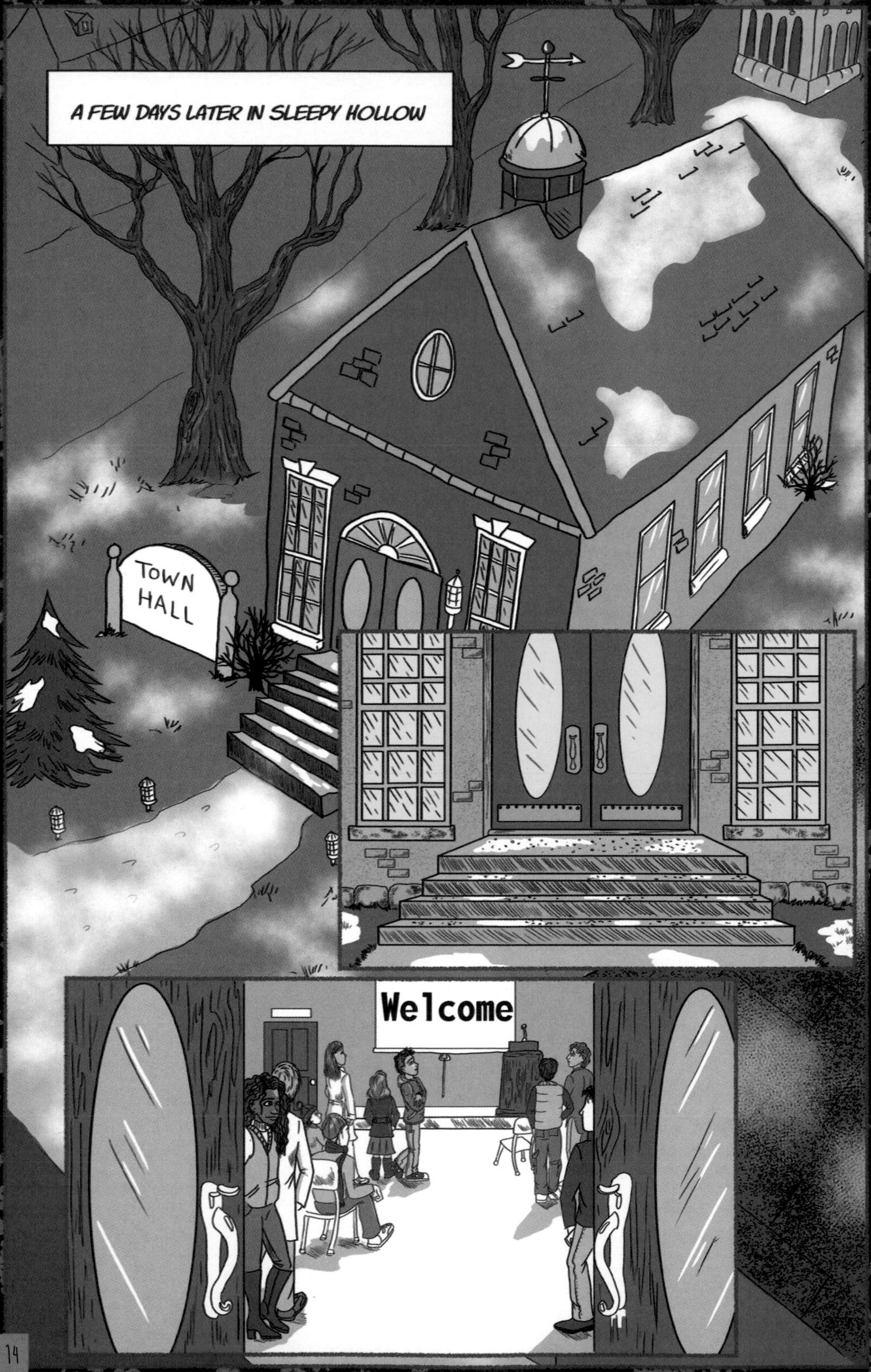
A FEW DAYS LATER IN SLEEPY HOLLOW
TOWN HALL
Welcome

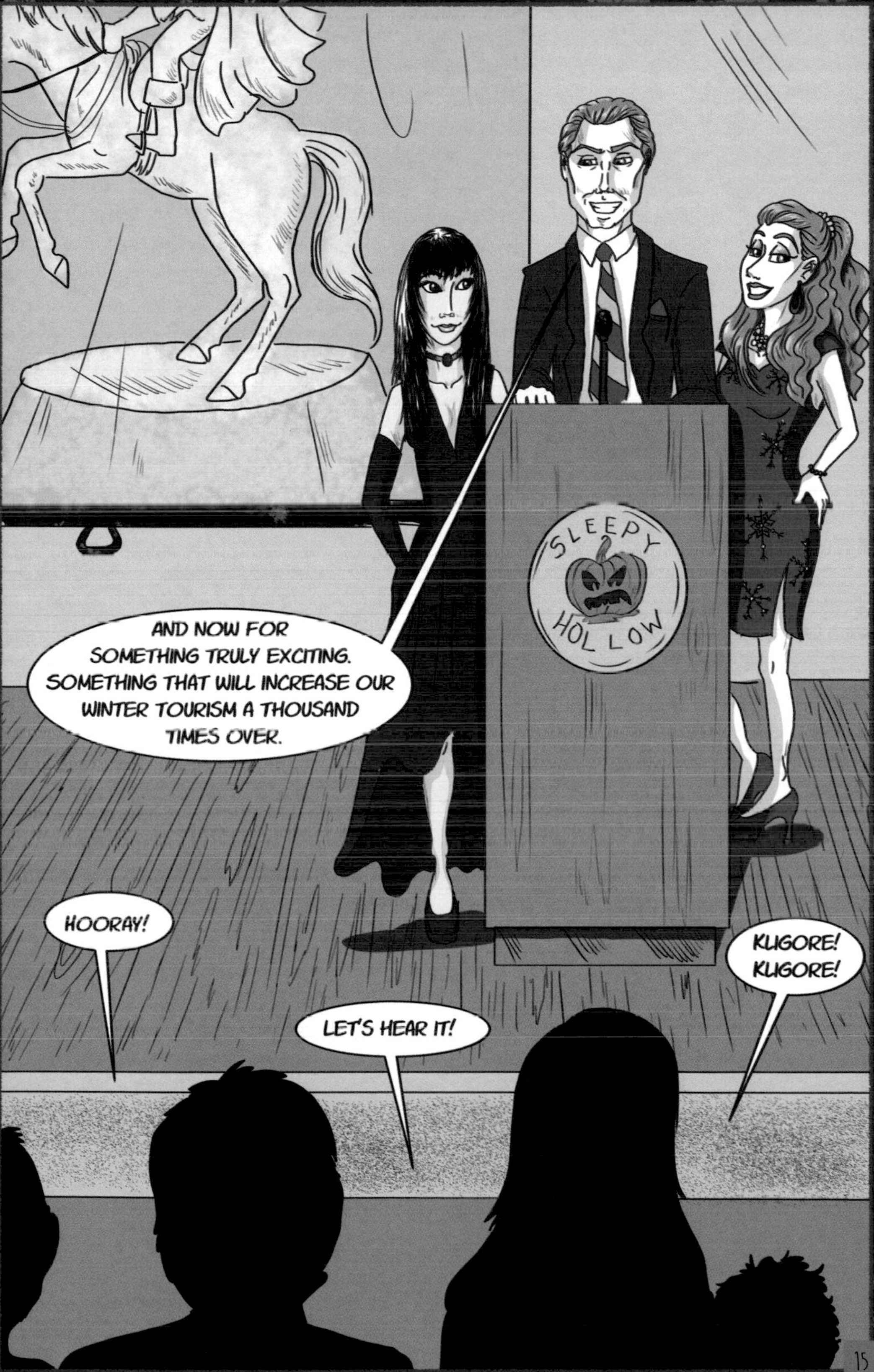
SLEEPY HOLLOW
AND NOW FOR SOMETHING TRULY EXCITING. SOMETHING THAT WILL INCREASE OUR WINTER TOURISM A THOUSAND TIMES OVER.
HOORAY!
LET'S HEAR IT!
KLIGORE! KLIGORE!

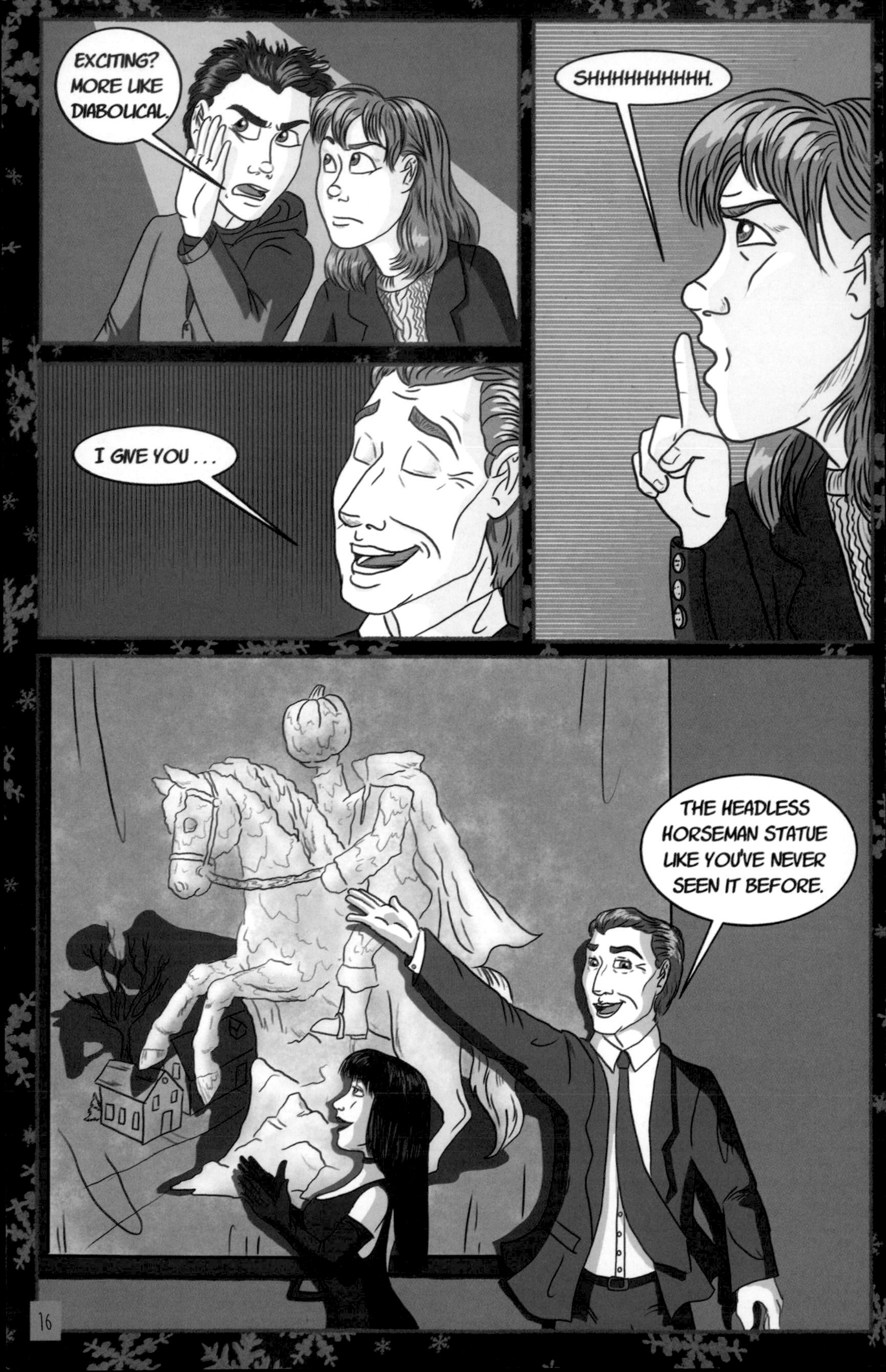
EXCITING? MORE LIKE DIABOLICAL.
SHHHHHHHHHH.
I GIVE YOU . . .
THE HEADLESS HORSEMAN STATUE LIKE YOU'VE NEVER SEEN IT BEFORE.

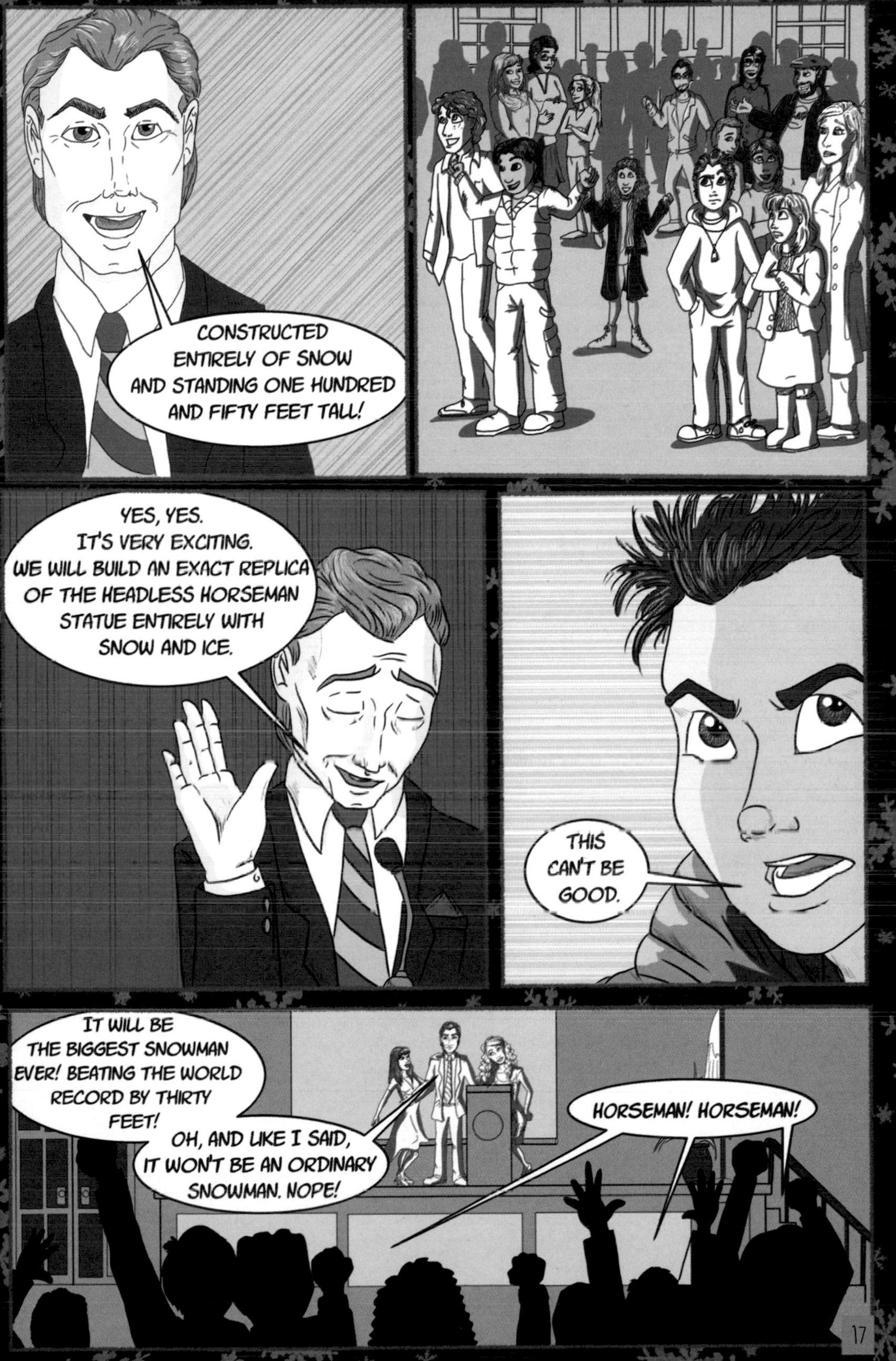
CONSTRUCTED ENTIRELY OF SNOW AND STANDING ONE HUNDRED AND FIFTY FEET TALL!
YES, YES. IT'S VERY EXCITING. WE WILL BUILD AN EXACT REPLICA OF THE HEADLESS HORSEMAN STATUE ENTIRELY WITH SNOW AND ICE.
THIS CAN'T BE GOOD.
IT WILL BE THE BIGGEST SNOWMAN EVER! BEATING THE WORLD RECORD BY THIRTY FEET!
OH, AND LIKE I SAID, IT WON'T BE AN ORDINARY SNOWMAN. NOPE!
HORSEMAN! HORSEMAN!

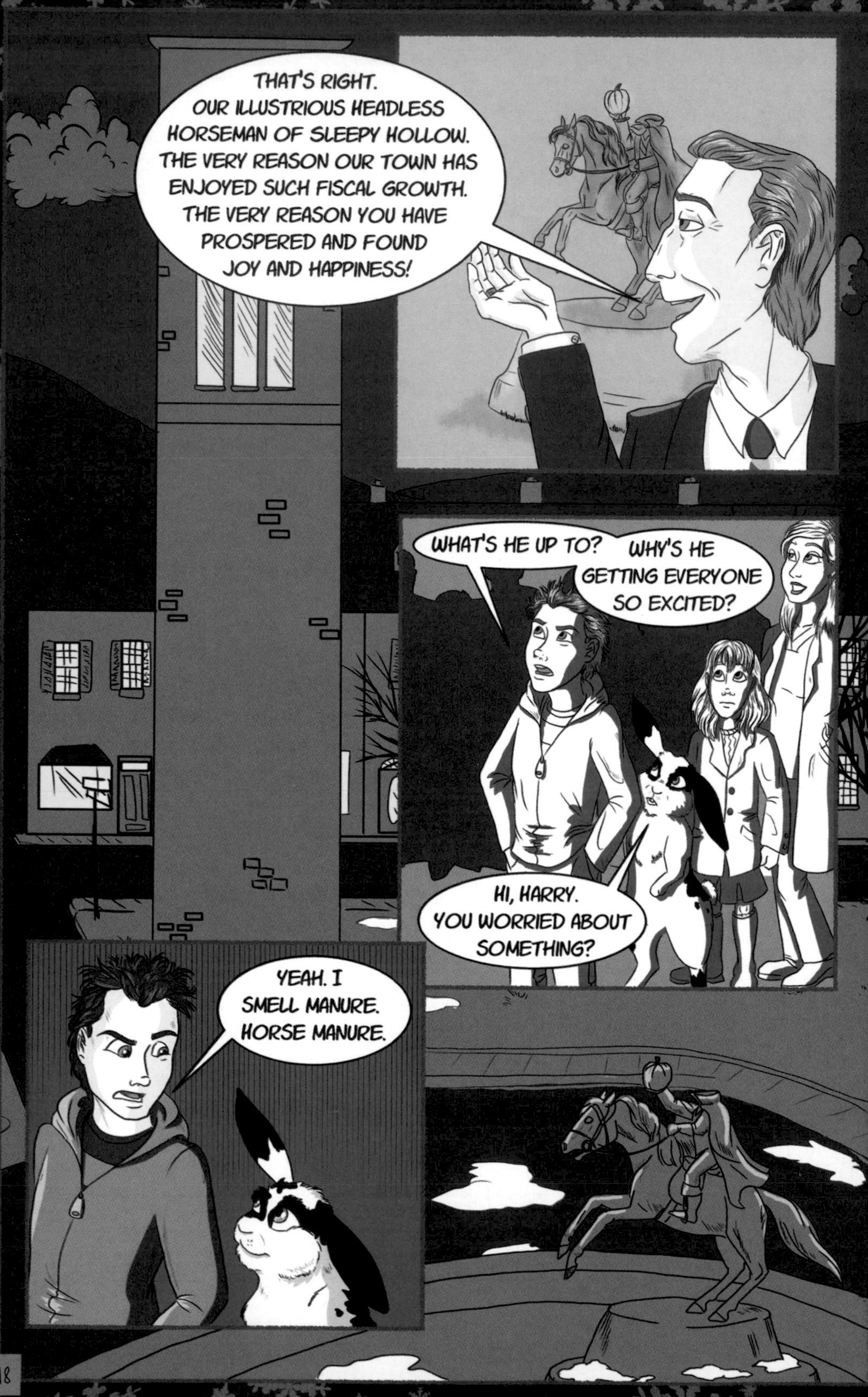
THAT'S RIGHT. OUR ILLUSTRIOUS HEADLESS HORSEMAN OF SLEEPY HOLLOW. THE VERY REASON OUR TOWN HAS ENJOYED SUCH FISCAL GROWTH. THE VERY REASON YOU HAVE PROSPERED AND FOUND JOY AND HAPPINESS!
WHAT'S HE UP TO?
WHY'S HE GETTING EVERYONE SO EXCITED?
HI, HARRY. YOU WORRIED ABOUT SOMETHING?
YEAH. I SMELL MANURE. HORSE MANURE.

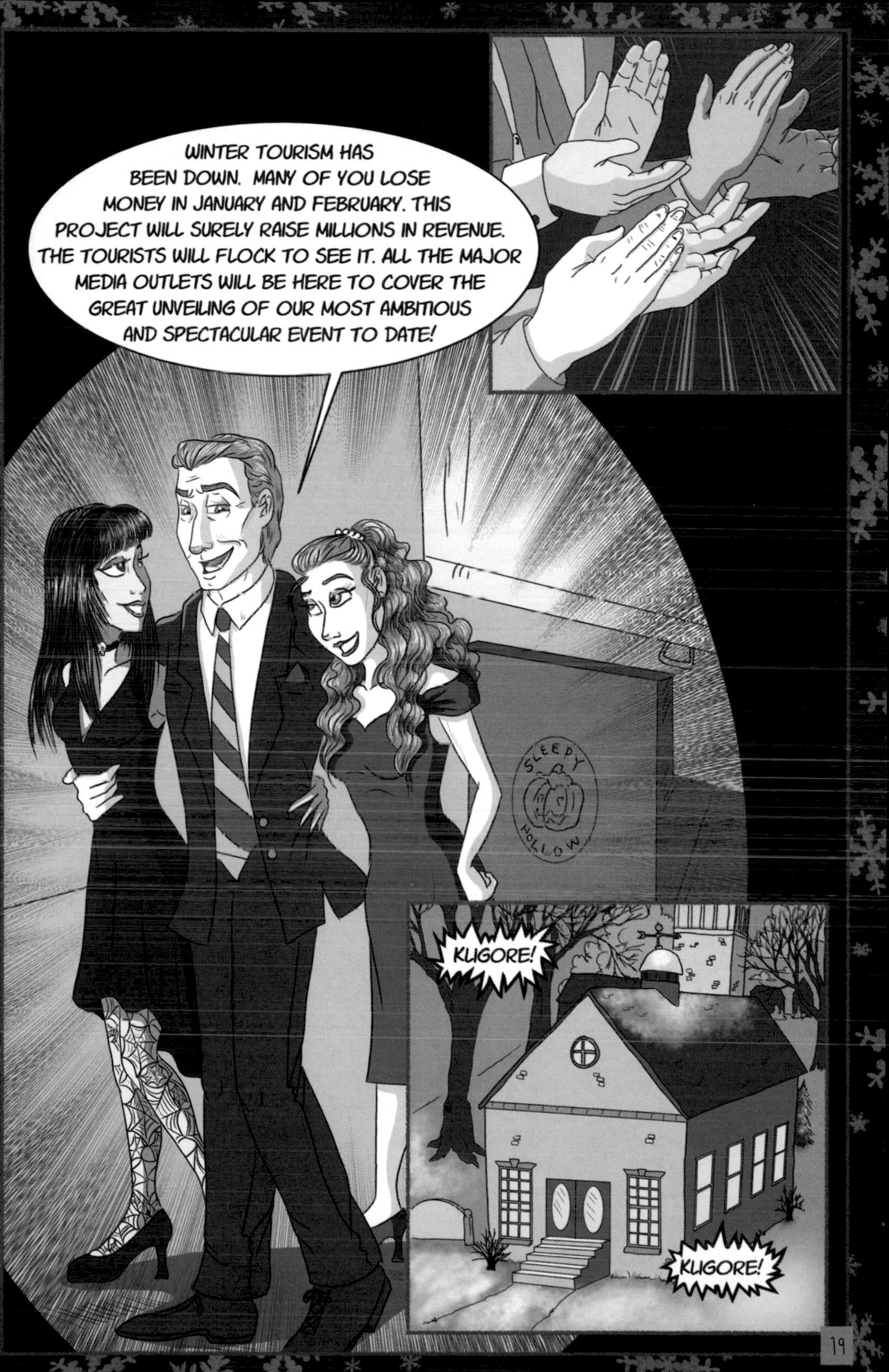
WINTER TOURISM HAS BEEN DOWN. MANY OF YOU LOSE MONEY IN JANUARY AND FEBRUARY. THIS PROJECT WILL SURELY RAISE MILLIONS IN REVENUE. THE TOURISTS WILL FLOCK TO SEE IT. ALL THE MAJOR MEDIA OUTLETS WILL BE HERE TO COVER THE GREAT UNVEILING OF OUR MOST AMBITIOUS AND SPECTACULAR EVENT TO DATE!
SLEEPY HOLLOW
KLIGORE!
KLIGORE!

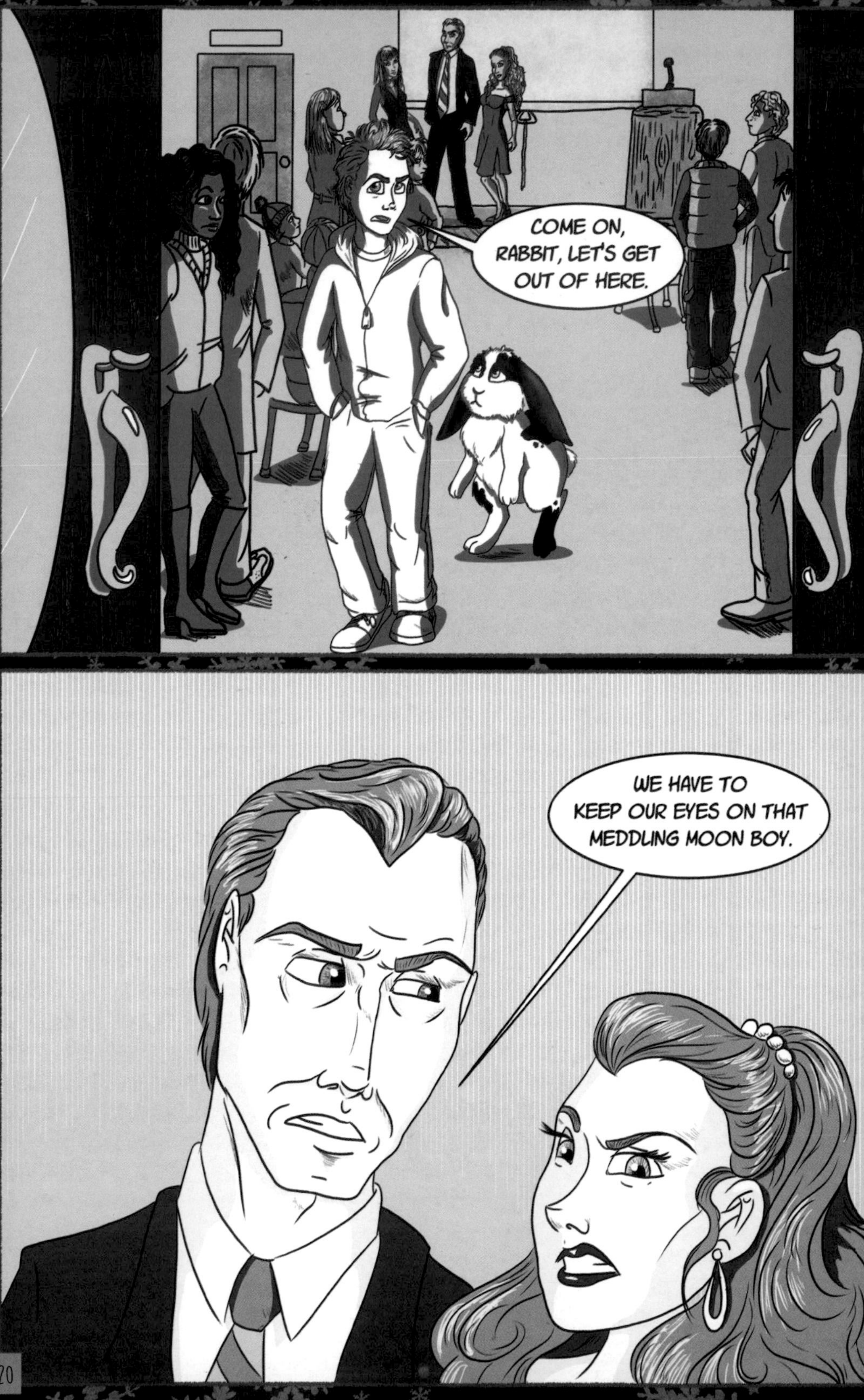
COME ON, RABBIT, LET'S GET OUT OF HERE.
WE HAVE TO KEEP OUR EYES ON THAT MEDDLING MOON BOY.

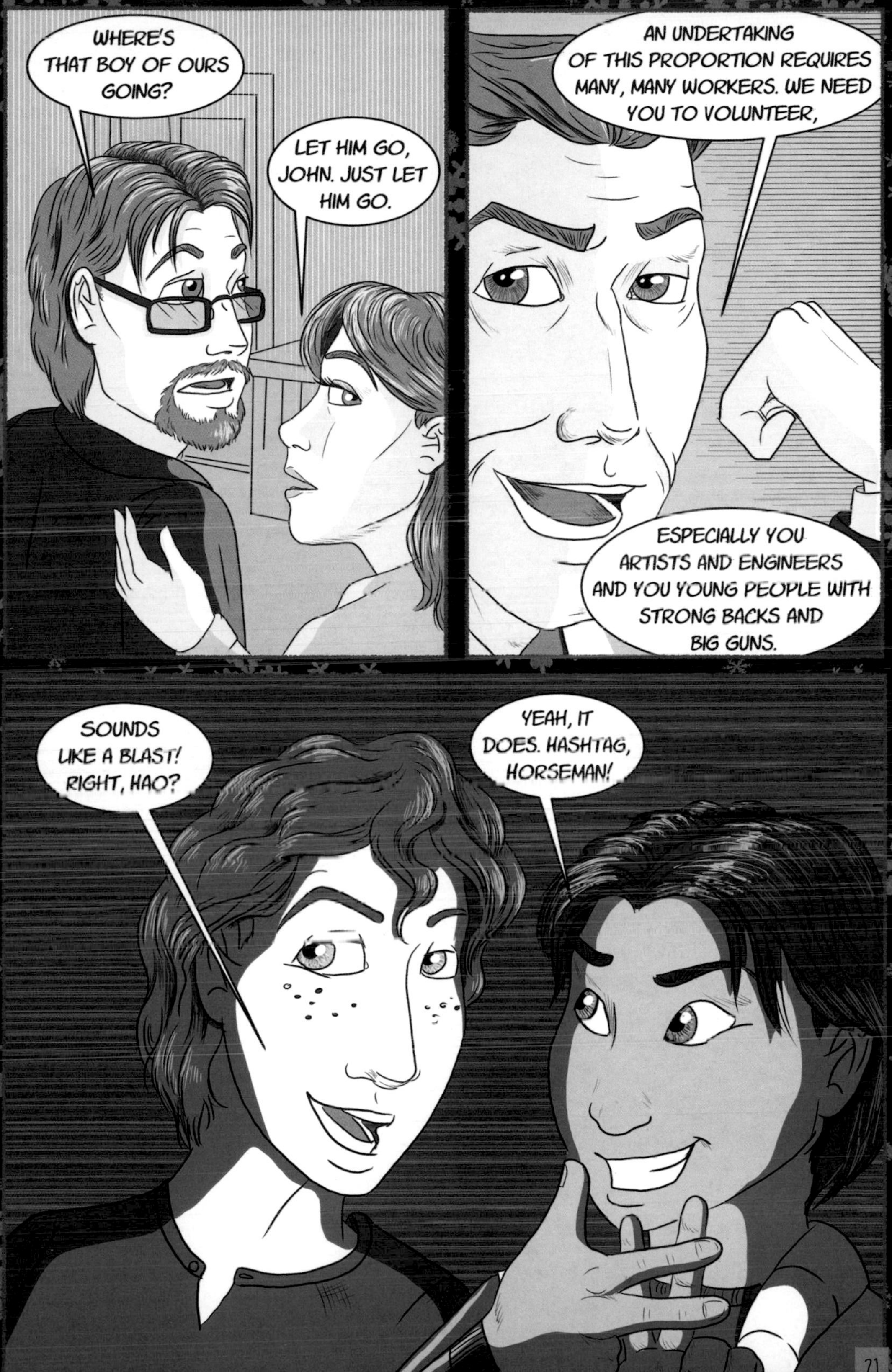
WHERE'S THAT BOY OF OURS GOING?
LET HIM GO, JOHN. JUST LET HIM GO.
AN UNDERTAKING OF THIS PROPORTION REQUIRES MANY, MANY WORKERS. WE NEED YOU TO VOLUNTEER,
ESPECIALLY YOU ARTISTS AND ENGINEERS AND YOU YOUNG PEOPLE WITH STRONG BACKS AND BIG GUNS.
SOUNDS LIKE A BLAST! RIGHT, HAO?
YEAH, IT DOES. HASHTAG, HORSEMAN!

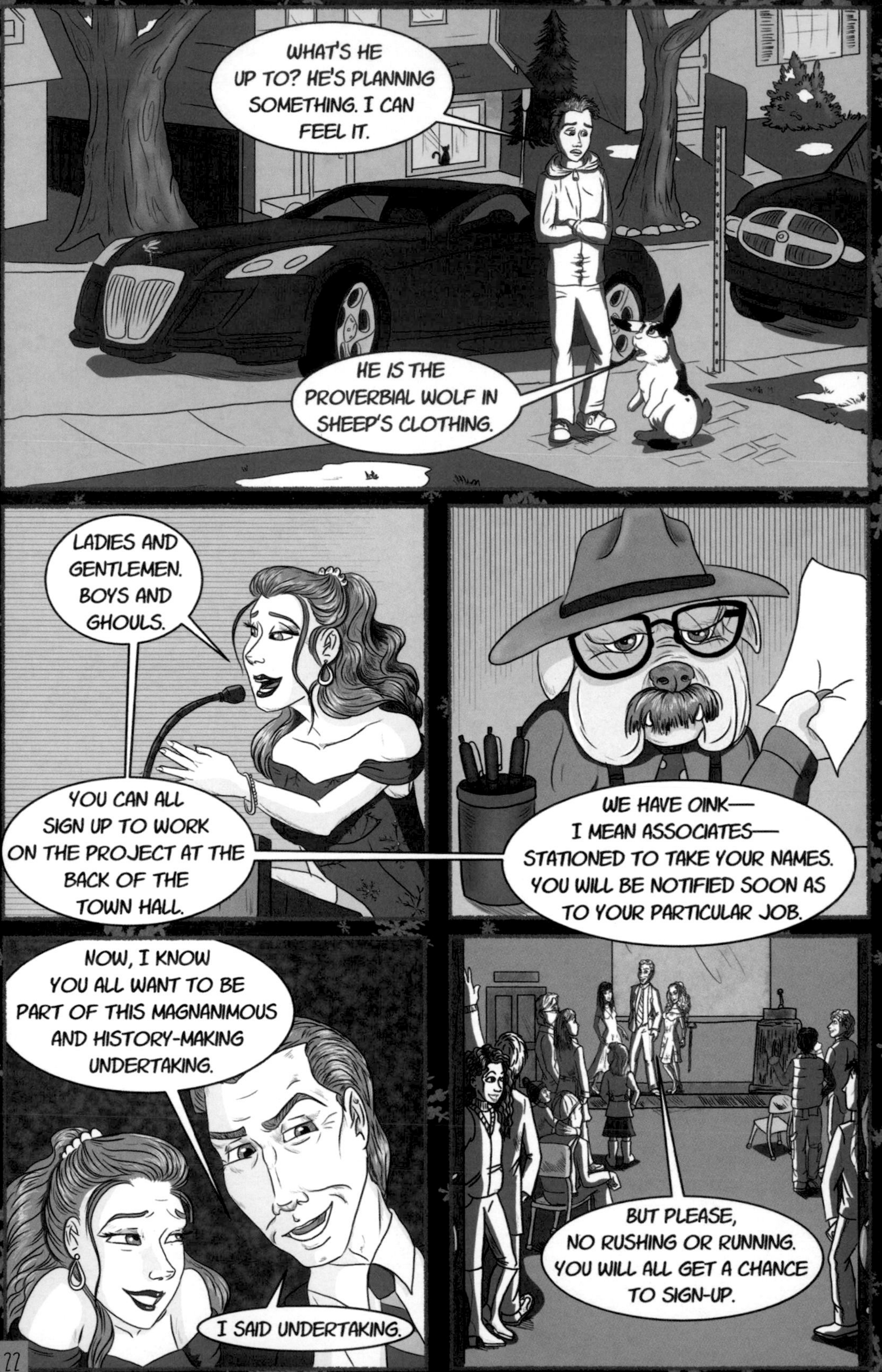

WHAT'S HE UP TO? HE'S PLANNING SOMETHING. I CAN FEEL IT.
HE IS THE PROVERBIAL WOLF IN SHEEP'S CLOTHING.
LADIES AND GENTLEMEN. BOYS AND GHOULS.
YOU CAN ALL SIGN UP TO WORK ON THE PROJECT AT THE BACK OF THE TOWN HALL.
WE HAVE OINK— I MEAN ASSOCIATES— STATIONED TO TAKE YOUR NAMES. YOU WILL BE NOTIFIED SOON AS TO YOUR PARTICULAR JOB.
NOW, I KNOW YOU ALL WANT TO BE PART OF THIS MAGNANIMOUS AND HISTORY-MAKING UNDERTAKING.
I SAID UNDERTAKING.
BUT PLEASE, NO RUSHING OR RUNNING. YOU WILL ALL GET A CHANCE TO SIGN-UP.

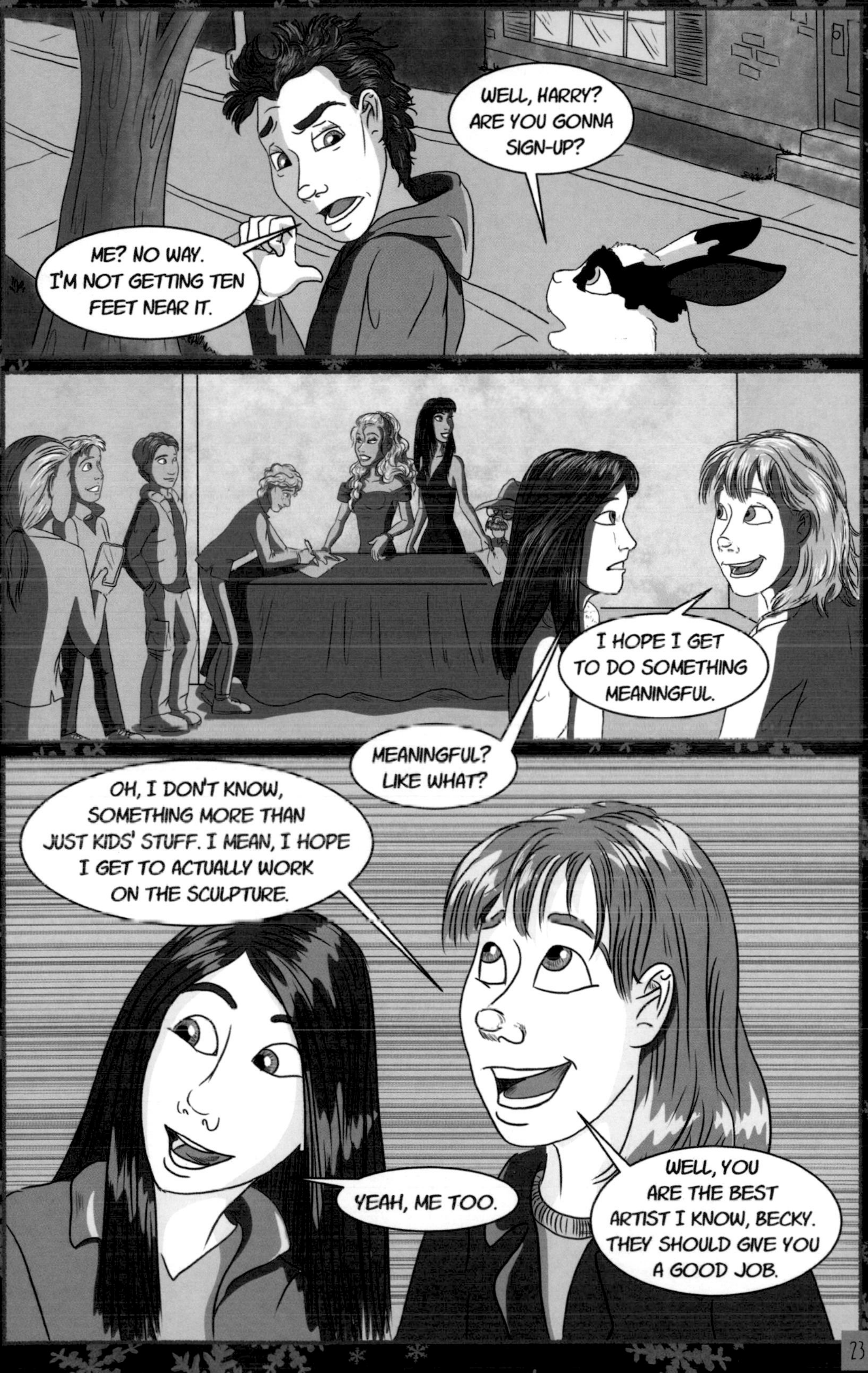
WELL, HARRY? ARE YOU GONNA SIGN-UP?
ME? NO WAY. I'M NOT GETTING TEN FEET NEAR IT.
I HOPE I GET TO DO SOMETHING MEANINGFUL.
MEANINGFUL? LIKE WHAT?
OH, I DON'T KNOW, SOMETHING MORE THAN JUST KIDS' STUFF. I MEAN, I HOPE I GET TO ACTUALLY WORK ON THE SCULPTURE.
WELL, YOU ARE THE BEST ARTIST I KNOW, BECKY. THEY SHOULD GIVE YOU A GOOD JOB.
YEAH, ME TOO.

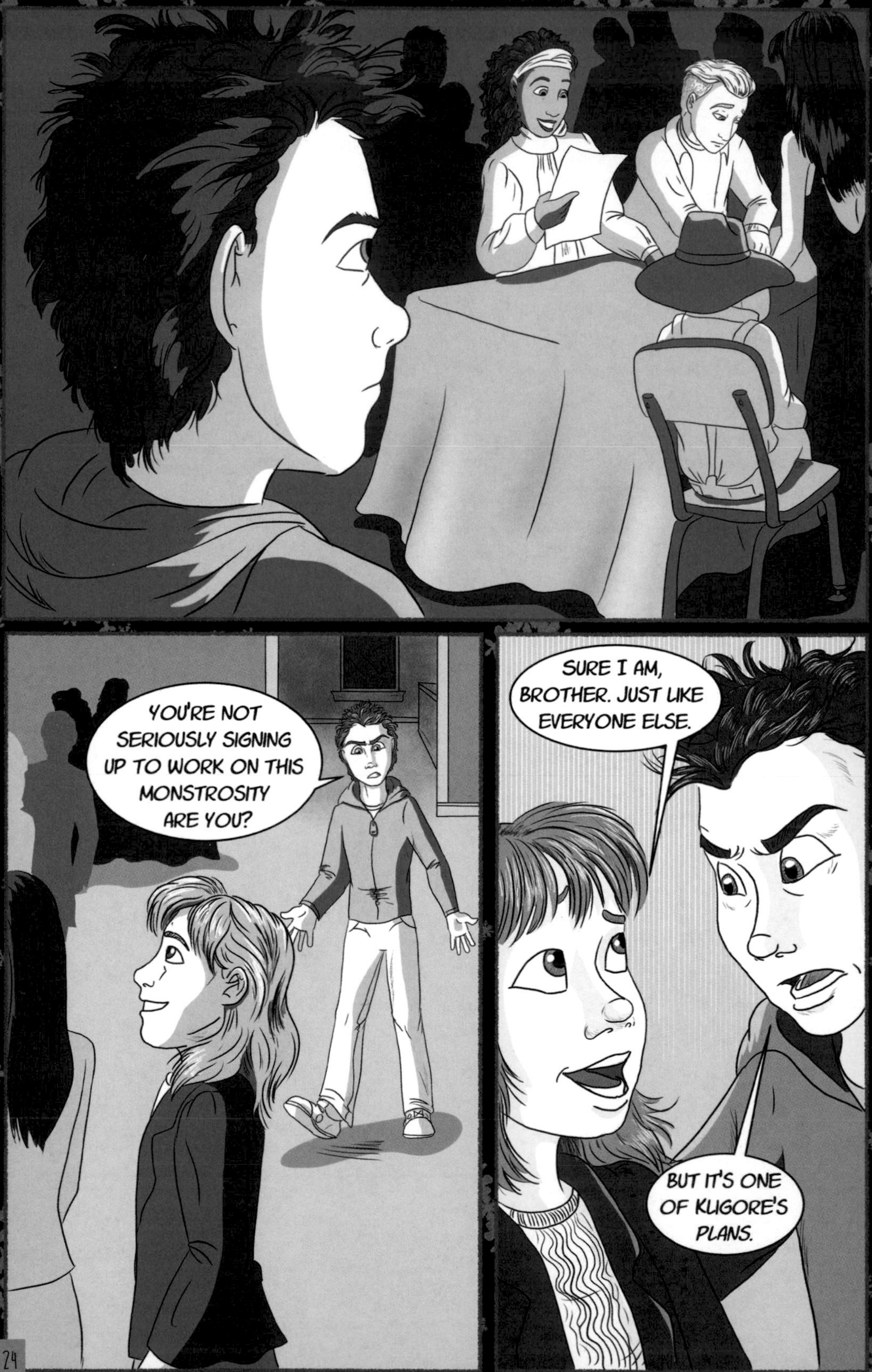
YOU'RE NOT SERIOUSLY SIGNING UP TO WORK ON THIS MONSTROSITY ARE YOU?
SURE I AM, BROTHER. JUST LIKE EVERYONE ELSE.
BUT IT'S ONE OF KLIGORE'S PLANS.

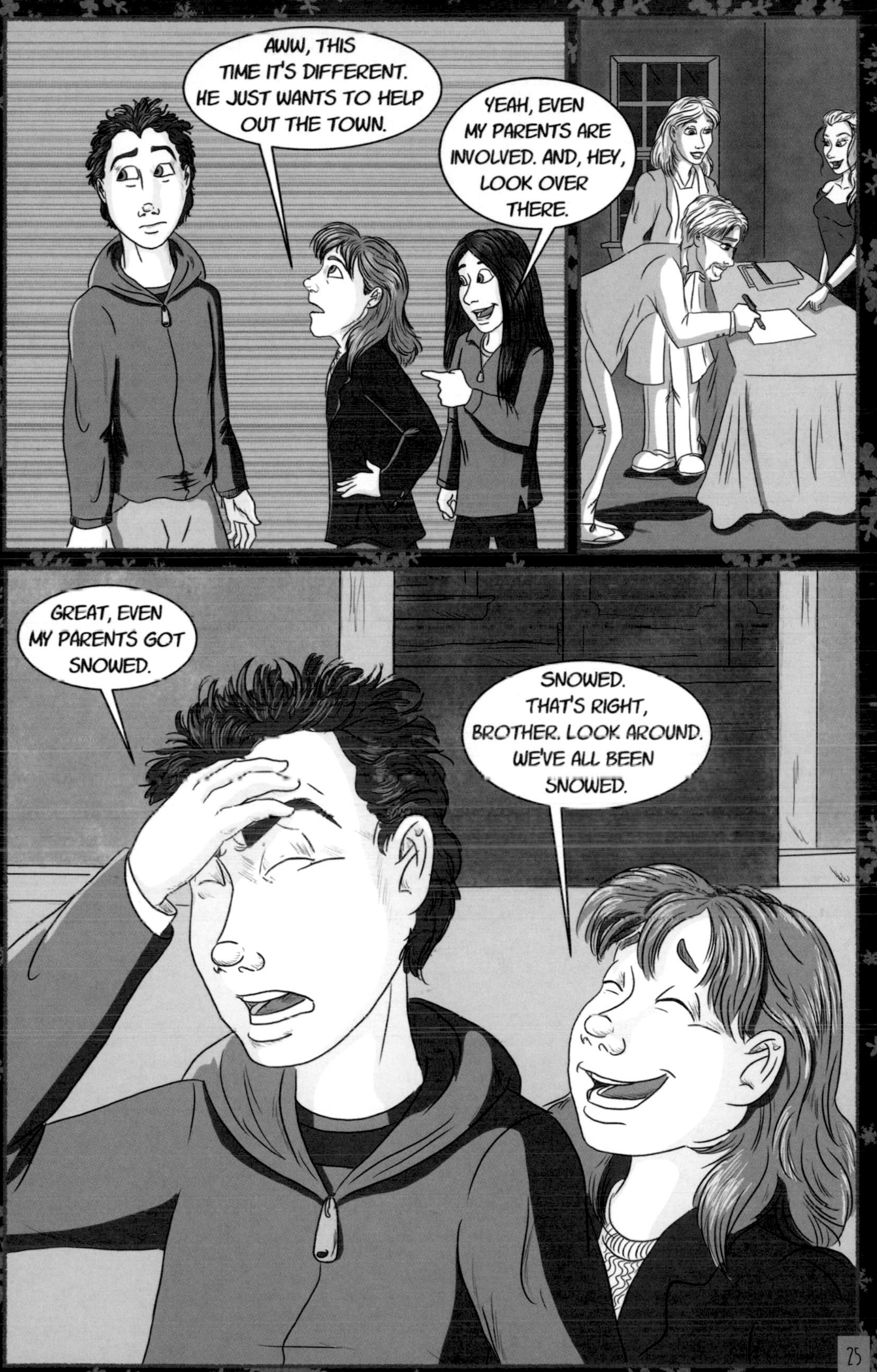
AWW, THIS TIME IT'S DIFFERENT. HE JUST WANTS TO HELP OUT THE TOWN.
YEAH, EVEN MY PARENTS ARE INVOLVED. AND, HEY, LOOK OVER THERE.
GREAT, EVEN MY PARENTS GOT SNOWED.
SNOWED. THAT'S RIGHT, BROTHER. LOOK AROUND. WE'VE ALL BEEN SNOWED.

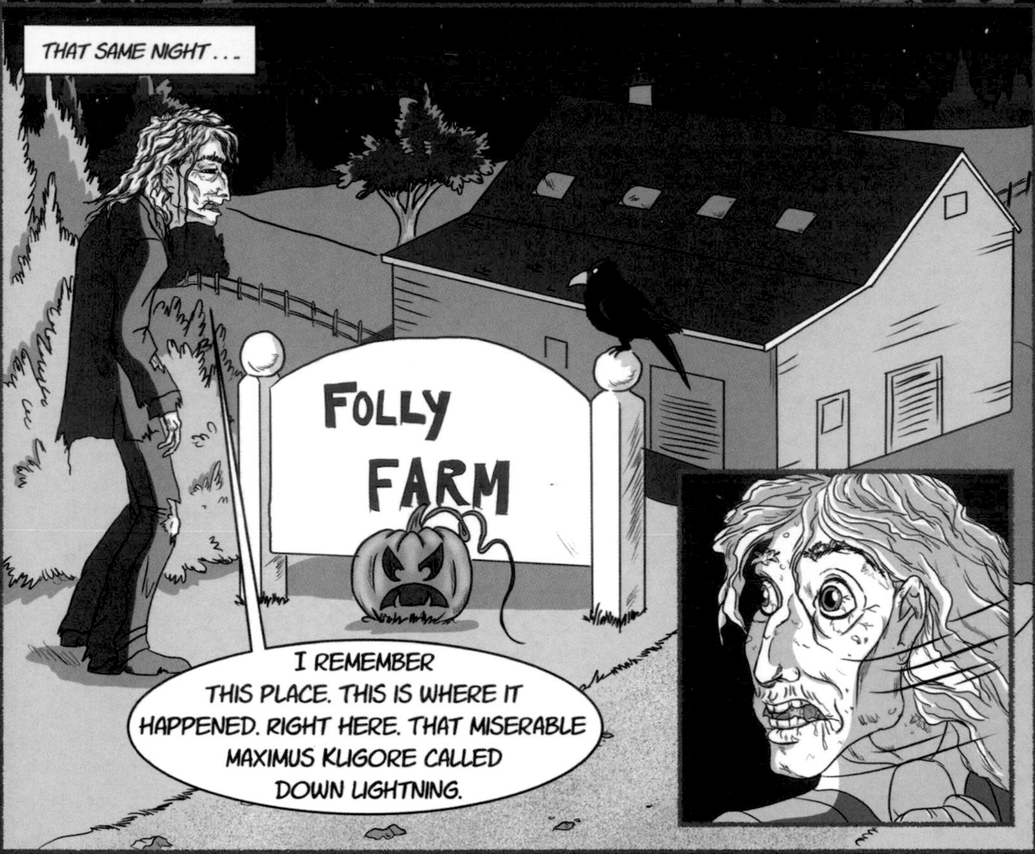
THAT SAME NIGHT . . .
FOLLY FARM
I REMEMBER THIS PLACE. THIS IS WHERE IT HAPPENED. RIGHT HERE. THAT MISERABLE MAXIMUS KLIGORE CALLED DOWN LIGHTNING.

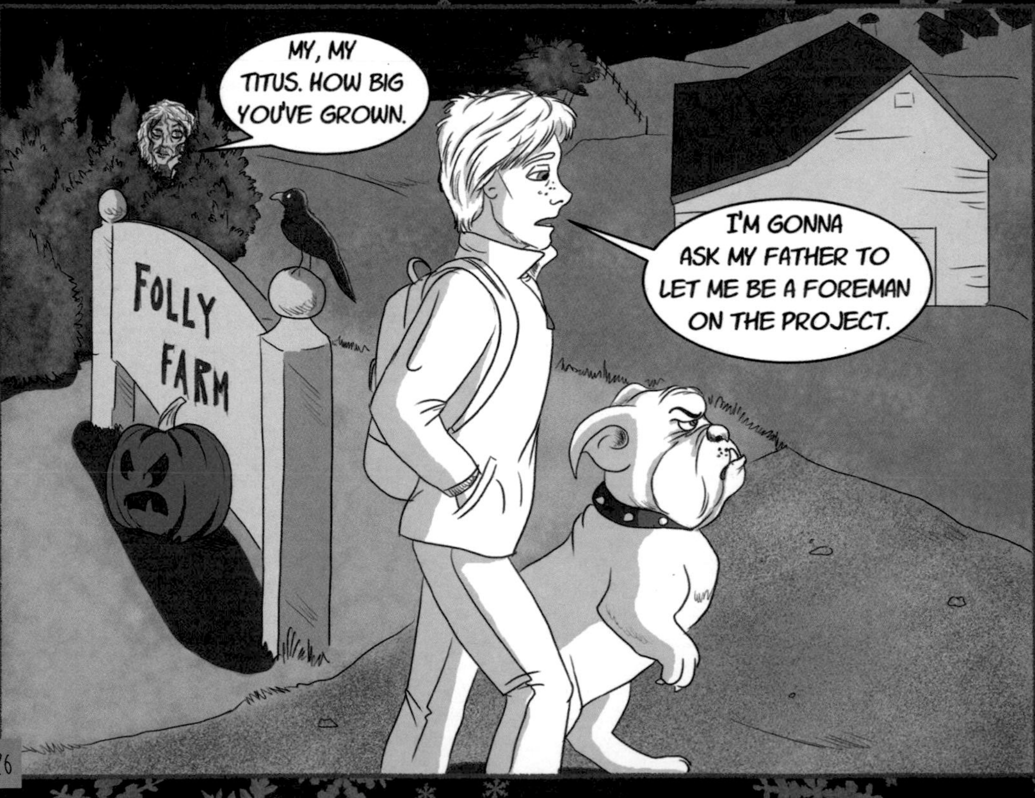
MY, MY TITUS. HOW BIG YOU'VE GROWN.
FOLLY FARM
I'M GONNA ASK MY FATHER TO LET ME BE A FOREMAN ON THE PROJECT.

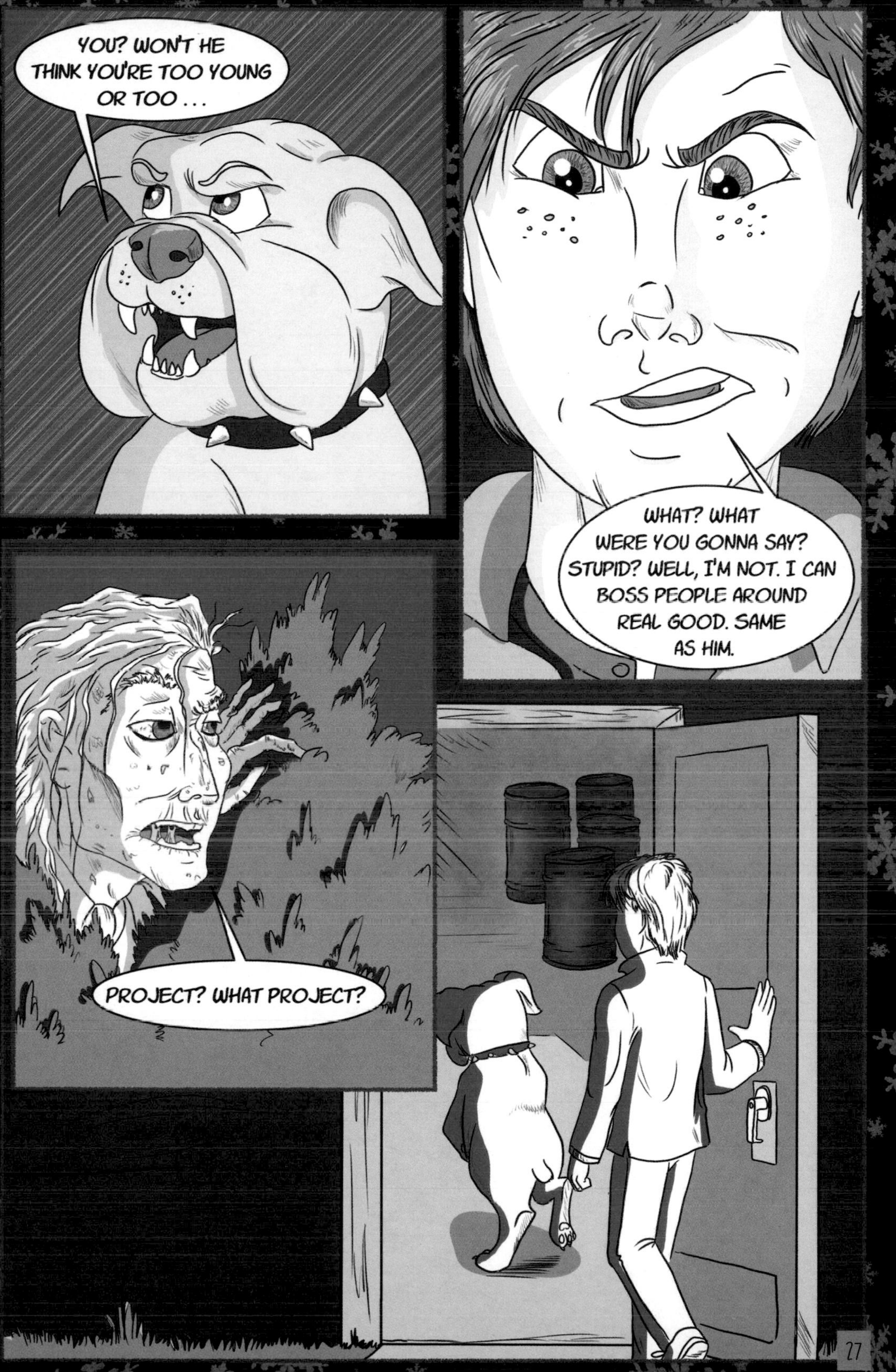
YOU? WON'T HE THINK YOU'RE TOO YOUNG OR TOO . . .
WHAT? WHAT WERE YOU GONNA SAY? STUPID? WELL, I'M NOT. I CAN BOSS PEOPLE AROUND REAL GOOD. SAME AS HIM.
PROJECT? WHAT PROJECT?

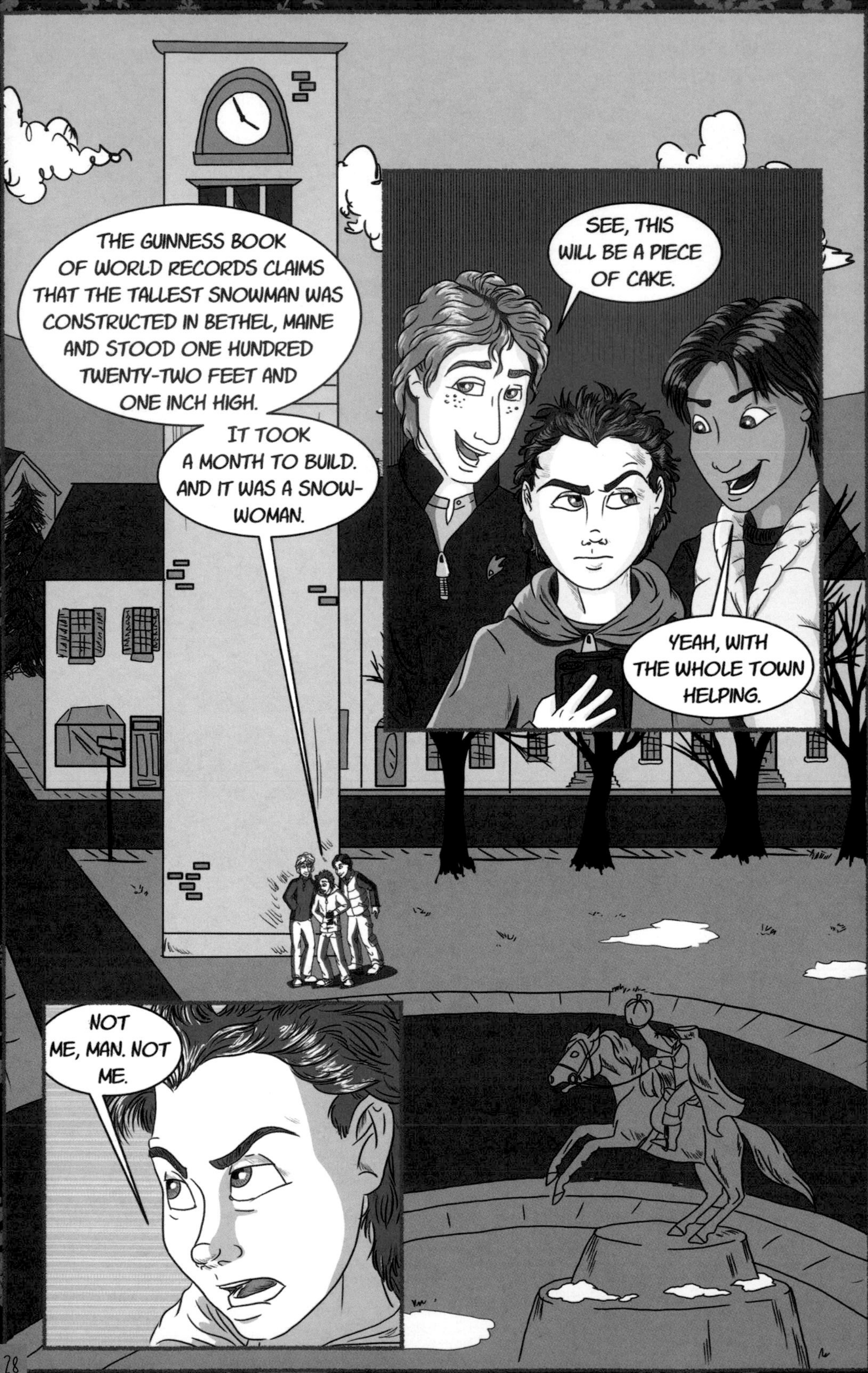
THE GUINNESS BOOK OF WORLD RECORDS CLAIMS THAT THE TALLEST SNOWMAN WAS CONSTRUCTED IN BETHEL, MAINE AND STOOD ONE HUNDRED TWENTY-TWO FEET AND ONE INCH HIGH.
IT TOOK A MONTH TO BUILD. AND IT WAS A SNOW-WOMAN.
SEE, THIS WILL BE A PIECE OF CAKE.
YEAH, WITH THE WHOLE TOWN HELPING.
NOT ME, MAN. NOT ME.

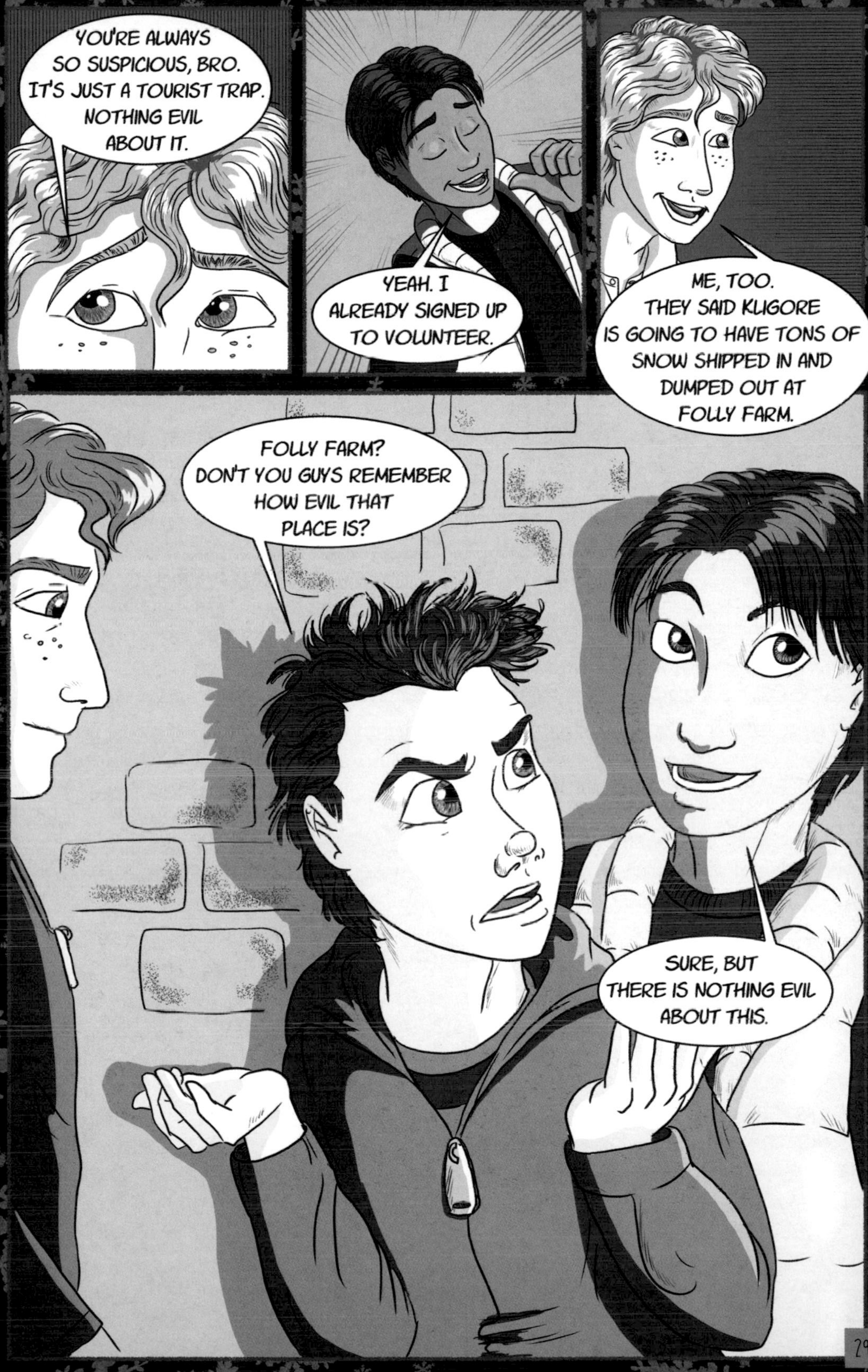
YOU'RE ALWAYS SO SUSPICIOUS, BRO. IT'S JUST A TOURIST TRAP. NOTHING EVIL ABOUT IT.
YEAH. I ALREADY SIGNED UP TO VOLUNTEER.
ME, TOO. THEY SAID KLIGORE IS GOING TO HAVE TONS OF SNOW SHIPPED IN AND DUMPED OUT AT FOLLY FARM.
FOLLY FARM? DON'T YOU GUYS REMEMBER HOW EVIL THAT PLACE IS?
SURE, BUT THERE IS NOTHING EVIL ABOUT THIS.

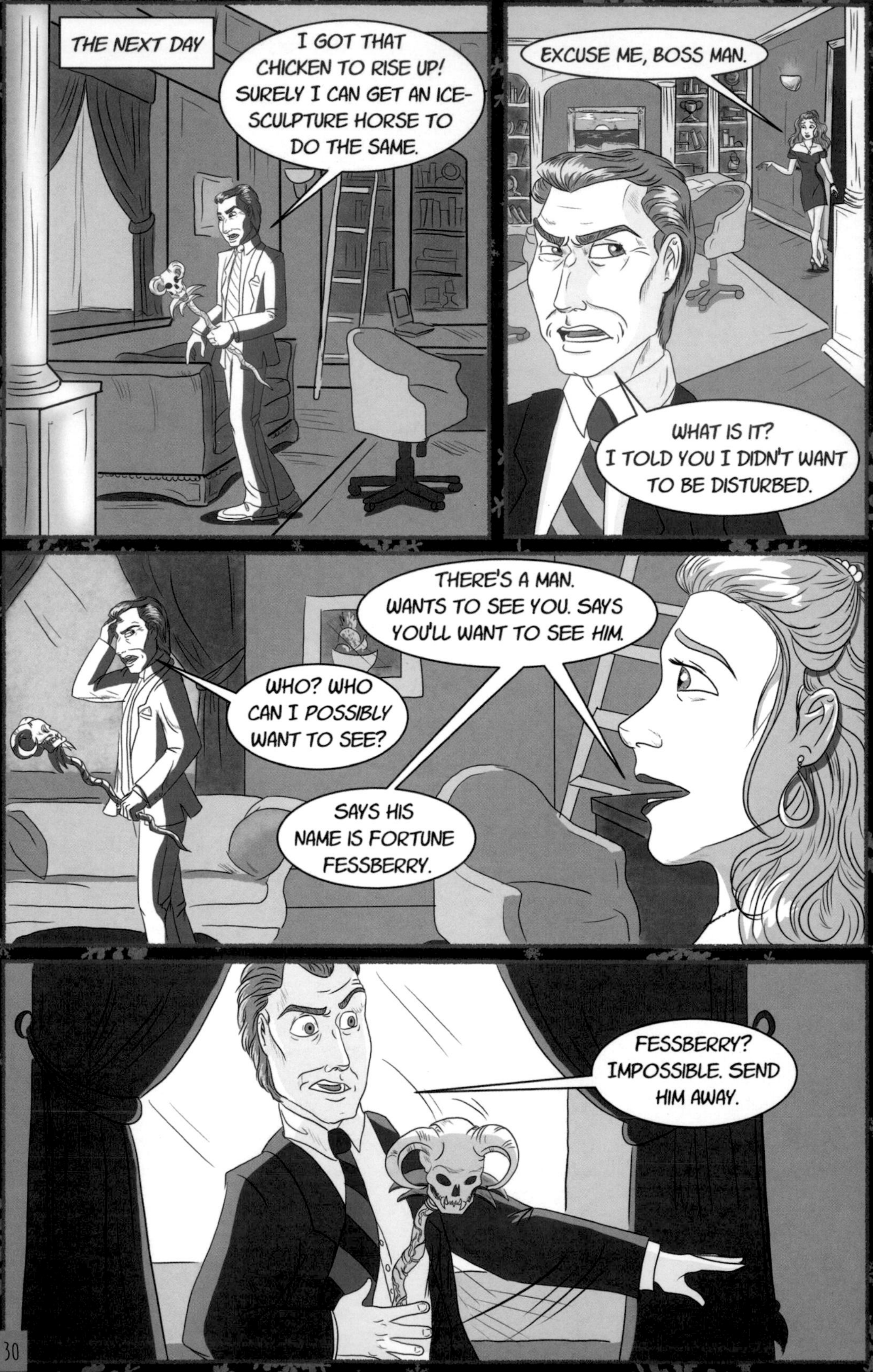
THE NEXT DAY
I GOT THAT CHICKEN TO RISE UP! SURELY I CAN GET AN ICE-SCULPTURE HORSE TO DO THE SAME.
EXCUSE ME, BOSS MAN.
WHAT IS IT? I TOLD YOU I DIDN'T WANT TO BE DISTURBED.
THERE'S A MAN. WANTS TO SEE YOU. SAYS YOU'LL WANT TO SEE HIM.
WHO? WHO CAN I POSSIBLY WANT TO SEE?
SAYS HIS NAME IS FORTUNE FESSBERRY.
FESSBERRY? IMPOSSIBLE. SEND HIM AWAY.

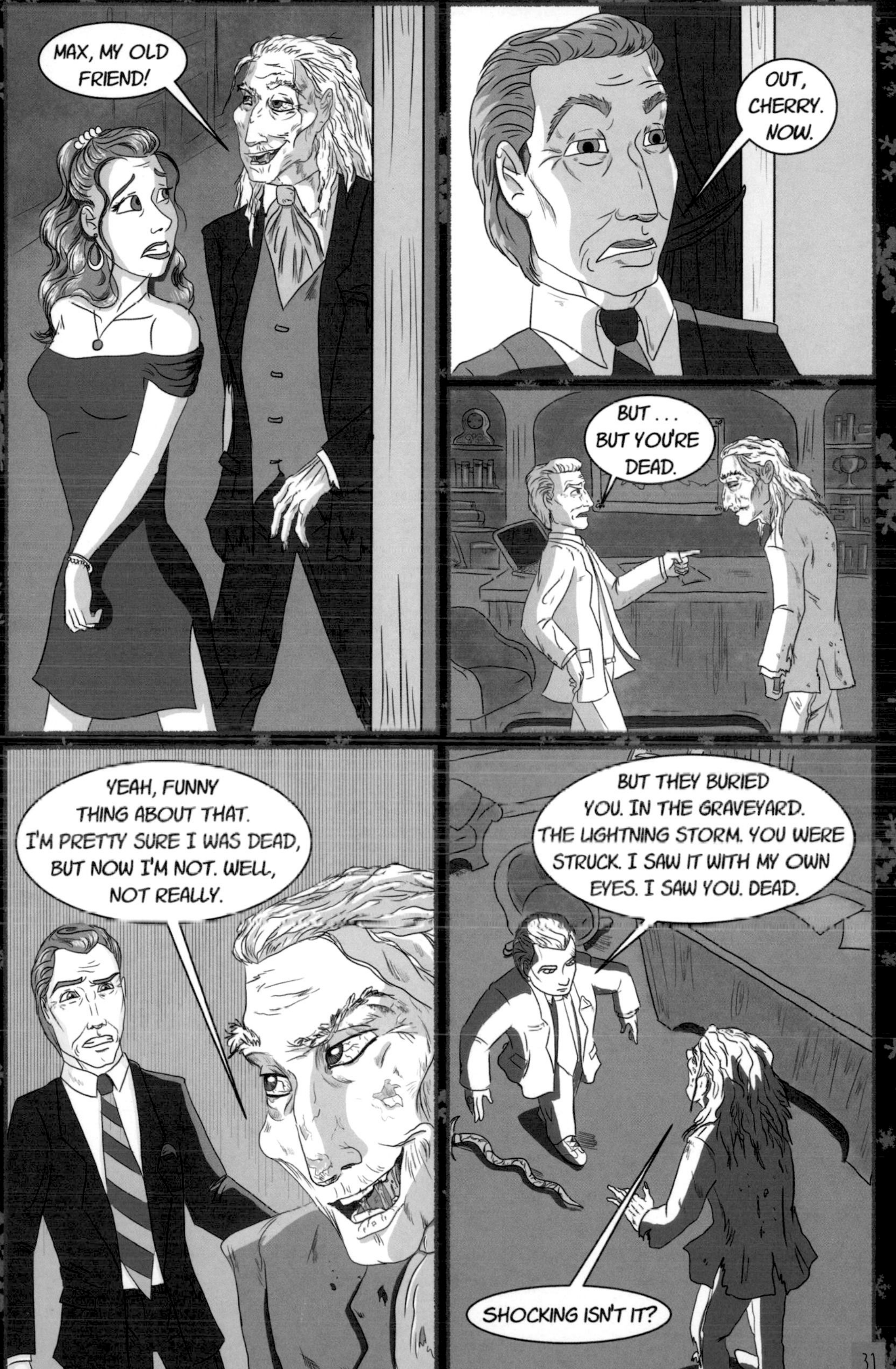
MAX, MY OLD FRIEND!
OUT, CHERRY. NOW.
BUT . . . BUT YOU'RE DEAD.
YEAH, FUNNY THING ABOUT THAT. I'M PRETTY SURE I WAS DEAD, BUT NOW I'M NOT. WELL, NOT REALLY.
BUT THEY BURIED YOU. IN THE GRAVEYARD. THE LIGHTNING STORM. YOU WERE STRUCK. I SAW IT WITH MY OWN EYES. I SAW YOU. DEAD.
SHOCKING ISN'T IT?

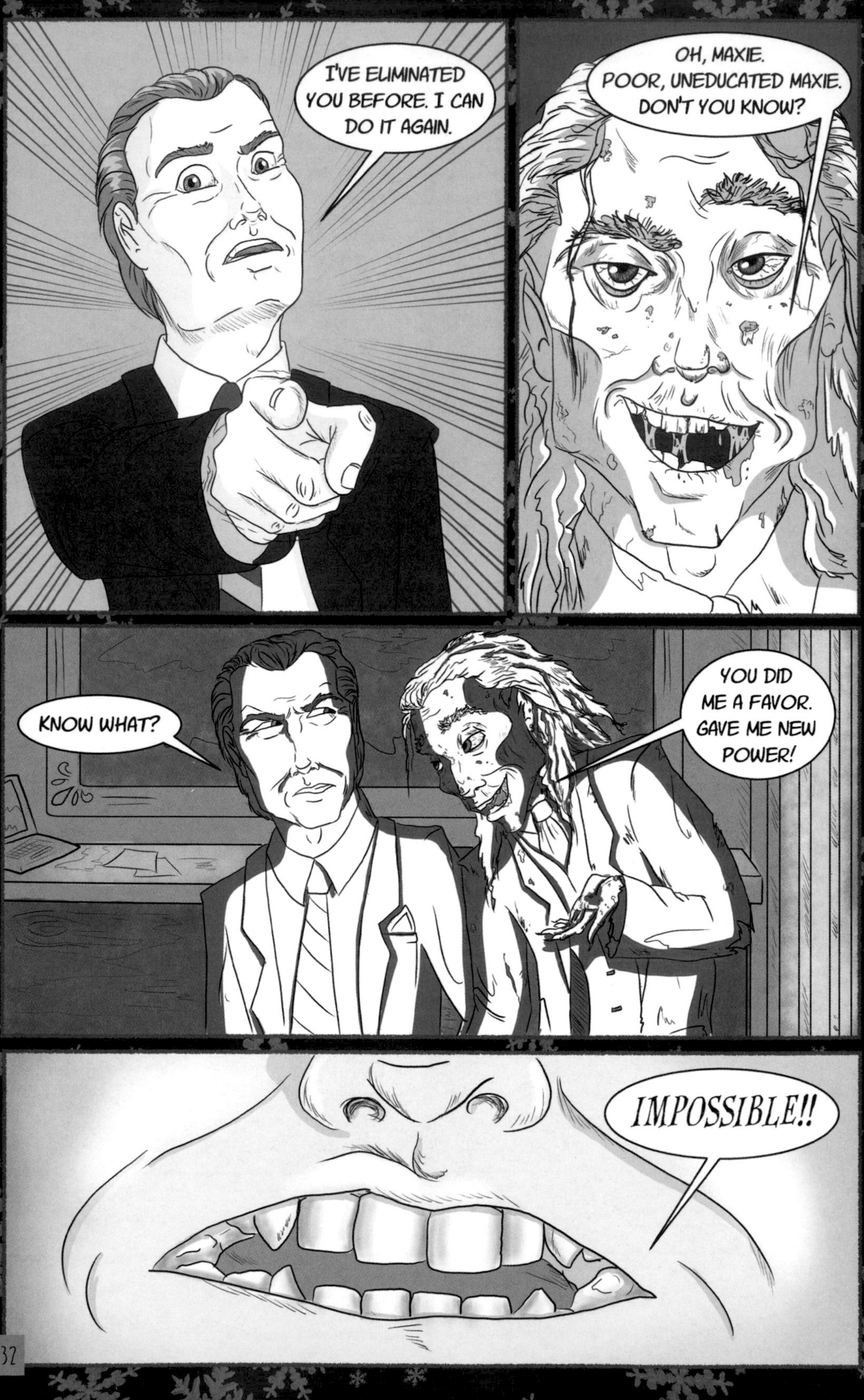
I'VE ELIMINATED YOU BEFORE. I CAN DO IT AGAIN.
OH, MAXIE. POOR, UNEDUCATED MAXIE. DON'T YOU KNOW?
KNOW WHAT?
YOU DID ME A FAVOR. GAVE ME NEW POWER!
IMPOSSIBLE!!

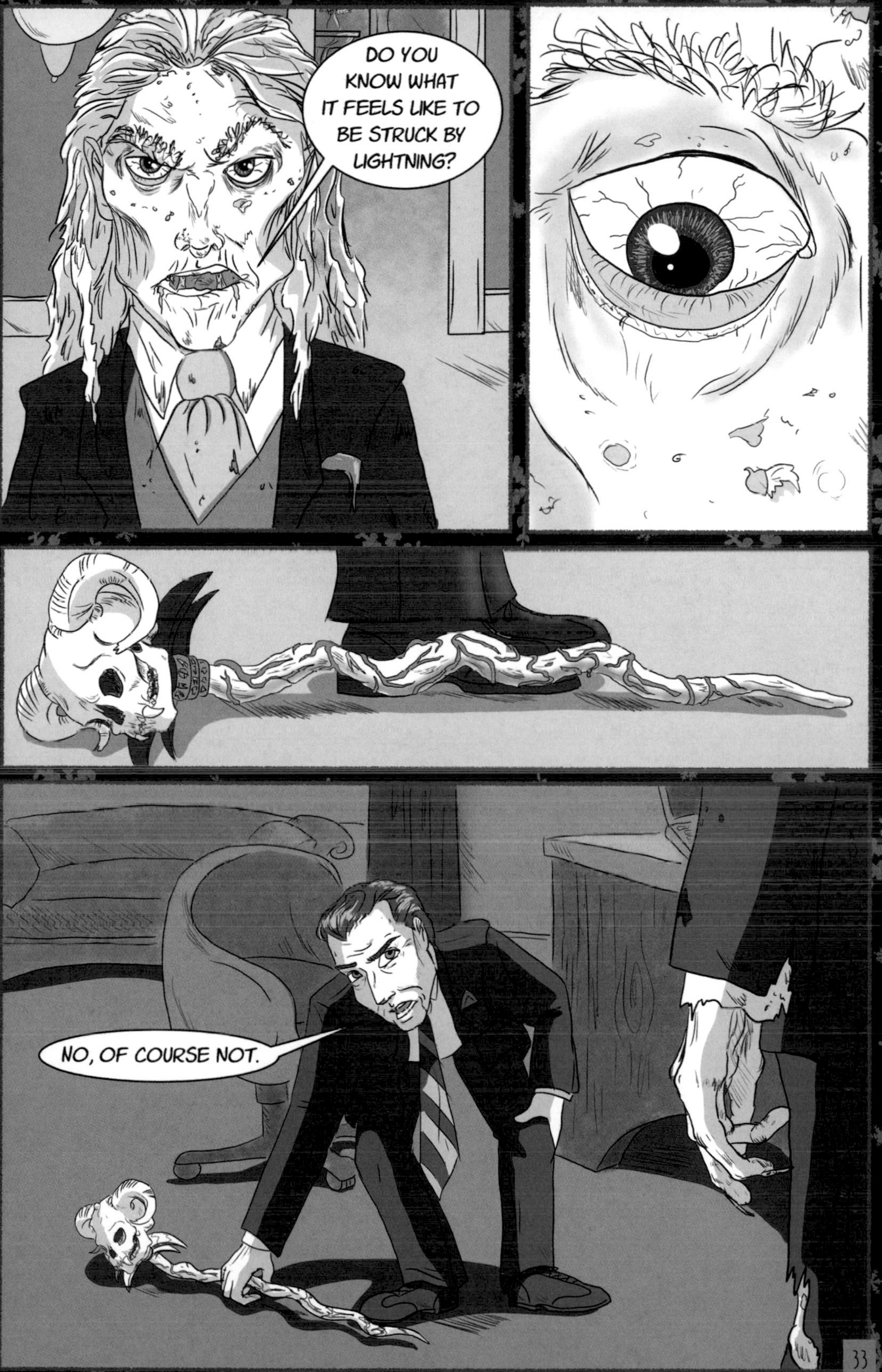
DO YOU KNOW WHAT IT FEELS LIKE TO BE STRUCK BY LIGHTNING?
NO, OF COURSE NOT.

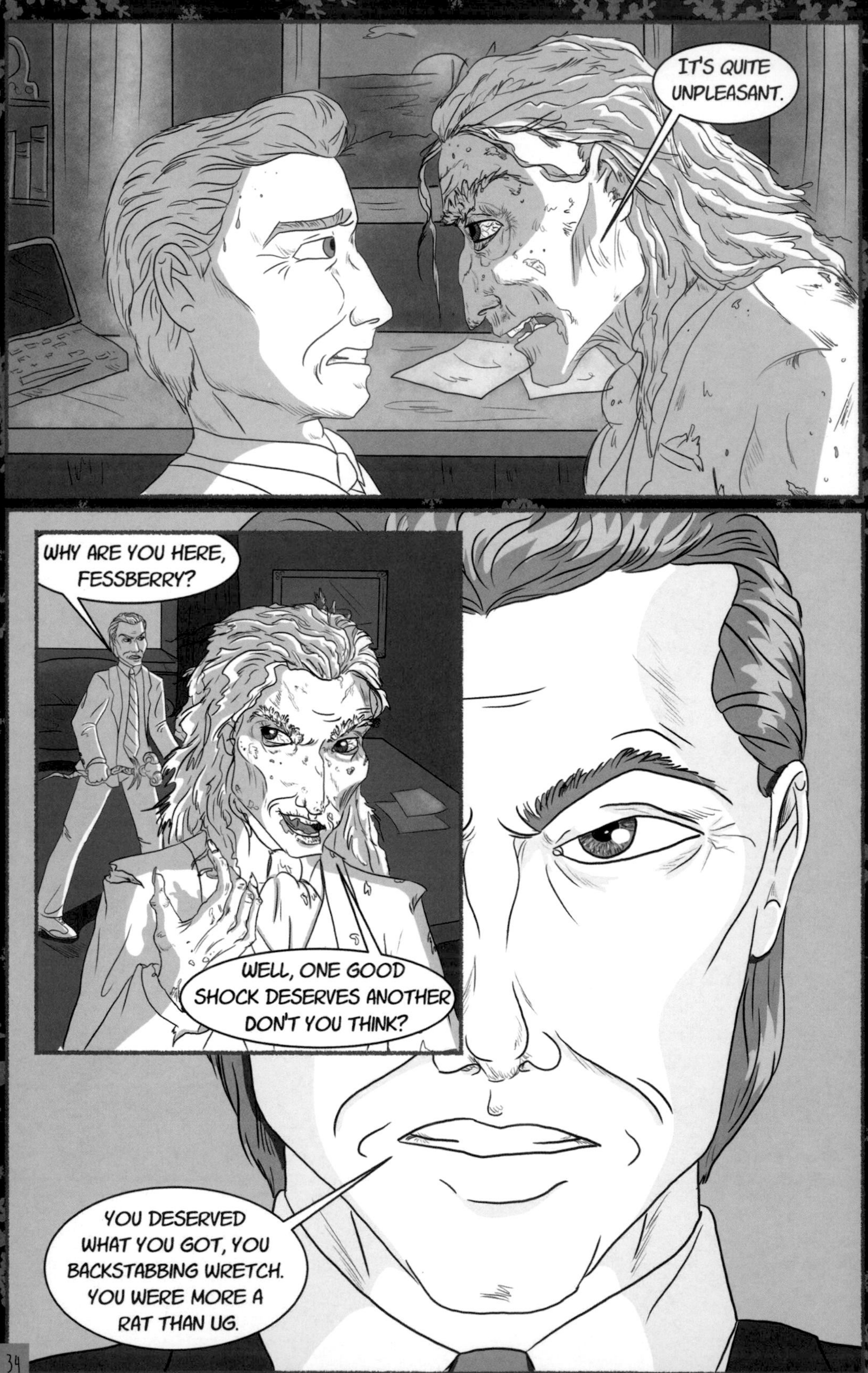
IT'S QUITE UNPLEASANT.
WHY ARE YOU HERE, FESSBERRY?
WELL, ONE GOOD SHOCK DESERVES ANOTHER DON'T YOU THINK?
YOU DESERVED WHAT YOU GOT, YOU BACKSTABBING WRETCH. YOU WERE MORE A RAT THAN UG.

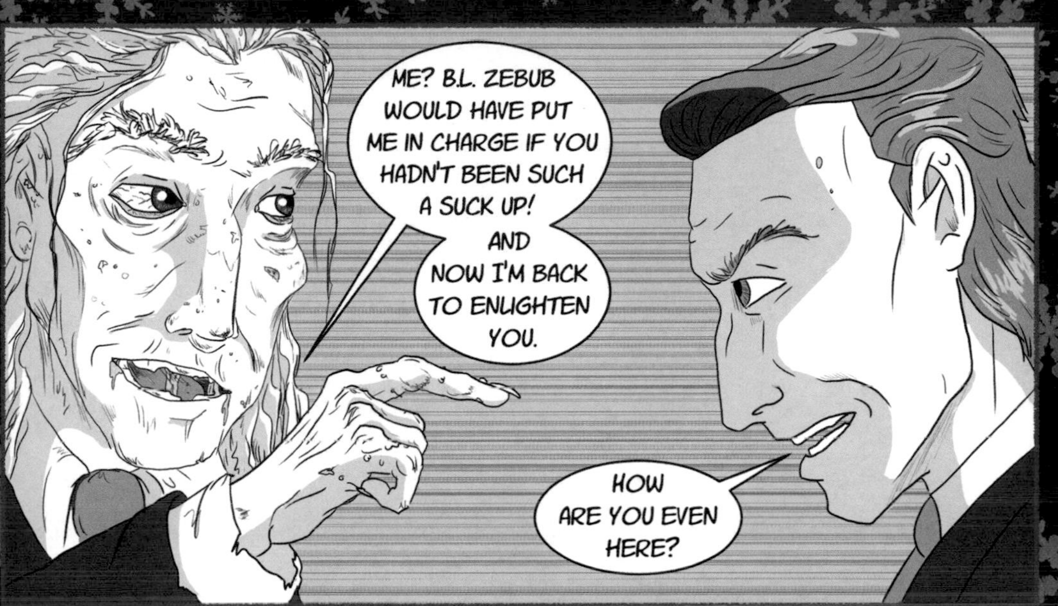
ME? B.L. ZEBUB WOULD HAVE PUT ME IN CHARGE IF YOU HADN'T BEEN SUCH A SUCK UP!
AND NOW I'M BACK TO ENLIGHTEN YOU.
HOW ARE YOU EVEN HERE?

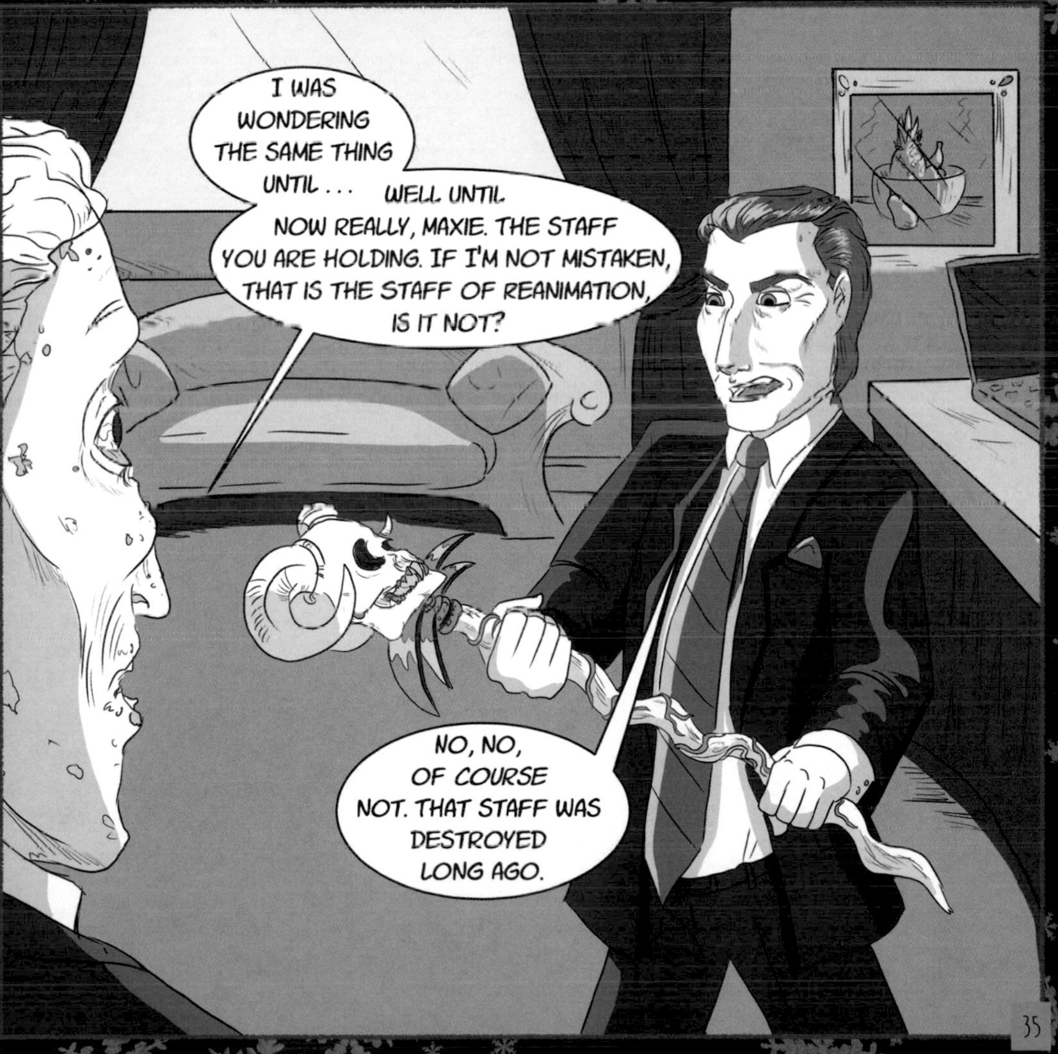
I WAS WONDERING THE SAME THING UNTIL . . . WELL UNTIL NOW REALLY, MAXIE. THE STAFF YOU ARE HOLDING. IF I'M NOT MISTAKEN, THAT IS THE STAFF OF REANIMATION, IS IT NOT?
NO, NO, OF COURSE NOT. THAT STAFF WAS DESTROYED LONG AGO.

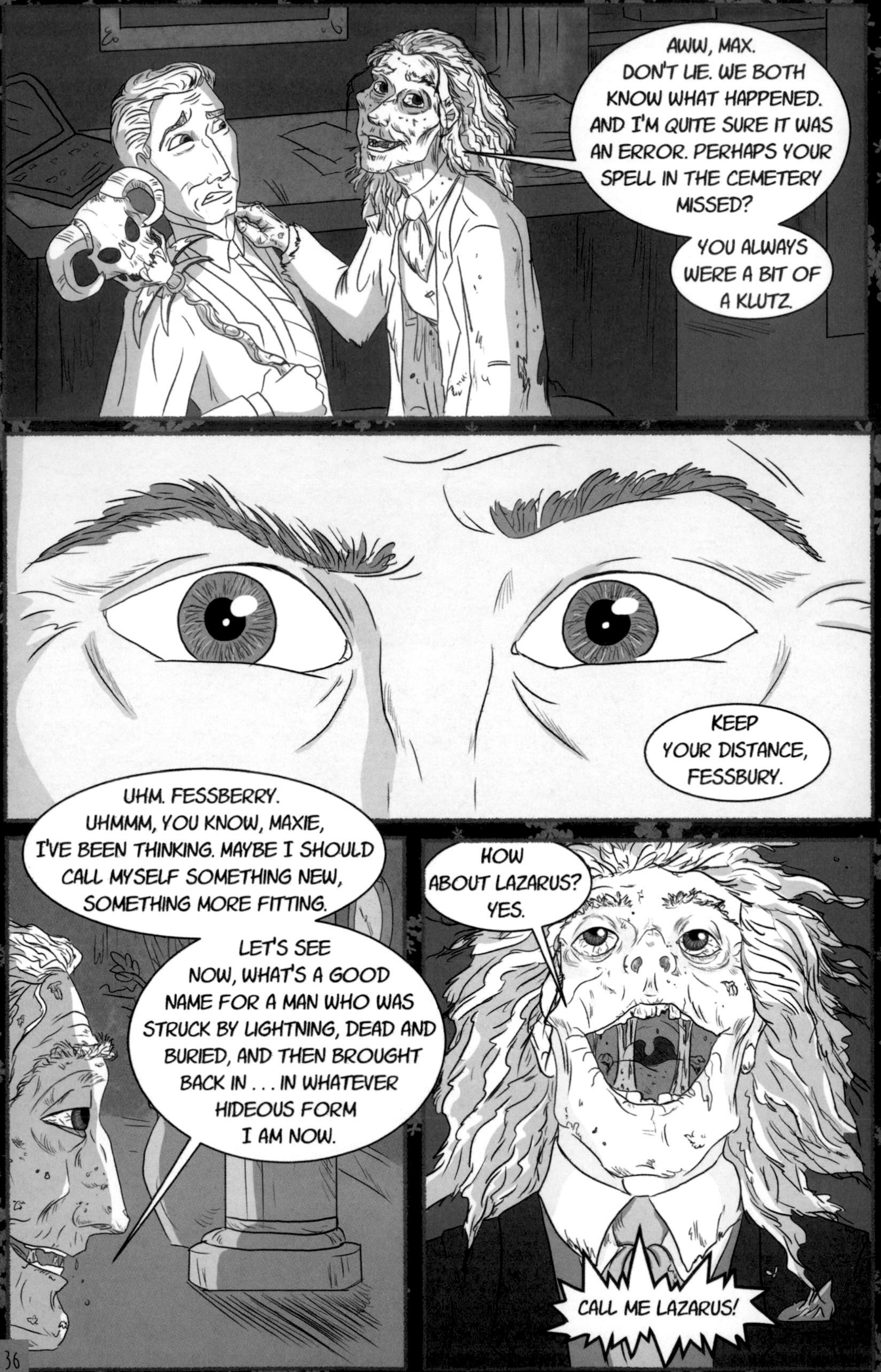
AWW, MAX. DON'T LIE. WE BOTH KNOW WHAT HAPPENED. AND I'M QUITE SURE IT WAS AN ERROR. PERHAPS YOUR SPELL IN THE CEMETERY MISSED?
YOU ALWAYS WERE A BIT OF A KLUTZ.
KEEP YOUR DISTANCE, FESSBURY.
UHM. FESSBERRY. UHMMM, YOU KNOW, MAXIE, I'VE BEEN THINKING. MAYBE I SHOULD CALL MYSELF SOMETHING NEW, SOMETHING MORE FITTING.
LET'S SEE NOW, WHAT'S A GOOD NAME FOR A MAN WHO WAS STRUCK BY LIGHTNING, DEAD AND BURIED, AND THEN BROUGHT BACK IN . . . IN WHATEVER HIDEOUS FORM I AM NOW.
HOW ABOUT LAZARUS? YES.
CALL ME LAZARUS!

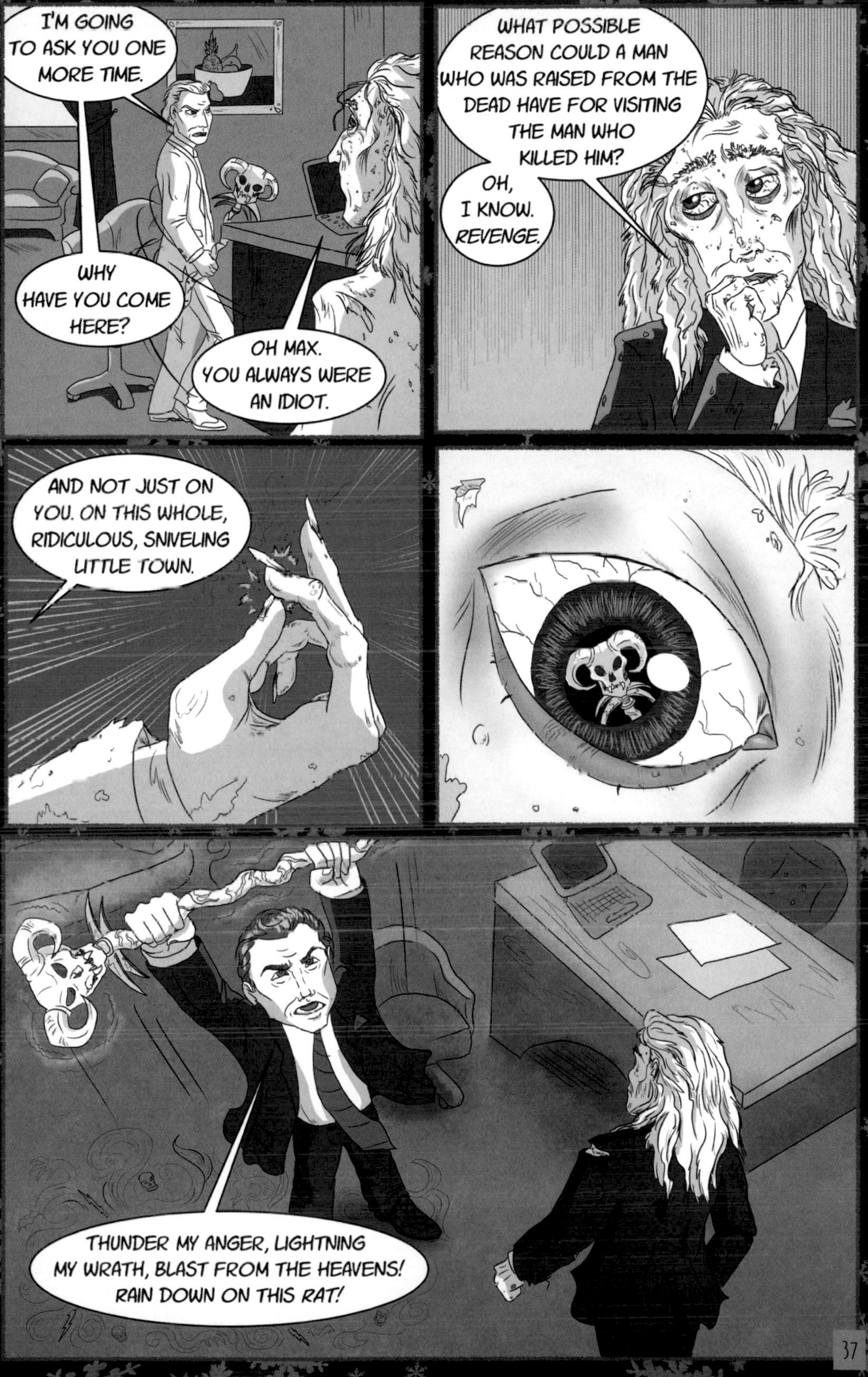
I'M GOING TO ASK YOU ONE MORE TIME.
WHY HAVE YOU COME HERE?
OH MAX. YOU ALWAYS WERE AN IDIOT.
WHAT POSSIBLE REASON COULD A MAN WHO WAS RAISED FROM THE DEAD HAVE FOR VISITING THE MAN WHO KILLED HIM?
OH, I KNOW. REVENGE.
AND NOT JUST ON YOU. ON THIS WHOLE, RIDICULOUS, SNIVELING LITTLE TOWN.
THUNDER MY ANGER, LIGHTNING MY WRATH, BLAST FROM THE HEAVENS! RAIN DOWN ON THIS RAT!

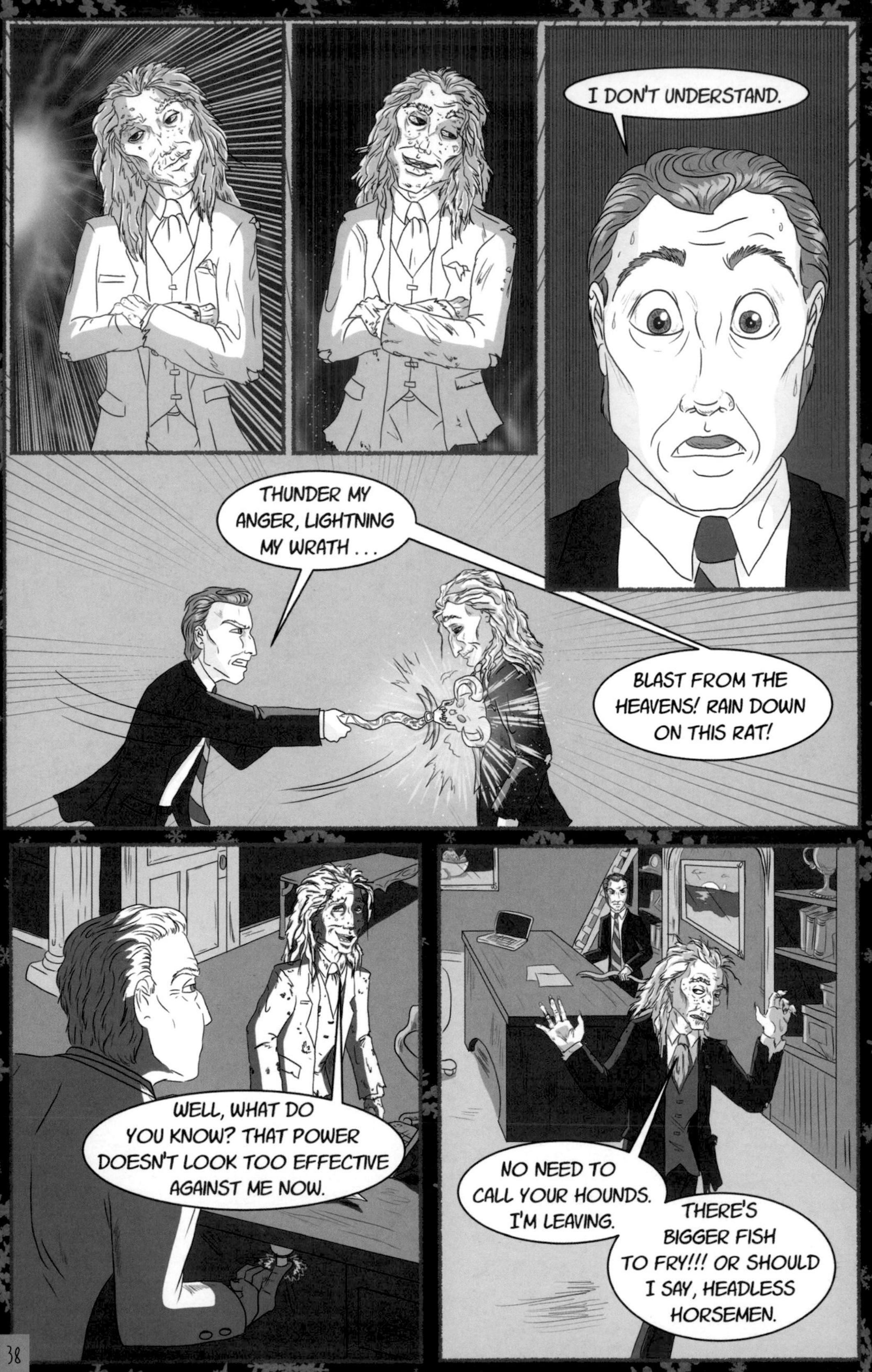
I DON'T UNDERSTAND.
THUNDER MY ANGER, LIGHTNING MY WRATH . . .
BLAST FROM THE HEAVENS! RAIN DOWN ON THIS RAT!
WELL, WHAT DO YOU KNOW? THAT POWER DOESN'T LOOK TOO EFFECTIVE AGAINST ME NOW.
NO NEED TO CALL YOUR HOUNDS. I'M LEAVING.
THERE'S BIGGER FISH TO FRY!!! OR SHOULD I SAY, HEADLESS HORSEMEN.

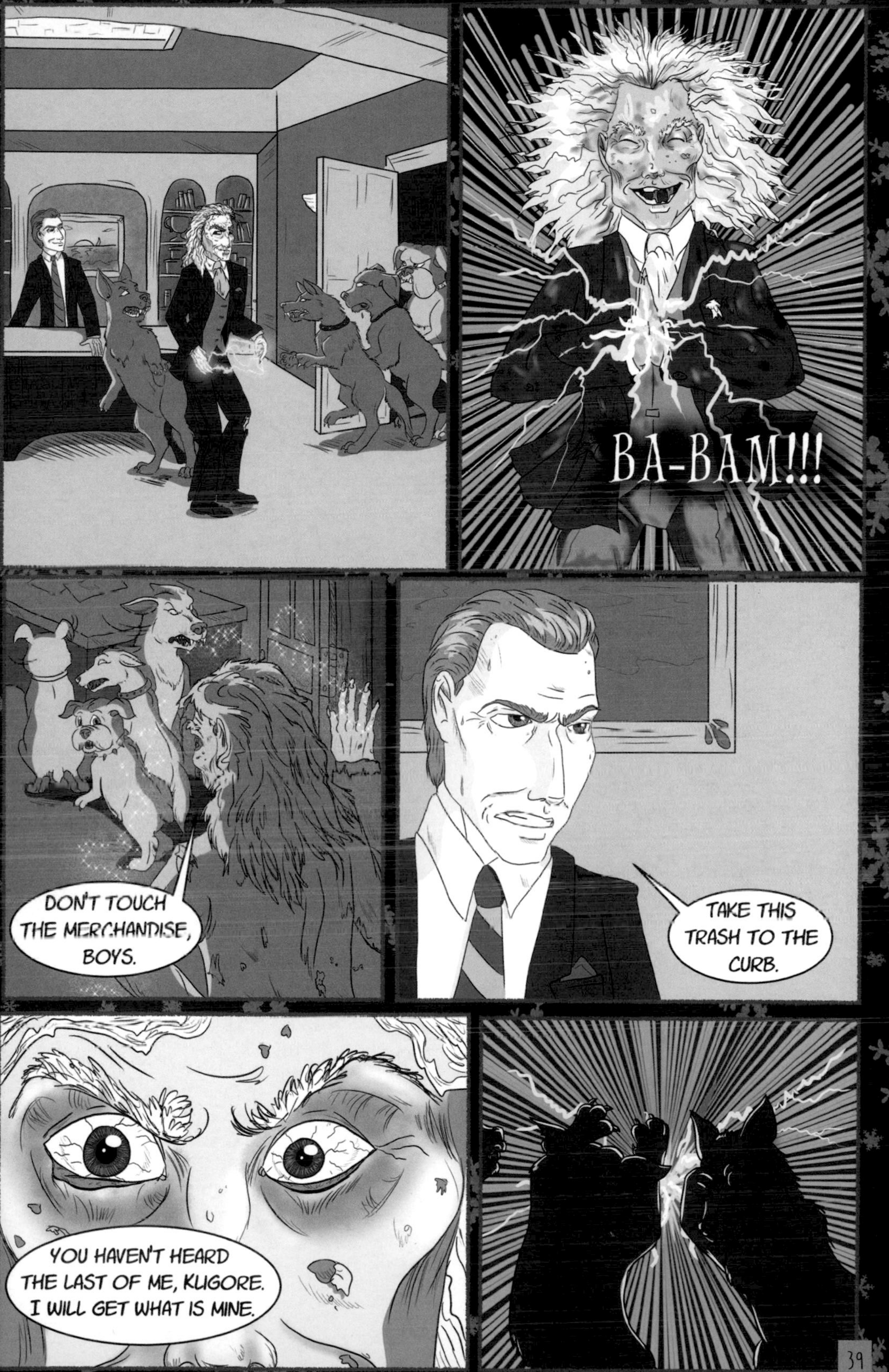
BA-BAM!!!
DON'T TOUCH THE MERCHANDISE, BOYS.
TAKE THIS TRASH TO THE CURB.
YOU HAVEN'T HEARD THE LAST OF ME, KLIGORE. I WILL GET WHAT IS MINE.

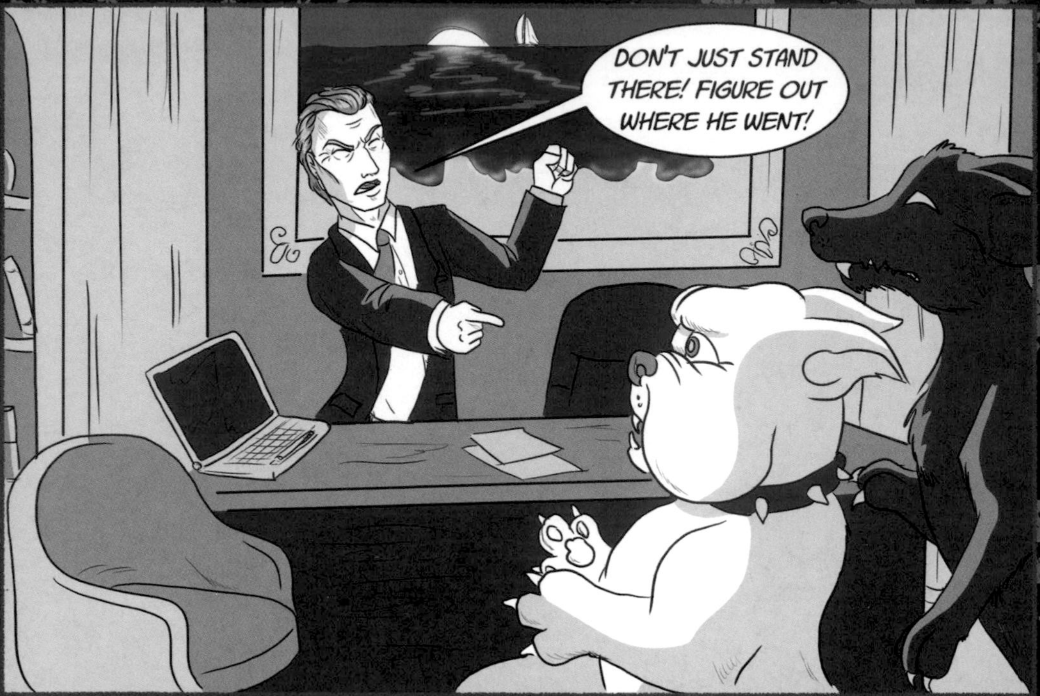
DON'T JUST STAND THERE! FIGURE OUT WHERE HE WENT!

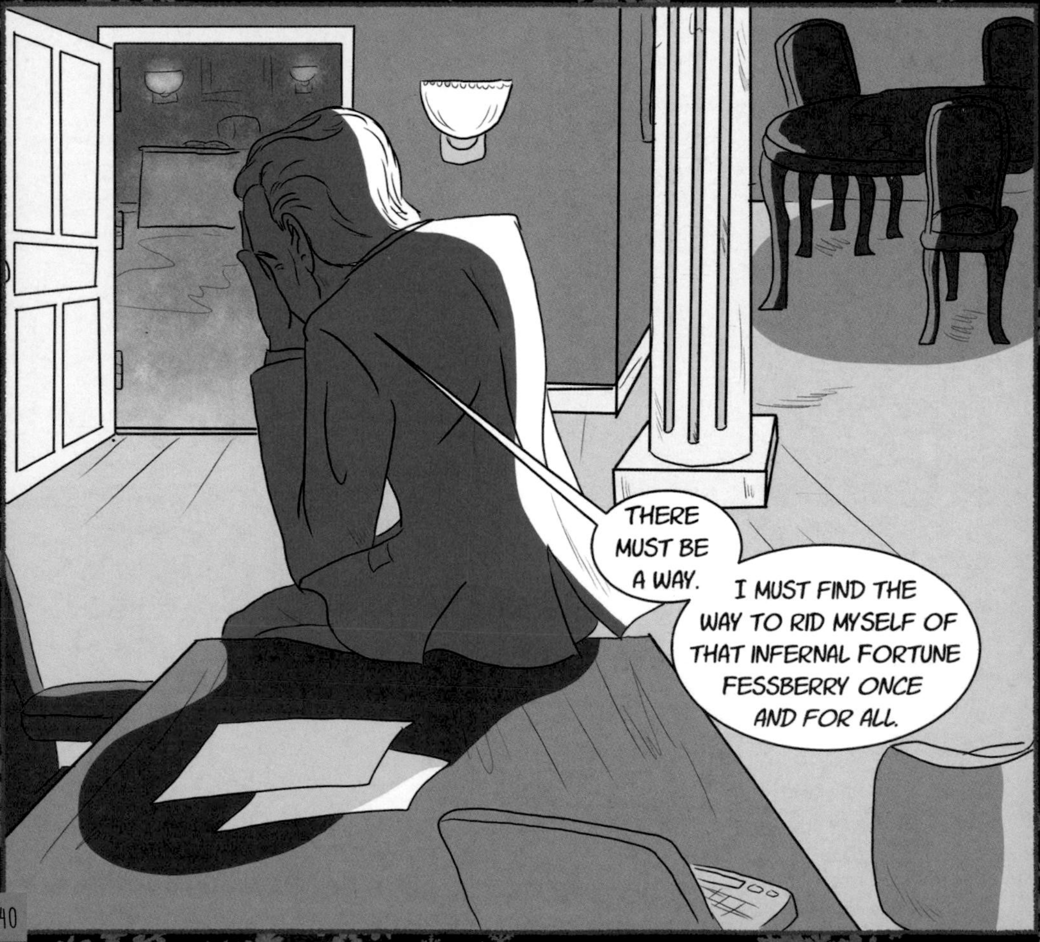
THERE MUST BE A WAY.
I MUST FIND THE WAY TO RID MYSELF OF THAT INFERNAL FORTUNE FESSBERRY ONCE AND FOR ALL.

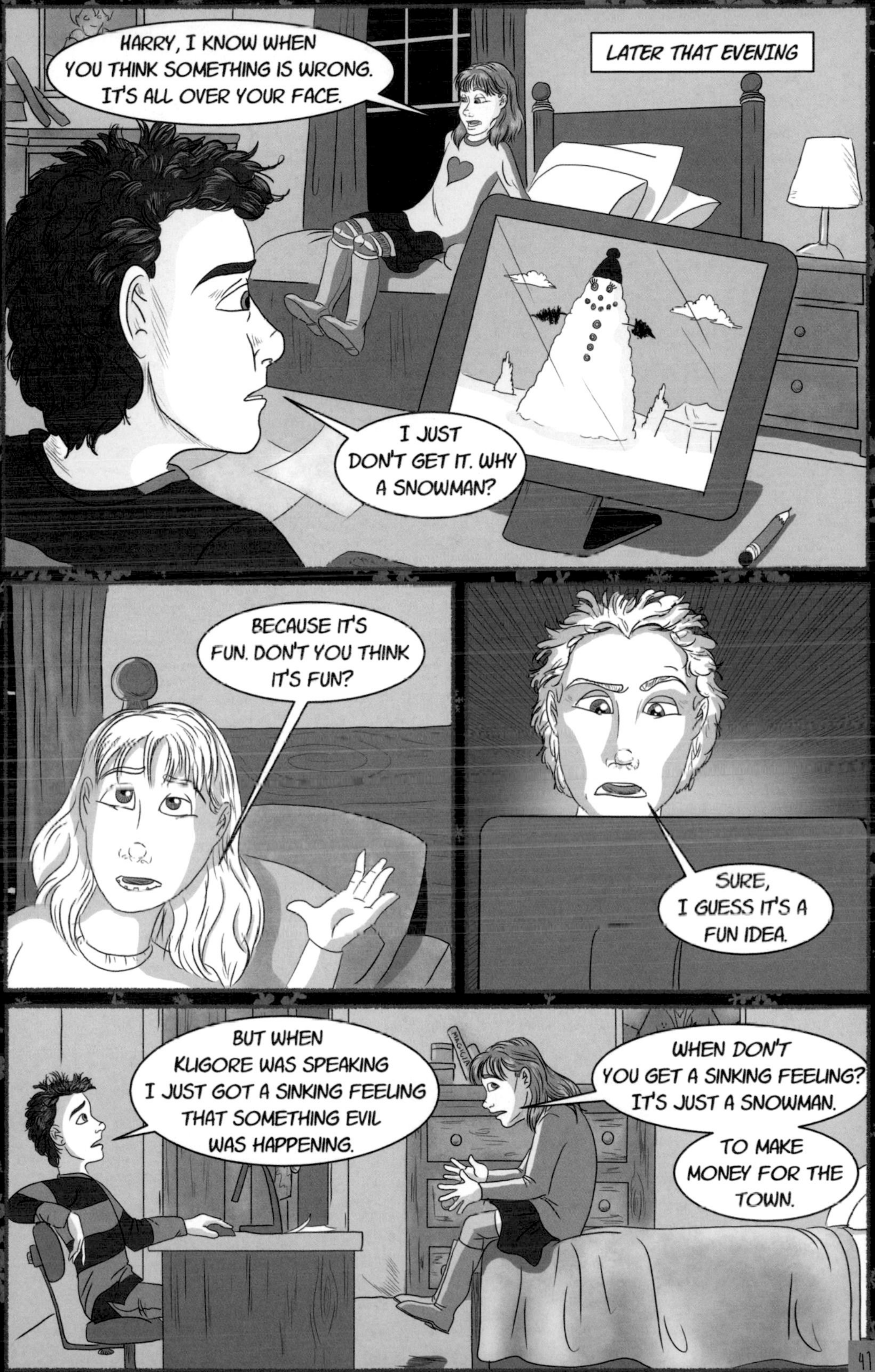
LATER THAT EVENING
HARRY, I KNOW WHEN YOU THINK SOMETHING IS WRONG. IT'S ALL OVER YOUR FACE.
I JUST DON'T GET IT. WHY A SNOWMAN?
BECAUSE IT'S FUN. DON'T YOU THINK IT'S FUN?
SURE, I GUESS IT'S A FUN IDEA.
BUT WHEN KLIGORE WAS SPEAKING I JUST GOT A SINKING FEELING THAT SOMETHING EVIL WAS HAPPENING.
WHEN DON'T YOU GET A SINKING FEELING? IT'S JUST A SNOWMAN.
TO MAKE MONEY FOR THE TOWN.

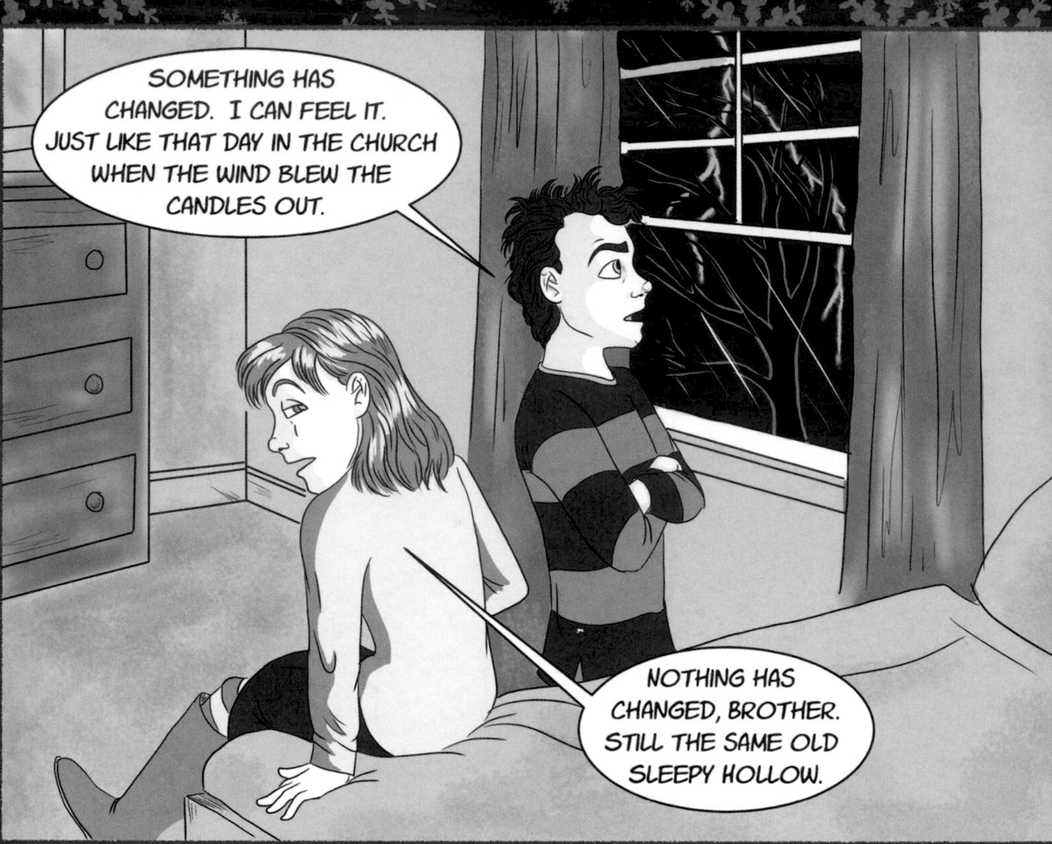
SOMETHING HAS CHANGED. I CAN FEEL IT. JUST LIKE THAT DAY IN THE CHURCH WHEN THE WIND BLEW THE CANDLES OUT.
NOTHING HAS CHANGED, BROTHER. STILL THE SAME OLD SLEEPY HOLLOW.

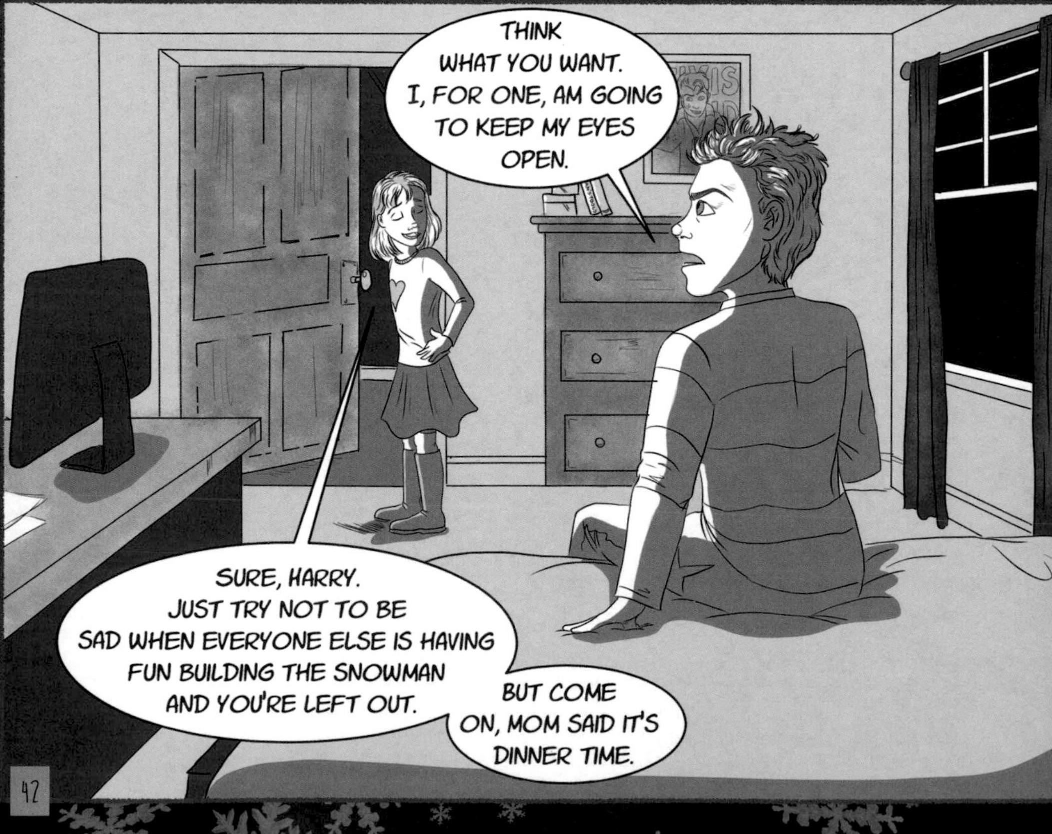
THINK WHAT YOU WANT. I, FOR ONE, AM GOING TO KEEP MY EYES OPEN.
SURE, HARRY. JUST TRY NOT TO BE SAD WHEN EVERYONE ELSE IS HAVING FUN BUILDING THE SNOWMAN AND YOU'RE LEFT OUT.
BUT COME ON, MOM SAID IT'S DINNER TIME.

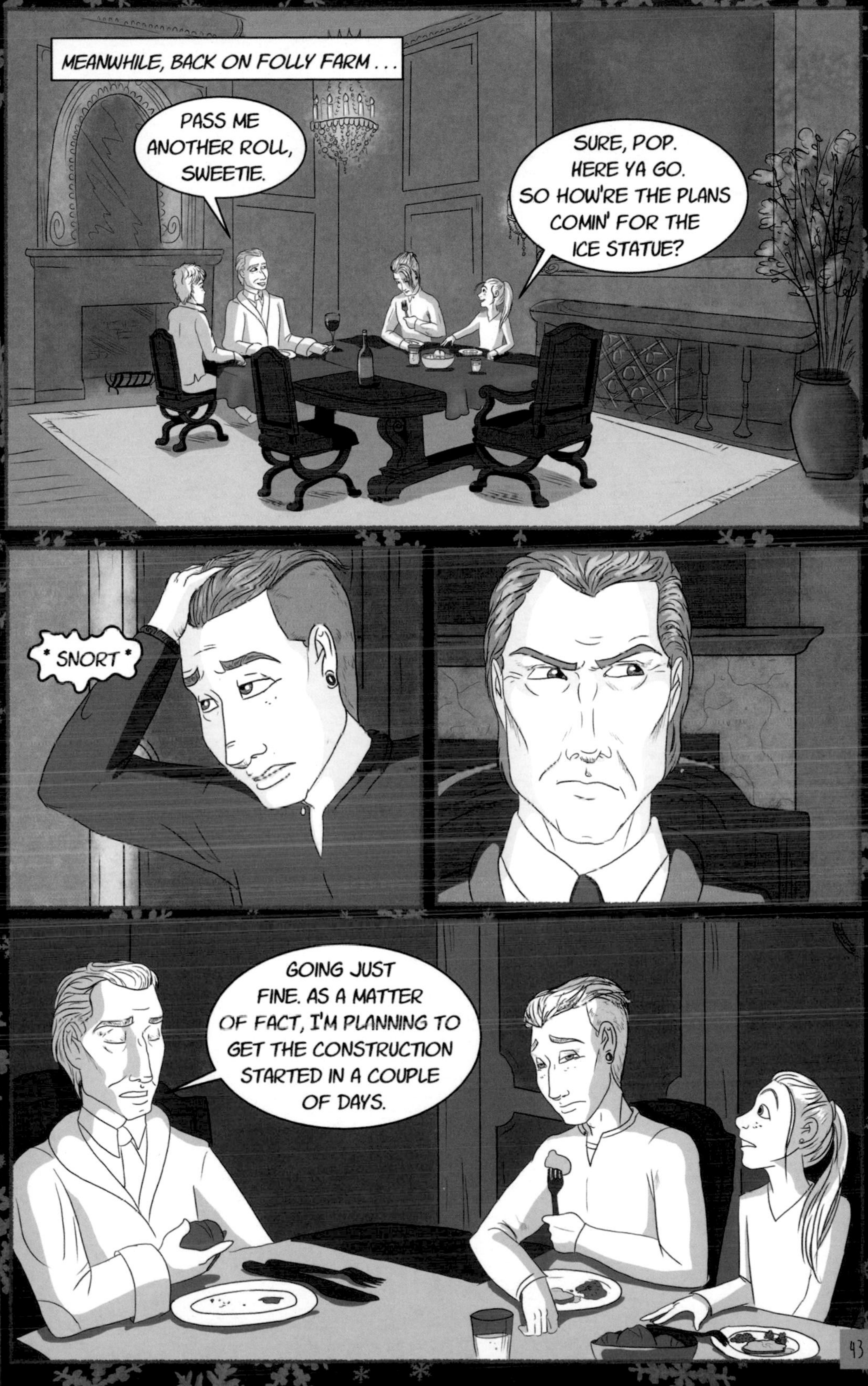
MEANWHILE, BACK ON FOLLY FARM . . .
PASS ME ANOTHER ROLL, SWEETIE.
SURE, POP. HERE YA GO. SO HOW'RE THE PLANS COMIN' FOR THE ICE STATUE?
* SNORT *
GOING JUST FINE. AS A MATTER OF FACT, I'M PLANNING TO GET THE CONSTRUCTION STARTED IN A COUPLE OF DAYS.

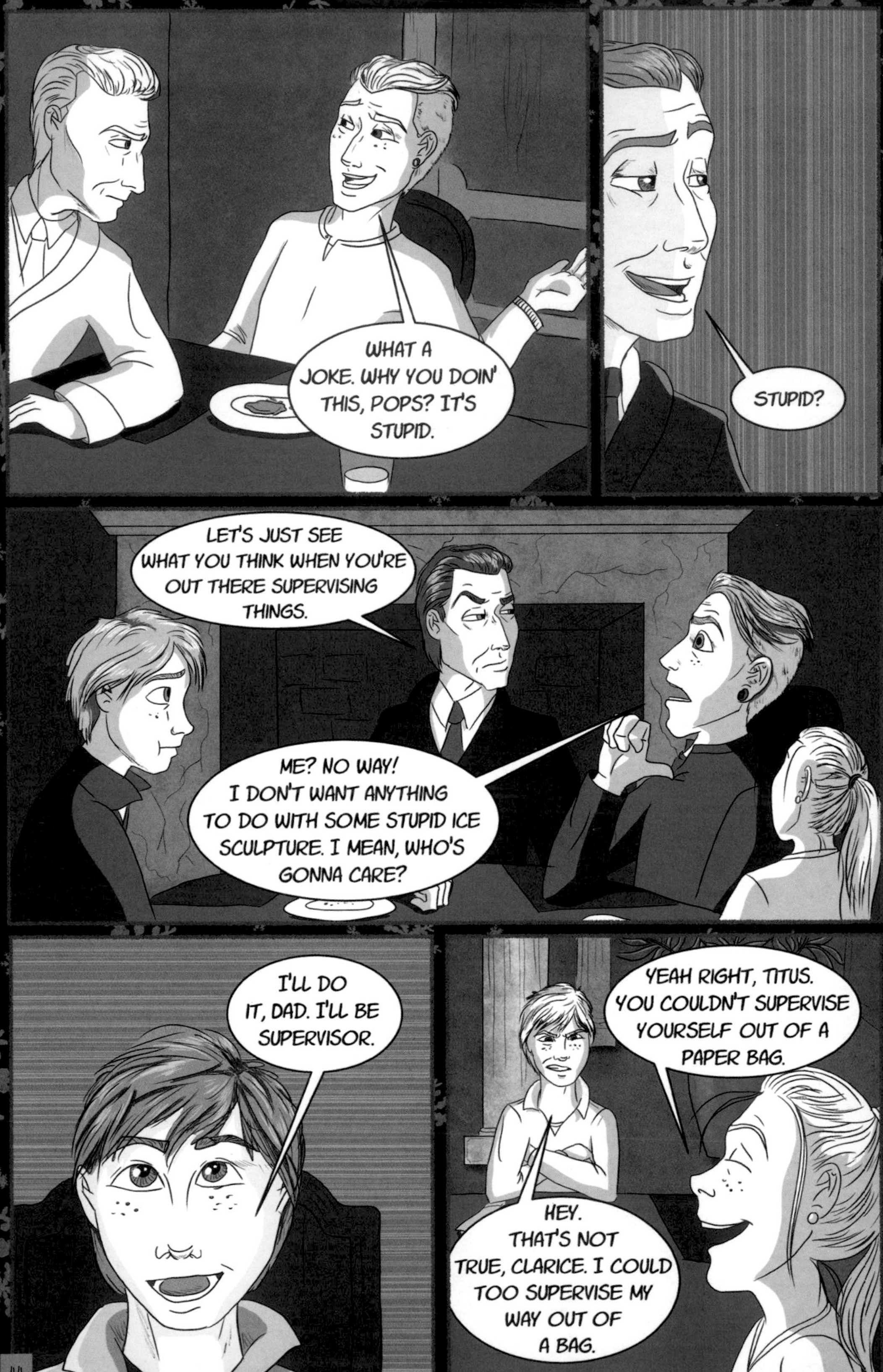
WHAT A JOKE. WHY YOU DOIN' THIS, POPS? IT'S STUPID.
STUPID?
LET'S JUST SEE WHAT YOU THINK WHEN YOU'RE OUT THERE SUPERVISING THINGS.
ME? NO WAY! I DON'T WANT ANYTHING TO DO WITH SOME STUPID ICE SCULPTURE. I MEAN, WHO'S GONNA CARE?
I'LL DO IT, DAD. I'LL BE SUPERVISOR.
YEAH RIGHT, TITUS. YOU COULDN'T SUPERVISE YOURSELF OUT OF A PAPER BAG.
HEY. THAT'S NOT TRUE, CLARICE. I COULD TOO SUPERVISE MY WAY OUT OF A BAG.

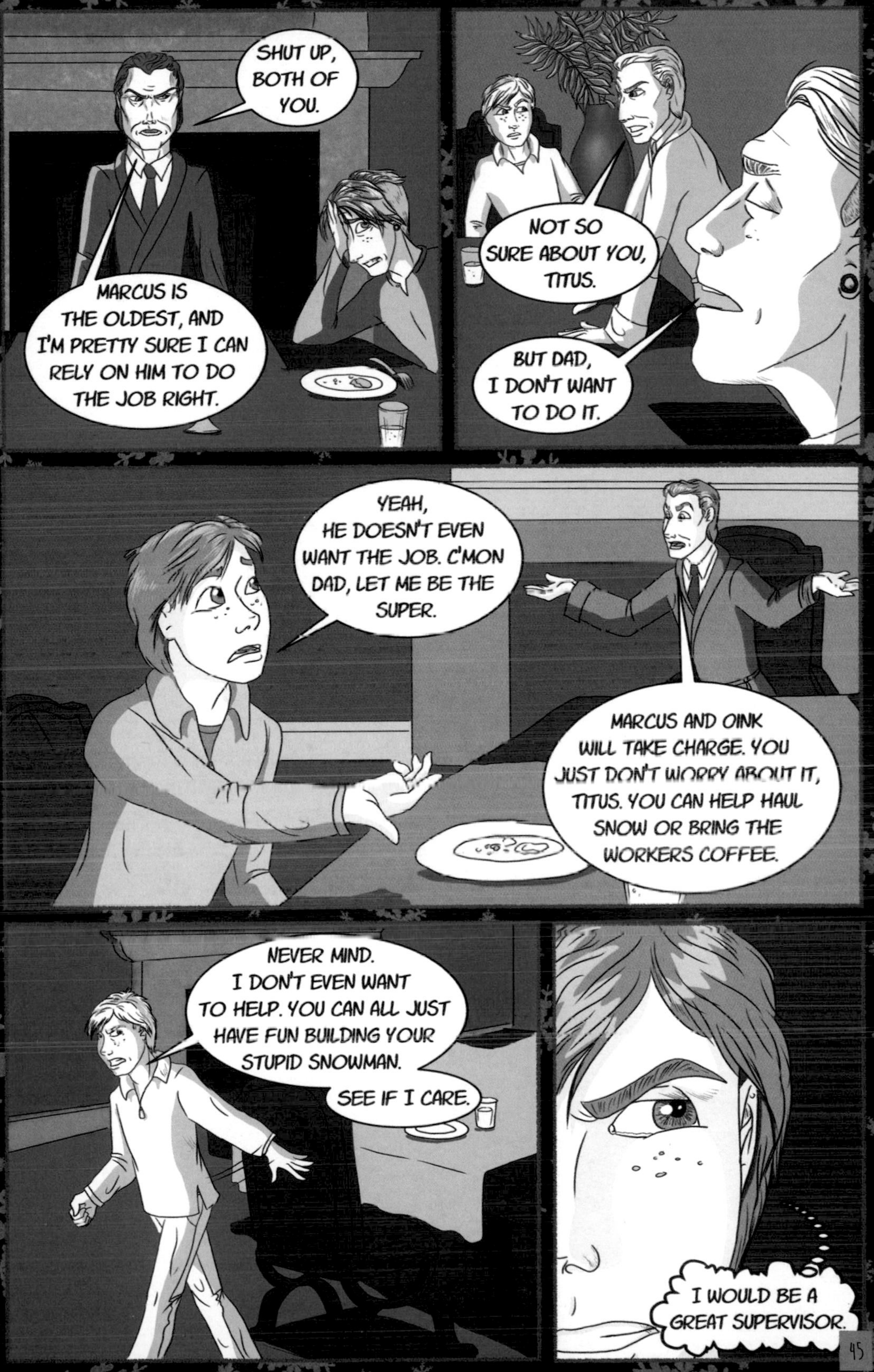
SHUT UP, BOTH OF YOU.
MARCUS IS THE OLDEST, AND I'M PRETTY SURE I CAN RELY ON HIM TO DO THE JOB RIGHT.
NOT SO SURE ABOUT YOU, TITUS.
BUT DAD, I DON'T WANT TO DO IT.
YEAH, HE DOESN'T EVEN WANT THE JOB. C'MON DAD, LET ME BE THE SUPER.
MARCUS AND OINK WILL TAKE CHARGE. YOU JUST DON'T WORRY ABOUT IT, TITUS. YOU CAN HELP HAUL SNOW OR BRING THE WORKERS COFFEE.
NEVER MIND. I DON'T EVEN WANT TO HELP. YOU CAN ALL JUST HAVE FUN BUILDING YOUR STUPID SNOWMAN.
SEE IF I CARE.
I WOULD BE A GREAT SUPERVISOR.

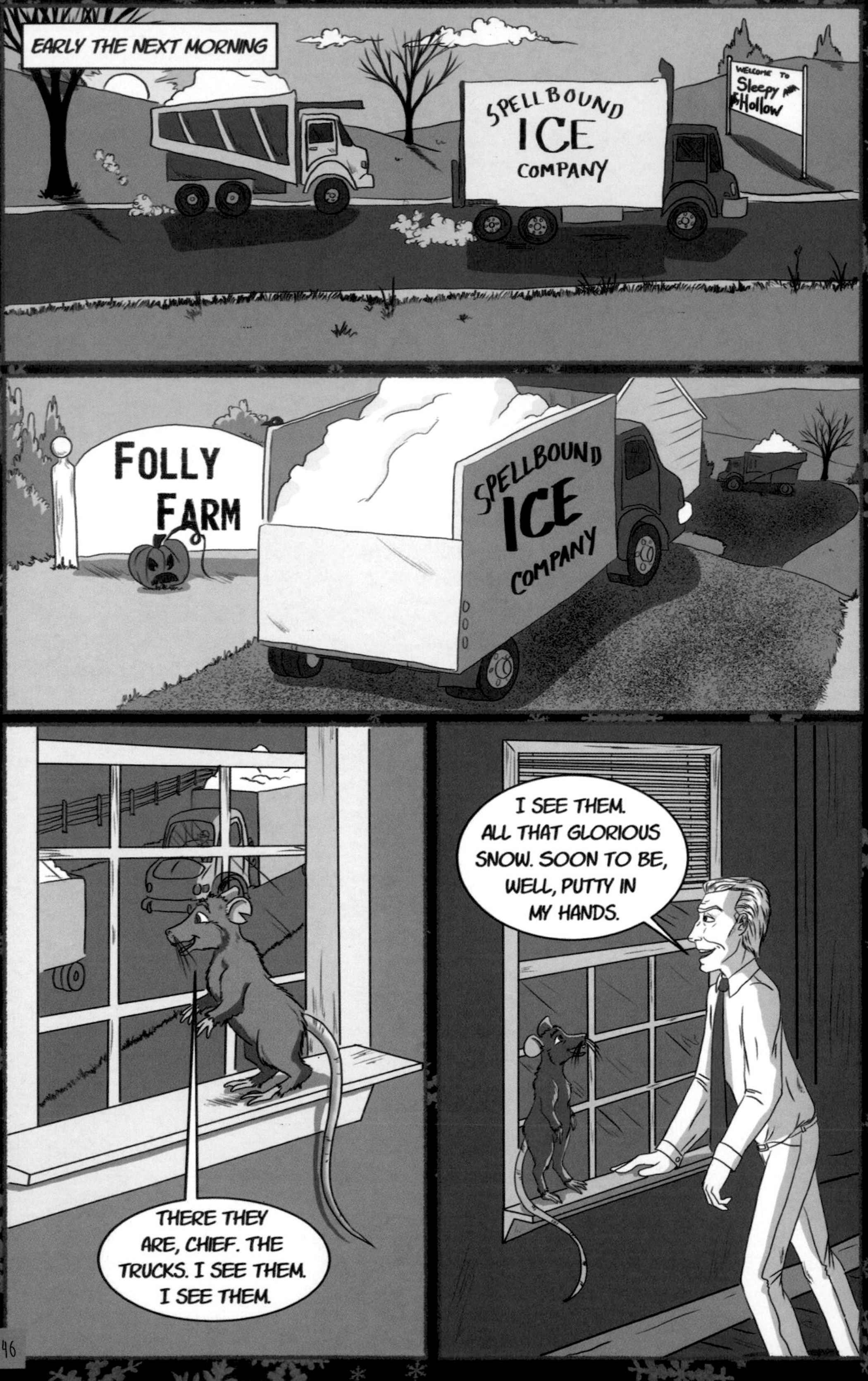
EARLY THE NEXT MORNING
SPELLBOUND ICE COMPANY
WELCOME TO Sleepy Hollow
FOLLY FARM
SPELLBOUND ICE COMPANY
THERE THEY ARE, CHIEF. THE TRUCKS. I SEE THEM. I SEE THEM.
I SEE THEM. ALL THAT GLORIOUS SNOW. SOON TO BE, WELL, PUTTY IN MY HANDS.

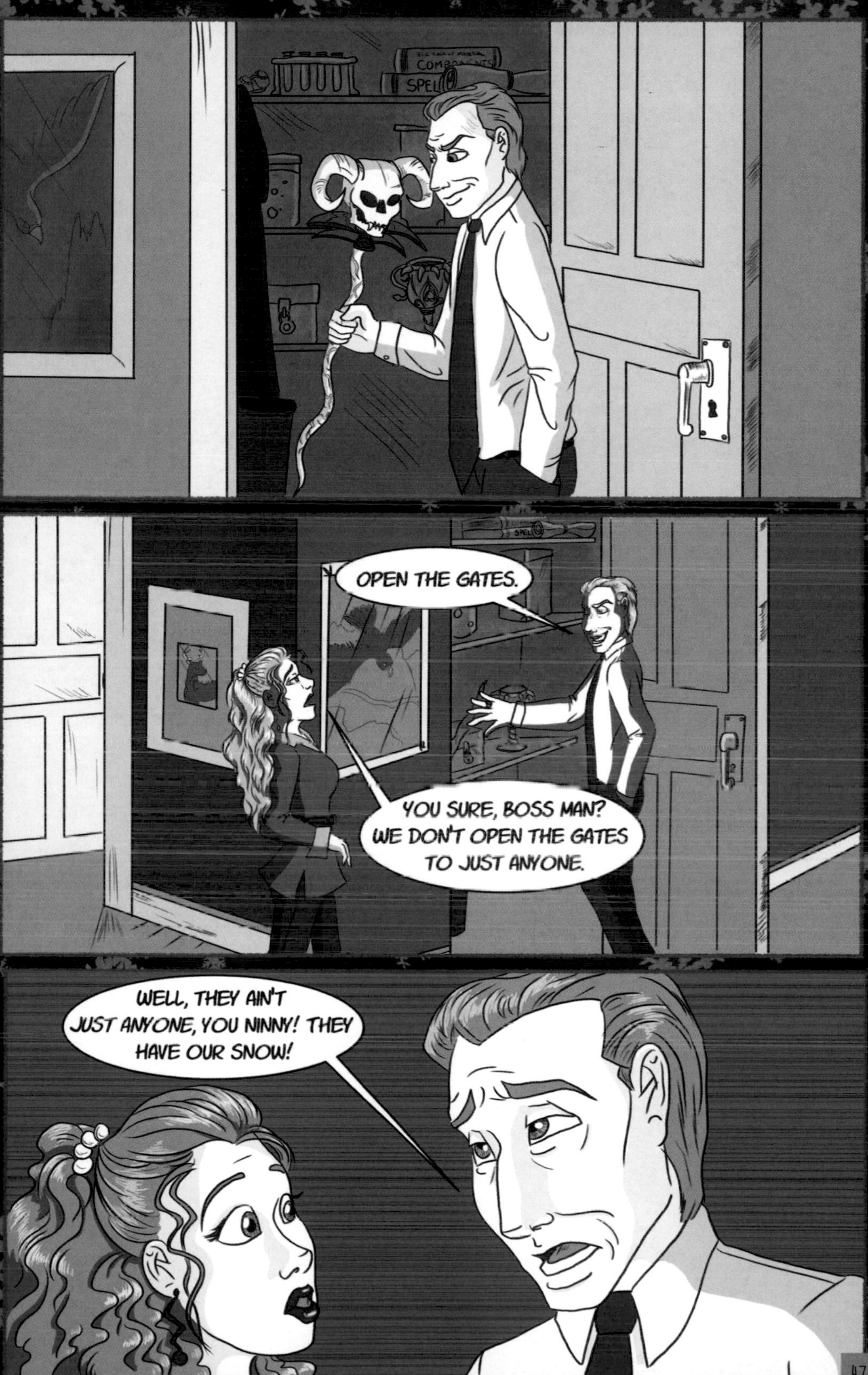
OPEN THE GATES.
YOU SURE, BOSS MAN? WE DON'T OPEN THE GATES TO JUST ANYONE.
WELL, THEY AIN'T JUST ANYONE, YOU NINNY! THEY HAVE OUR SNOW!

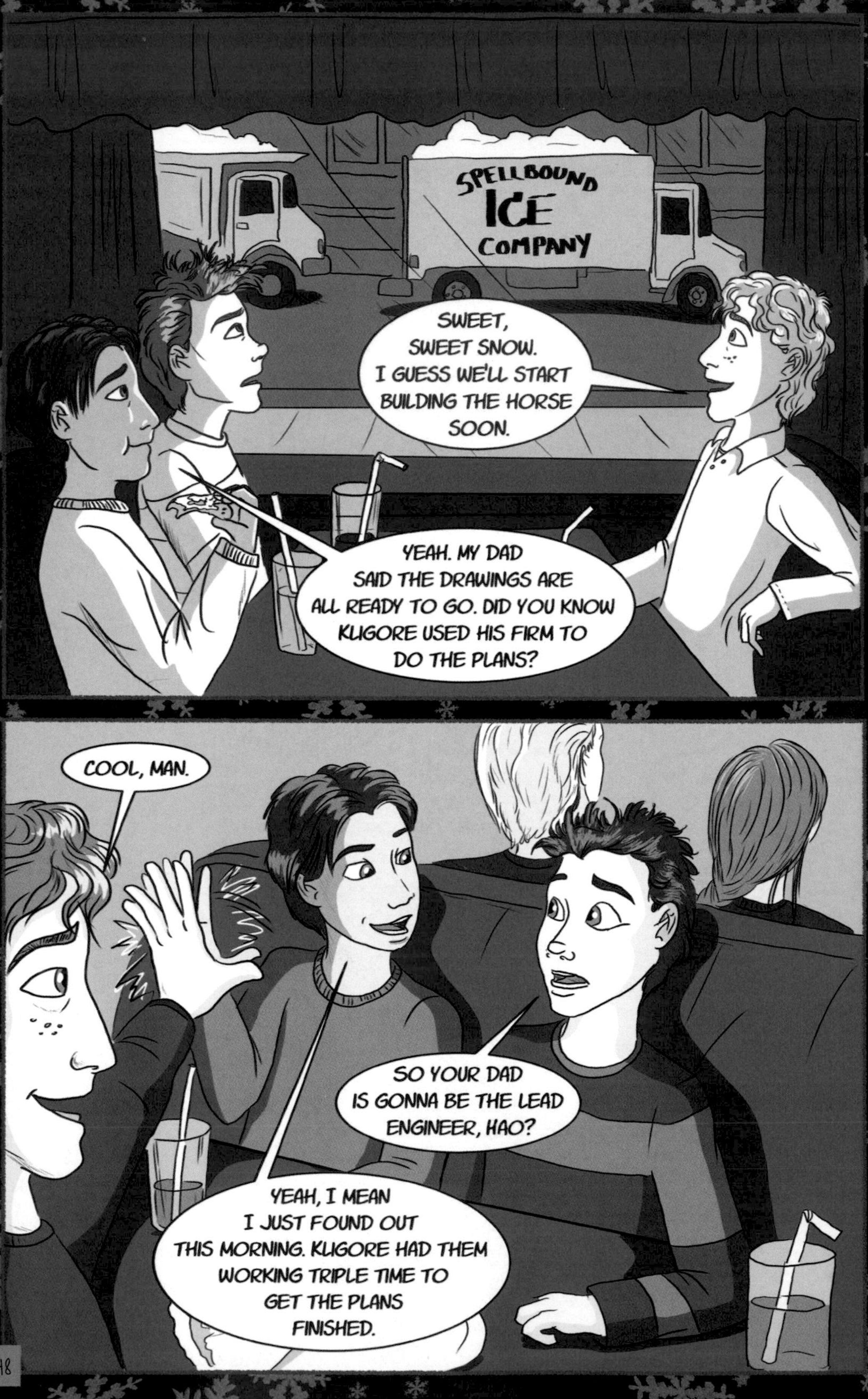
SPELLBOUND ICE COMPANY
SWEET, SWEET SNOW. I GUESS WE'LL START BUILDING THE HORSE SOON.
YEAH. MY DAD SAID THE DRAWINGS ARE ALL READY TO GO. DID YOU KNOW KLIGORE USED HIS FIRM TO DO THE PLANS?
COOL, MAN.
SO YOUR DAD IS GONNA BE THE LEAD ENGINEER, HAO?
YEAH, I MEAN I JUST FOUND OUT THIS MORNING. KLIGORE HAD THEM WORKING TRIPLE TIME TO GET THE PLANS FINISHED.

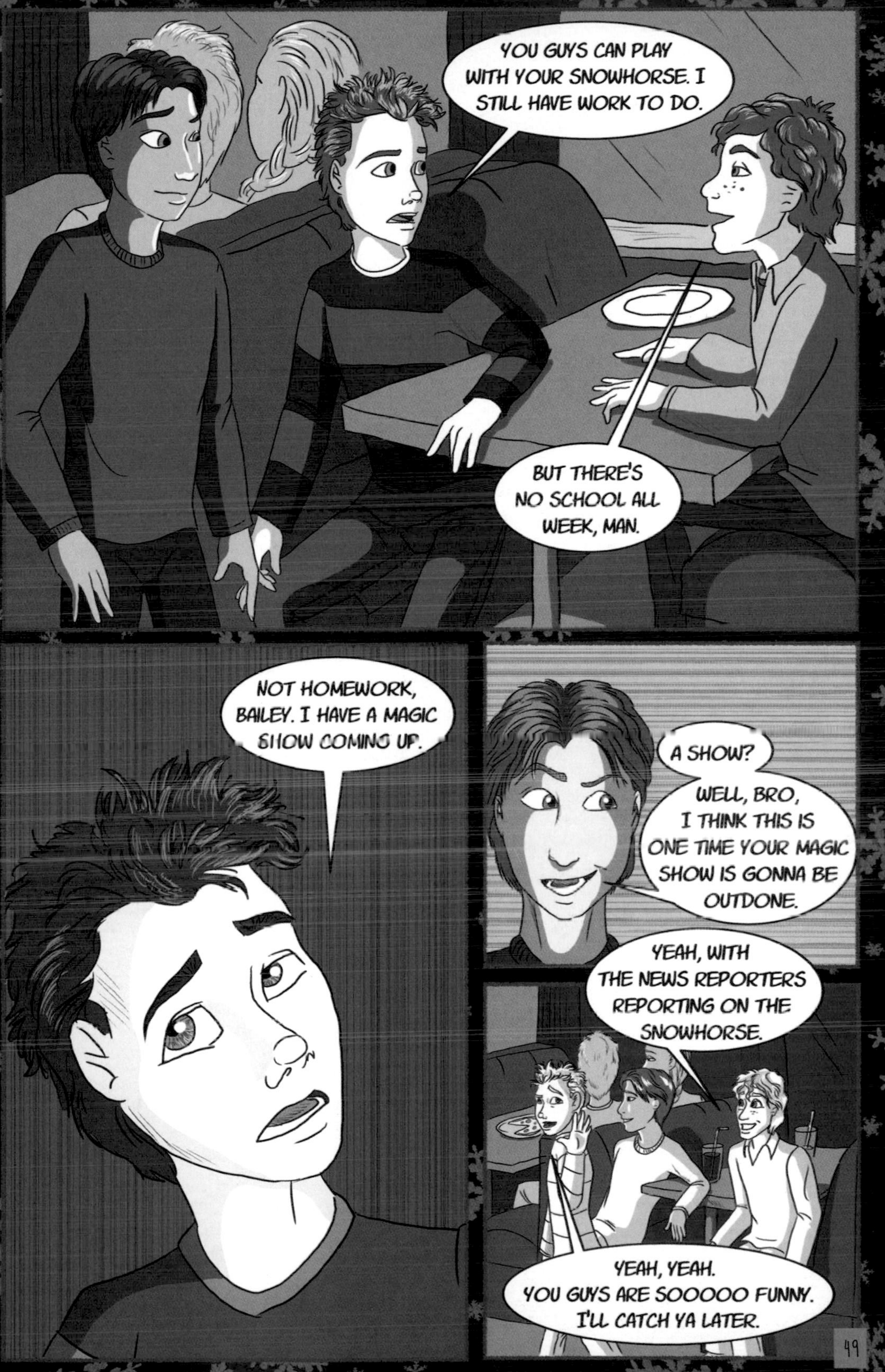
YOU GUYS CAN PLAY WITH YOUR SNOWHORSE. I STILL HAVE WORK TO DO.
BUT THERE'S NO SCHOOL ALL WEEK, MAN.
NOT HOMEWORK, BAILEY. I HAVE A MAGIC SHOW COMING UP.
A SHOW?
WELL, BRO, I THINK THIS IS ONE TIME YOUR MAGIC SHOW IS GONNA BE OUTDONE.
YEAH, WITH THE NEWS REPORTERS REPORTING ON THE SNOWHORSE.
YEAH, YEAH. YOU GUYS ARE SOOOOO FUNNY. I'LL CATCH YA LATER.

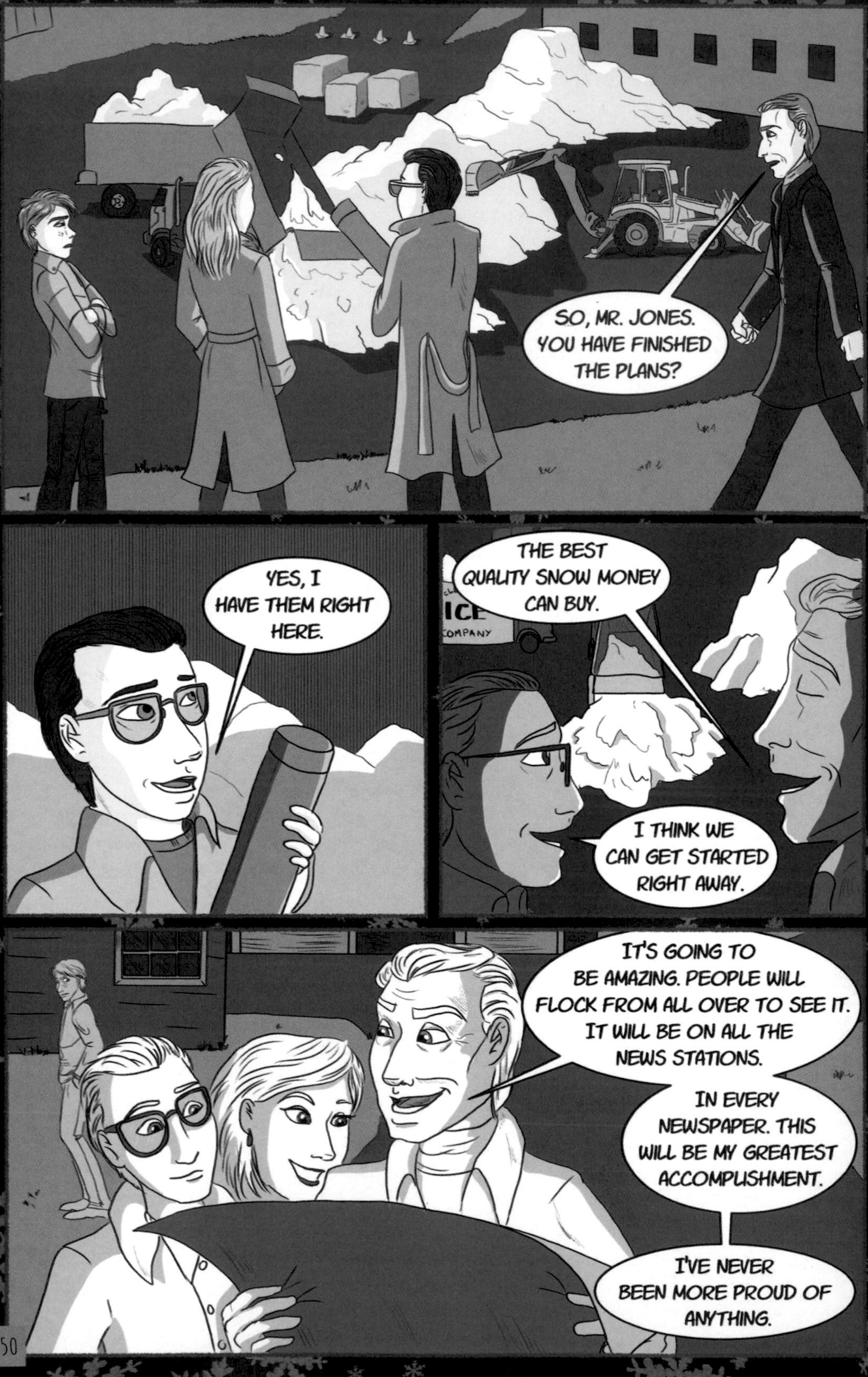
SO, MR. JONES. YOU HAVE FINISHED THE PLANS?
YES, I HAVE THEM RIGHT HERE.
THE BEST QUALITY SNOW MONEY CAN BUY.
ICE
COMPANY
I THINK WE CAN GET STARTED RIGHT AWAY.
IT'S GOING TO BE AMAZING. PEOPLE WILL FLOCK FROM ALL OVER TO SEE IT. IT WILL BE ON ALL THE NEWS STATIONS.
IN EVERY NEWSPAPER. THIS WILL BE MY GREATEST ACCOMPLISHMENT.
I'VE NEVER BEEN MORE PROUD OF ANYTHING.

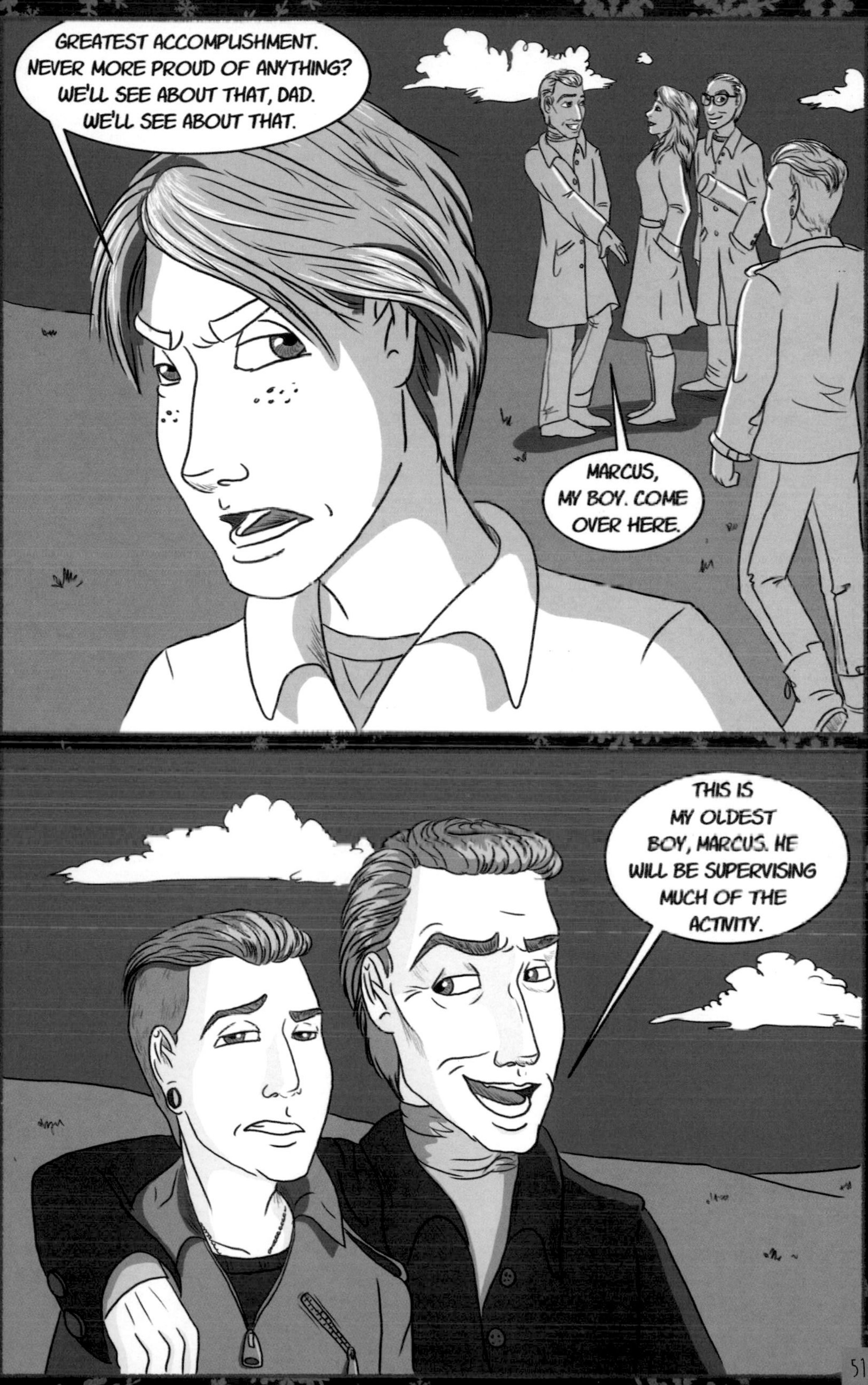
GREATEST ACCOMPLISHMENT. NEVER MORE PROUD OF ANYTHING? WE'LL SEE ABOUT THAT, DAD. WE'LL SEE ABOUT THAT.
MARCUS, MY BOY. COME OVER HERE.
THIS IS MY OLDEST BOY, MARCUS. HE WILL BE SUPERVISING MUCH OF THE ACTIVITY.

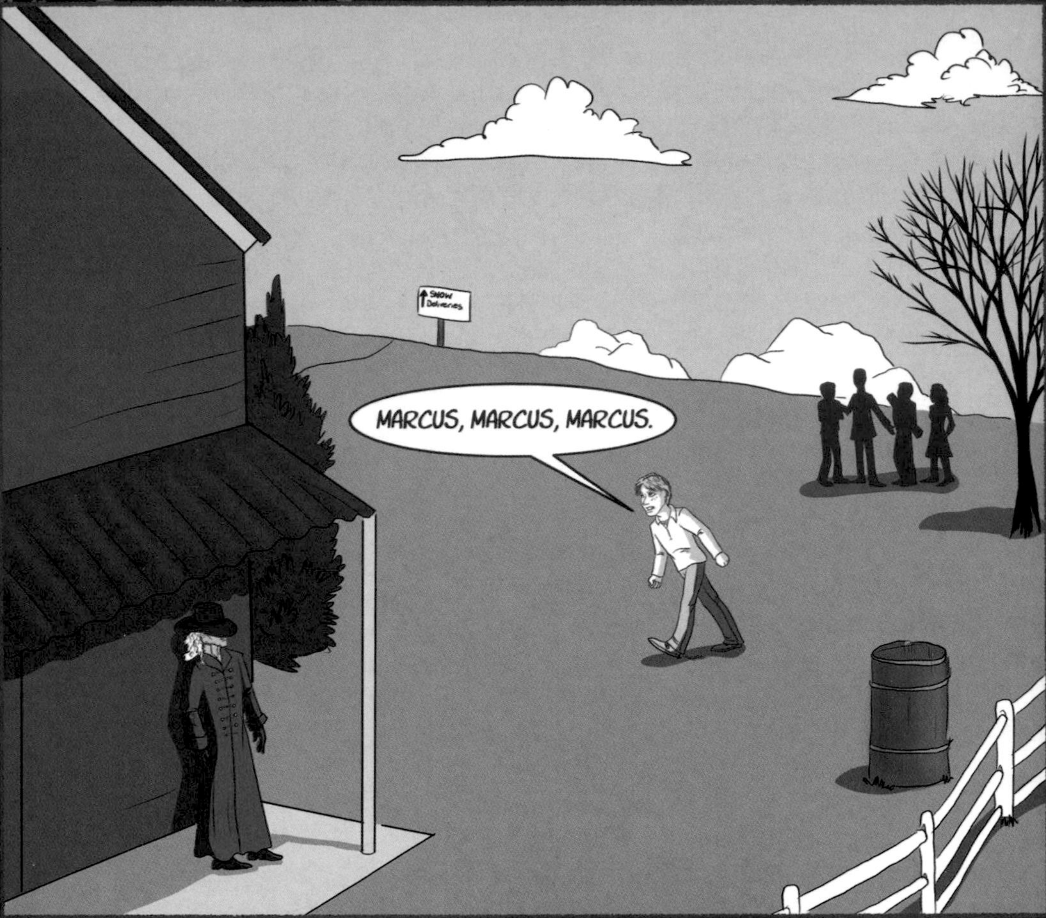
SNOW Deliveries
MARCUS, MARCUS, MARCUS.

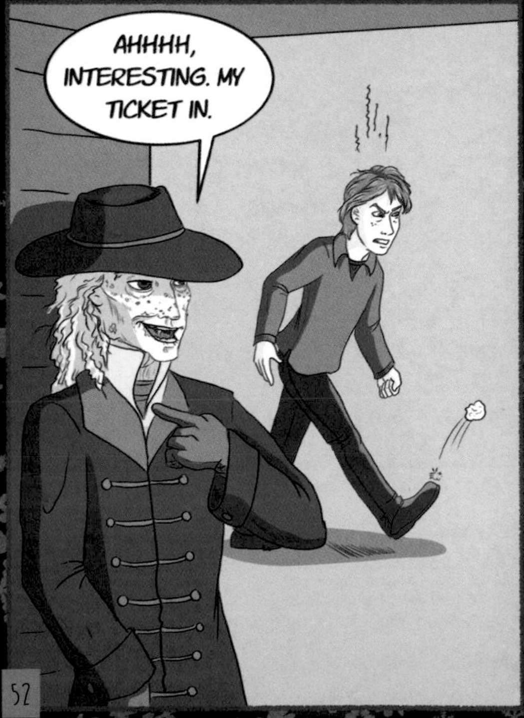
AHHHH, INTERESTING. MY TICKET IN.

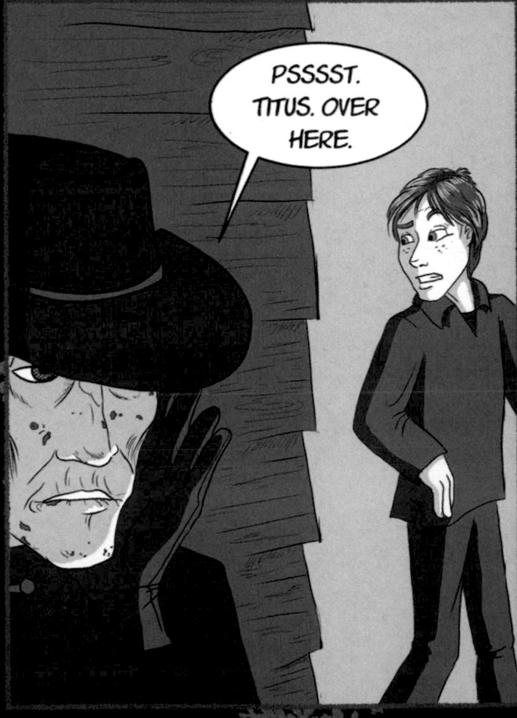
PSSSST. TITUS. OVER HERE.

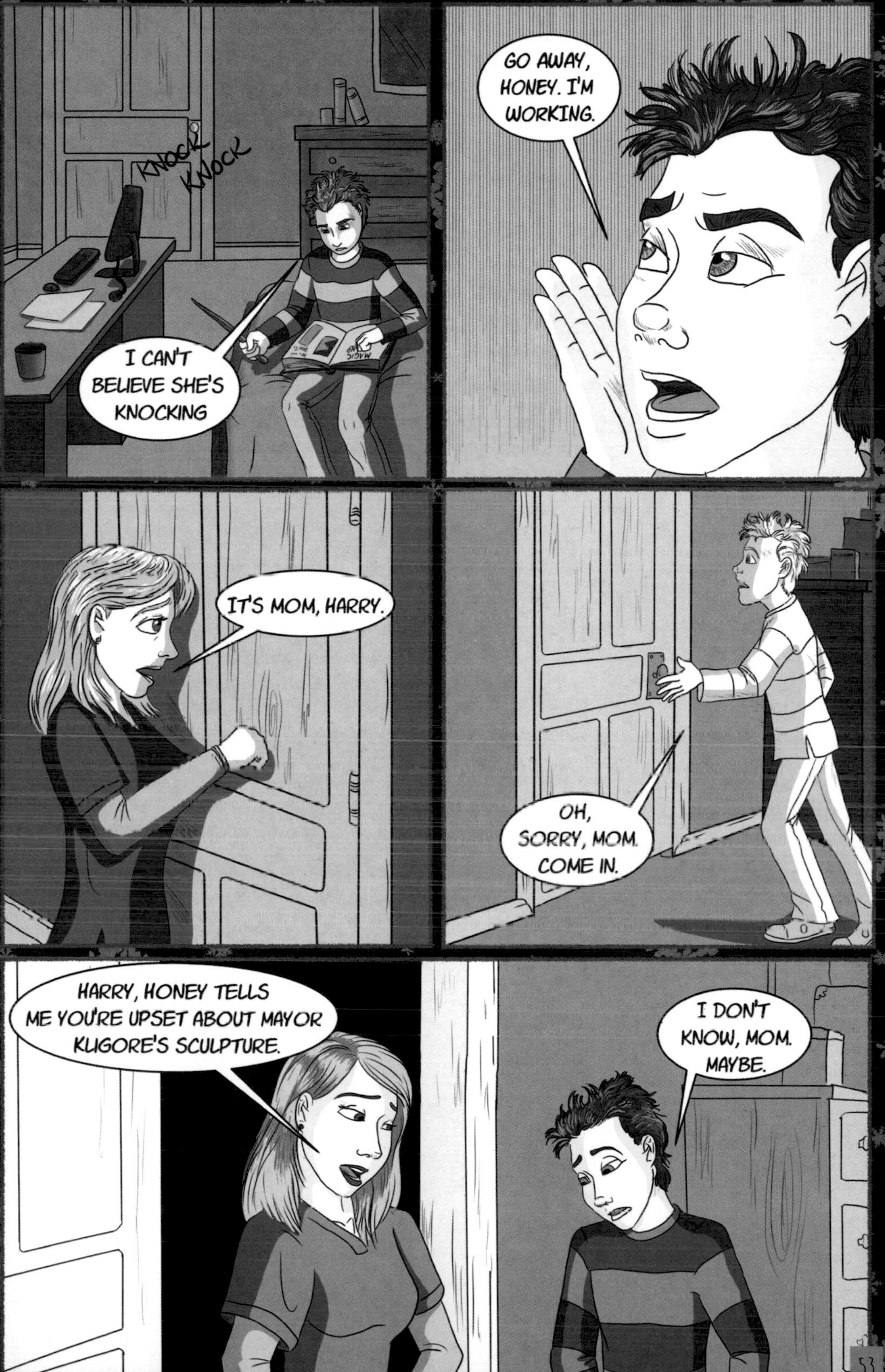
KNOCK KNOCK
I CAN'T BELIEVE SHE'S KNOCKING
GO AWAY, HONEY. I'M WORKING.
IT'S MOM, HARRY.
OH, SORRY, MOM. COME IN.
HARRY, HONEY TELLS ME YOU'RE UPSET ABOUT MAYOR KLIGORE'S SCULPTURE.
I DON'T KNOW, MOM. MAYBE.

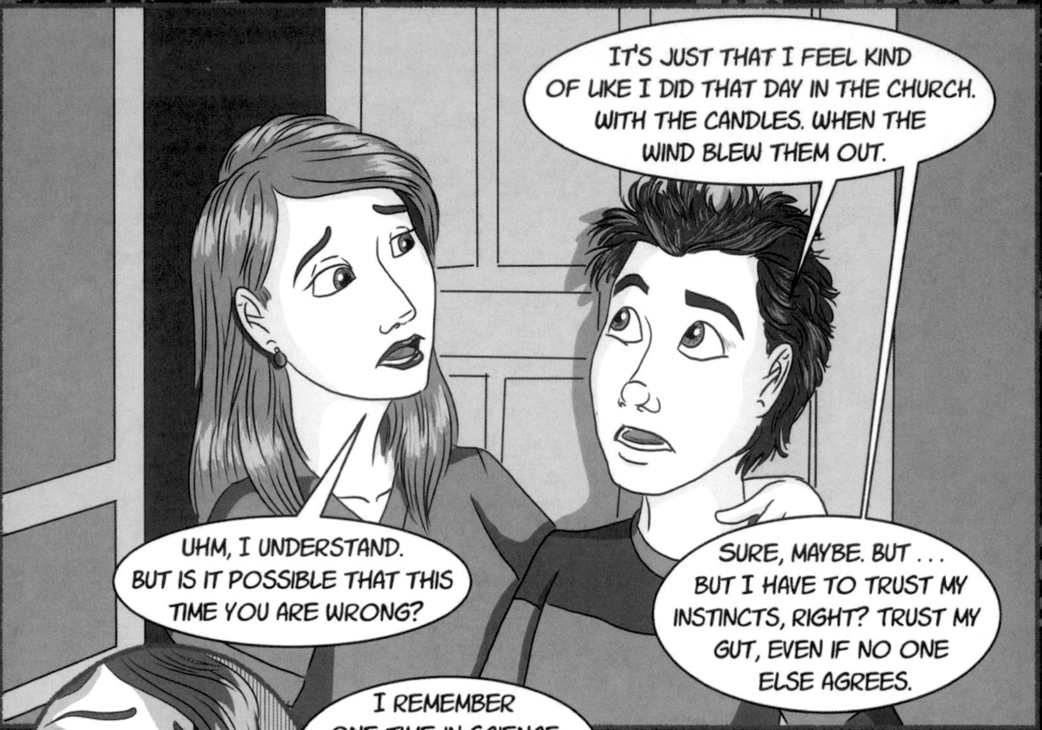
IT'S JUST THAT I FEEL KIND OF LIKE I DID THAT DAY IN THE CHURCH. WITH THE CANDLES. WHEN THE WIND BLEW THEM OUT.
UHM, I UNDERSTAND. BUT IS IT POSSIBLE THAT THIS TIME YOU ARE WRONG?
SURE, MAYBE. BUT . . . BUT I HAVE TO TRUST MY INSTINCTS, RIGHT? TRUST MY GUT, EVEN IF NO ONE ELSE AGREES.

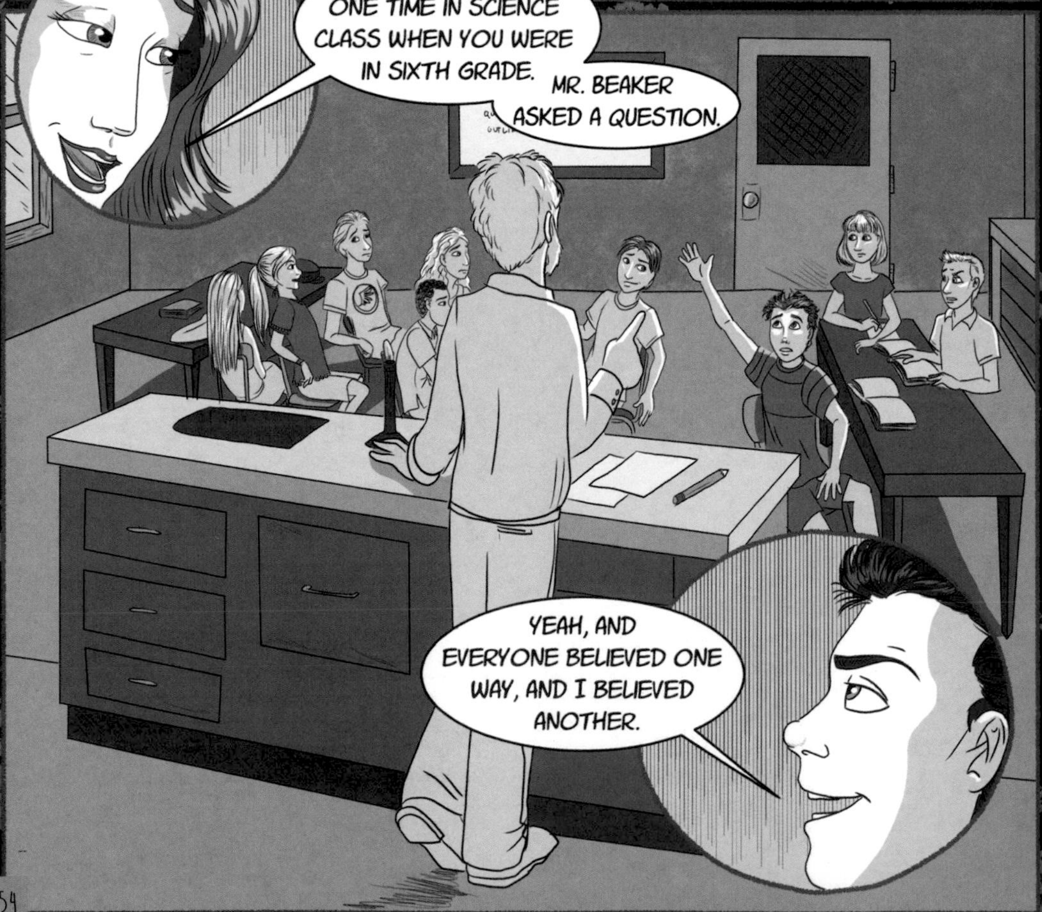
I REMEMBER ONE TIME IN SCIENCE CLASS WHEN YOU WERE IN SIXTH GRADE.
MR. BEAKER ASKED A QUESTION.
YEAH, AND EVERYONE BELIEVED ONE WAY, AND I BELIEVED ANOTHER.

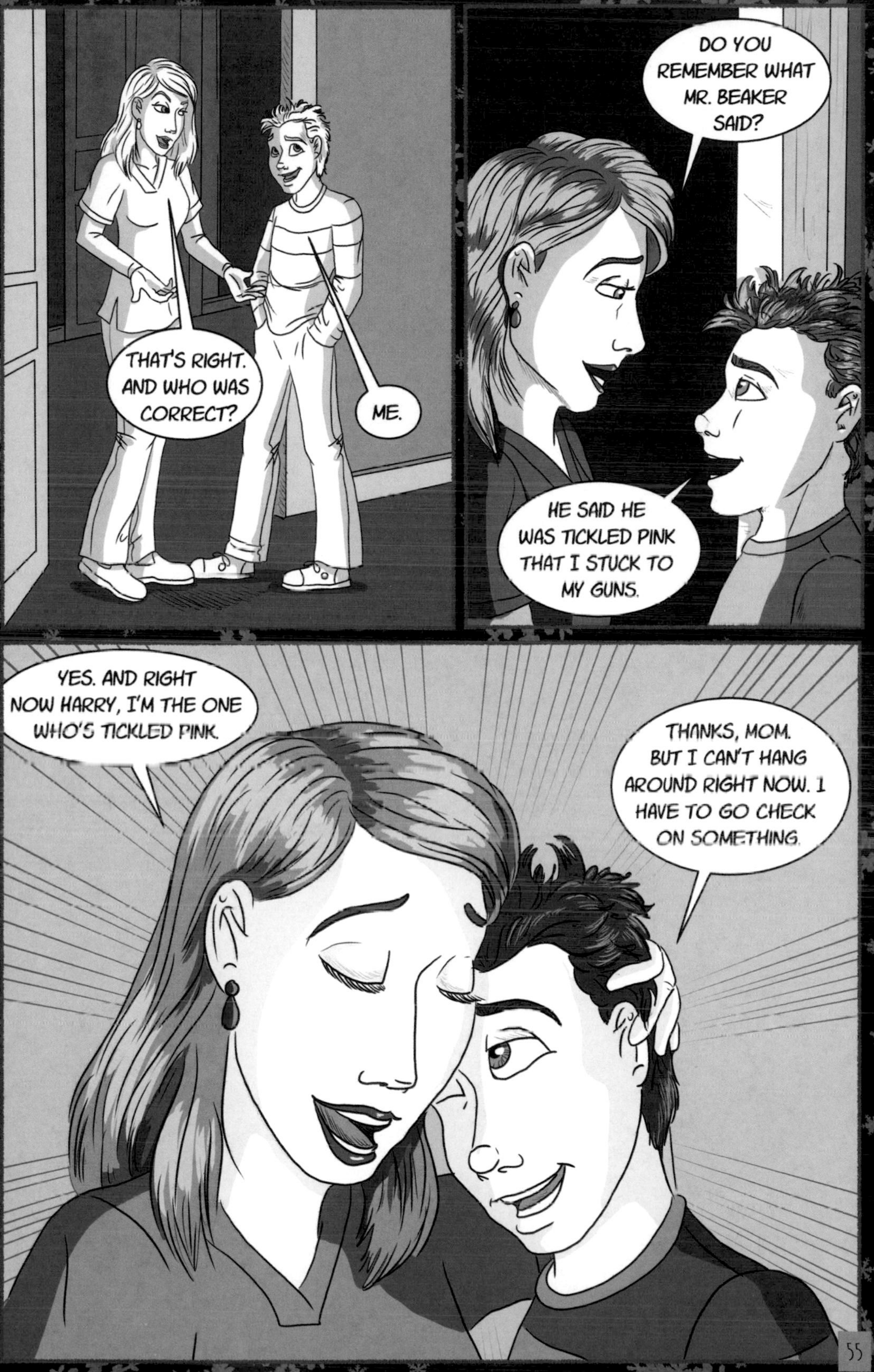
THAT'S RIGHT. AND WHO WAS CORRECT?
ME.
DO YOU REMEMBER WHAT MR. BEAKER SAID?
HE SAID HE WAS TICKLED PINK THAT I STUCK TO MY GUNS.
YES. AND RIGHT NOW HARRY, I'M THE ONE WHO'S TICKLED PINK.
THANKS, MOM. BUT I CAN'T HANG AROUND RIGHT NOW. I HAVE TO GO CHECK ON SOMETHING.

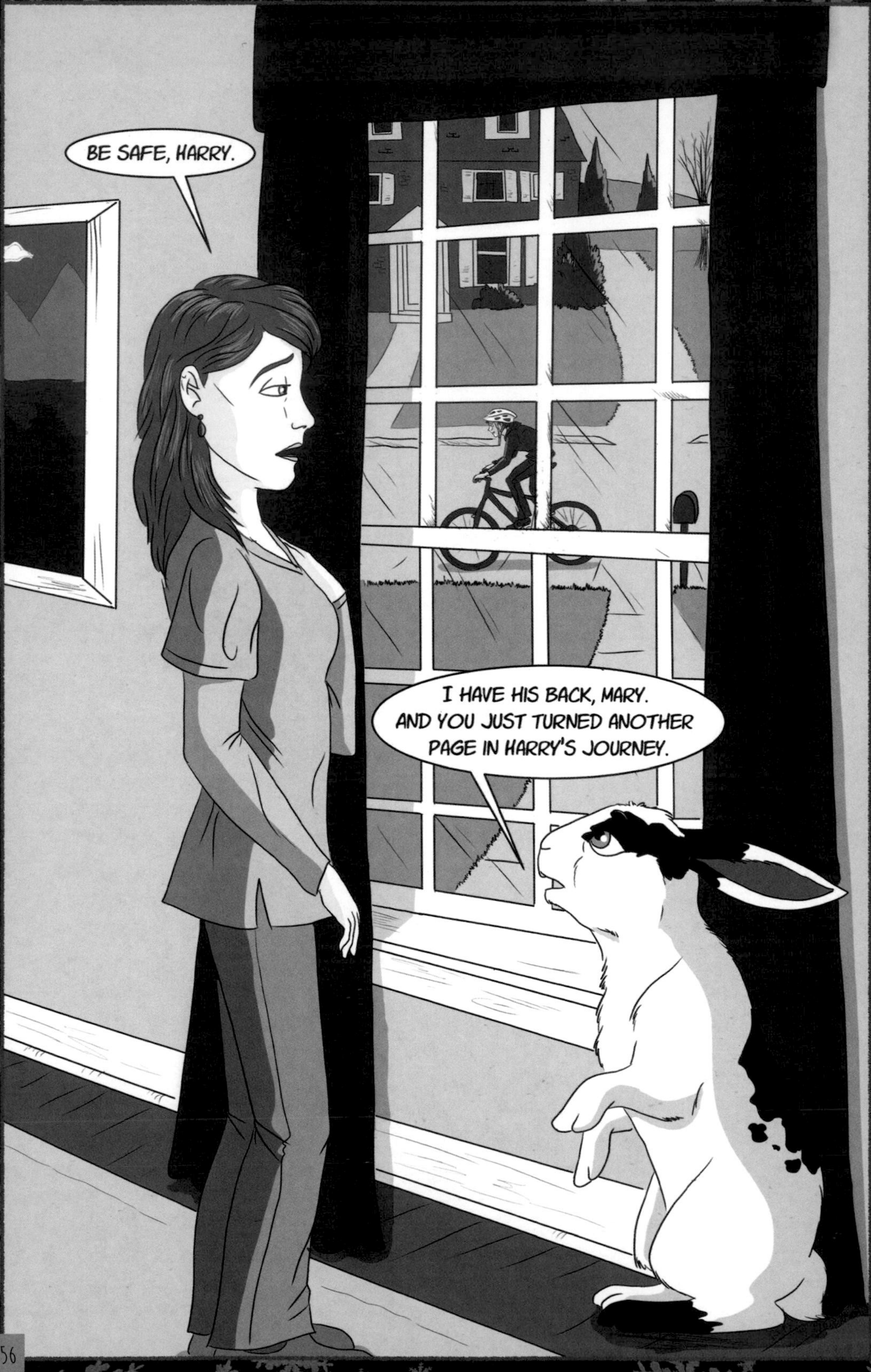
BE SAFE, HARRY.
I HAVE HIS BACK, MARY. AND YOU JUST TURNED ANOTHER PAGE IN HARRY'S JOURNEY.

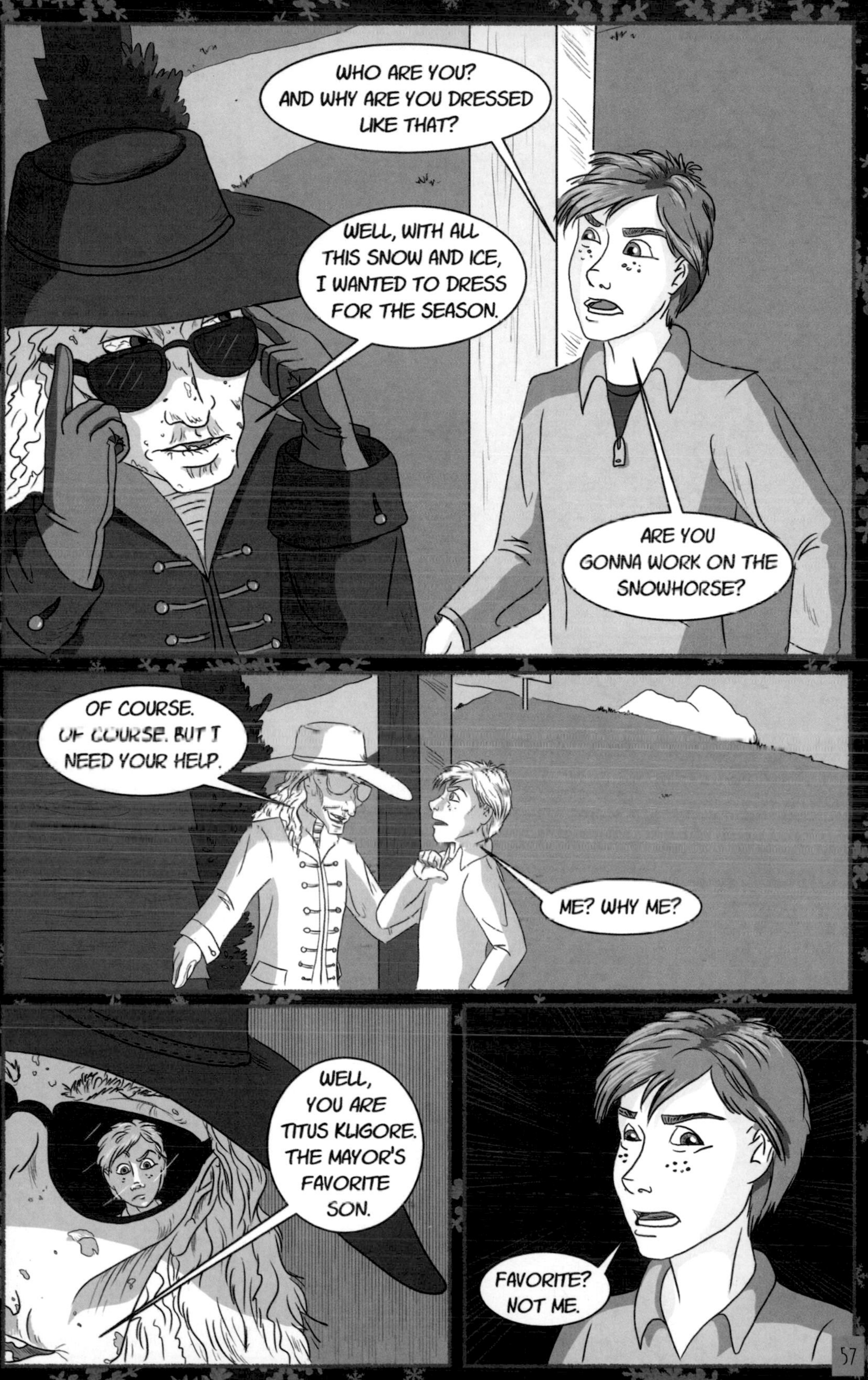
WHO ARE YOU? AND WHY ARE YOU DRESSED LIKE THAT?
WELL, WITH ALL THIS SNOW AND ICE, I WANTED TO DRESS FOR THE SEASON.
ARE YOU GONNA WORK ON THE SNOWHORSE?
OF COURSE. OF COURSE. BUT I NEED YOUR HELP.
ME? WHY ME?
WELL, YOU ARE TITUS KLIGORE. THE MAYOR'S FAVORITE SON.
FAVORITE? NOT ME.

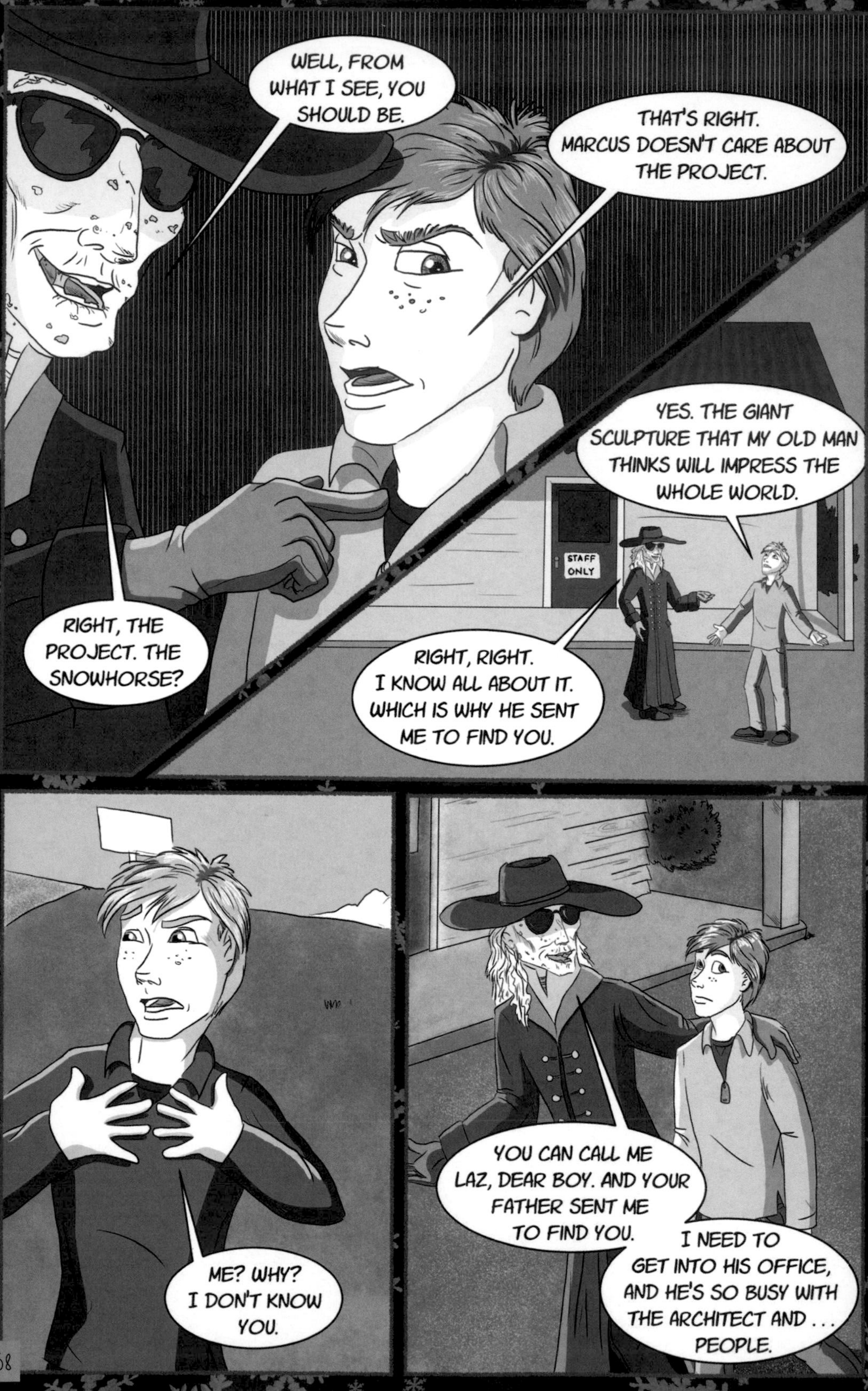

WELL, FROM WHAT I SEE, YOU SHOULD BE.
THAT'S RIGHT. MARCUS DOESN'T CARE ABOUT THE PROJECT.
RIGHT, THE PROJECT. THE SNOWHORSE?
YES. THE GIANT SCULPTURE THAT MY OLD MAN THINKS WILL IMPRESS THE WHOLE WORLD.
STAFF ONLY
RIGHT, RIGHT. I KNOW ALL ABOUT IT. WHICH IS WHY HE SENT ME TO FIND YOU.
ME? WHY? I DON'T KNOW YOU.
YOU CAN CALL ME LAZ, DEAR BOY. AND YOUR FATHER SENT ME TO FIND YOU.
I NEED TO GET INTO HIS OFFICE, AND HE'S SO BUSY WITH THE ARCHITECT AND . . . PEOPLE.

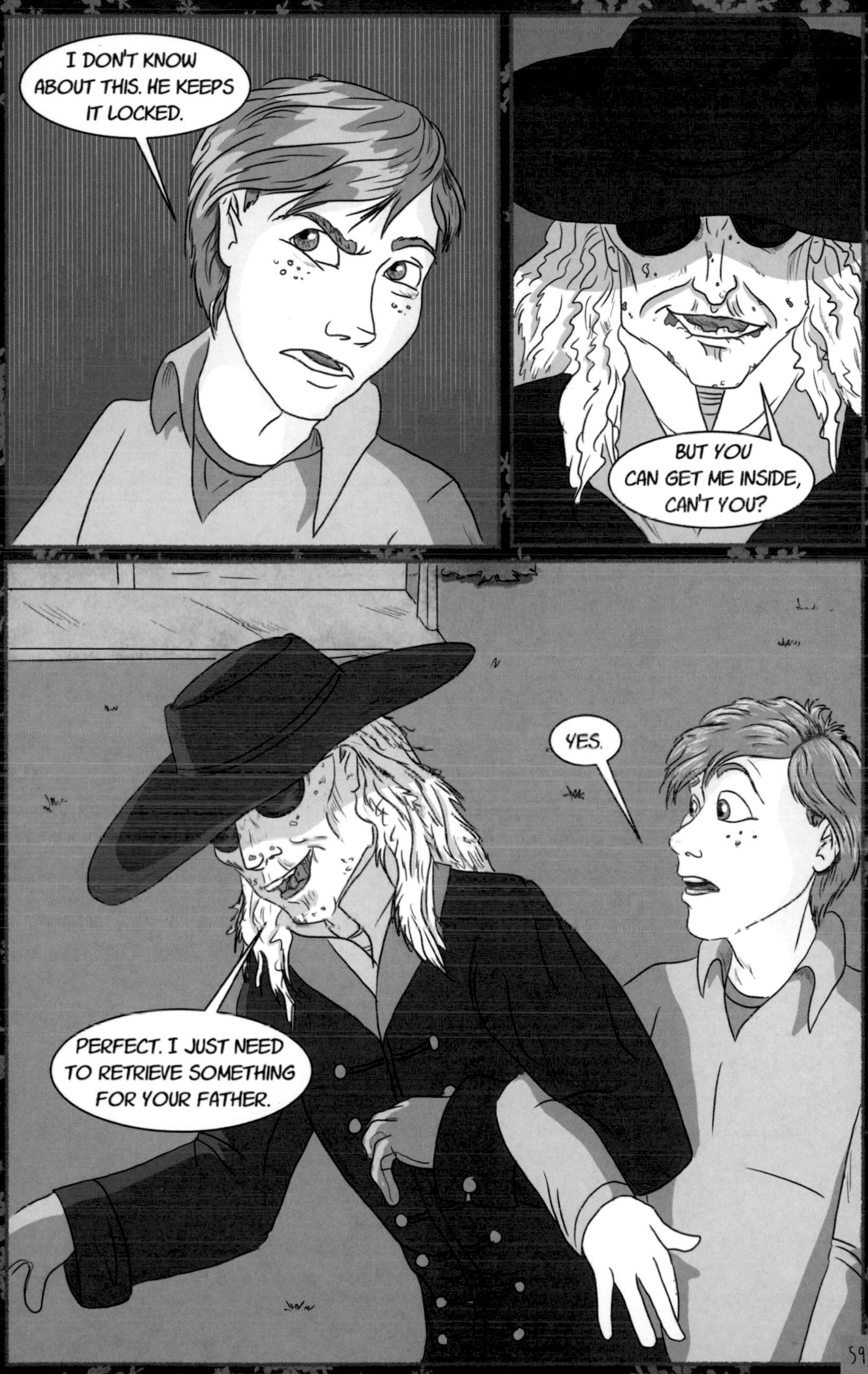
I DON'T KNOW ABOUT THIS. HE KEEPS IT LOCKED.
BUT YOU CAN GET ME INSIDE, CAN'T YOU?
YES.
PERFECT. I JUST NEED TO RETRIEVE SOMETHING FOR YOUR FATHER.

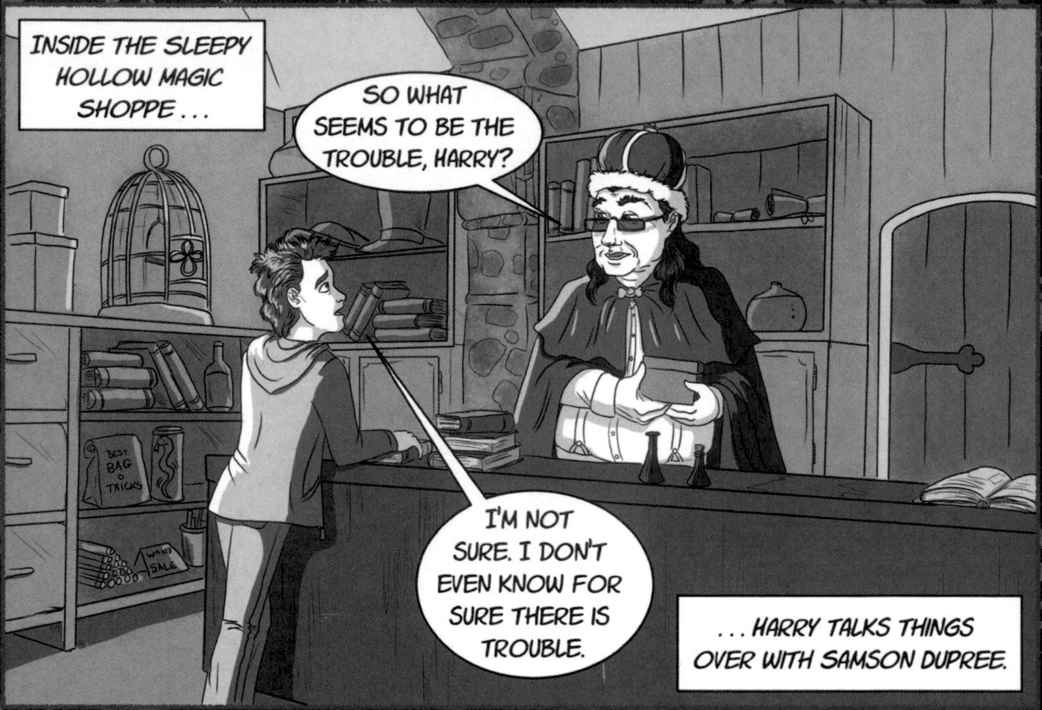
INSIDE THE SLEEPY HOLLOW MAGIC SHOPPE . . .
SO WHAT SEEMS TO BE THE TROUBLE, HARRY?
BEST BAG O TRICKS
WAND SALE
I'M NOT SURE. I DON'T EVEN KNOW FOR SURE THERE IS TROUBLE.
. . . HARRY TALKS THINGS OVER WITH SAMSON DUPREE.

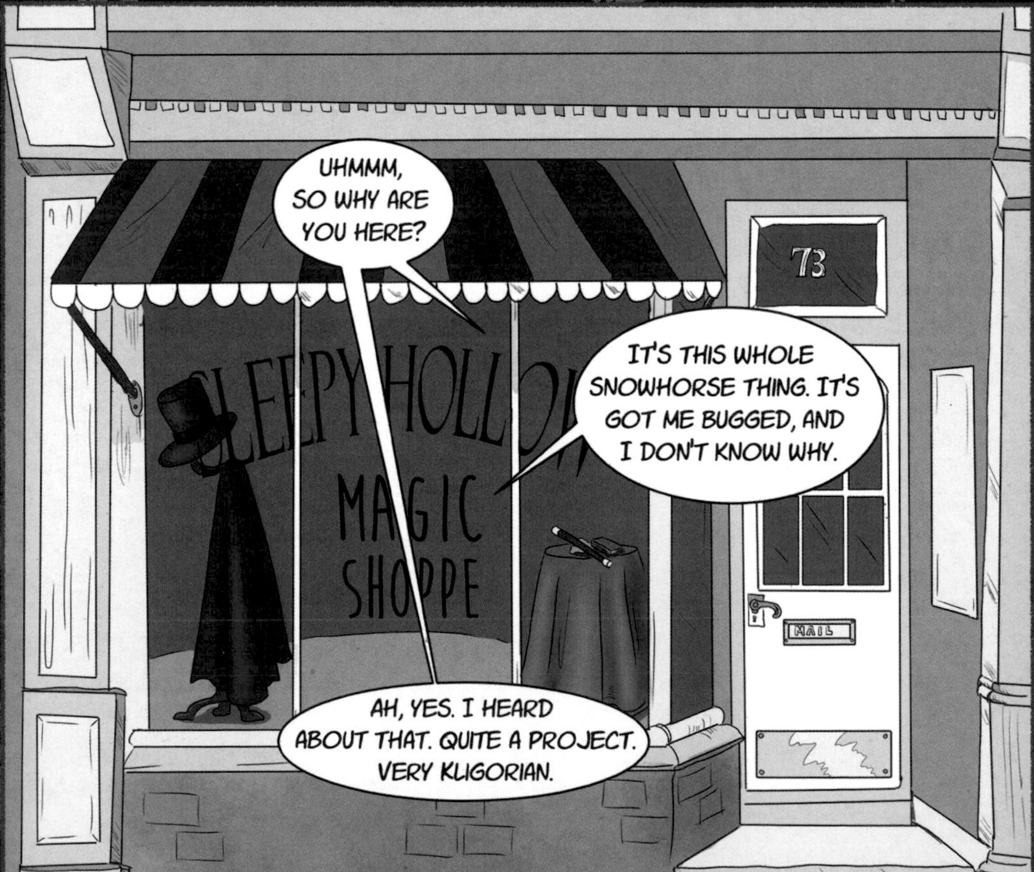
UHMMM, SO WHY ARE YOU HERE?
73
IT'S THIS WHOLE SNOWHORSE THING. IT'S GOT ME BUGGED, AND I DON'T KNOW WHY.
MAGIC SHOPPE
MAIL
AH, YES. I HEARD ABOUT THAT. QUITE A PROJECT. VERY KLIGORIAN.

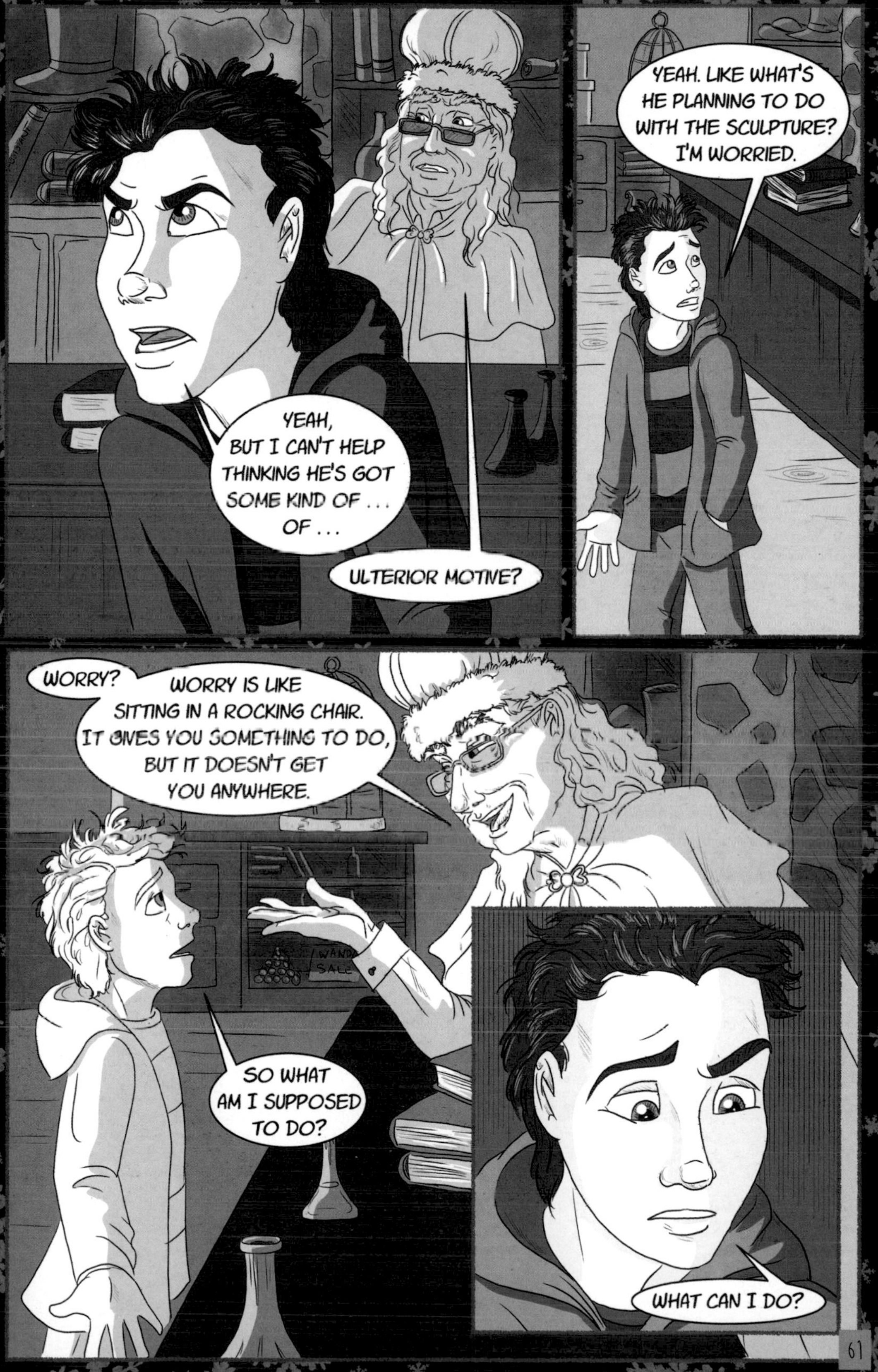
YEAH, BUT I CAN'T HELP THINKING HE'S GOT SOME KIND OF . . . OF . . .
ULTERIOR MOTIVE?
YEAH. LIKE WHAT'S HE PLANNING TO DO WITH THE SCULPTURE? I'M WORRIED.
WORRY?
WORRY IS LIKE SITTING IN A ROCKING CHAIR. IT GIVES YOU SOMETHING TO DO, BUT IT DOESN'T GET YOU ANYWHERE.
SO WHAT AM I SUPPOSED TO DO?
WHAT CAN I DO?

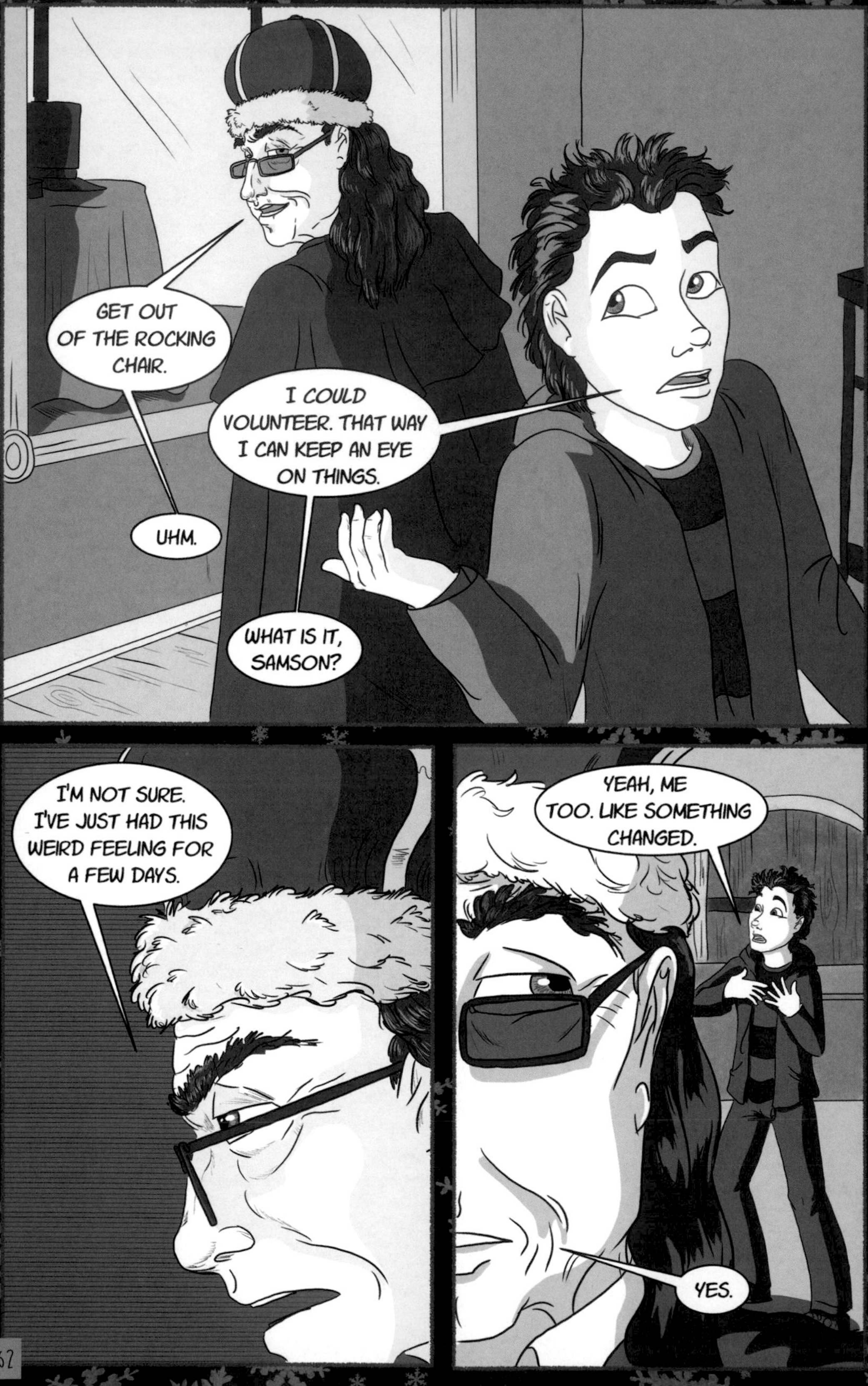
GET OUT OF THE ROCKING CHAIR.
UHM.
I COULD VOLUNTEER. THAT WAY I CAN KEEP AN EYE ON THINGS.
WHAT IS IT, SAMSON?
I'M NOT SURE. I'VE JUST HAD THIS WEIRD FEELING FOR A FEW DAYS.
YEAH, ME TOO. LIKE SOMETHING CHANGED.
YES.

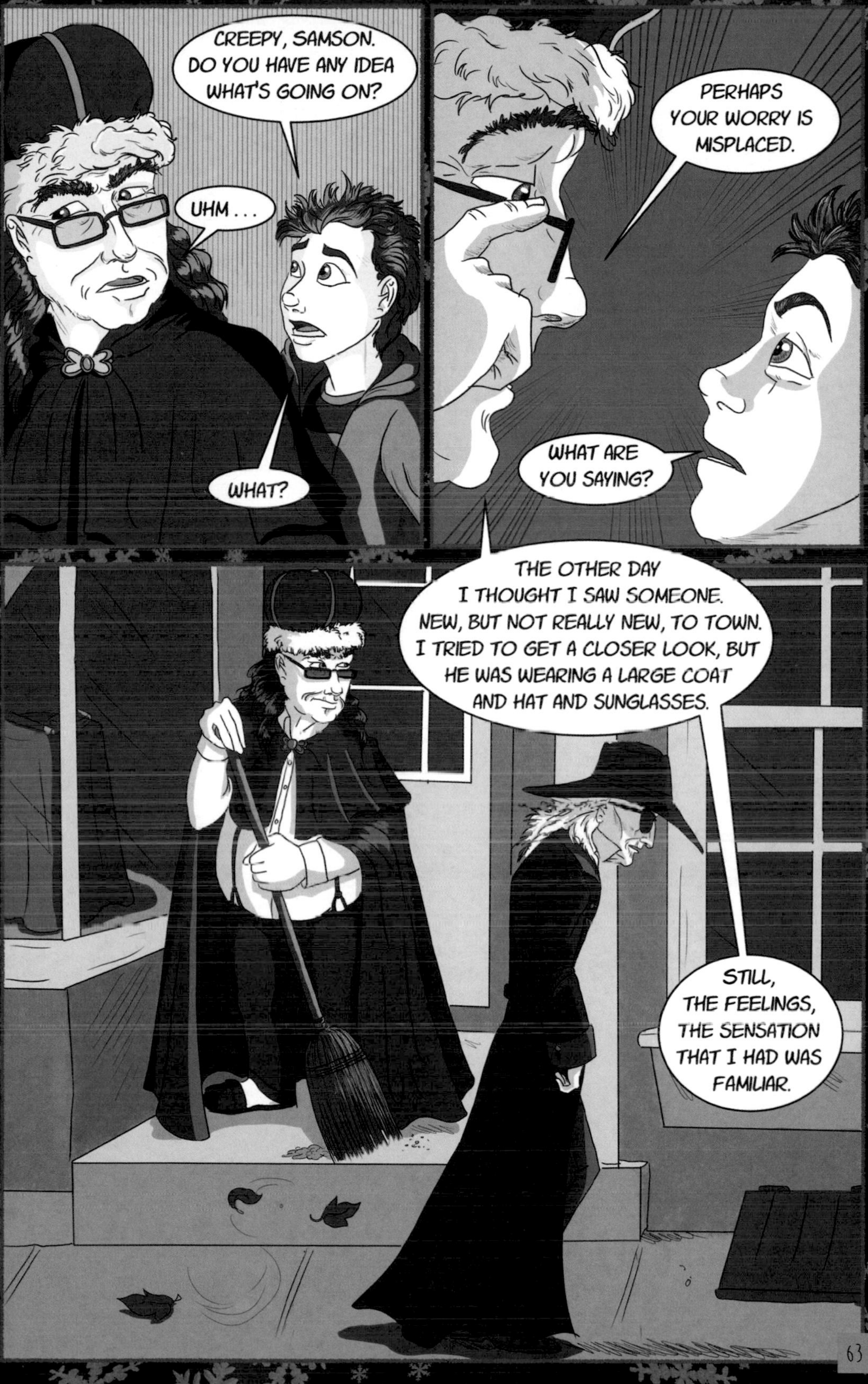
CREEPY, SAMSON. DO YOU HAVE ANY IDEA WHAT'S GOING ON?
UHM . . .
WHAT?
PERHAPS YOUR WORRY IS MISPLACED.
WHAT ARE YOU SAYING?
THE OTHER DAY I THOUGHT I SAW SOMEONE. NEW, BUT NOT REALLY NEW, TO TOWN. I TRIED TO GET A CLOSER LOOK, BUT HE WAS WEARING A LARGE COAT AND HAT AND SUNGLASSES.
STILL, THE FEELINGS, THE SENSATION THAT I HAD WAS FAMILIAR.

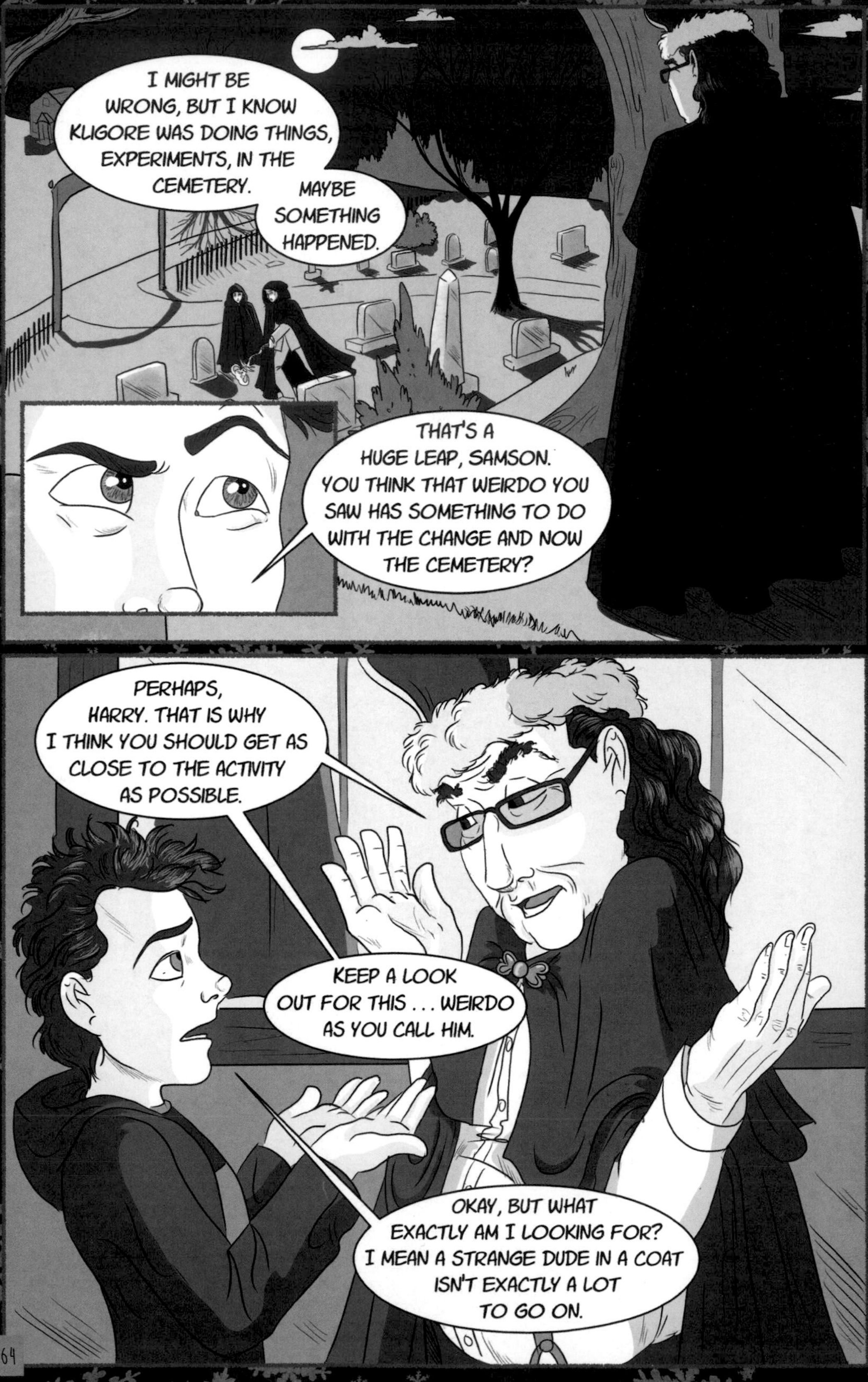
I MIGHT BE WRONG, BUT I KNOW KLIGORE WAS DOING THINGS, EXPERIMENTS, IN THE CEMETERY.
MAYBE SOMETHING HAPPENED.
THAT'S A HUGE LEAP, SAMSON. YOU THINK THAT WEIRDO YOU SAW HAS SOMETHING TO DO WITH THE CHANGE AND NOW THE CEMETERY?
PERHAPS, HARRY. THAT IS WHY I THINK YOU SHOULD GET AS CLOSE TO THE ACTIVITY AS POSSIBLE.
KEEP A LOOK OUT FOR THIS . . . WEIRDO AS YOU CALL HIM.
OKAY, BUT WHAT EXACTLY AM I LOOKING FOR? I MEAN A STRANGE DUDE IN A COAT ISN'T EXACTLY A LOT TO GO ON.

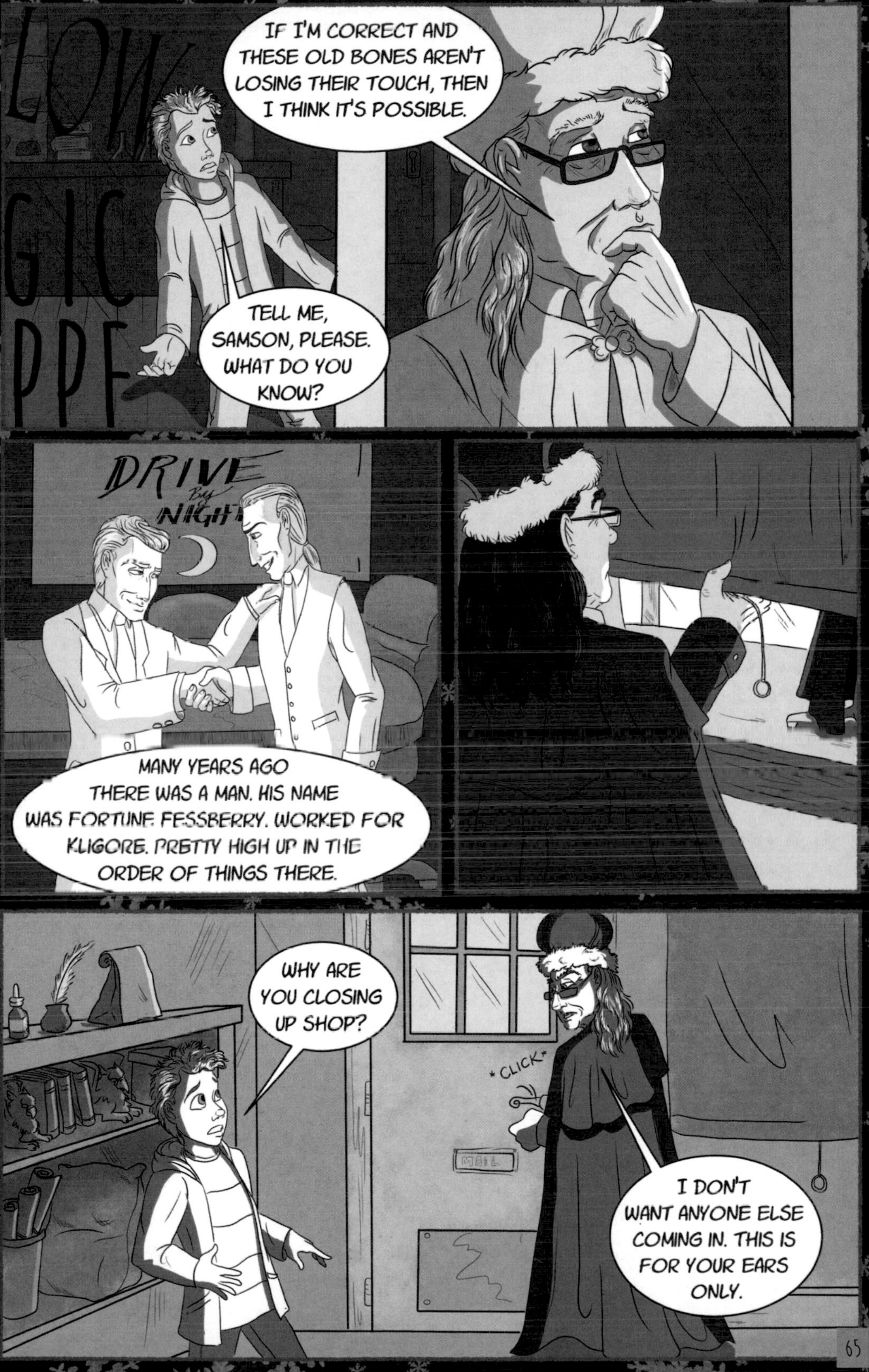
LOW
GIC
PPF
IF I'M CORRECT AND THESE OLD BONES AREN'T LOSING THEIR TOUCH, THEN I THINK IT'S POSSIBLE.
TELL ME, SAMSON, PLEASE. WHAT DO YOU KNOW?
DRIVE By NIGHT
MANY YEARS AGO THERE WAS A MAN. HIS NAME WAS FORTUNE FESSBERRY. WORKED FOR KLIGORE. PRETTY HIGH UP IN THE ORDER OF THINGS THERE.
WHY ARE YOU CLOSING UP SHOP?
CLICK
MAIL
I DON'T WANT ANYONE ELSE COMING IN. THIS IS FOR YOUR EARS ONLY.

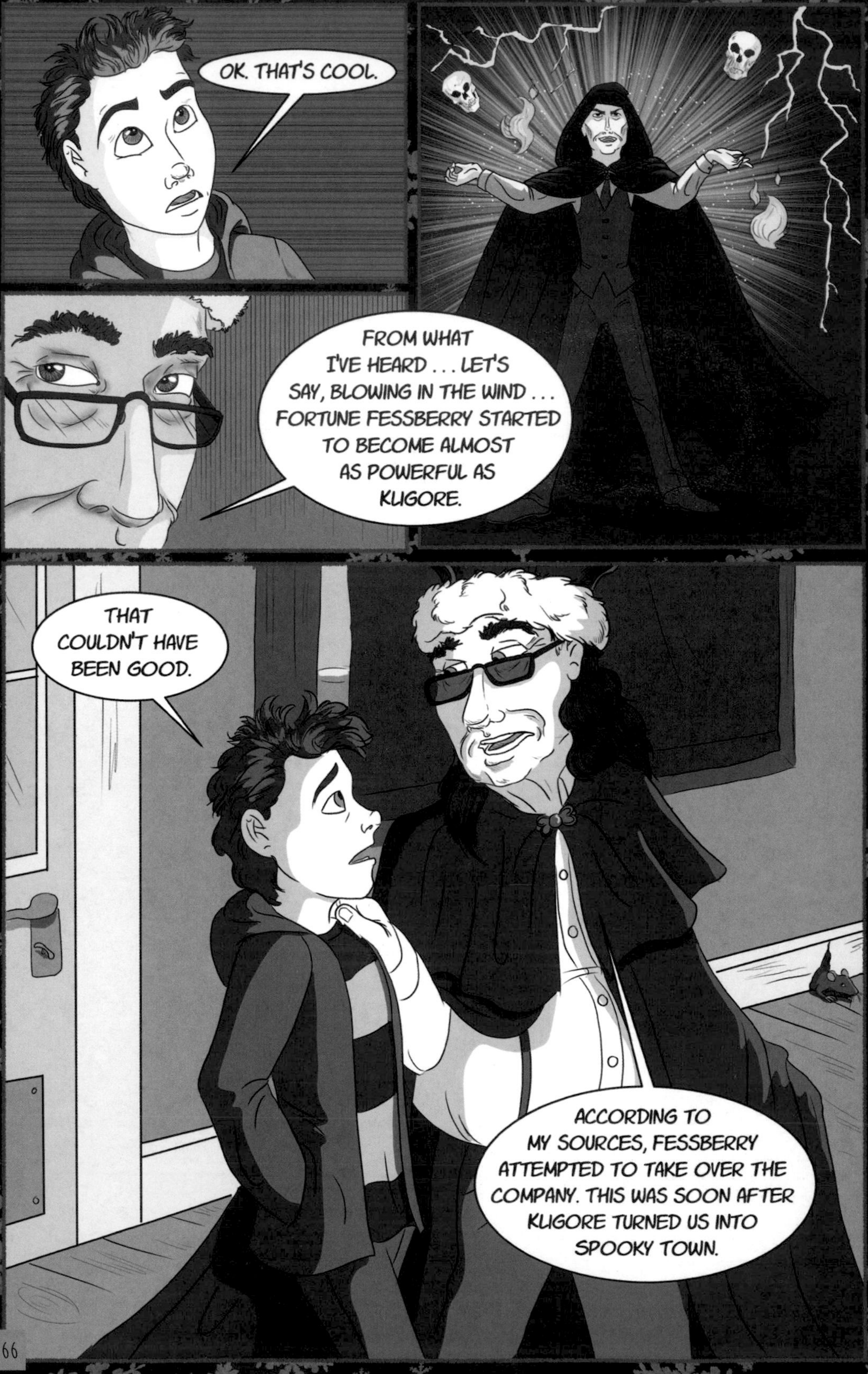
OK. THAT'S COOL.
FROM WHAT I'VE HEARD . . . LET'S SAY, BLOWING IN THE WIND . . . FORTUNE FESSBERRY STARTED TO BECOME ALMOST AS POWERFUL AS KLIGORE.
THAT COULDN'T HAVE BEEN GOOD.
ACCORDING TO MY SOURCES, FESSBERRY ATTEMPTED TO TAKE OVER THE COMPANY. THIS WAS SOON AFTER KLIGORE TURNED US INTO SPOOKY TOWN.

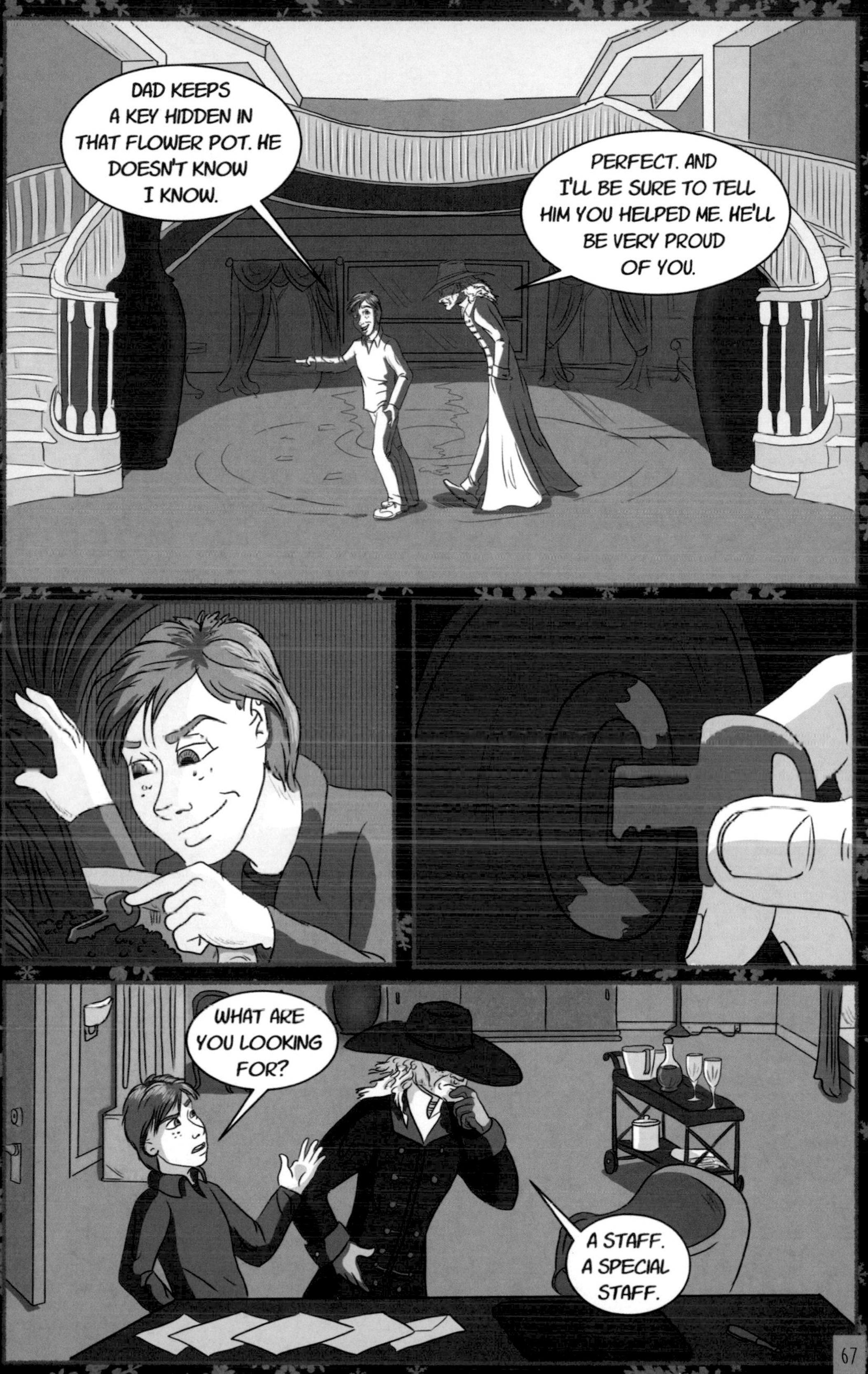
DAD KEEPS A KEY HIDDEN IN THAT FLOWER POT. HE DOESN'T KNOW I KNOW.
PERFECT. AND I'LL BE SURE TO TELL HIM YOU HELPED ME. HE'LL BE VERY PROUD OF YOU.
WHAT ARE YOU LOOKING FOR?
A STAFF. A SPECIAL STAFF.

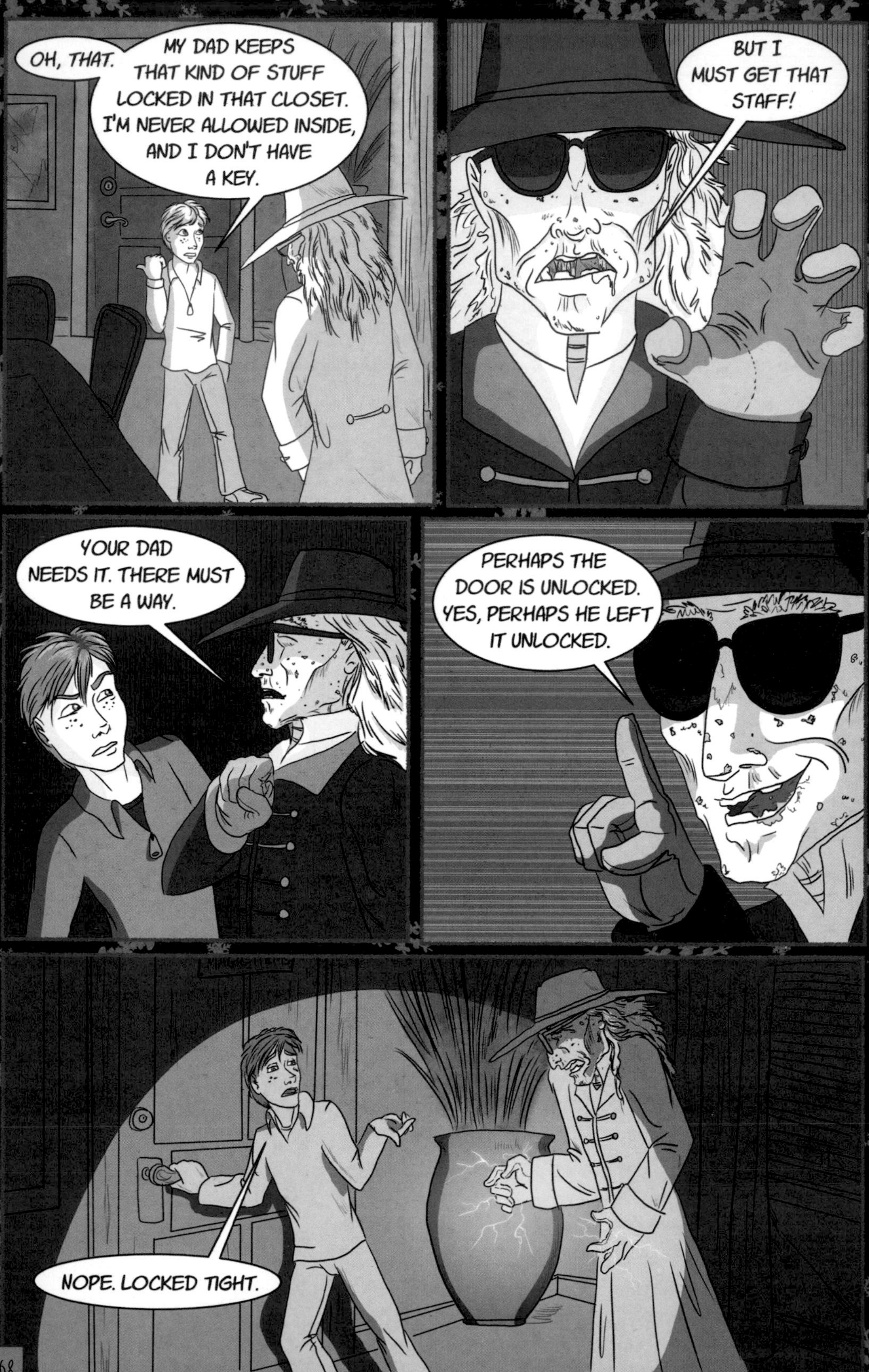
OH, THAT.
MY DAD KEEPS THAT KIND OF STUFF LOCKED IN THAT CLOSET. I'M NEVER ALLOWED INSIDE, AND I DON'T HAVE A KEY.
BUT I MUST GET THAT STAFF!
YOUR DAD NEEDS IT. THERE MUST BE A WAY.
PERHAPS THE DOOR IS UNLOCKED. YES, PERHAPS HE LEFT IT UNLOCKED.
NOPE. LOCKED TIGHT.

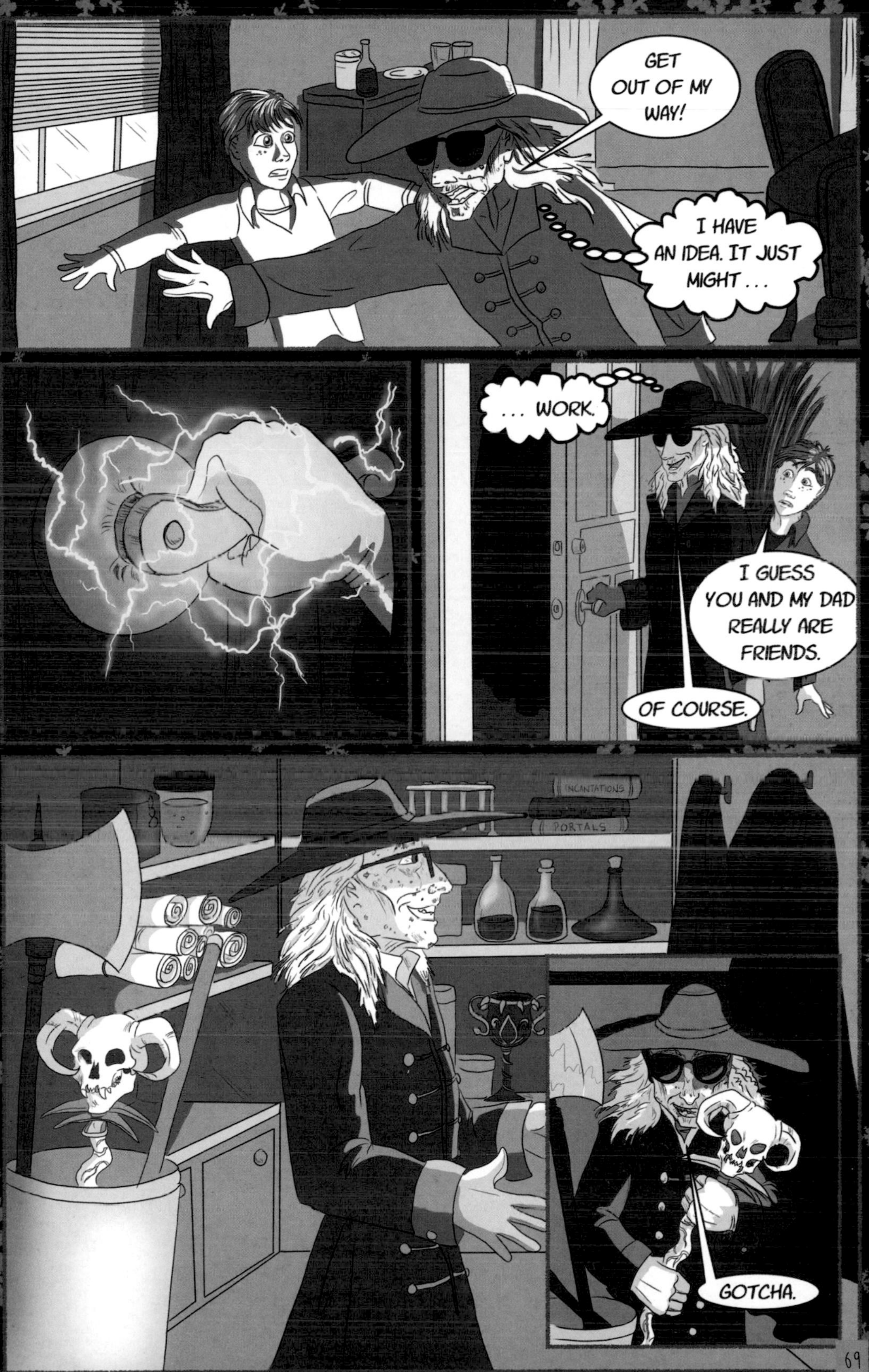
GET OUT OF MY WAY!
I HAVE AN IDEA. IT JUST MIGHT . . .
. . . WORK.
I GUESS YOU AND MY DAD REALLY ARE FRIENDS.
OF COURSE.
INCANTATIONS
PORTALS
GOTCHA.

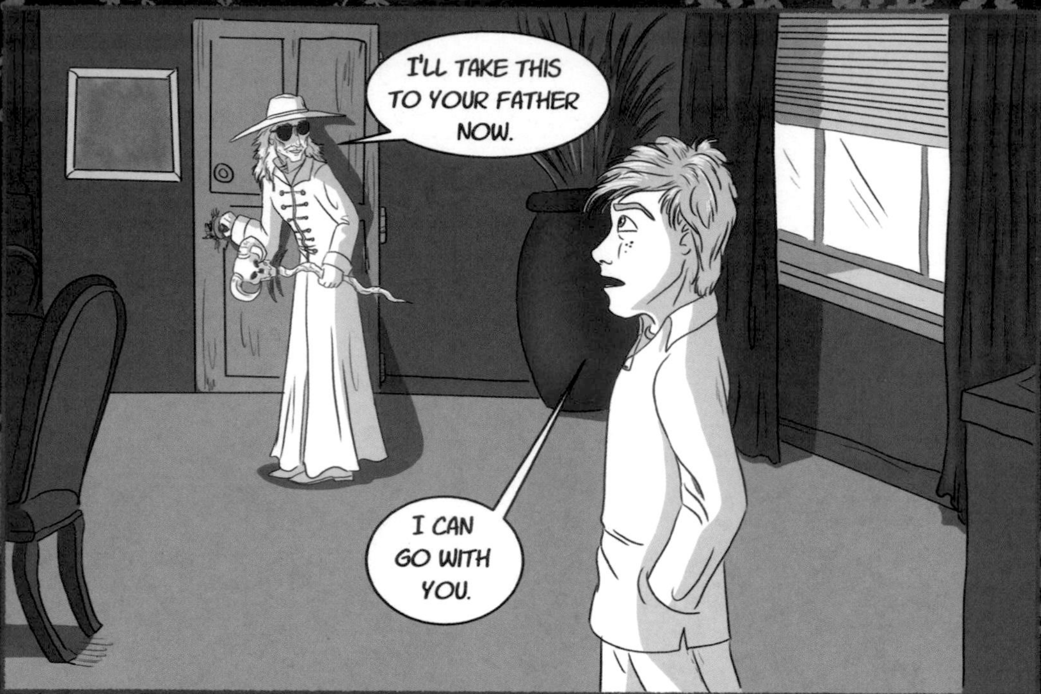
I'LL TAKE THIS TO YOUR FATHER NOW.
I CAN GO WITH YOU.

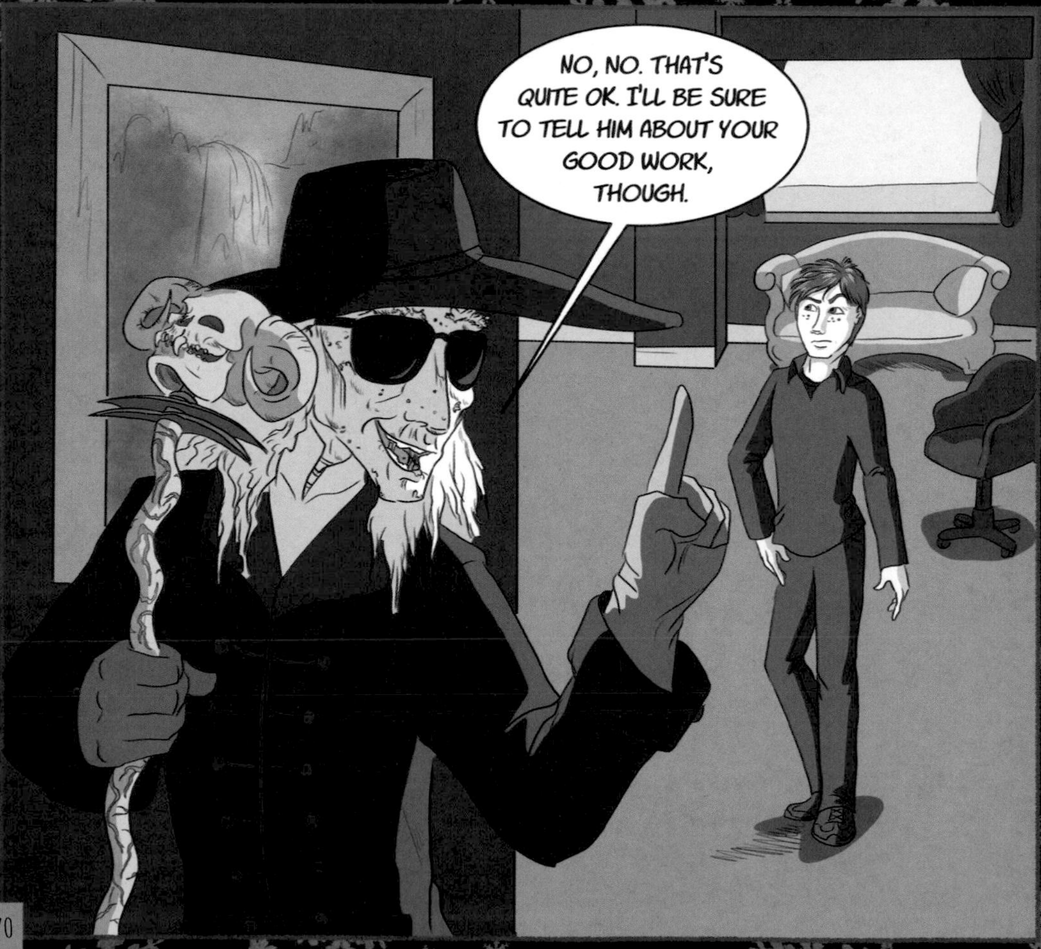
NO, NO. THAT'S QUITE OK. I'LL BE SURE TO TELL HIM ABOUT YOUR GOOD WORK, THOUGH.

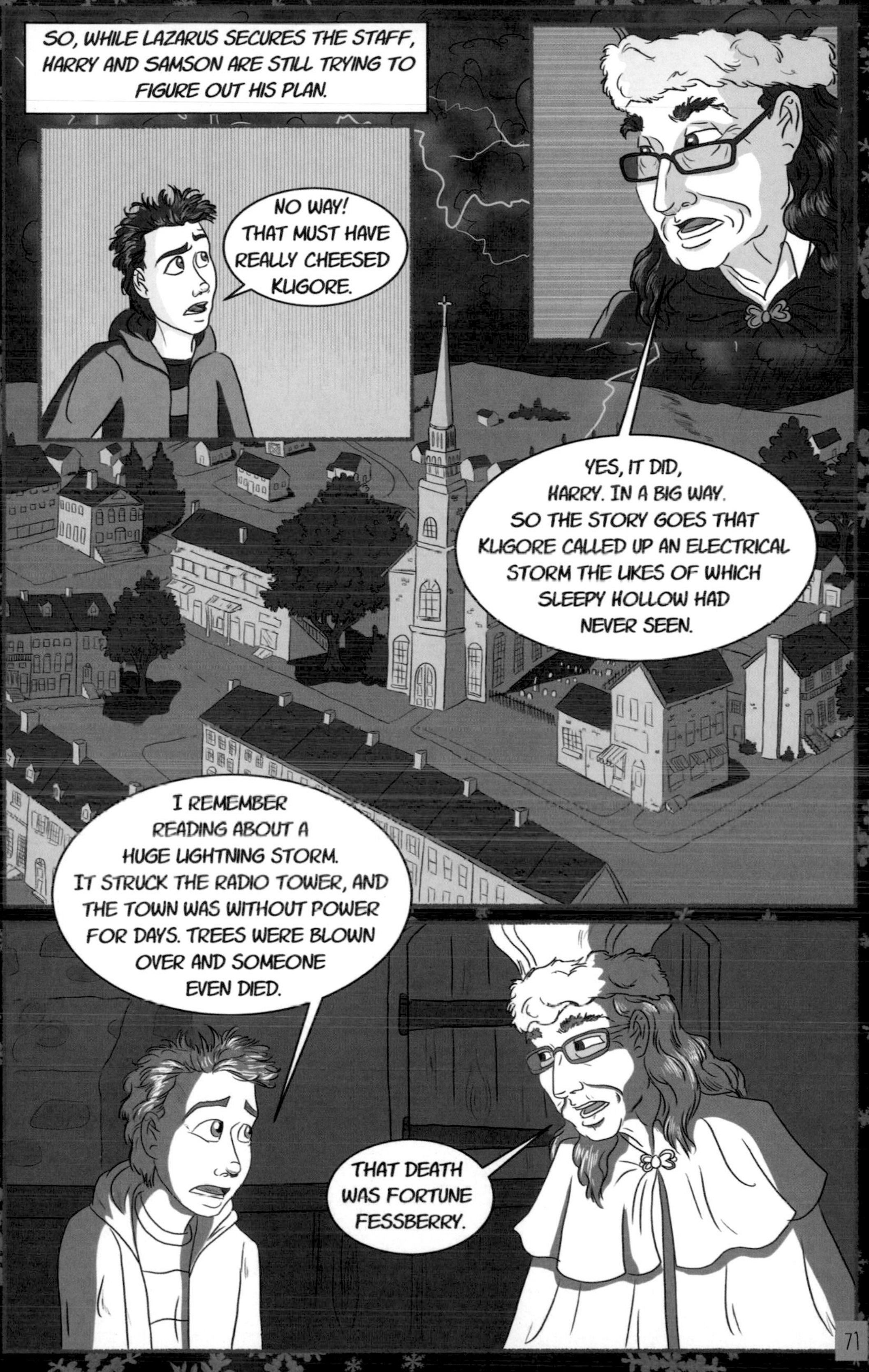

SO, WHILE LAZARUS SECURES THE STAFF, HARRY AND SAMSON ARE STILL TRYING TO FIGURE OUT HIS PLAN.
NO WAY! THAT MUST HAVE REALLY CHEESED KLIGORE.
YES, IT DID, HARRY. IN A BIG WAY. SO THE STORY GOES THAT KLIGORE CALLED UP AN ELECTRICAL STORM THE LIKES OF WHICH SLEEPY HOLLOW HAD NEVER SEEN.
I REMEMBER READING ABOUT A HUGE LIGHTNING STORM. IT STRUCK THE RADIO TOWER, AND THE TOWN WAS WITHOUT POWER FOR DAYS. TREES WERE BLOWN OVER AND SOMEONE EVEN DIED.
THAT DEATH WAS FORTUNE FESSBERRY.

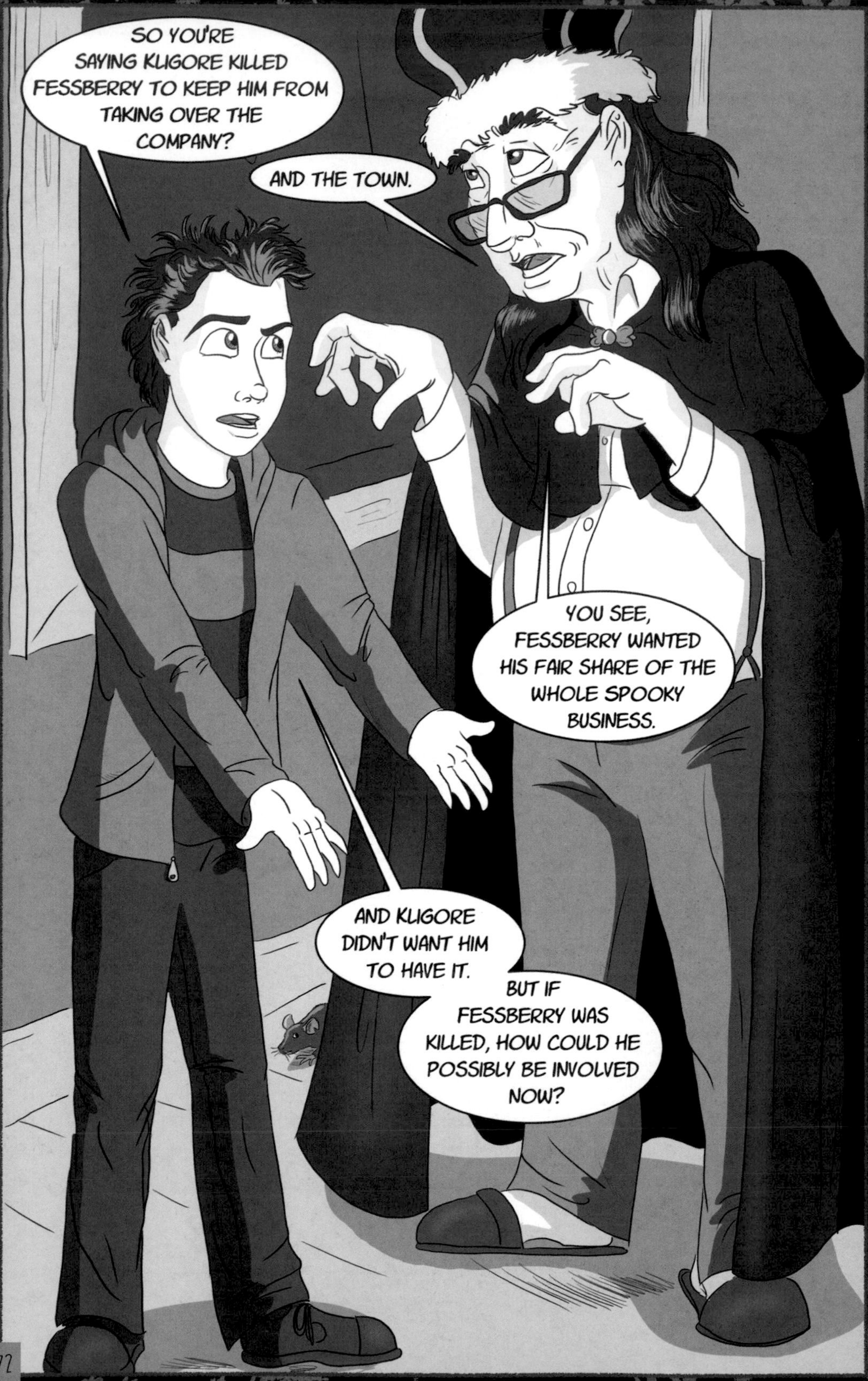
SO YOU'RE SAYING KLIGORE KILLED FESSBERRY TO KEEP HIM FROM TAKING OVER THE COMPANY?
AND THE TOWN.
YOU SEE, FESSBERRY WANTED HIS FAIR SHARE OF THE WHOLE SPOOKY BUSINESS.
AND KLIGORE DIDN'T WANT HIM TO HAVE IT.
BUT IF FESSBERRY WAS KILLED, HOW COULD HE POSSIBLY BE INVOLVED NOW?

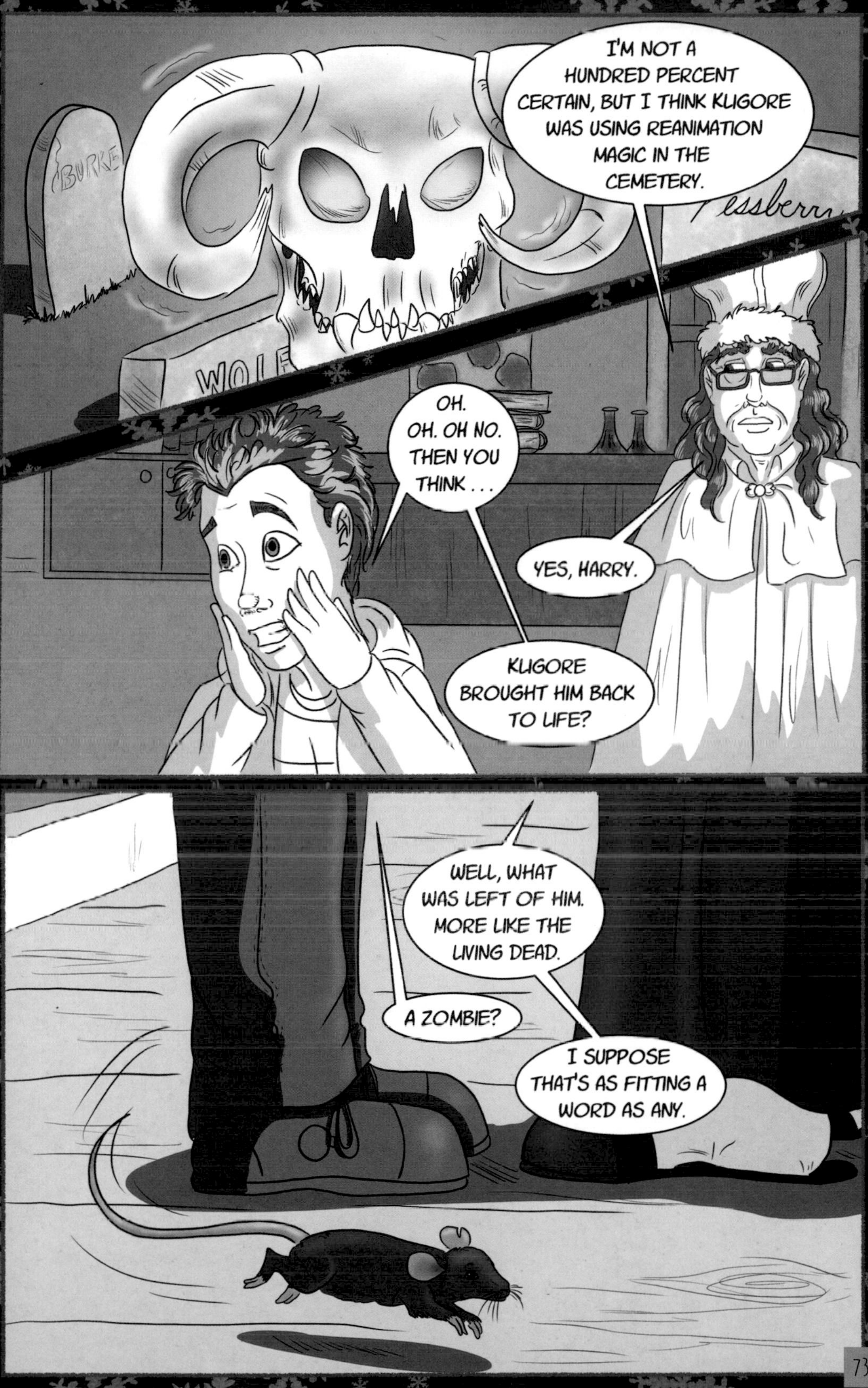
BURKE
I'M NOT A HUNDRED PERCENT CERTAIN, BUT I THINK KLIGORE WAS USING REANIMATION MAGIC IN THE CEMETERY.
WOLF
OH. OH. OH NO. THEN YOU THINK . . .
YES, HARRY.
KLIGORE BROUGHT HIM BACK TO LIFE?
WELL, WHAT WAS LEFT OF HIM. MORE LIKE THE LIVING DEAD.
A ZOMBIE?
I SUPPOSE THAT'S AS FITTING A WORD AS ANY.

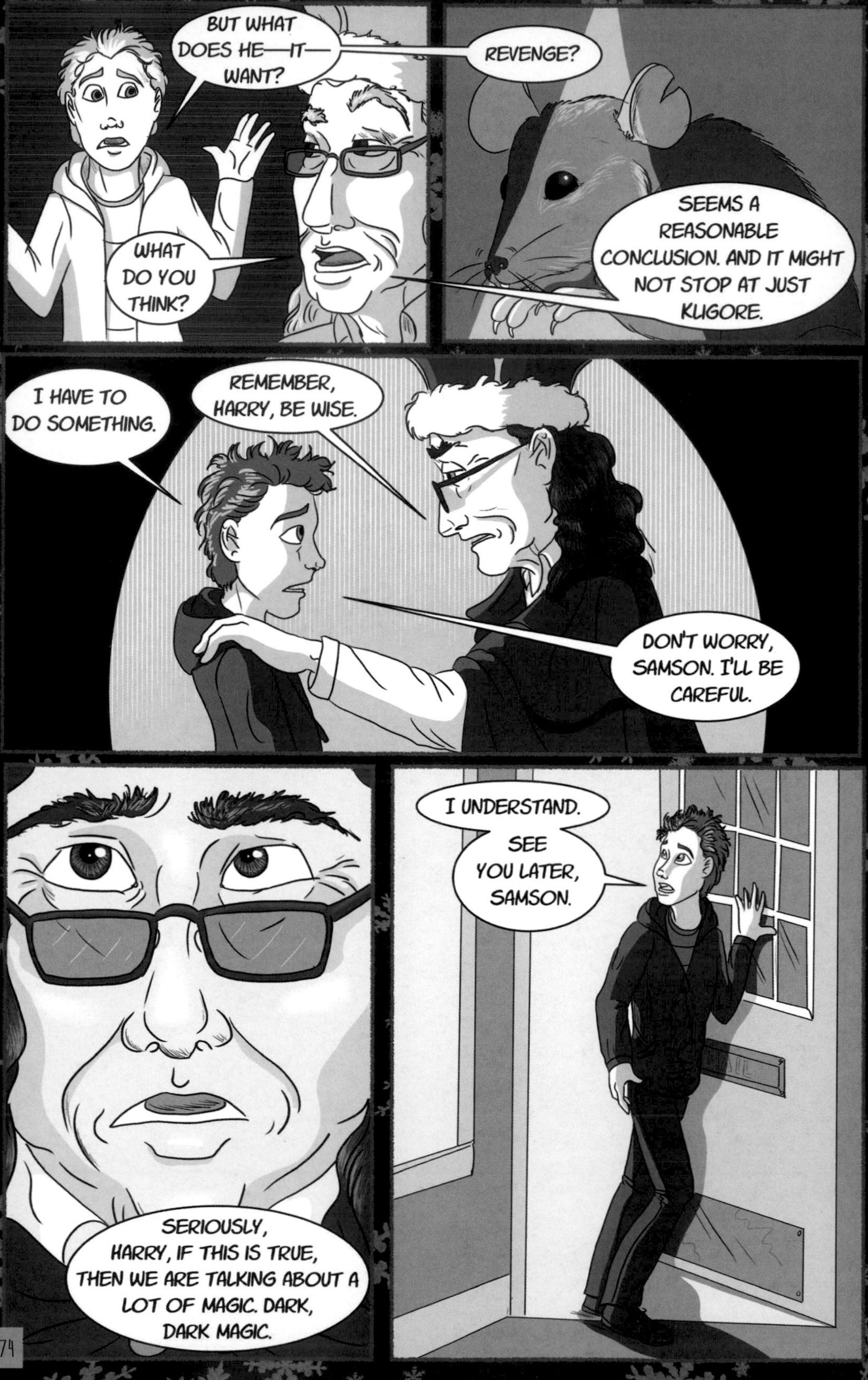
BUT WHAT DOES HE—IT—WANT?
REVENGE?
WHAT DO YOU THINK?
SEEMS A REASONABLE CONCLUSION. AND IT MIGHT NOT STOP AT JUST KLIGORE.
I HAVE TO DO SOMETHING.
REMEMBER, HARRY, BE WISE.
DON'T WORRY, SAMSON. I'LL BE CAREFUL.
SERIOUSLY, HARRY, IF THIS IS TRUE, THEN WE ARE TALKING ABOUT A LOT OF MAGIC. DARK, DARK MAGIC.
I UNDERSTAND.
SEE YOU LATER, SAMSON.

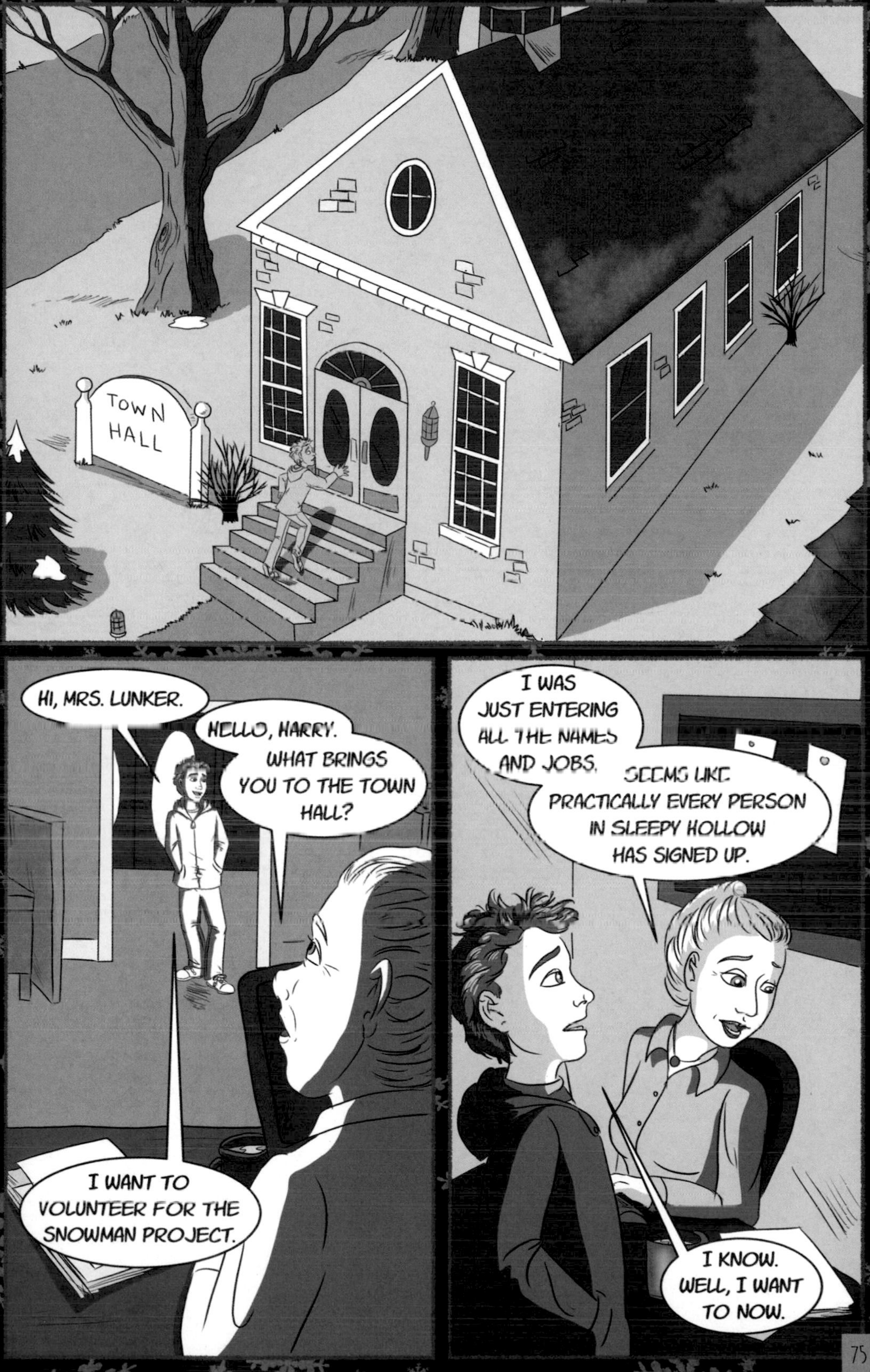
TOWN HALL
HI, MRS. LUNKER.
HELLO, HARRY. WHAT BRINGS YOU TO THE TOWN HALL?
I WANT TO VOLUNTEER FOR THE SNOWMAN PROJECT.
I WAS JUST ENTERING ALL THE NAMES AND JOBS.
SEEMS LIKE PRACTICALLY EVERY PERSON IN SLEEPY HOLLOW HAS SIGNED UP.
I KNOW. WELL, I WANT TO NOW.

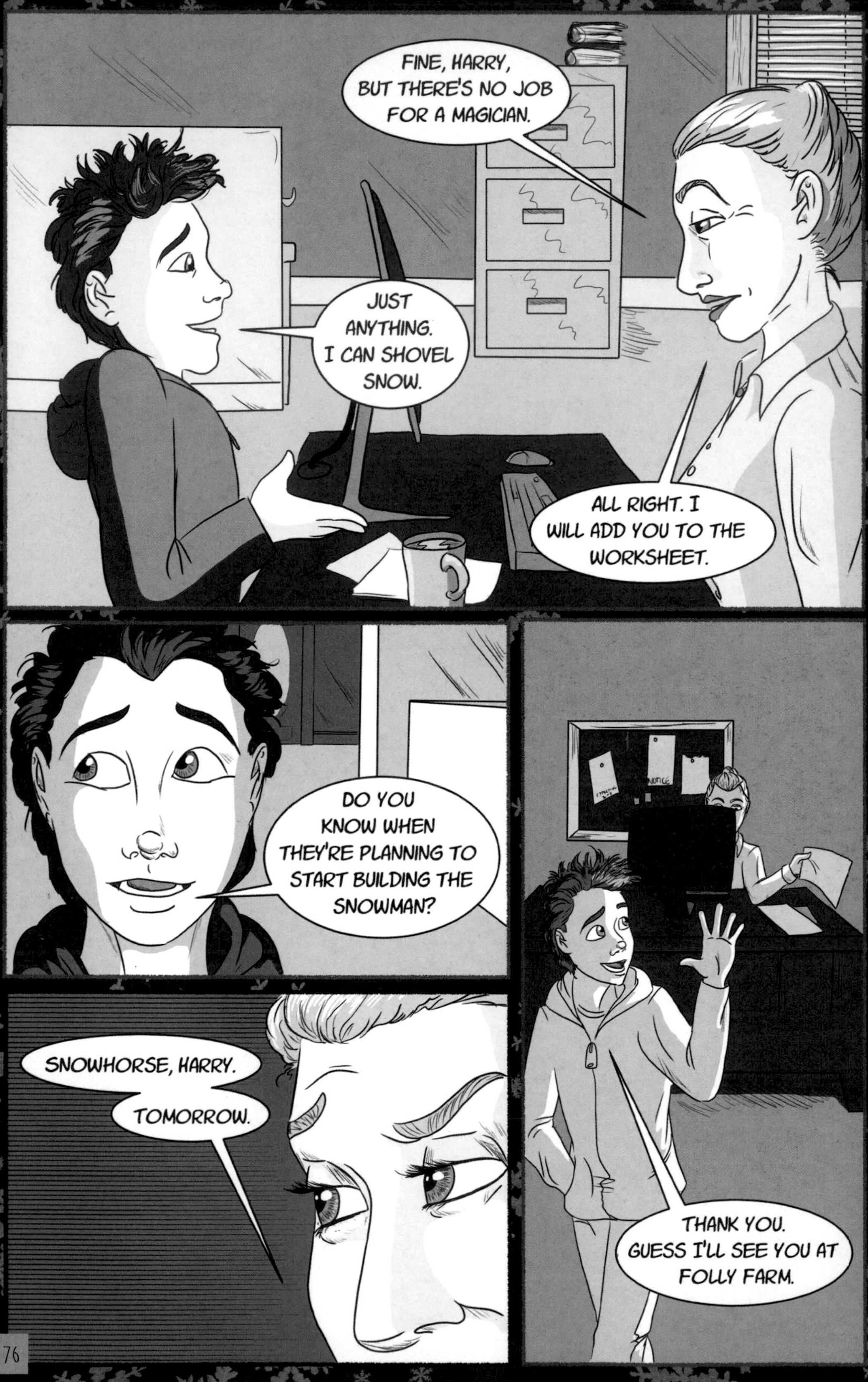
FINE, HARRY, BUT THERE'S NO JOB FOR A MAGICIAN.
JUST ANYTHING. I CAN SHOVEL SNOW.
ALL RIGHT. I WILL ADD YOU TO THE WORKSHEET.
DO YOU KNOW WHEN THEY'RE PLANNING TO START BUILDING THE SNOWMAN?
SNOWHORSE, HARRY.
TOMORROW.
THANK YOU. GUESS I'LL SEE YOU AT FOLLY FARM.

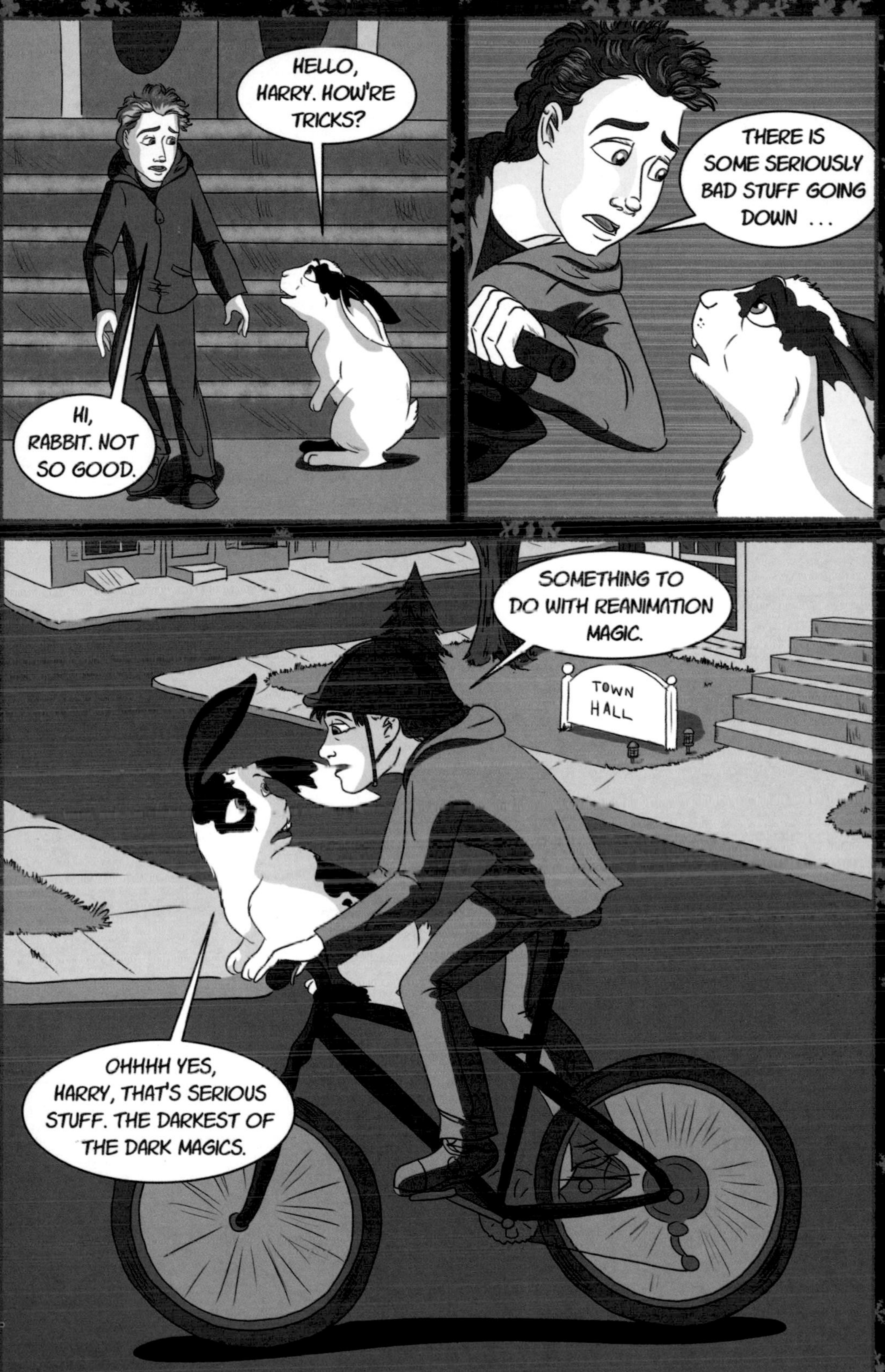
HELLO, HARRY. HOW'RE TRICKS?
HI, RABBIT. NOT SO GOOD.
THERE IS SOME SERIOUSLY BAD STUFF GOING DOWN . . .
SOMETHING TO DO WITH REANIMATION MAGIC.
TOWN HALL
OHHHH YES, HARRY, THAT'S SERIOUS STUFF. THE DARKEST OF THE DARK MAGICS.

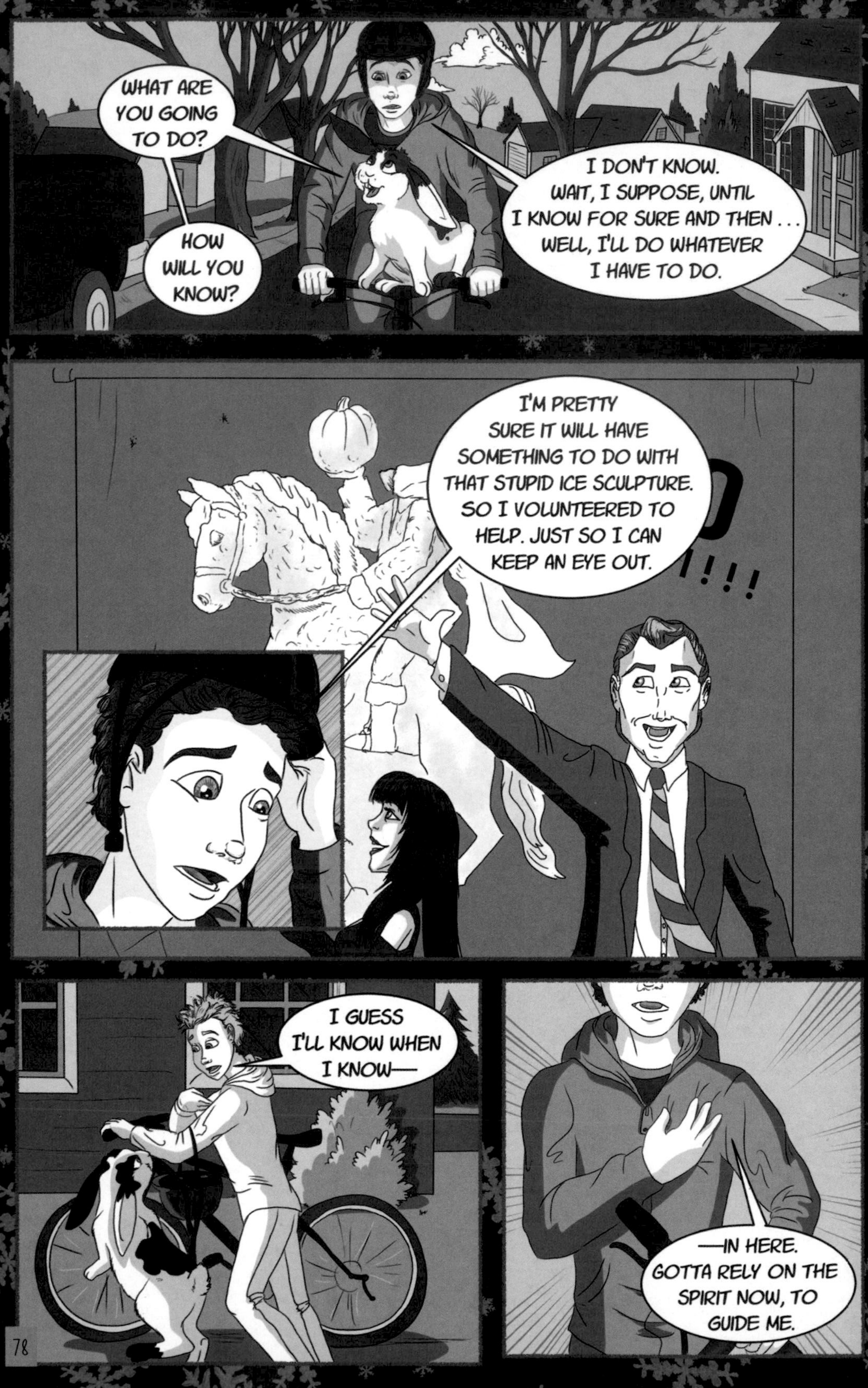
WHAT ARE YOU GOING TO DO?
I DON'T KNOW. WAIT, I SUPPOSE, UNTIL I KNOW FOR SURE AND THEN . . . WELL, I'LL DO WHATEVER I HAVE TO DO.
HOW WILL YOU KNOW?
I'M PRETTY SURE IT WILL HAVE SOMETHING TO DO WITH THAT STUPID ICE SCULPTURE. SO I VOLUNTEERED TO HELP. JUST SO I CAN KEEP AN EYE OUT.
!!!!
I GUESS I'LL KNOW WHEN I KNOW—
—IN HERE. GOTTA RELY ON THE SPIRIT NOW, TO GUIDE ME.

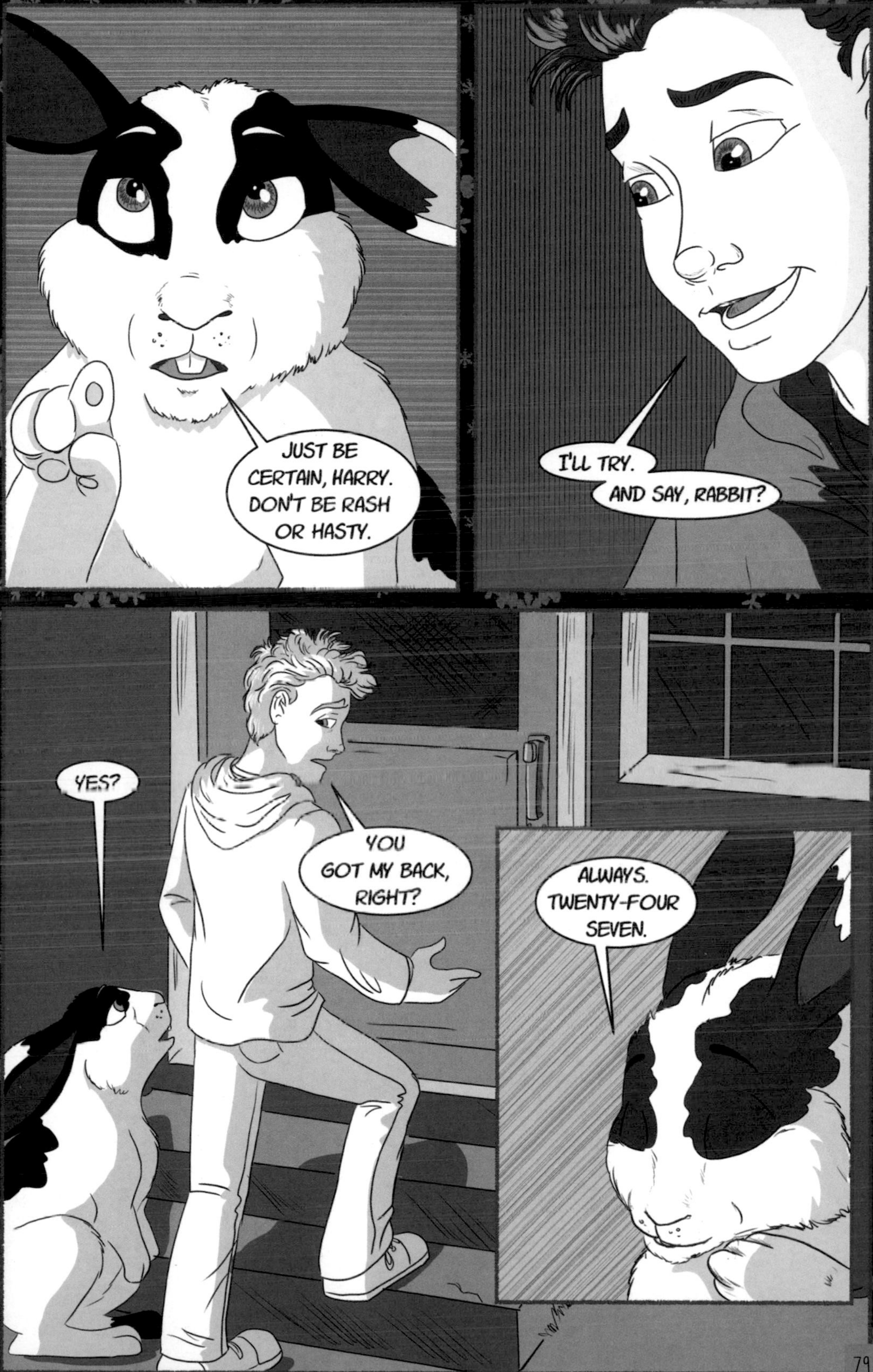
JUST BE CERTAIN, HARRY. DON'T BE RASH OR HASTY.
I'LL TRY.
AND SAY, RABBIT?
YES?
YOU GOT MY BACK, RIGHT?
ALWAYS. TWENTY-FOUR SEVEN.

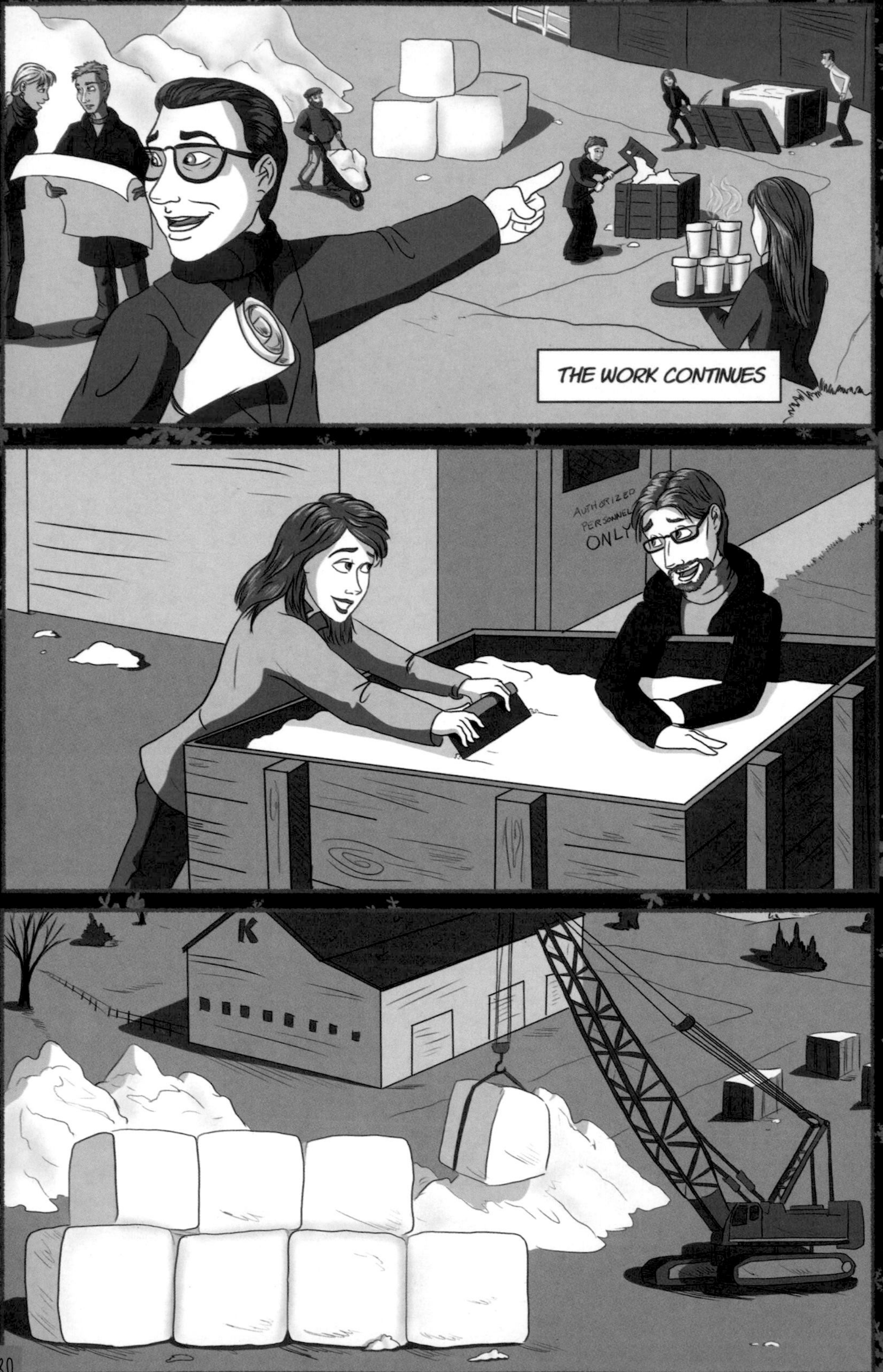
THE WORK CONTINUES
AUTHORIZED PERSONNEL ONLY
K

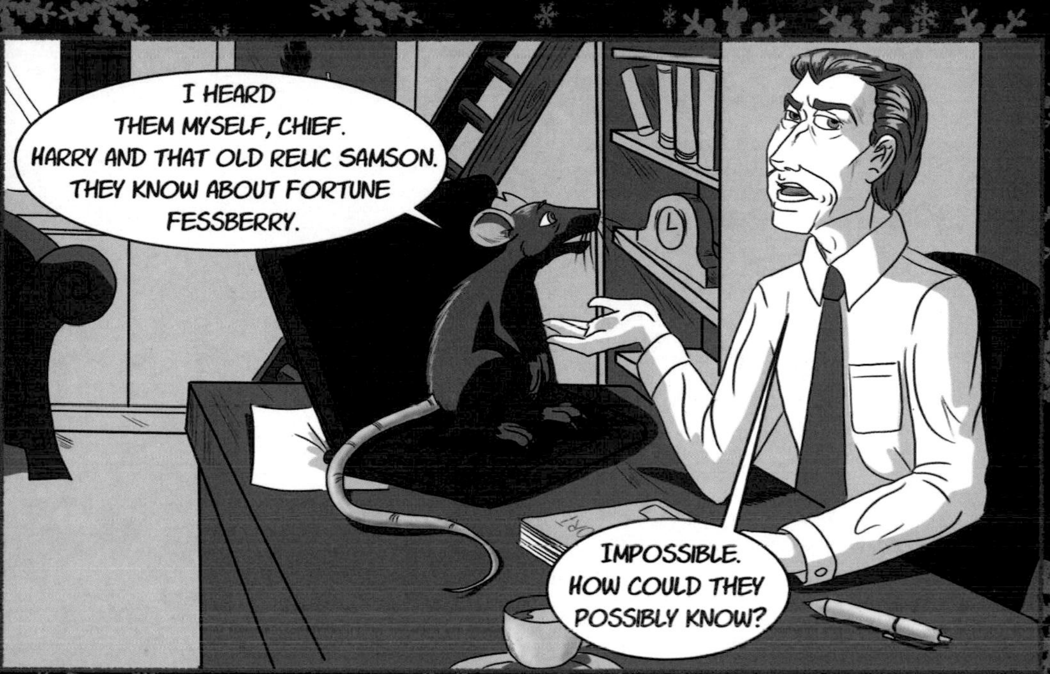
I HEARD THEM MYSELF, CHIEF. HARRY AND THAT OLD RELIC SAMSON. THEY KNOW ABOUT FORTUNE FESSBERRY.
IMPOSSIBLE. HOW COULD THEY POSSIBLY KNOW?

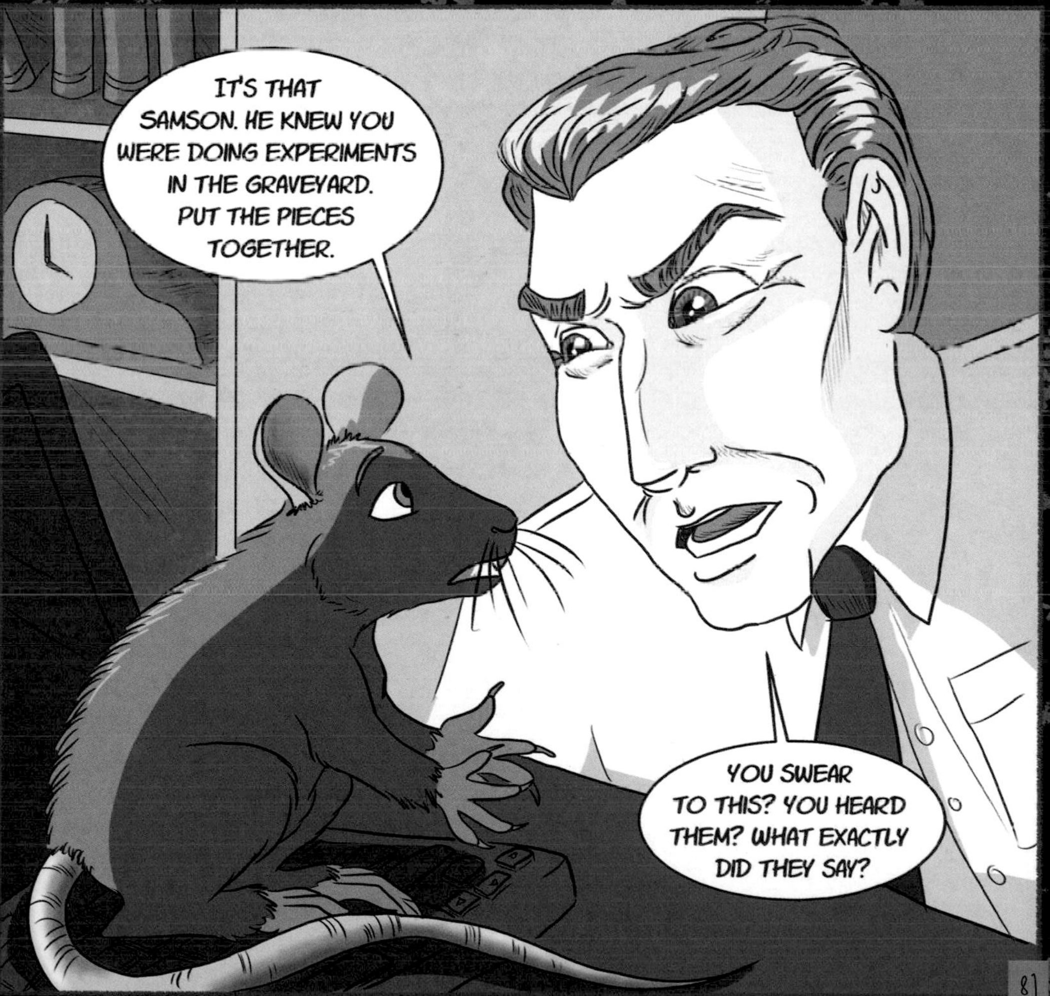
IT'S THAT SAMSON. HE KNEW YOU WERE DOING EXPERIMENTS IN THE GRAVEYARD. PUT THE PIECES TOGETHER.
YOU SWEAR TO THIS? YOU HEARD THEM? WHAT EXACTLY DID THEY SAY?

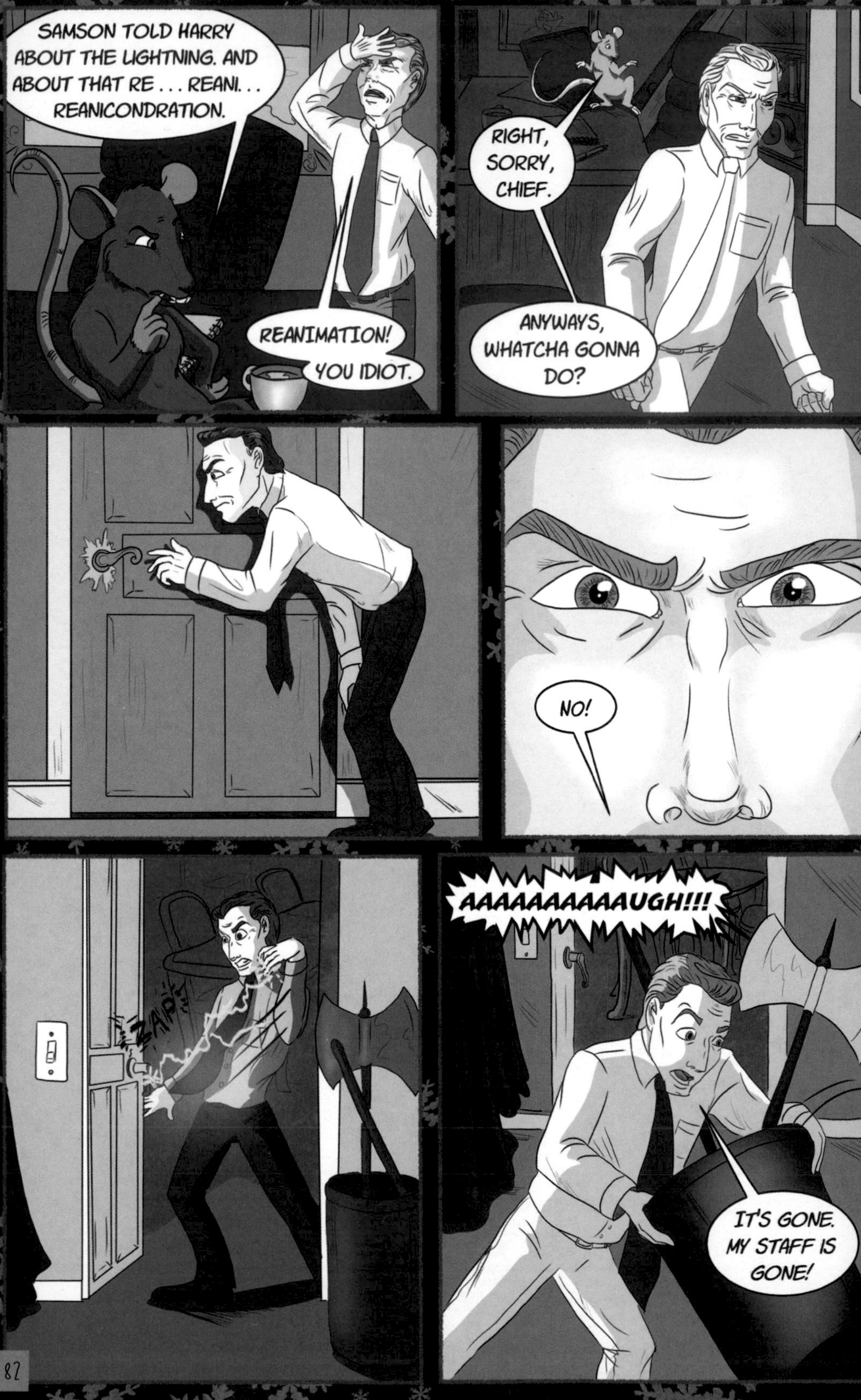
SAMSON TOLD HARRY ABOUT THE LIGHTNING. AND ABOUT THAT RE . . . REANI. . . REANICONDRATION.
REANIMATION!
YOU IDIOT.
RIGHT, SORRY, CHIEF.
ANYWAYS, WHATCHA GONNA DO?
NO!
ZAP!
AAAAAAAAAAUGH!!!
IT'S GONE. MY STAFF IS GONE!

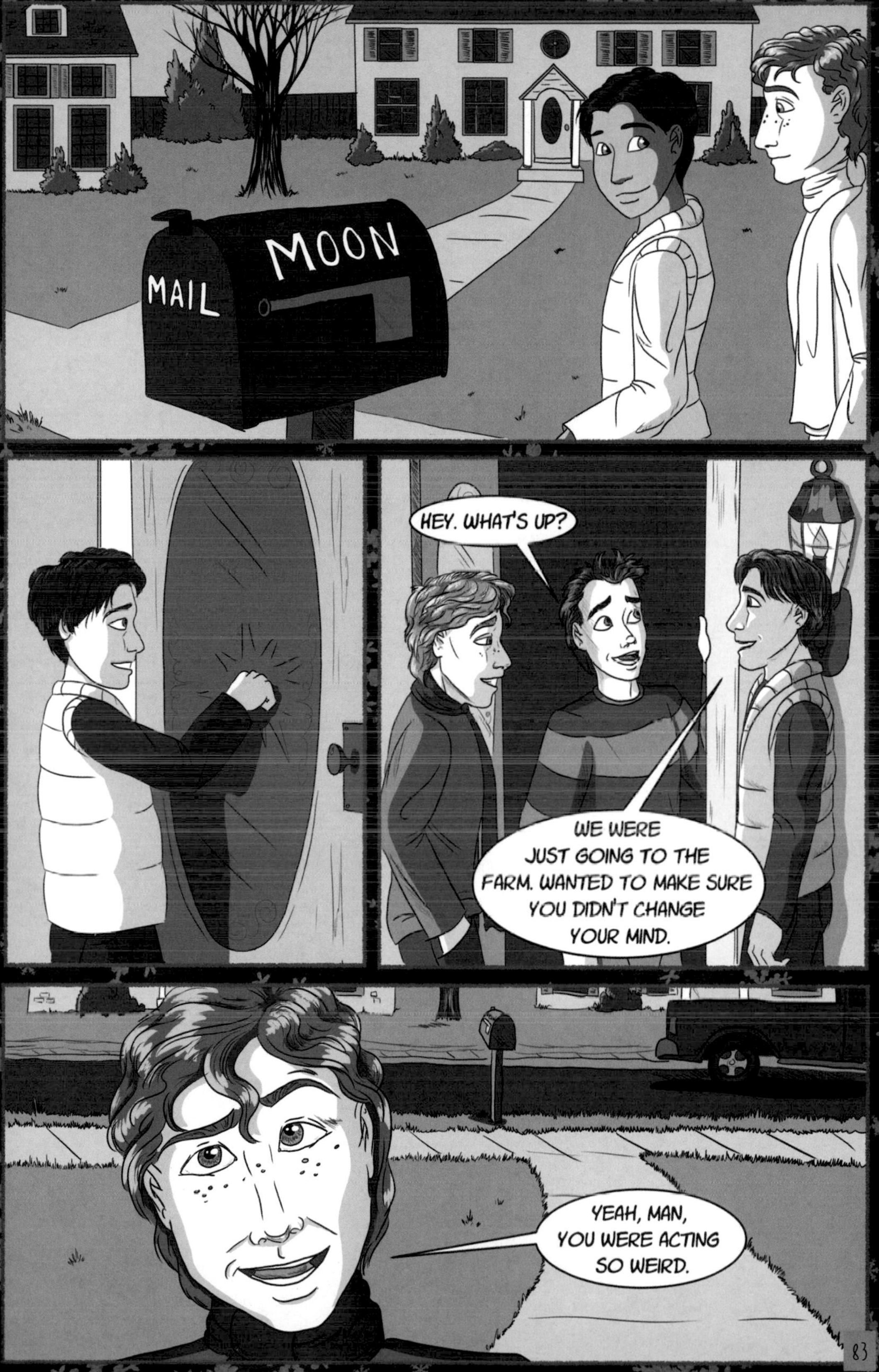
MAIL
MOON
HEY. WHAT'S UP?
WE WERE JUST GOING TO THE FARM. WANTED TO MAKE SURE YOU DIDN'T CHANGE YOUR MIND.
YEAH, MAN, YOU WERE ACTING SO WEIRD.

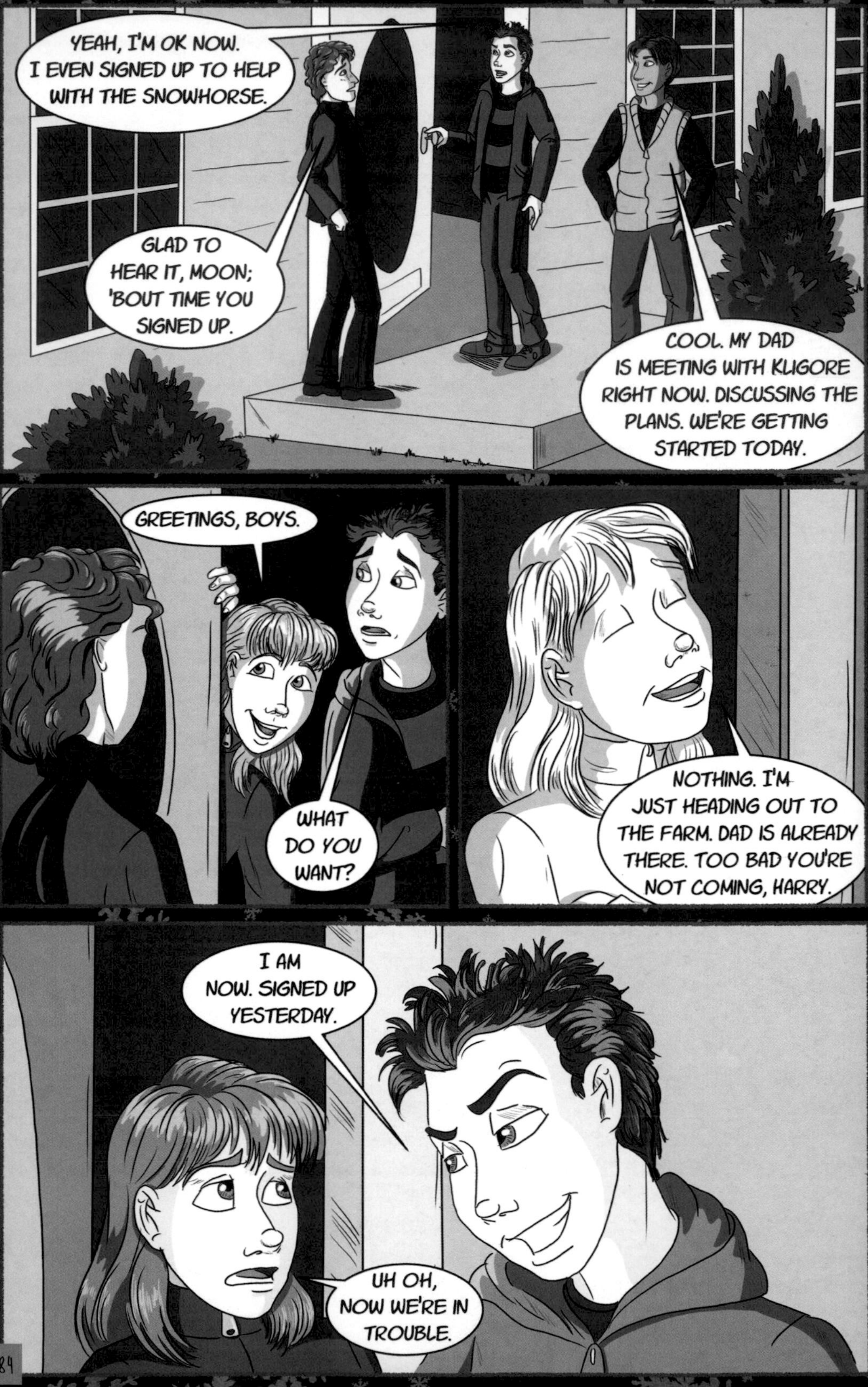

YEAH, I'M OK NOW. I EVEN SIGNED UP TO HELP WITH THE SNOWHORSE.
GLAD TO HEAR IT, MOON; 'BOUT TIME YOU SIGNED UP.
COOL. MY DAD IS MEETING WITH KLIGORE RIGHT NOW. DISCUSSING THE PLANS. WE'RE GETTING STARTED TODAY.
GREETINGS, BOYS.
WHAT DO YOU WANT?
NOTHING. I'M JUST HEADING OUT TO THE FARM. DAD IS ALREADY THERE. TOO BAD YOU'RE NOT COMING, HARRY.
I AM NOW. SIGNED UP YESTERDAY.
UH OH, NOW WE'RE IN TROUBLE.

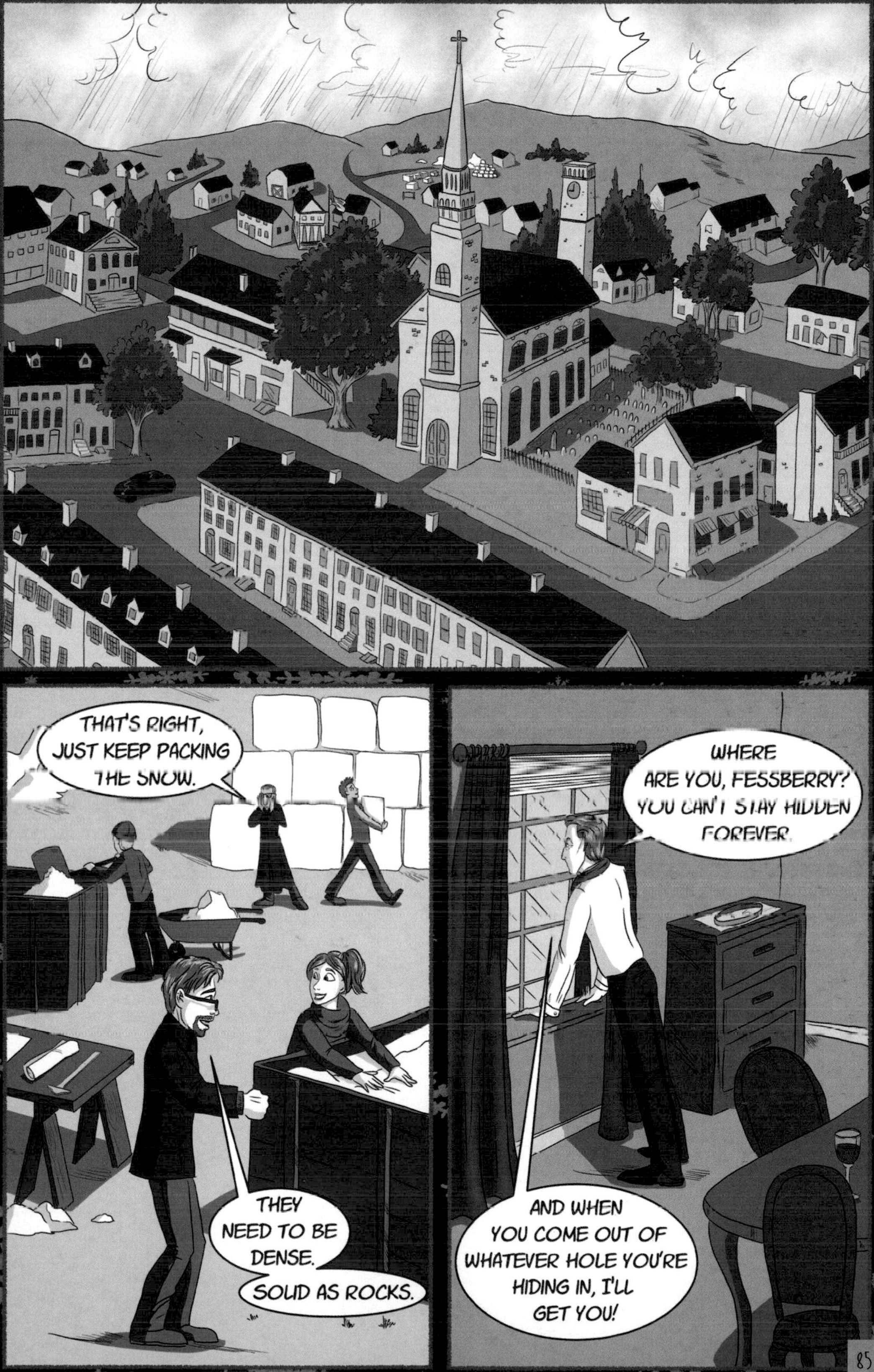
THAT'S RIGHT, JUST KEEP PACKING THE SNOW.
THEY NEED TO BE DENSE.
SOLID AS ROCKS.
WHERE ARE YOU, FESSBERRY? YOU CAN'T STAY HIDDEN FOREVER.
AND WHEN YOU COME OUT OF WHATEVER HOLE YOU'RE HIDING IN, I'LL GET YOU!

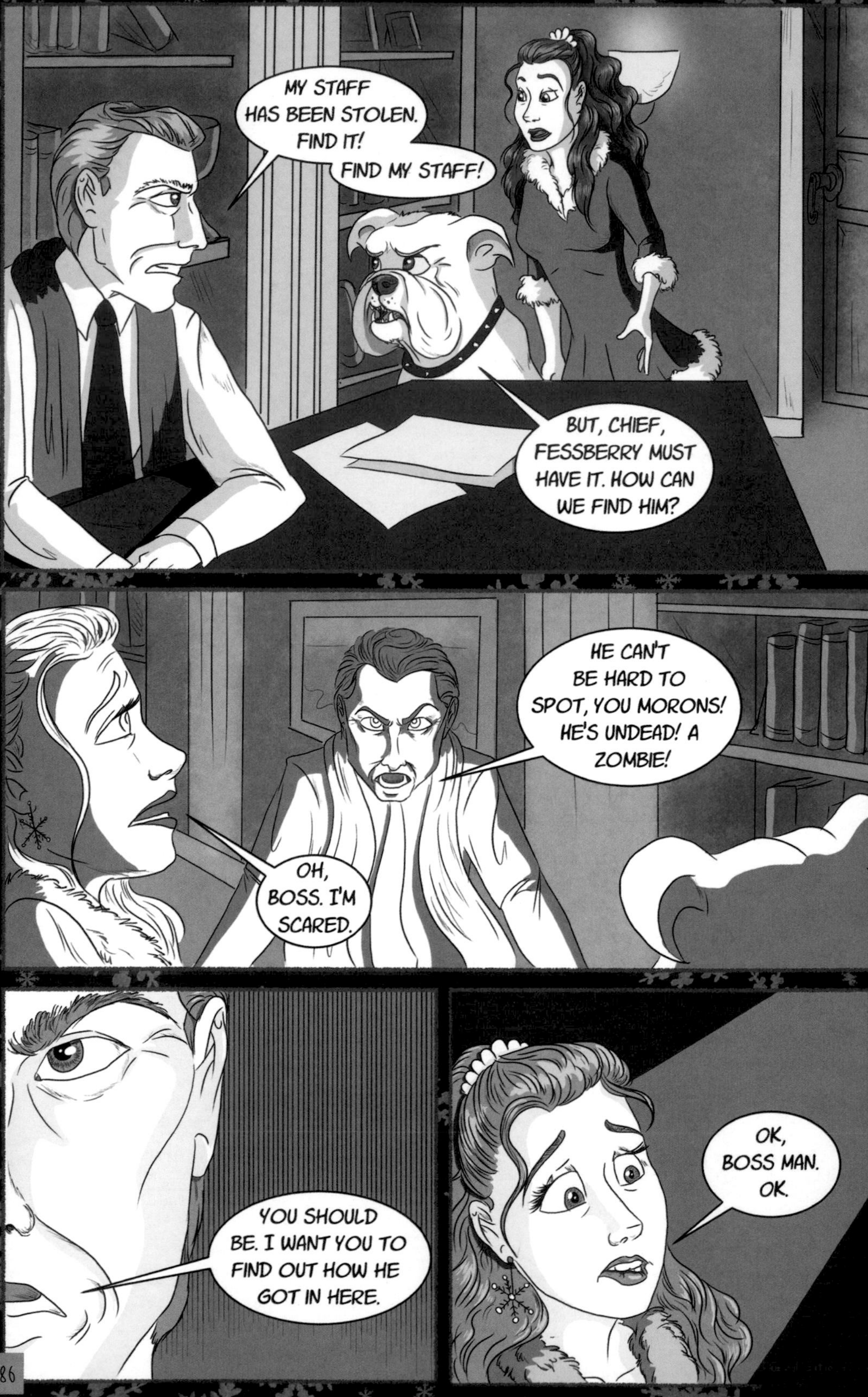
MY STAFF HAS BEEN STOLEN. FIND IT!
FIND MY STAFF!
BUT, CHIEF, FESSBERRY MUST HAVE IT. HOW CAN WE FIND HIM?
HE CAN'T BE HARD TO SPOT, YOU MORONS! HE'S UNDEAD! A ZOMBIE!
OH, BOSS. I'M SCARED.
YOU SHOULD BE. I WANT YOU TO FIND OUT HOW HE GOT IN HERE.
OK, BOSS MAN. OK.

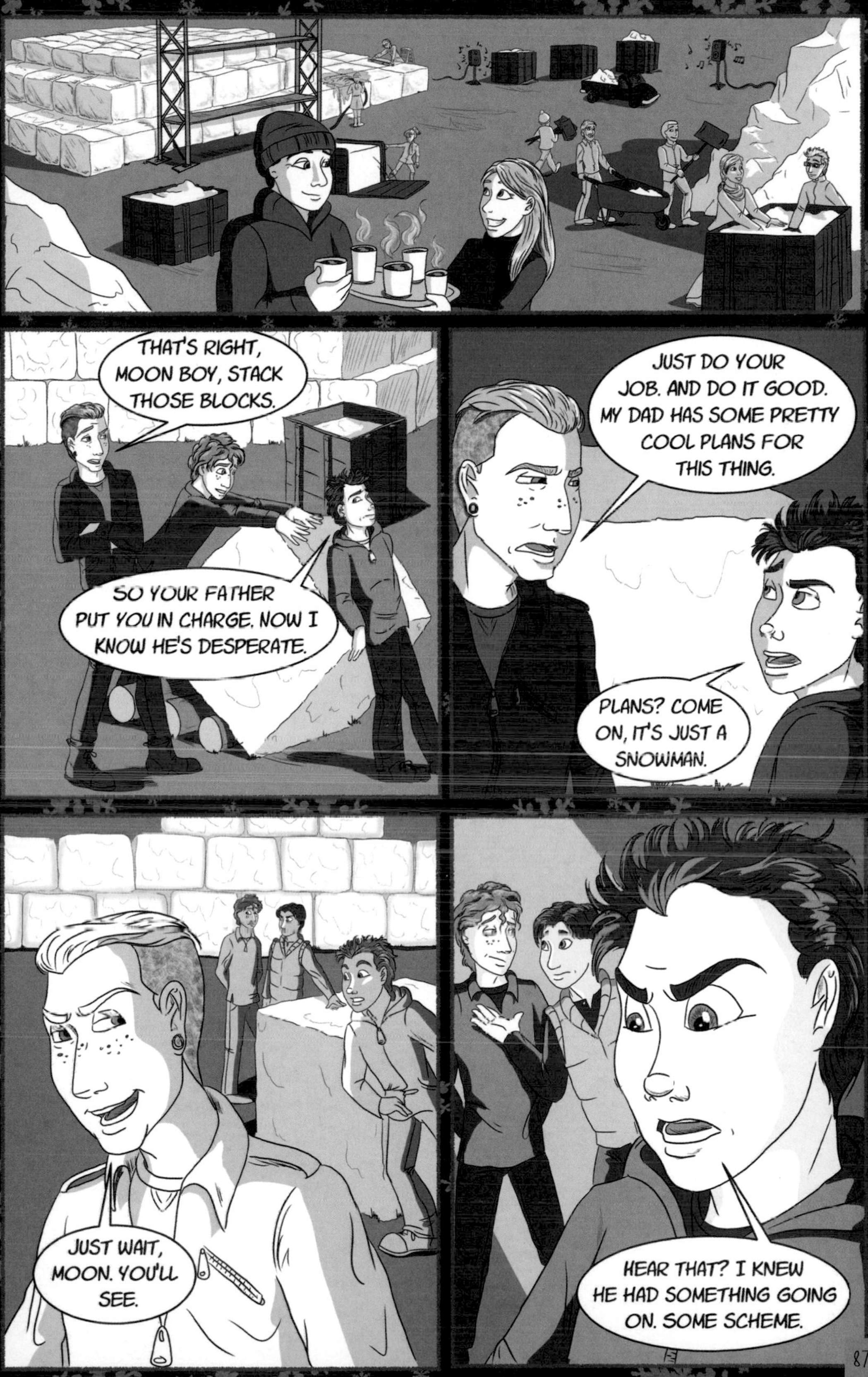
THAT'S RIGHT, MOON BOY, STACK THOSE BLOCKS.
SO YOUR FATHER PUT YOU IN CHARGE. NOW I KNOW HE'S DESPERATE.
JUST DO YOUR JOB. AND DO IT GOOD. MY DAD HAS SOME PRETTY COOL PLANS FOR THIS THING.
PLANS? COME ON, IT'S JUST A SNOWMAN.
JUST WAIT, MOON. YOU'LL SEE.
HEAR THAT? I KNEW HE HAD SOMETHING GOING ON. SOME SCHEME.

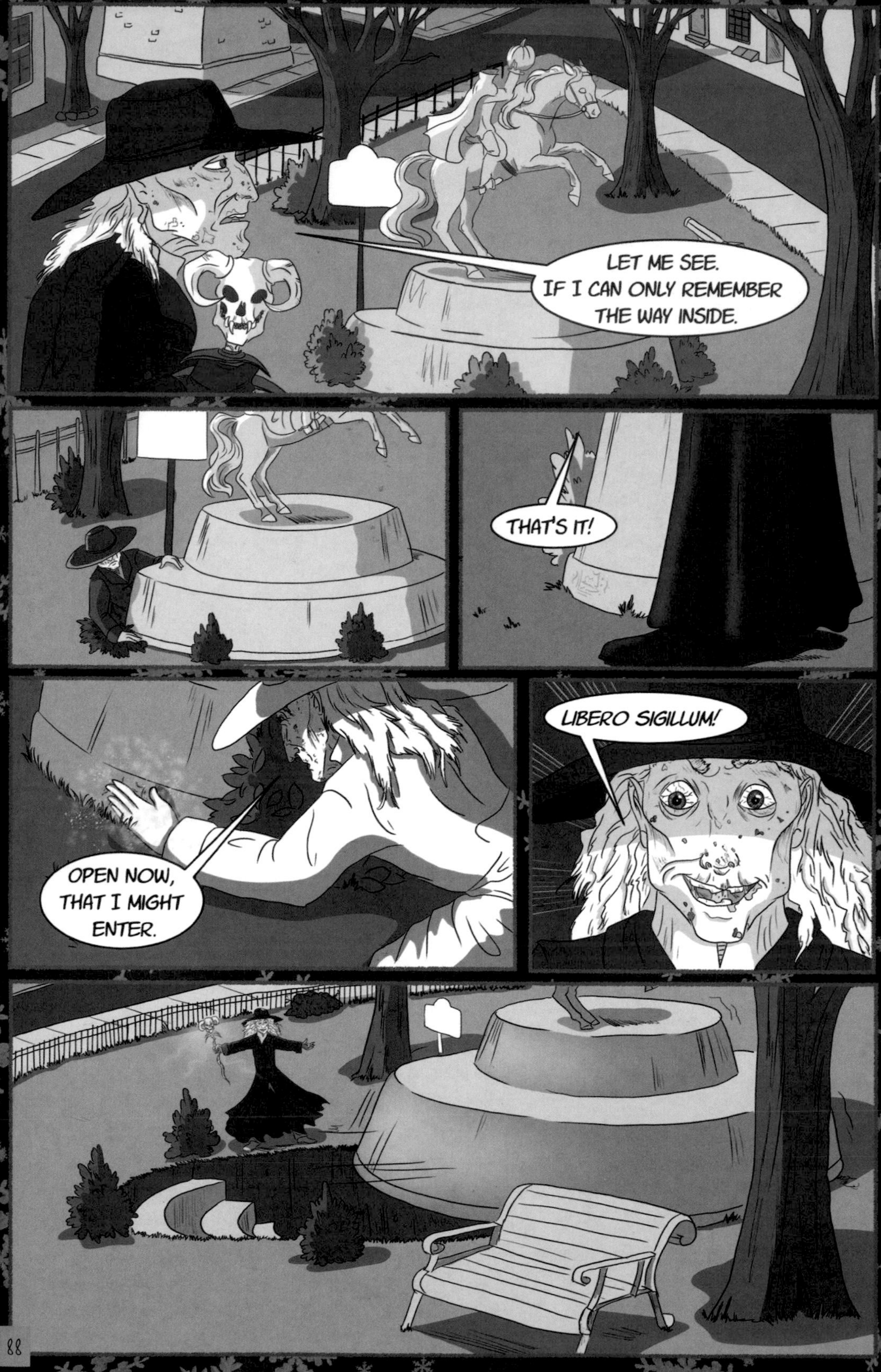
LET ME SEE.
IF I CAN ONLY REMEMBER
THE WAY INSIDE.
THAT'S IT!
OPEN NOW,
THAT I MIGHT
ENTER.
LIBERO SIGILLUM!

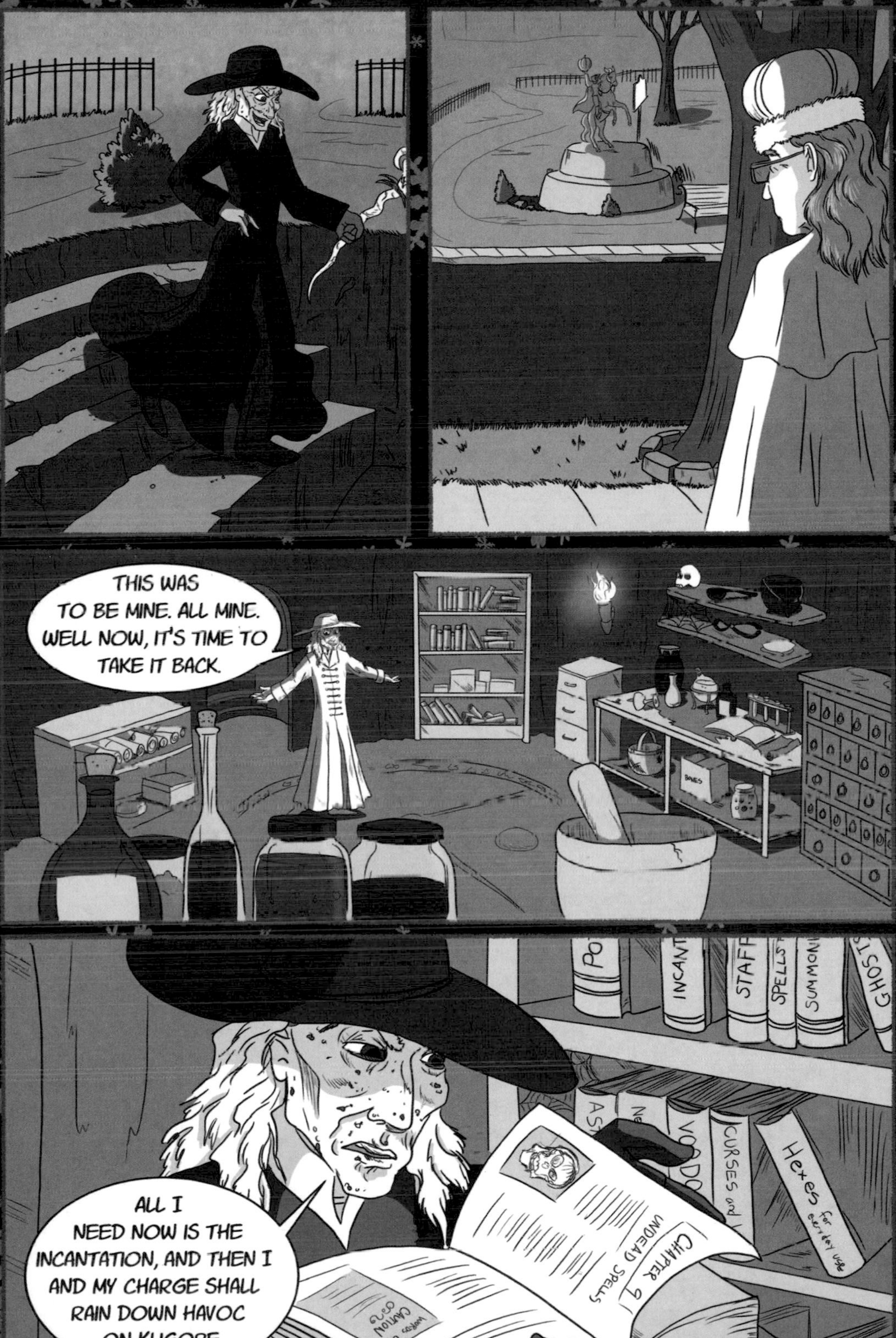
THIS WAS TO BE MINE. ALL MINE. WELL NOW, IT'S TIME TO TAKE IT BACK.
BONES
STAFF
CURSES and
Hexes for everyday use
CHAPTER 9
UNDEAD SPELLS
WORDS OF CAUTION
ALL I NEED NOW IS THE INCANTATION, AND THEN I AND MY CHARGE SHALL RAIN DOWN HAVOC ON KILGORE.

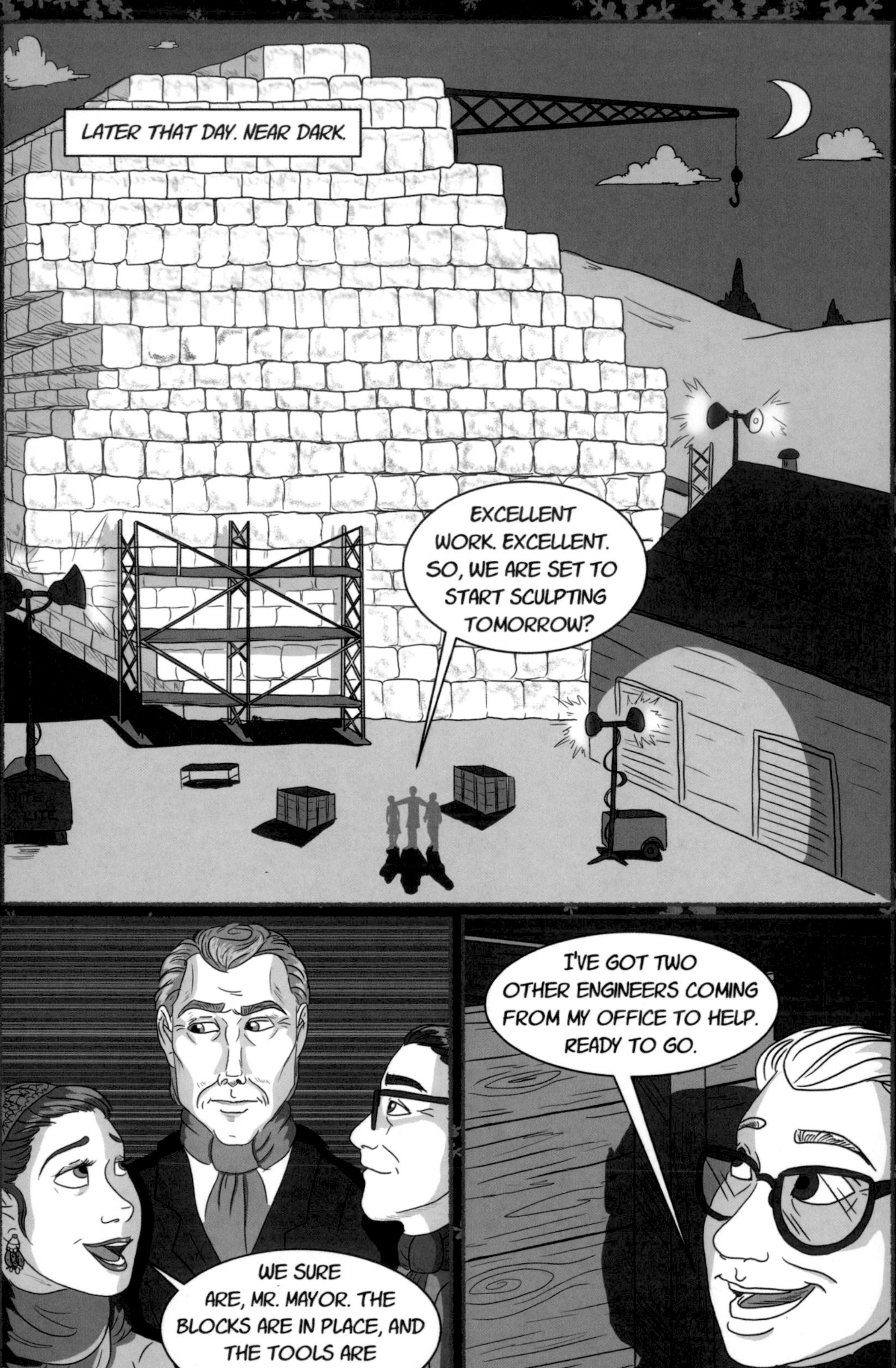
LATER THAT DAY. NEAR DARK.
EXCELLENT WORK. EXCELLENT. SO, WE ARE SET TO START SCULPTING TOMORROW?
WE SURE ARE, MR. MAYOR. THE BLOCKS ARE IN PLACE, AND THE TOOLS ARE ASSEMBLED.
I'VE GOT TWO OTHER ENGINEERS COMING FROM MY OFFICE TO HELP. READY TO GO.

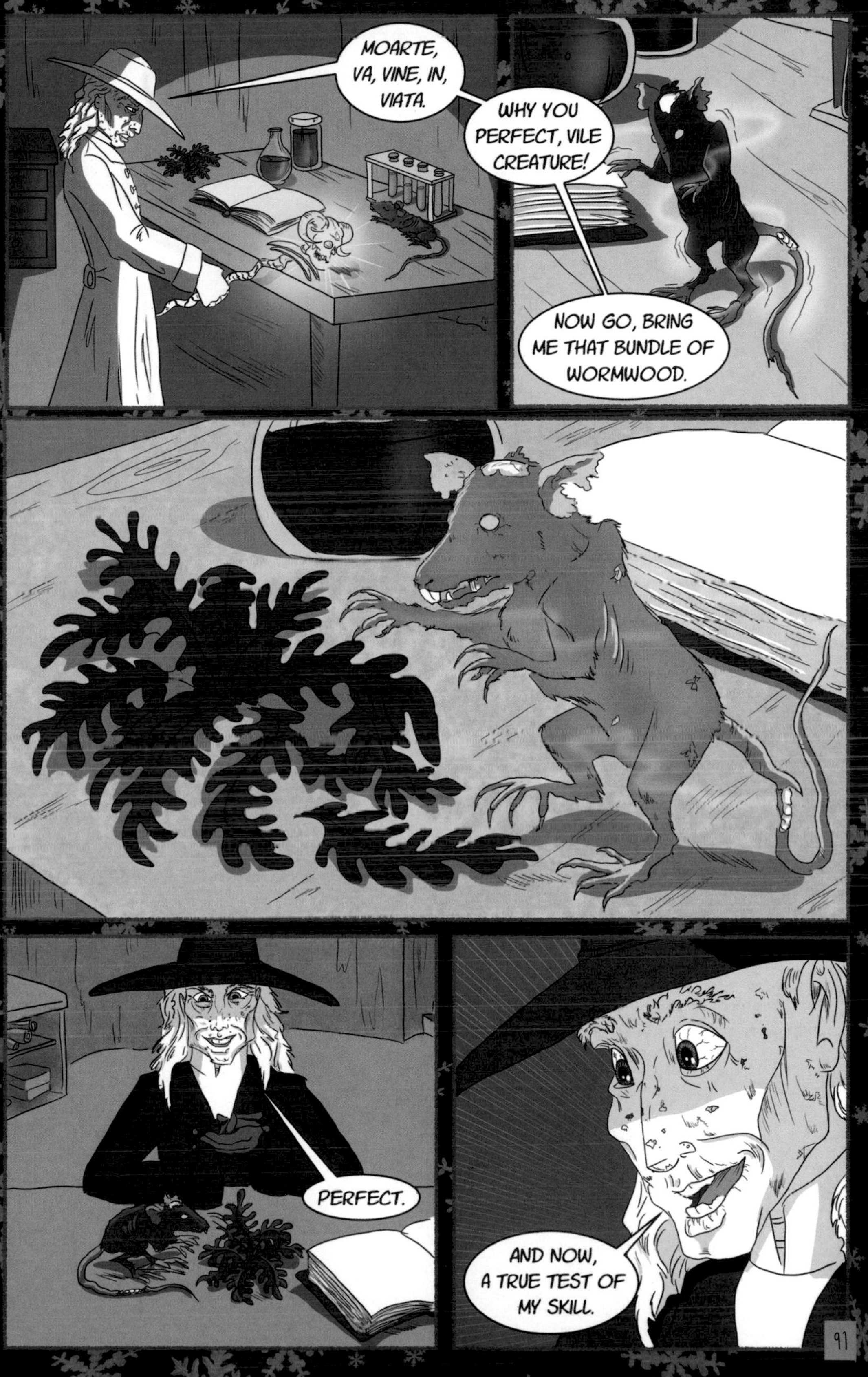
MOARTE, VA, VINE, IN, VIATA.
WHY YOU PERFECT, VILE CREATURE!
NOW GO, BRING ME THAT BUNDLE OF WORMWOOD.
PERFECT.
AND NOW, A TRUE TEST OF MY SKILL.

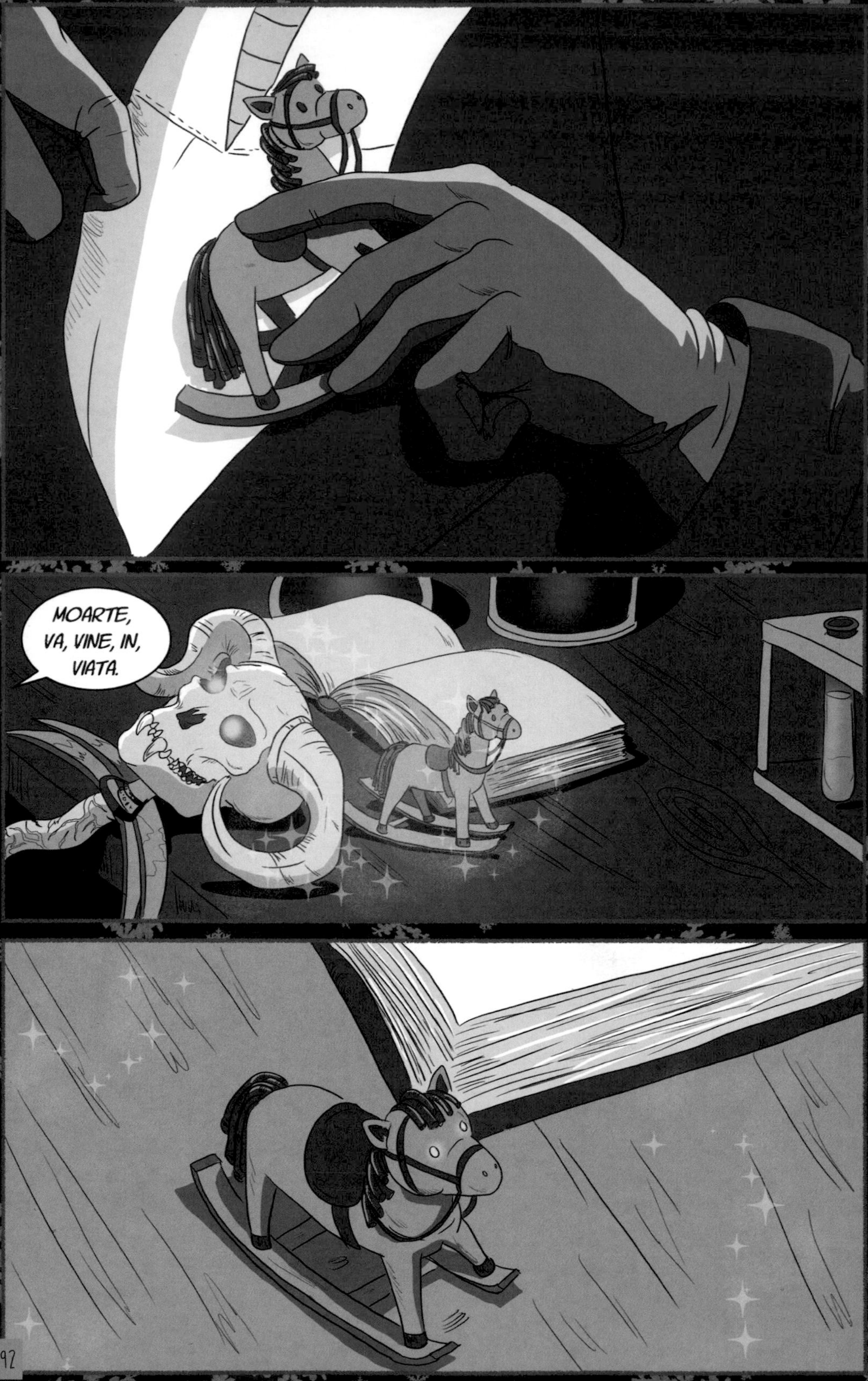
MOARTE, VA, VINE, IN, VIATA.

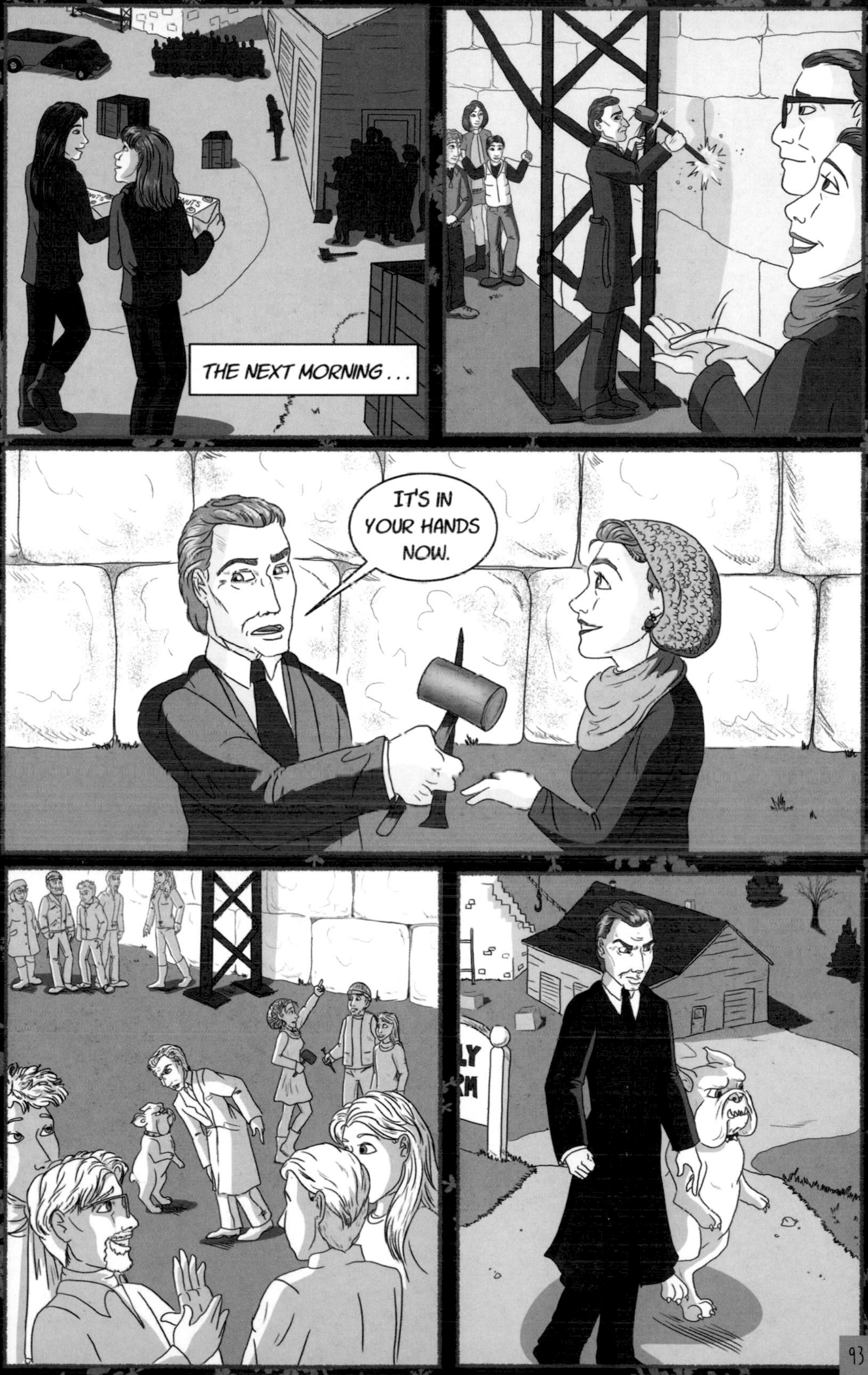
THE NEXT MORNING . . .
IT'S IN YOUR HANDS NOW.

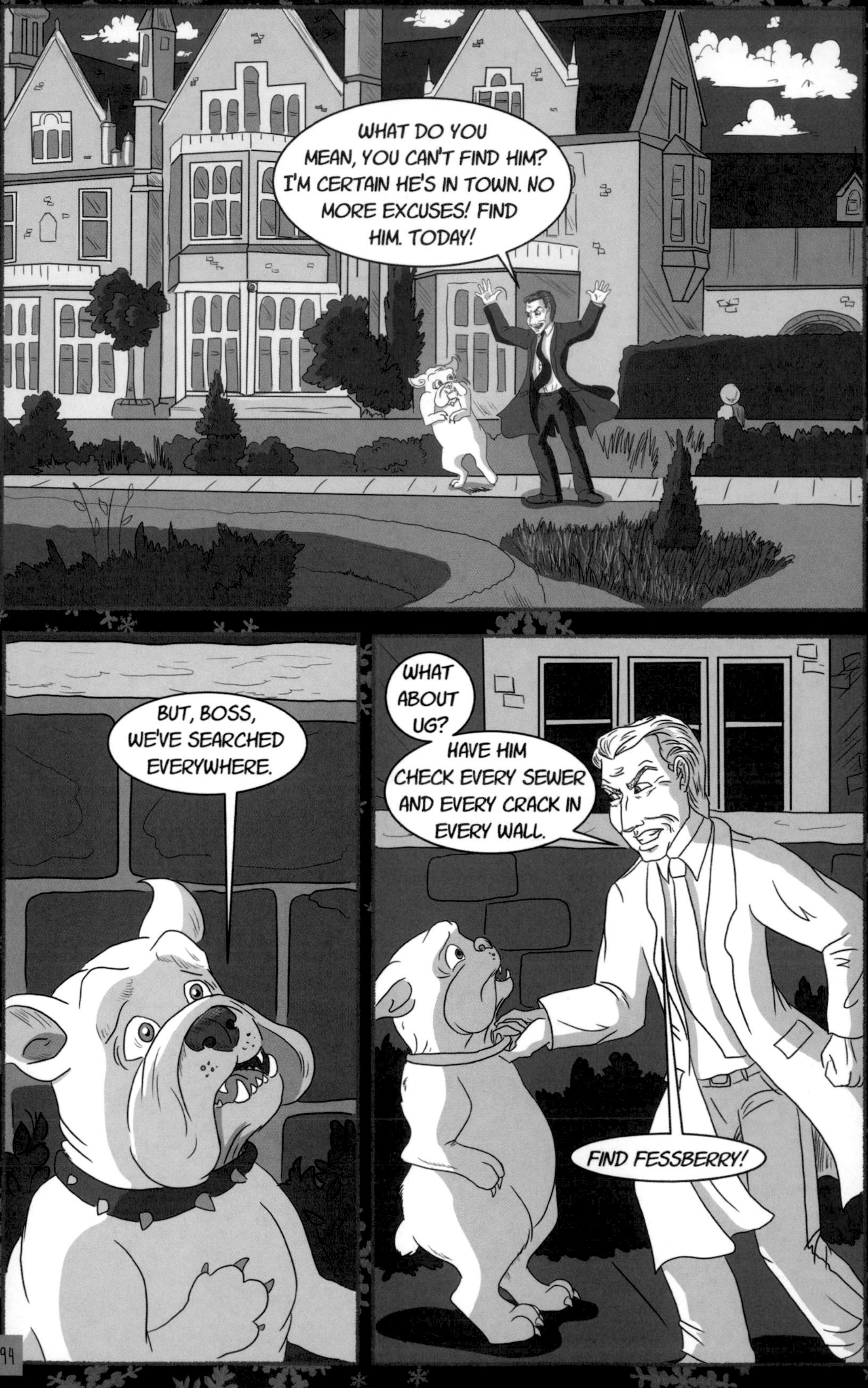
WHAT DO YOU MEAN, YOU CAN'T FIND HIM? I'M CERTAIN HE'S IN TOWN. NO MORE EXCUSES! FIND HIM. TODAY!
BUT, BOSS, WE'VE SEARCHED EVERYWHERE.
WHAT ABOUT UG?
HAVE HIM CHECK EVERY SEWER AND EVERY CRACK IN EVERY WALL.
FIND FESSBERRY!

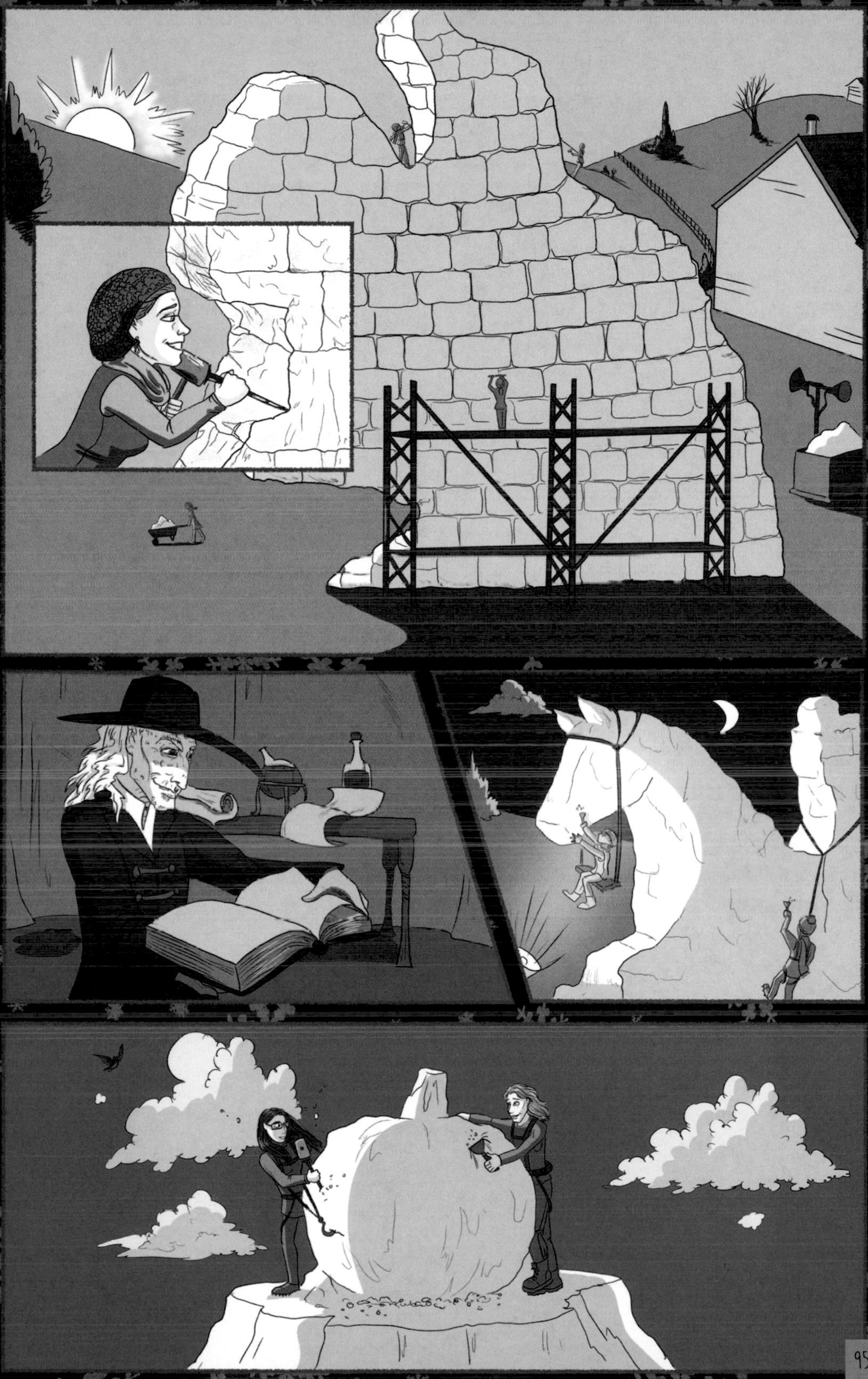

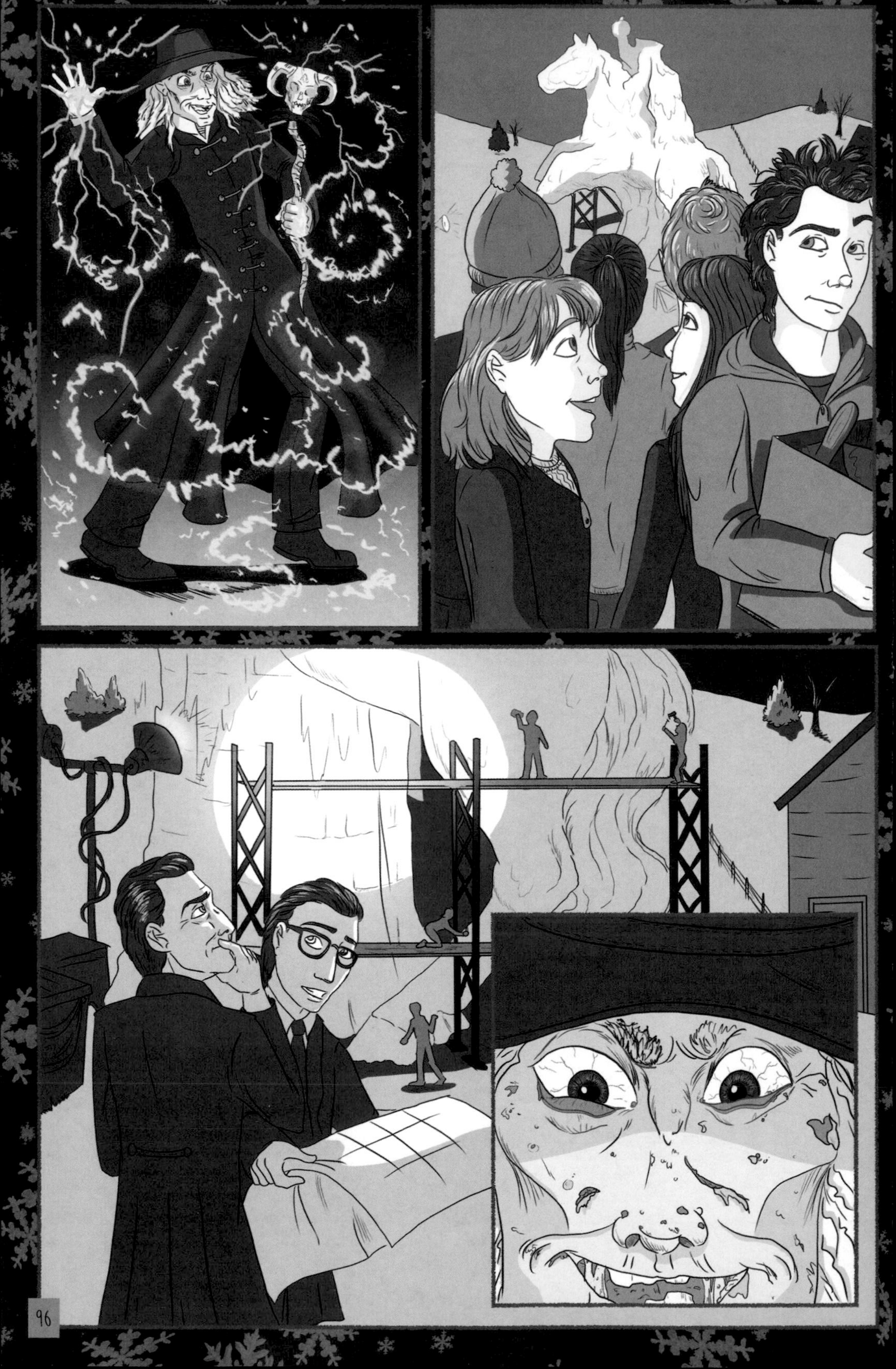

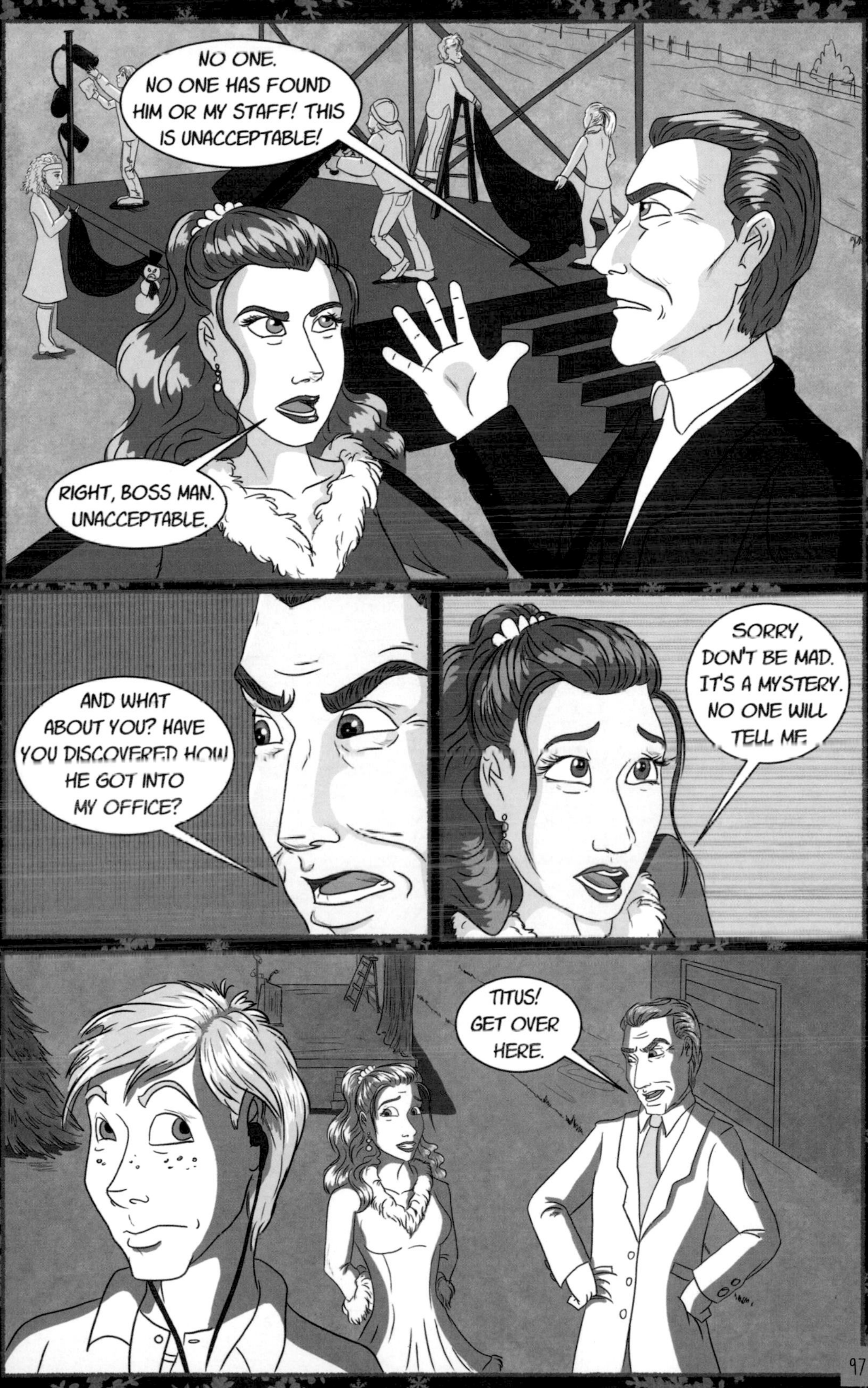
NO ONE.
NO ONE HAS FOUND HIM OR MY STAFF! THIS IS UNACCEPTABLE!
RIGHT, BOSS MAN. UNACCEPTABLE.
AND WHAT ABOUT YOU? HAVE YOU DISCOVERED HOW HE GOT INTO MY OFFICE?
SORRY, DON'T BE MAD. IT'S A MYSTERY. NO ONE WILL TELL ME.
TITUS! GET OVER HERE.

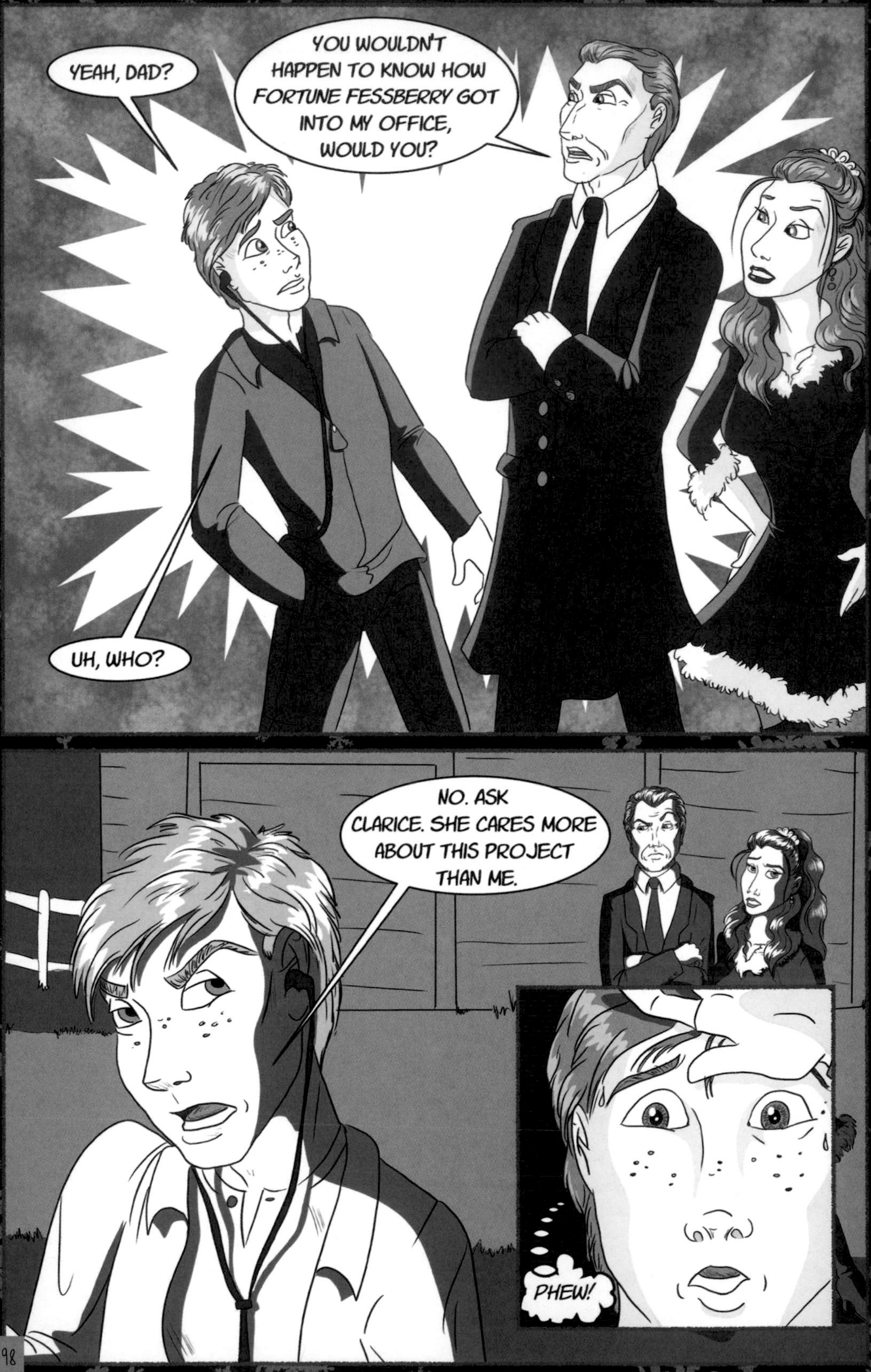
YEAH, DAD?
YOU WOULDN'T HAPPEN TO KNOW HOW FORTUNE FESSBERRY GOT INTO MY OFFICE, WOULD YOU?
UH, WHO?
NO. ASK CLARICE. SHE CARES MORE ABOUT THIS PROJECT THAN ME.
PHEW!

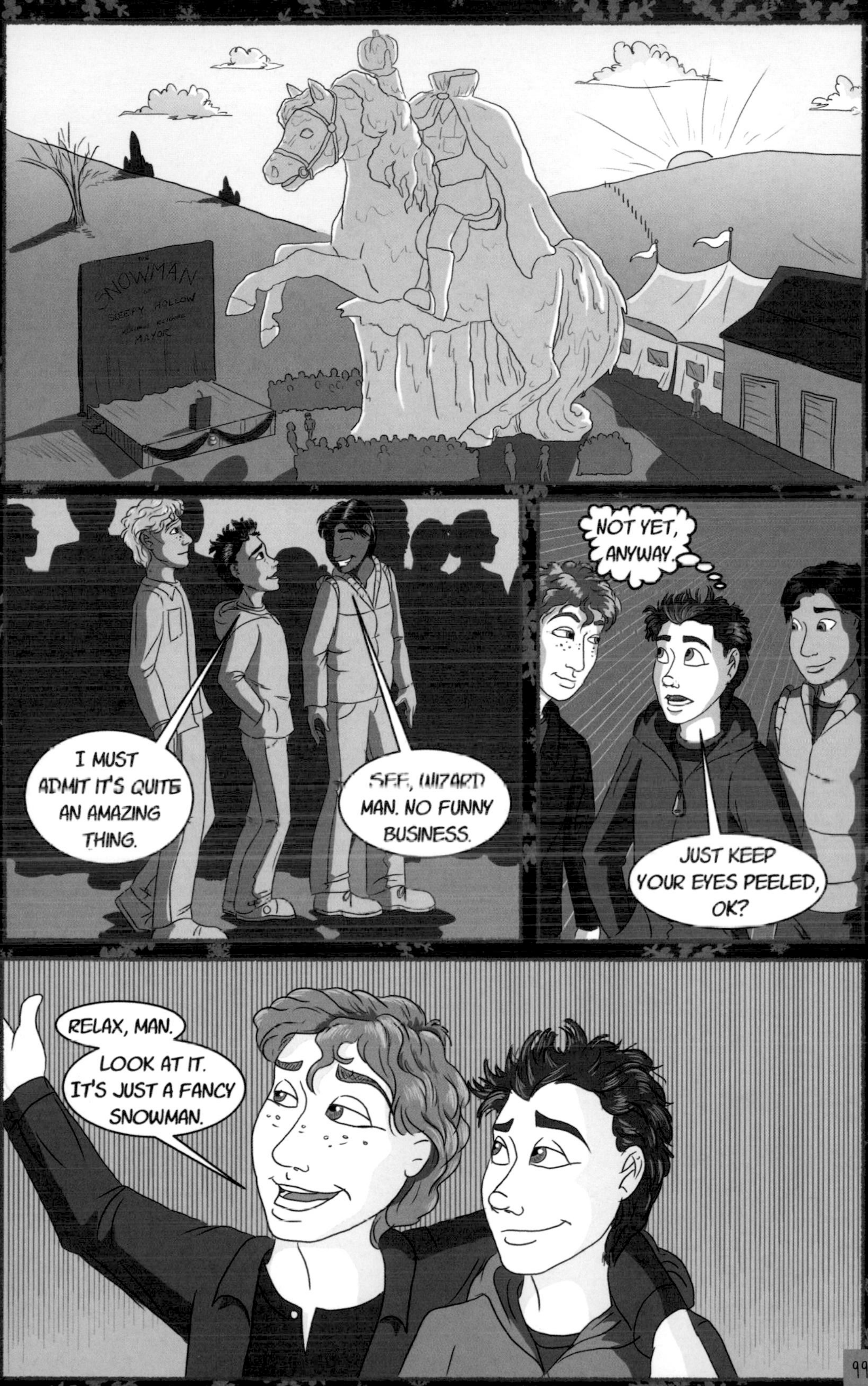
SNOWMAN
SLEEPY HOLLOW
MAYOR
I MUST ADMIT IT'S QUITE AN AMAZING THING.
SEE, WIZARD MAN. NO FUNNY BUSINESS.
NOT YET, ANYWAY.
JUST KEEP YOUR EYES PEELED, OK?
RELAX, MAN.
LOOK AT IT. IT'S JUST A FANCY SNOWMAN.

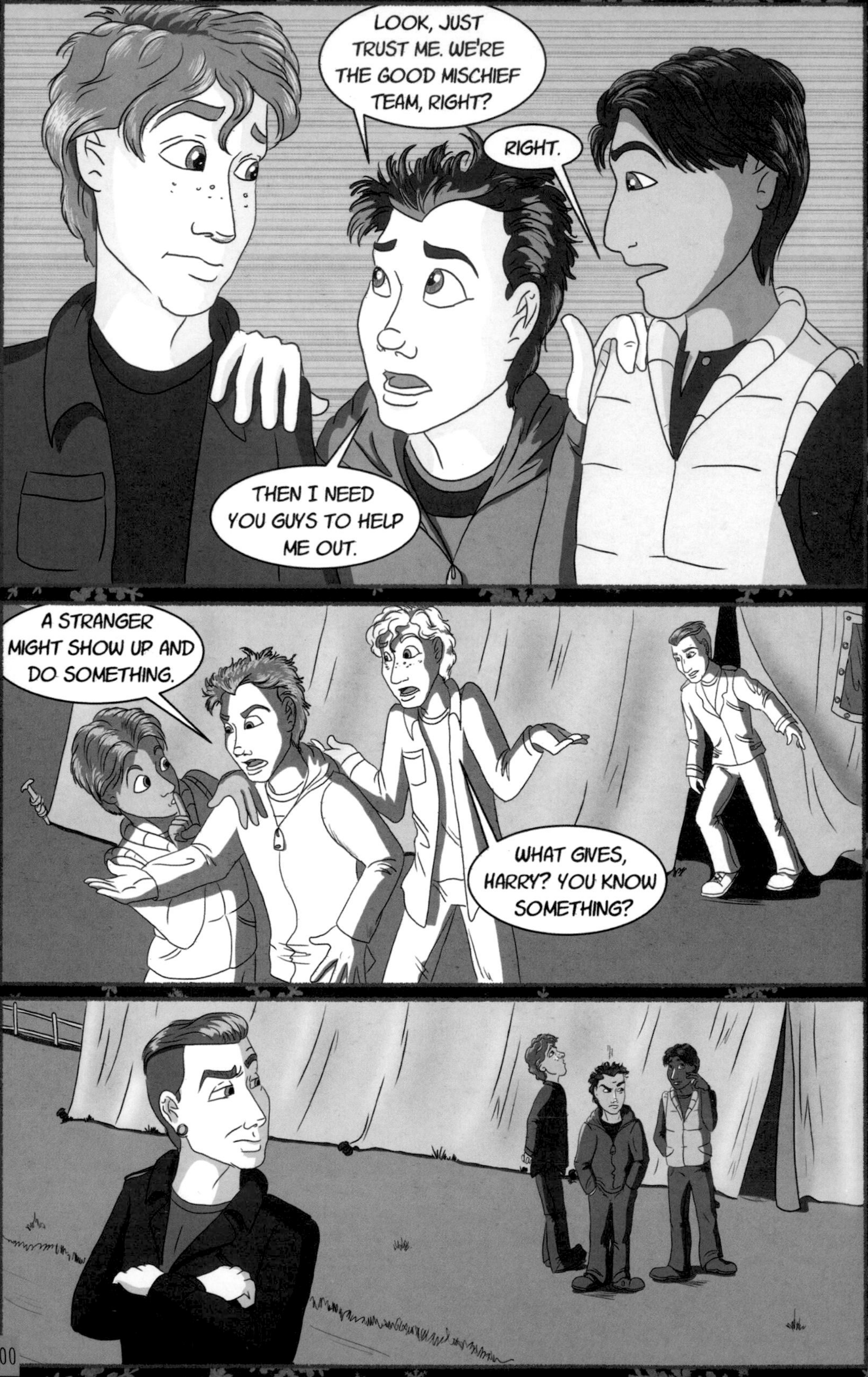
LOOK, JUST TRUST ME. WE'RE THE GOOD MISCHIEF TEAM, RIGHT?
RIGHT.
THEN I NEED YOU GUYS TO HELP ME OUT.
A STRANGER MIGHT SHOW UP AND DO SOMETHING.
WHAT GIVES, HARRY? YOU KNOW SOMETHING?

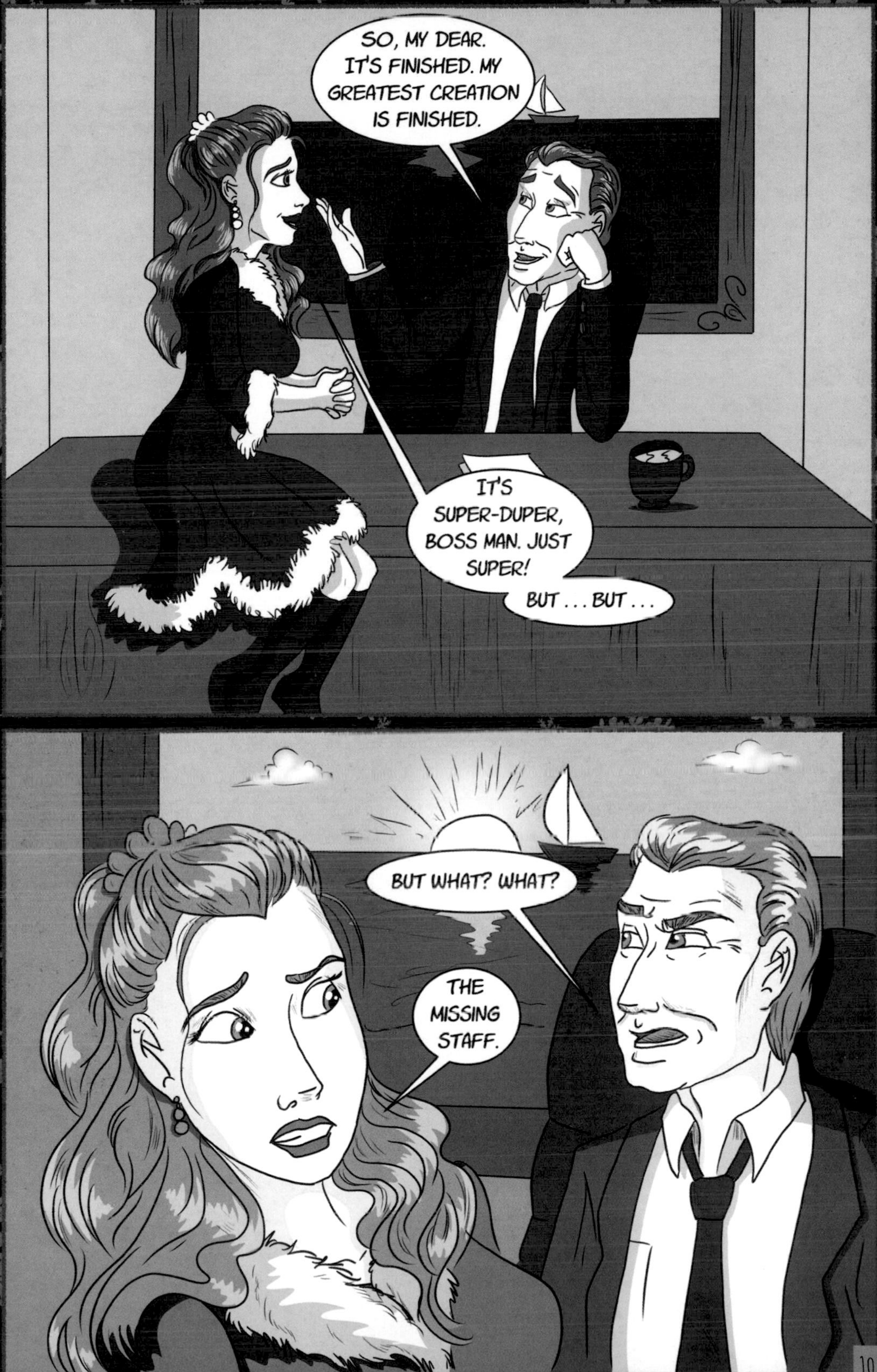
SO, MY DEAR. IT'S FINISHED. MY GREATEST CREATION IS FINISHED.
IT'S SUPER-DUPER, BOSS MAN. JUST SUPER!
BUT . . . BUT . . .
BUT WHAT? WHAT?
THE MISSING STAFF.

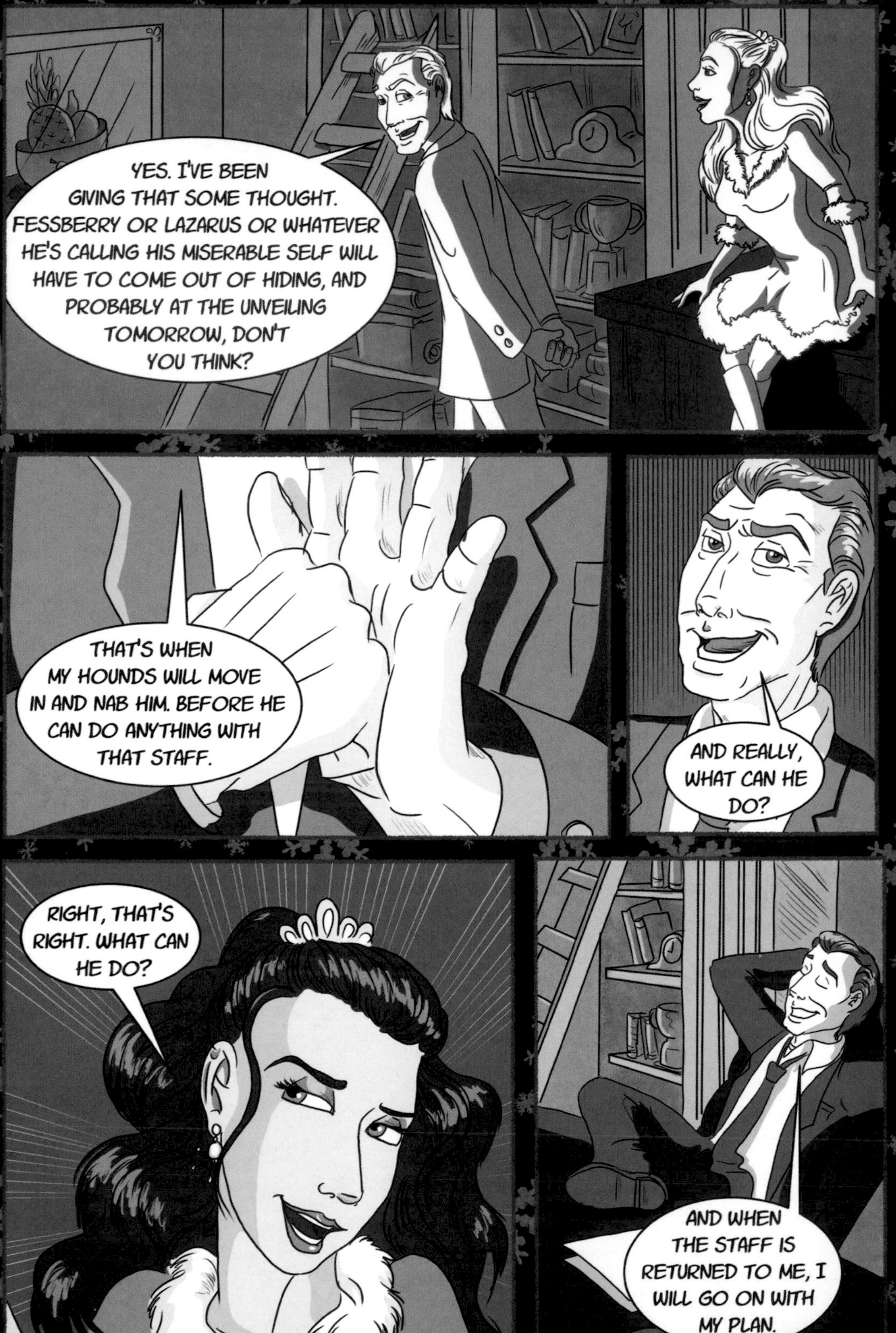
YES. I'VE BEEN GIVING THAT SOME THOUGHT. FESSBERRY OR LAZARUS OR WHATEVER HE'S CALLING HIS MISERABLE SELF WILL HAVE TO COME OUT OF HIDING, AND PROBABLY AT THE UNVEILING TOMORROW, DON'T YOU THINK?
THAT'S WHEN MY HOUNDS WILL MOVE IN AND NAB HIM. BEFORE HE CAN DO ANYTHING WITH THAT STAFF.
AND REALLY, WHAT CAN HE DO?
RIGHT, THAT'S RIGHT. WHAT CAN HE DO?
AND WHEN THE STAFF IS RETURNED TO ME, I WILL GO ON WITH MY PLAN.

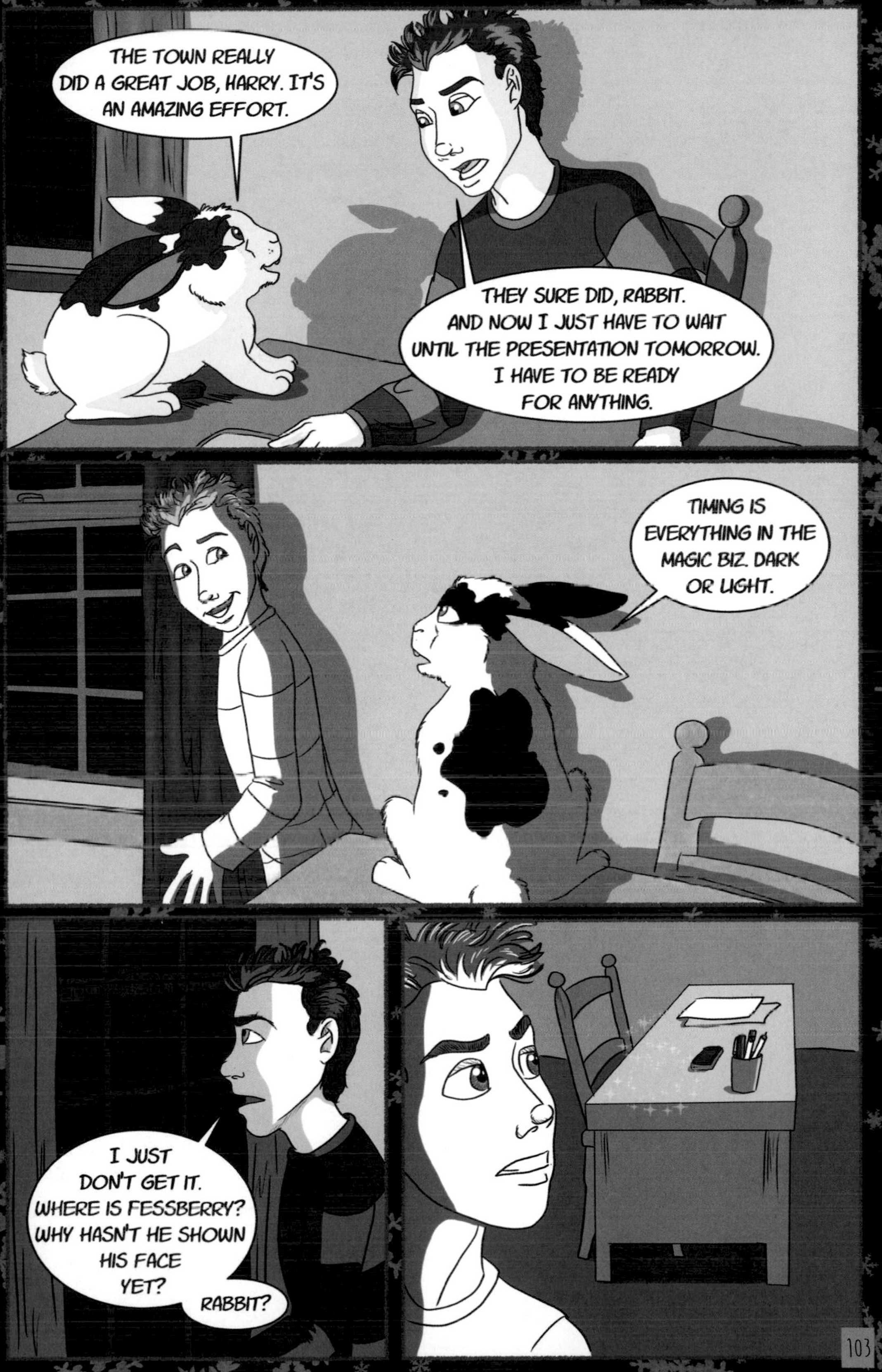
THE TOWN REALLY DID A GREAT JOB, HARRY. IT'S AN AMAZING EFFORT.
THEY SURE DID, RABBIT. AND NOW I JUST HAVE TO WAIT UNTIL THE PRESENTATION TOMORROW. I HAVE TO BE READY FOR ANYTHING.
TIMING IS EVERYTHING IN THE MAGIC BIZ. DARK OR LIGHT.
I JUST DON'T GET IT. WHERE IS FESSBERRY? WHY HASN'T HE SHOWN HIS FACE YET?
RABBIT?

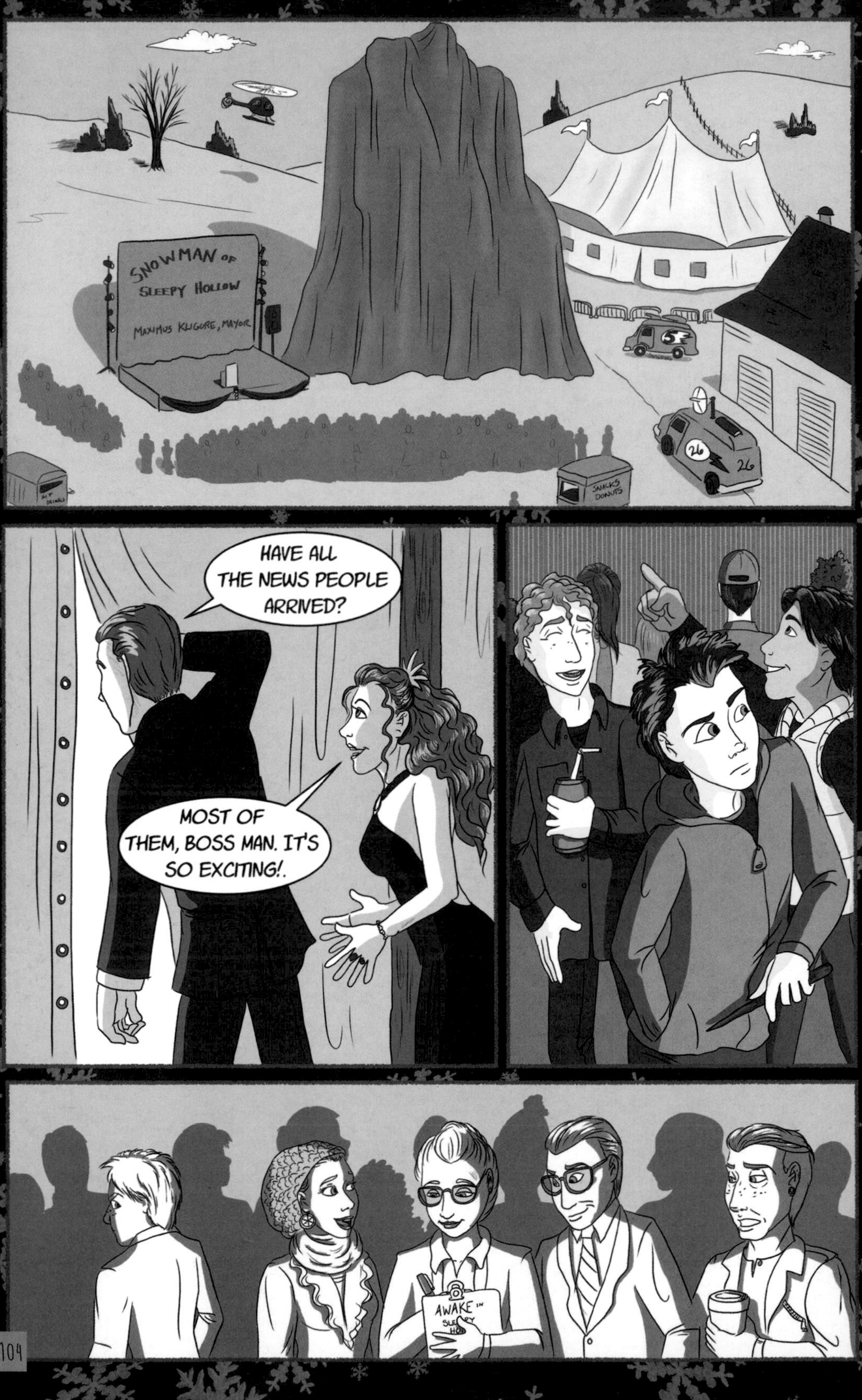
SNOWMAN OF SLEEPY HOLLOW
MAXIMUS KILGORE, MAYOR
SNACKS DONUTS
HAVE ALL THE NEWS PEOPLE ARRIVED?
MOST OF THEM, BOSS MAN. IT'S SO EXCITING!.
AWAKE IN

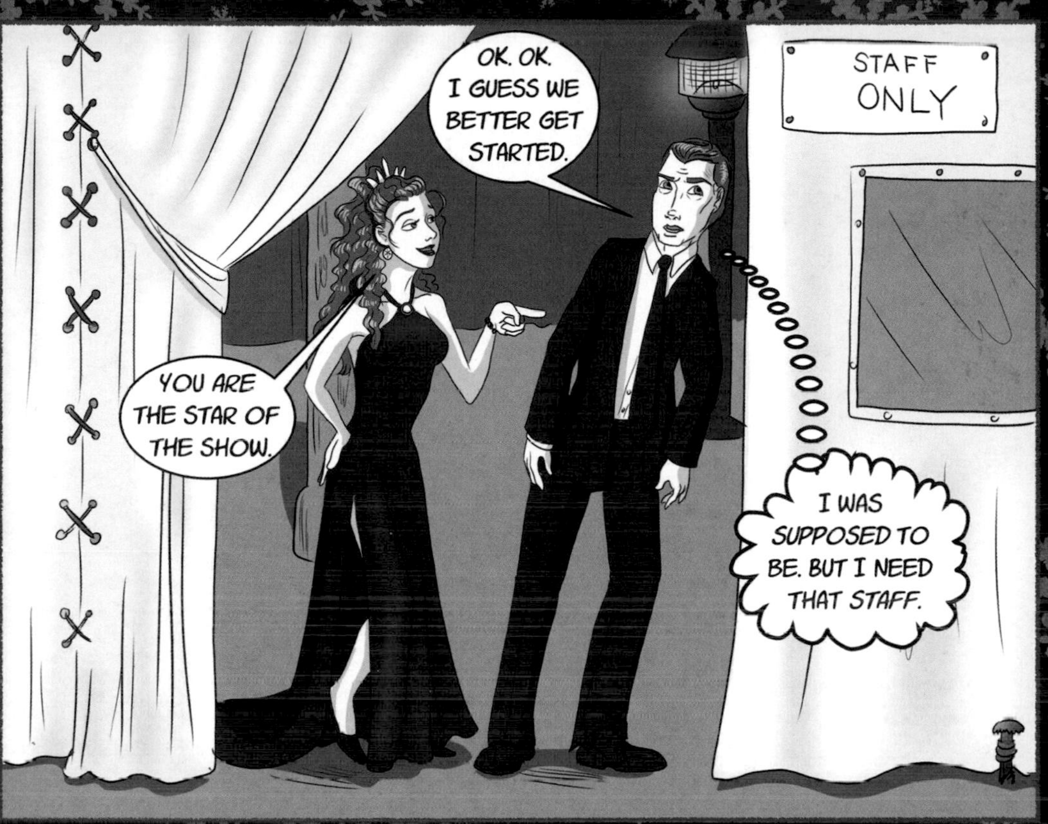
STAFF ONLY
OK. OK. I GUESS WE BETTER GET STARTED.
YOU ARE THE STAR OF THE SHOW.
I WAS SUPPOSED TO BE. BUT I NEED THAT STAFF.
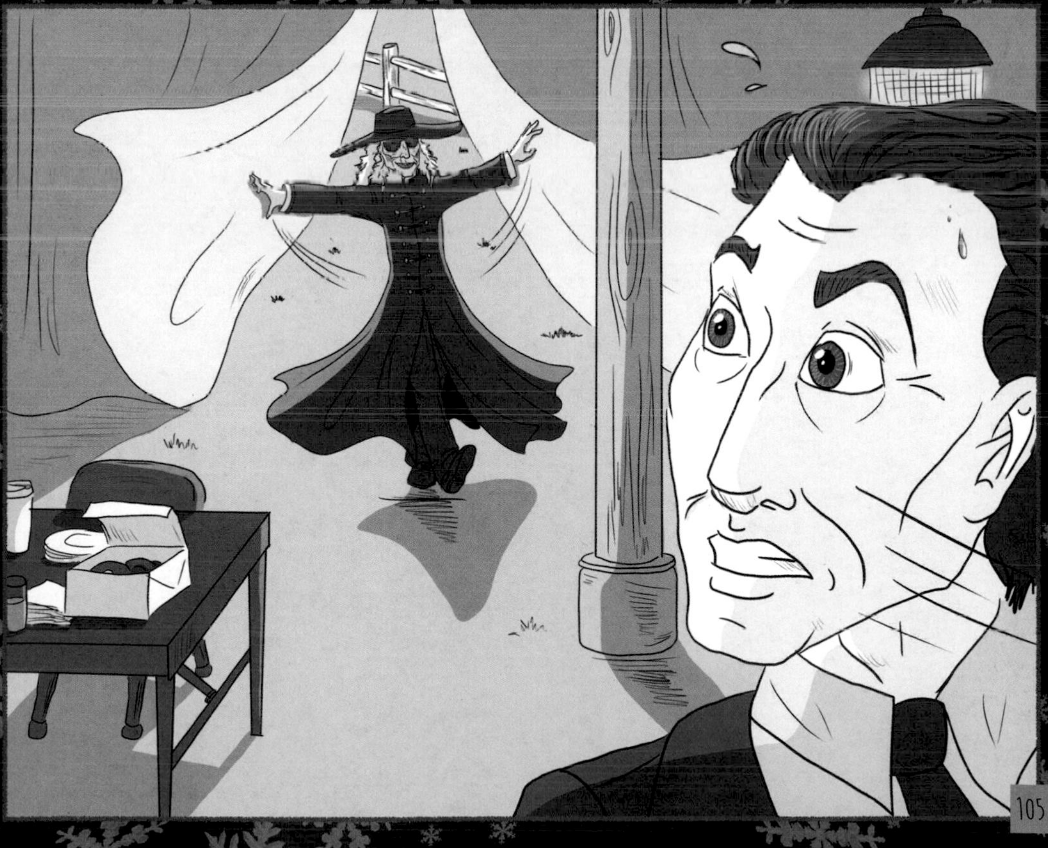

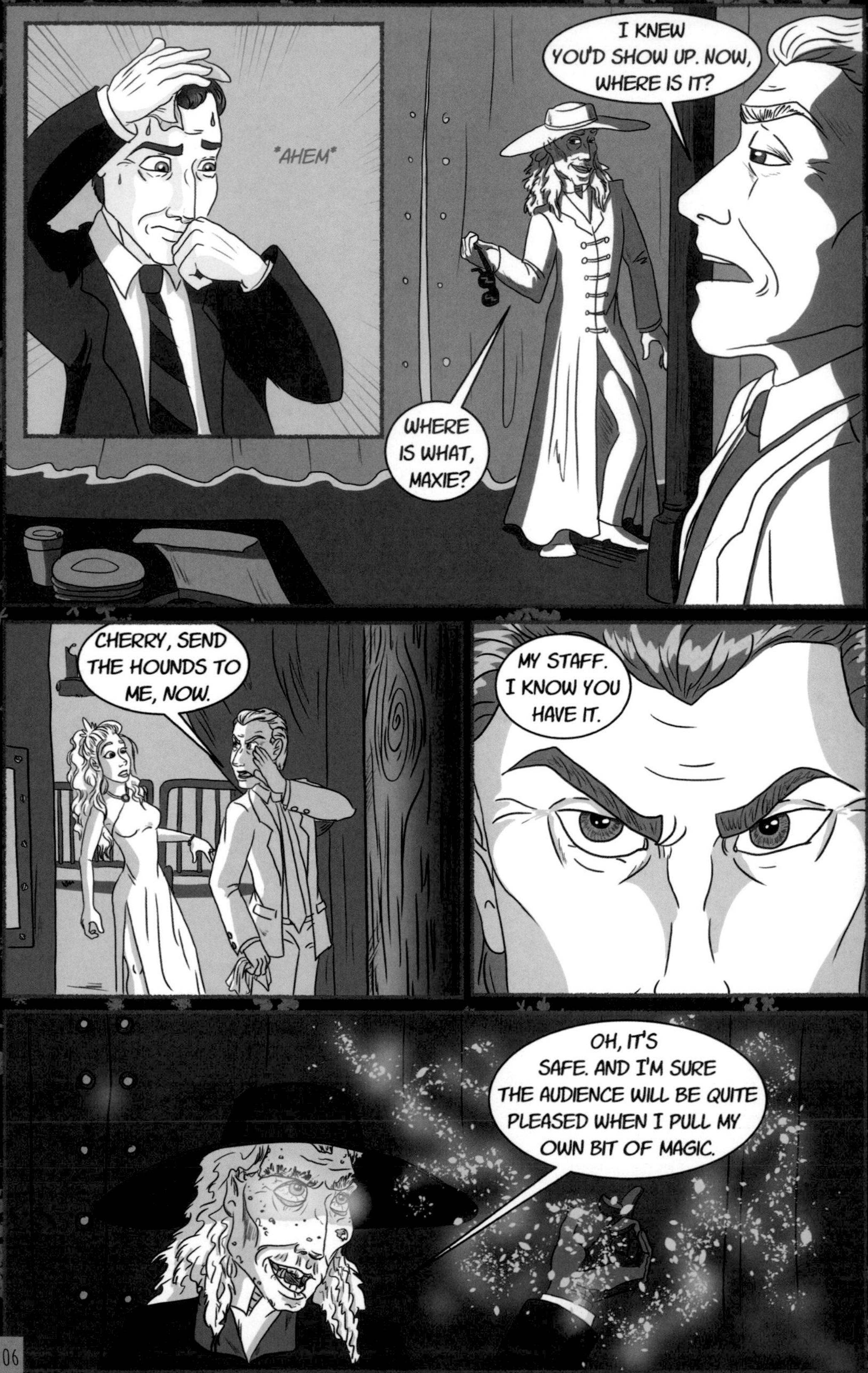
AHEM
I KNEW YOU'D SHOW UP. NOW, WHERE IS IT?
WHERE IS WHAT, MAXIE?
CHERRY, SEND THE HOUNDS TO ME, NOW.
MY STAFF. I KNOW YOU HAVE IT.
OH, IT'S SAFE. AND I'M SURE THE AUDIENCE WILL BE QUITE PLEASED WHEN I PULL MY OWN BIT OF MAGIC.

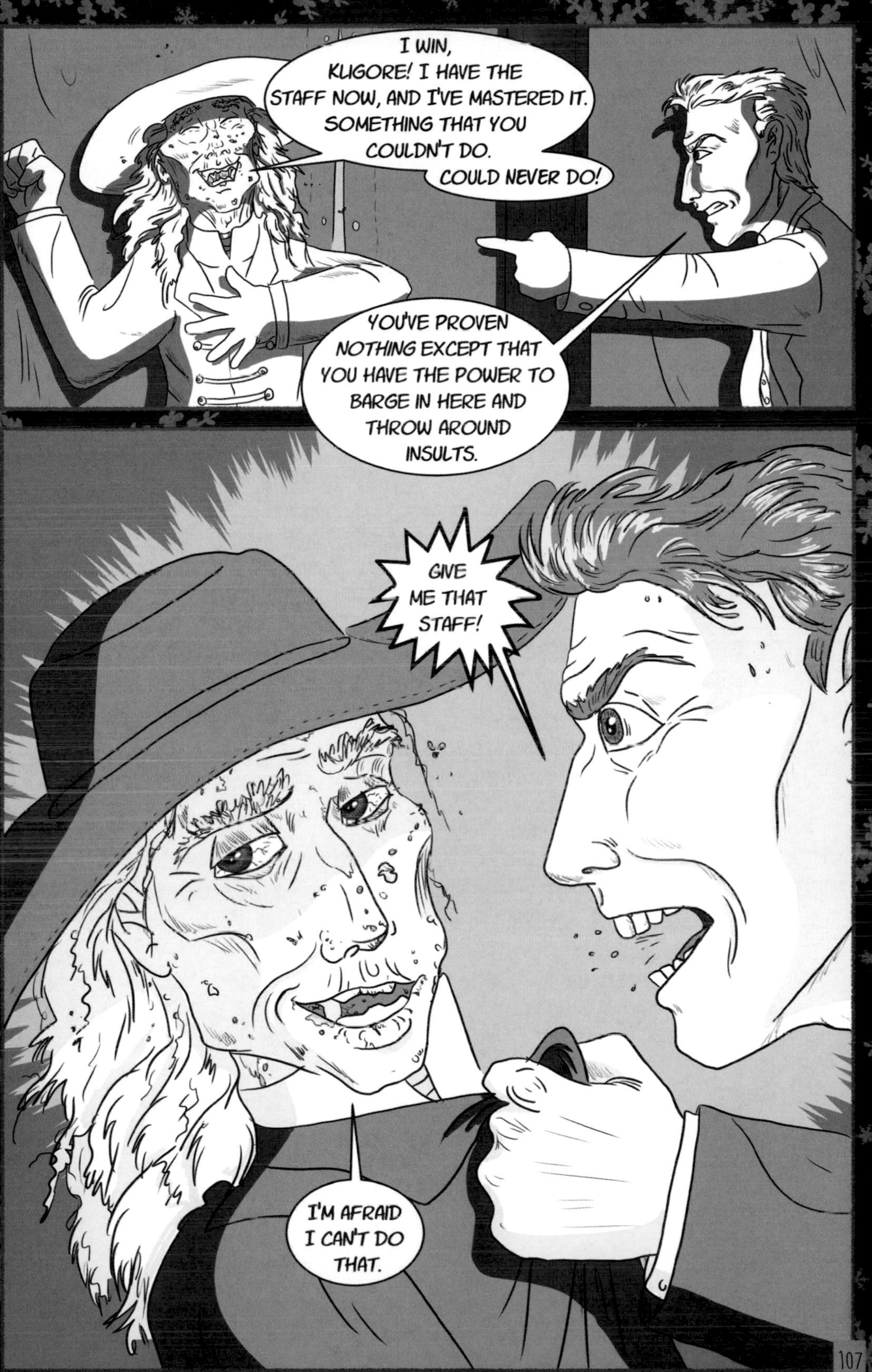
I WIN, KLIGORE! I HAVE THE STAFF NOW, AND I'VE MASTERED IT. SOMETHING THAT YOU COULDN'T DO.
COULD NEVER DO!
YOU'VE PROVEN NOTHING EXCEPT THAT YOU HAVE THE POWER TO BARGE IN HERE AND THROW AROUND INSULTS.
GIVE ME THAT STAFF!
I'M AFRAID I CAN'T DO THAT.

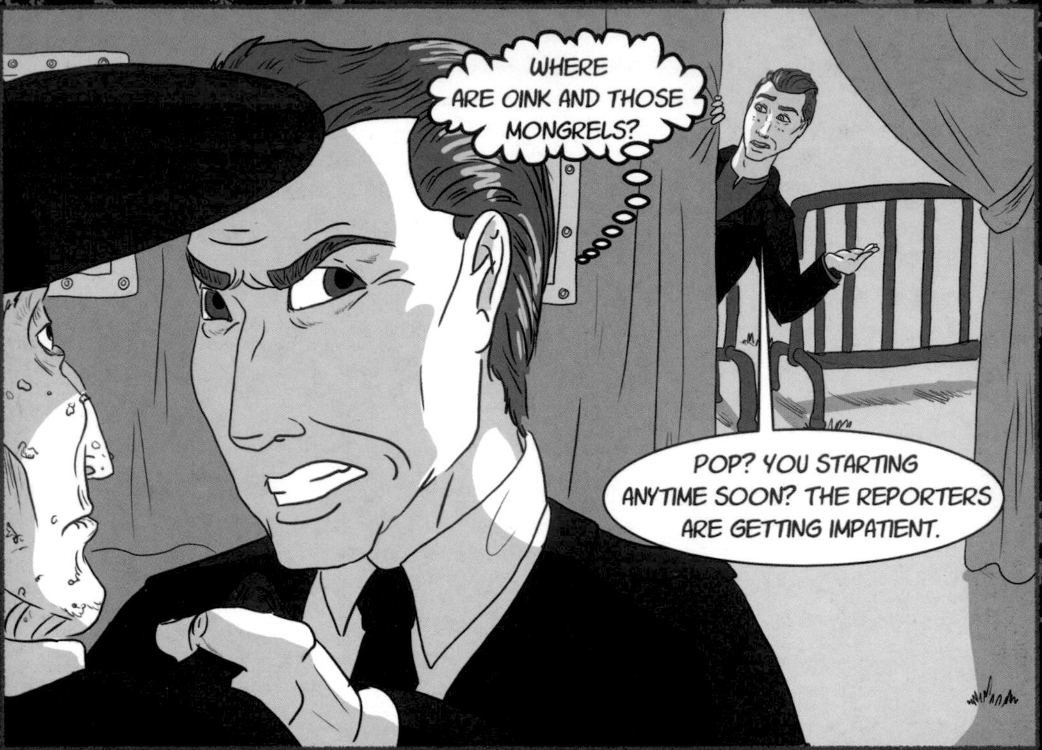
WHERE ARE OINK AND THOSE MONGRELS?
POP? YOU STARTING ANYTIME SOON? THE REPORTERS ARE GETTING IMPATIENT.

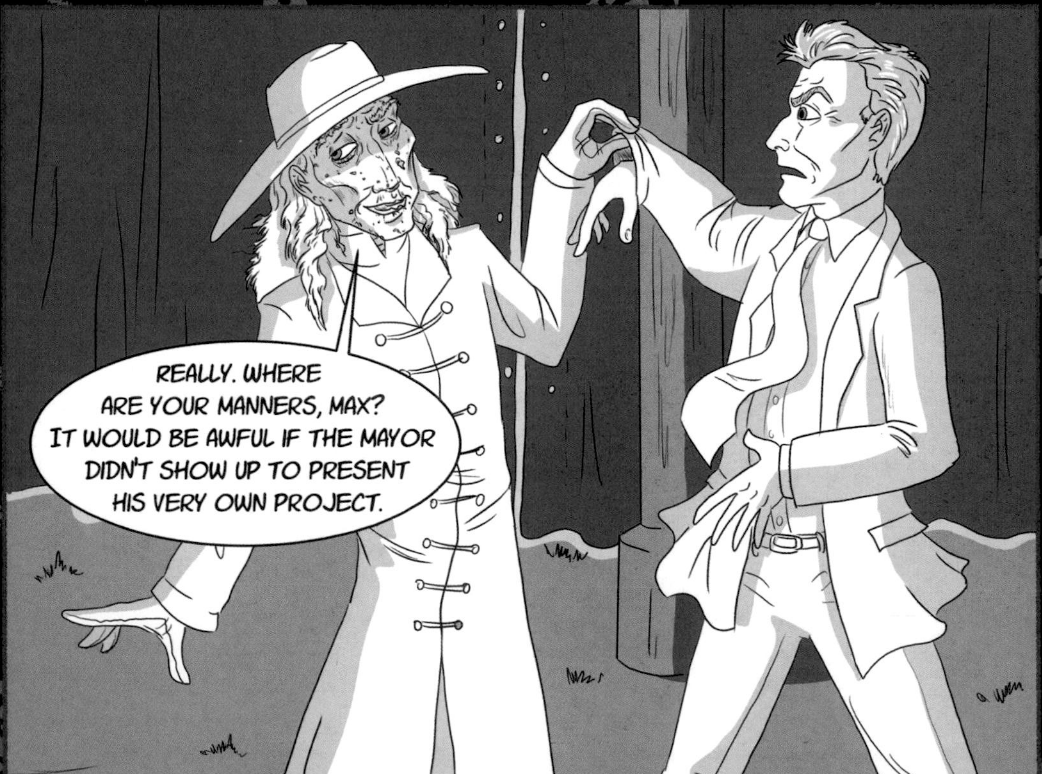
REALLY. WHERE ARE YOUR MANNERS, MAX? IT WOULD BE AWFUL IF THE MAYOR DIDN'T SHOW UP TO PRESENT HIS VERY OWN PROJECT.

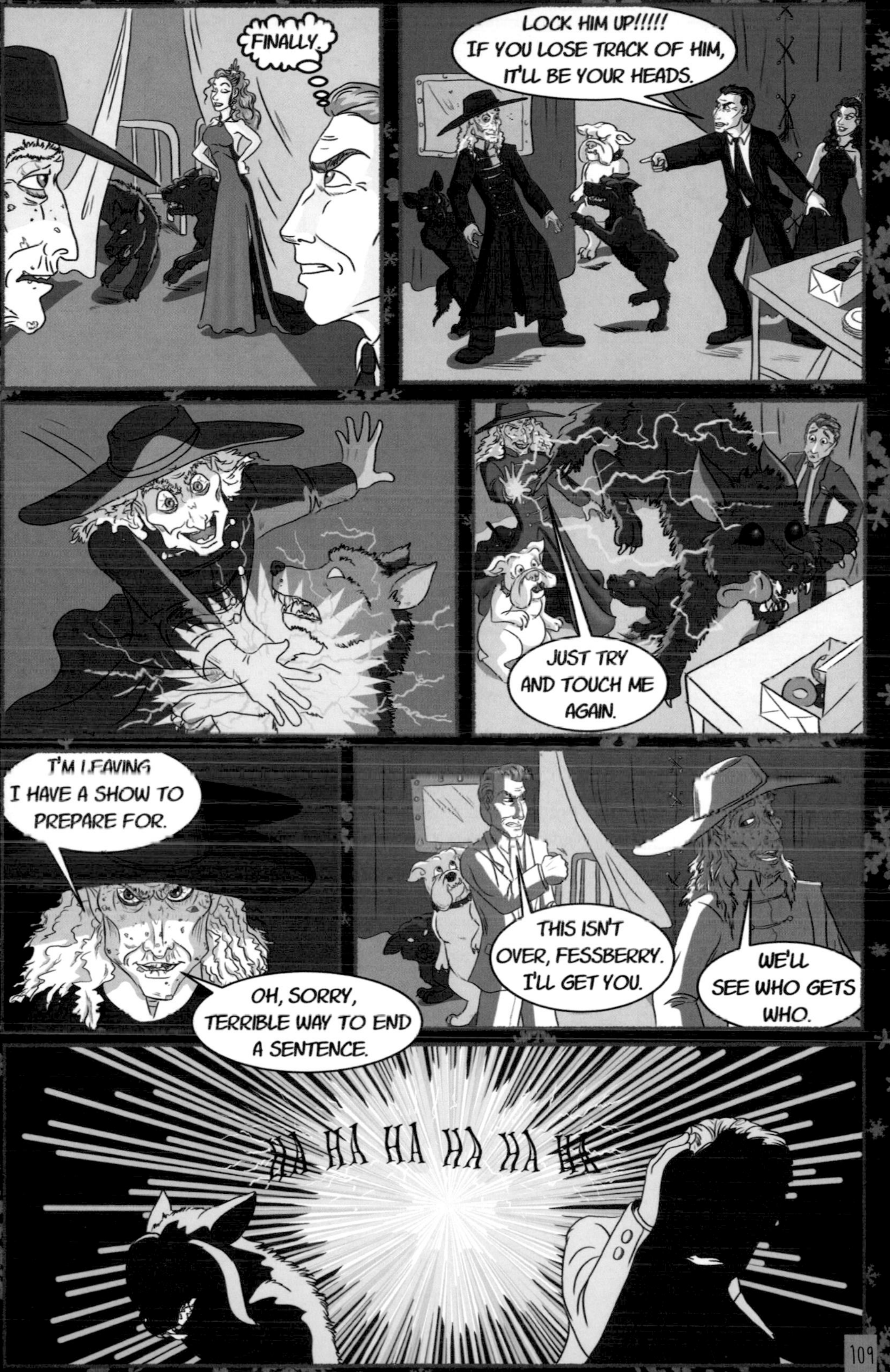
FINALLY.
LOCK HIM UP!!!!!
IF YOU LOSE TRACK OF HIM,
IT'LL BE YOUR HEADS.
JUST TRY
AND TOUCH ME
AGAIN.
I'M LEAVING
I HAVE A SHOW TO
PREPARE FOR.
OH, SORRY,
TERRIBLE WAY TO END
A SENTENCE.
THIS ISN'T
OVER, FESSBERRY.
I'LL GET YOU.
WE'LL
SEE WHO GETS
WHO.
HA HA HA HA HA HA

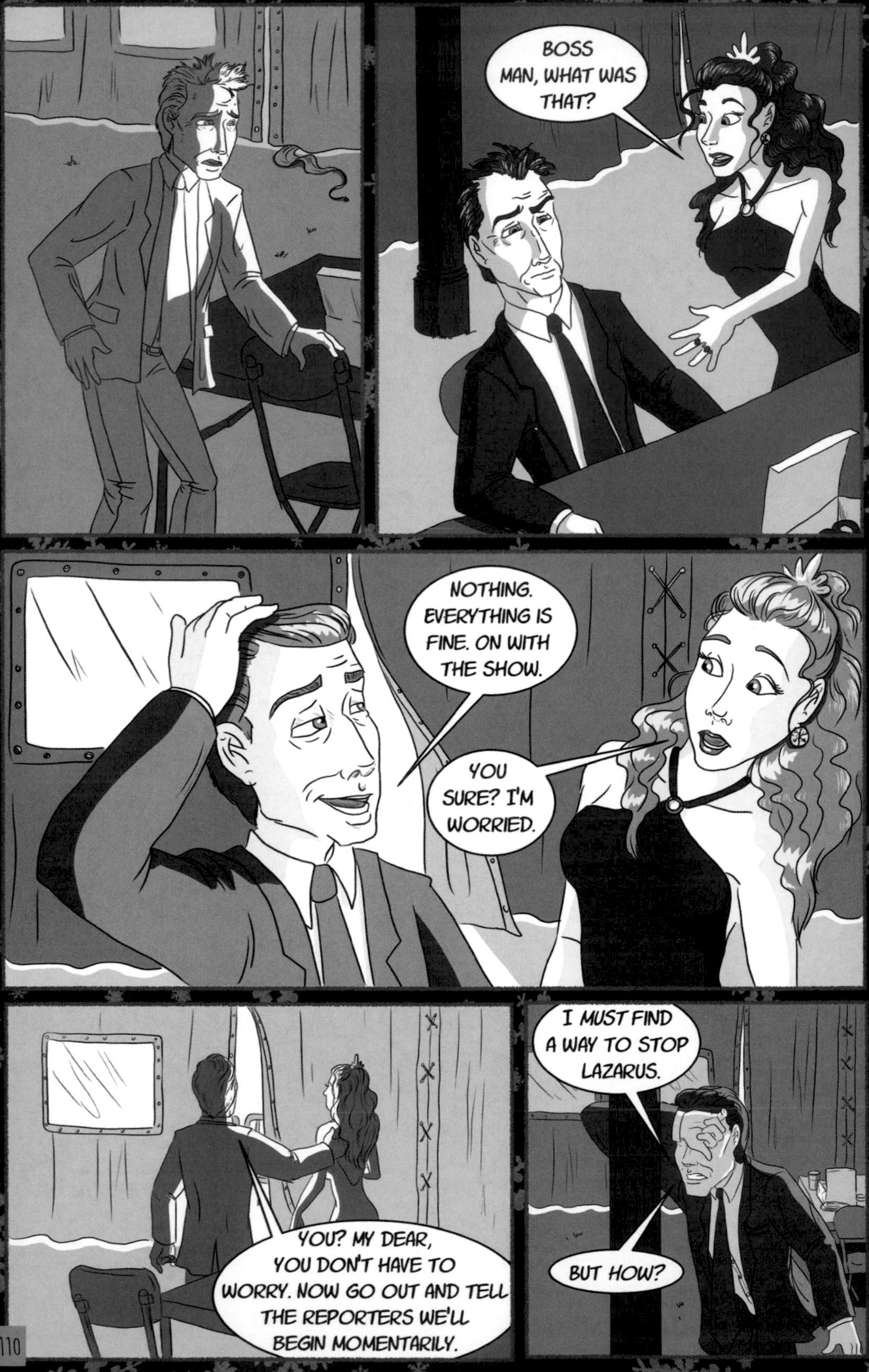
BOSS MAN, WHAT WAS THAT?
NOTHING. EVERYTHING IS FINE. ON WITH THE SHOW.
YOU SURE? I'M WORRIED.
YOU? MY DEAR, YOU DON'T HAVE TO WORRY. NOW GO OUT AND TELL THE REPORTERS WE'LL BEGIN MOMENTARILY.
I MUST FIND A WAY TO STOP LAZARUS.
BUT HOW?

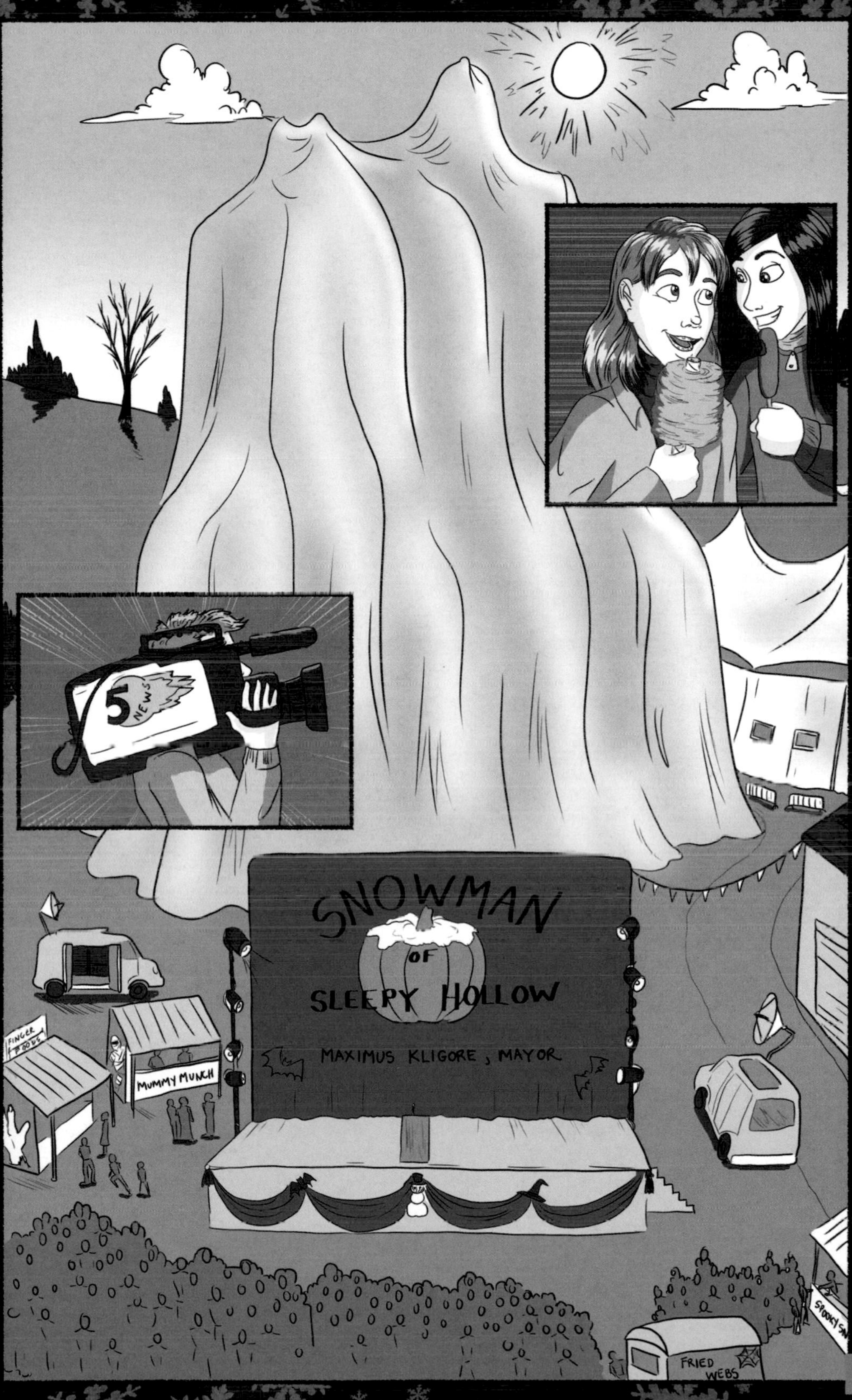

5 NEWS
SNOWMAN OF SLEEPY HOLLOW
MAXIMUS KLIGORE, MAYOR
FINGER FOODS
MUMMY MUNCH
FRIED WEBS

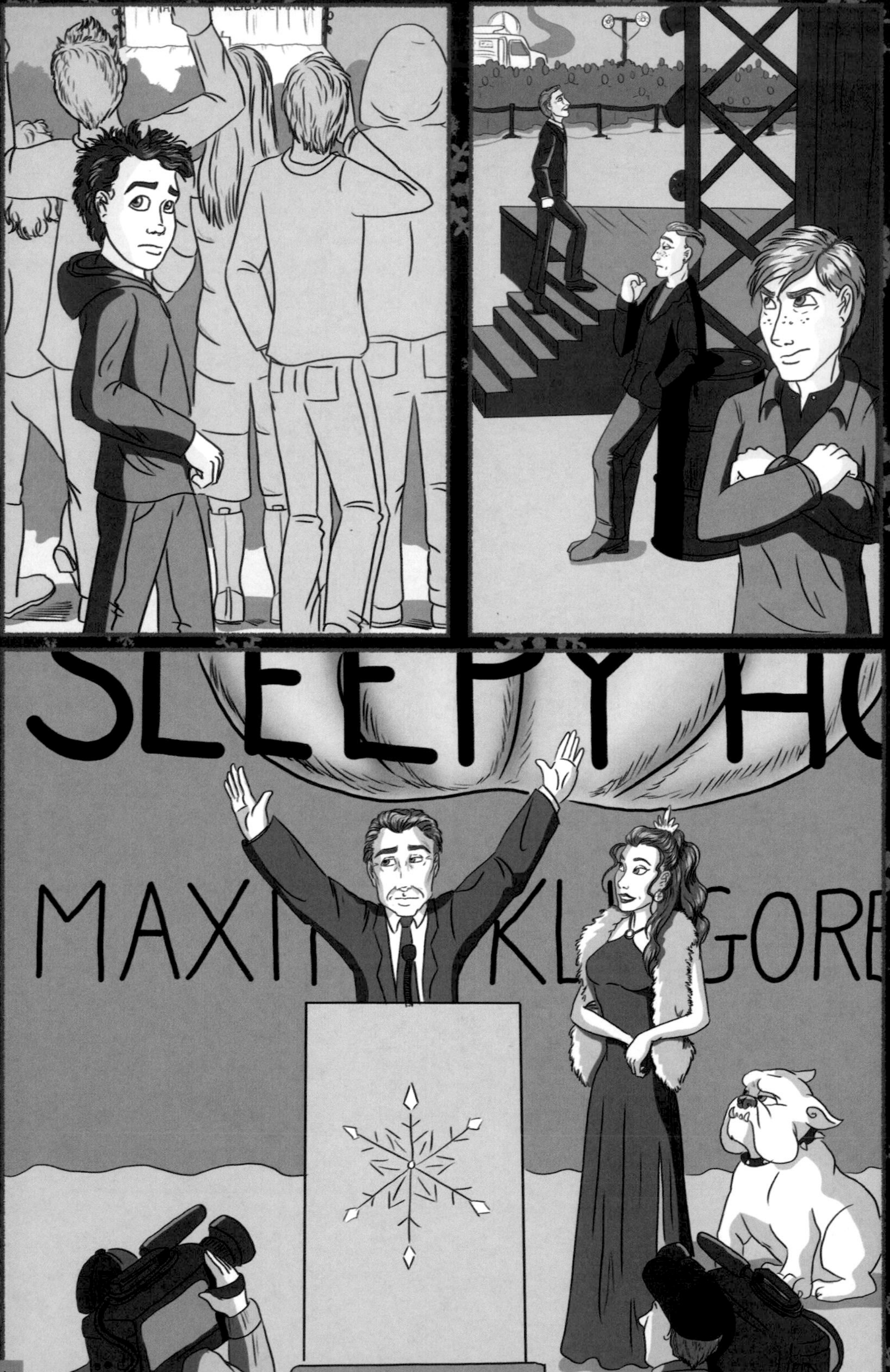
SLEEPY HO
MAXI
KL
GORE

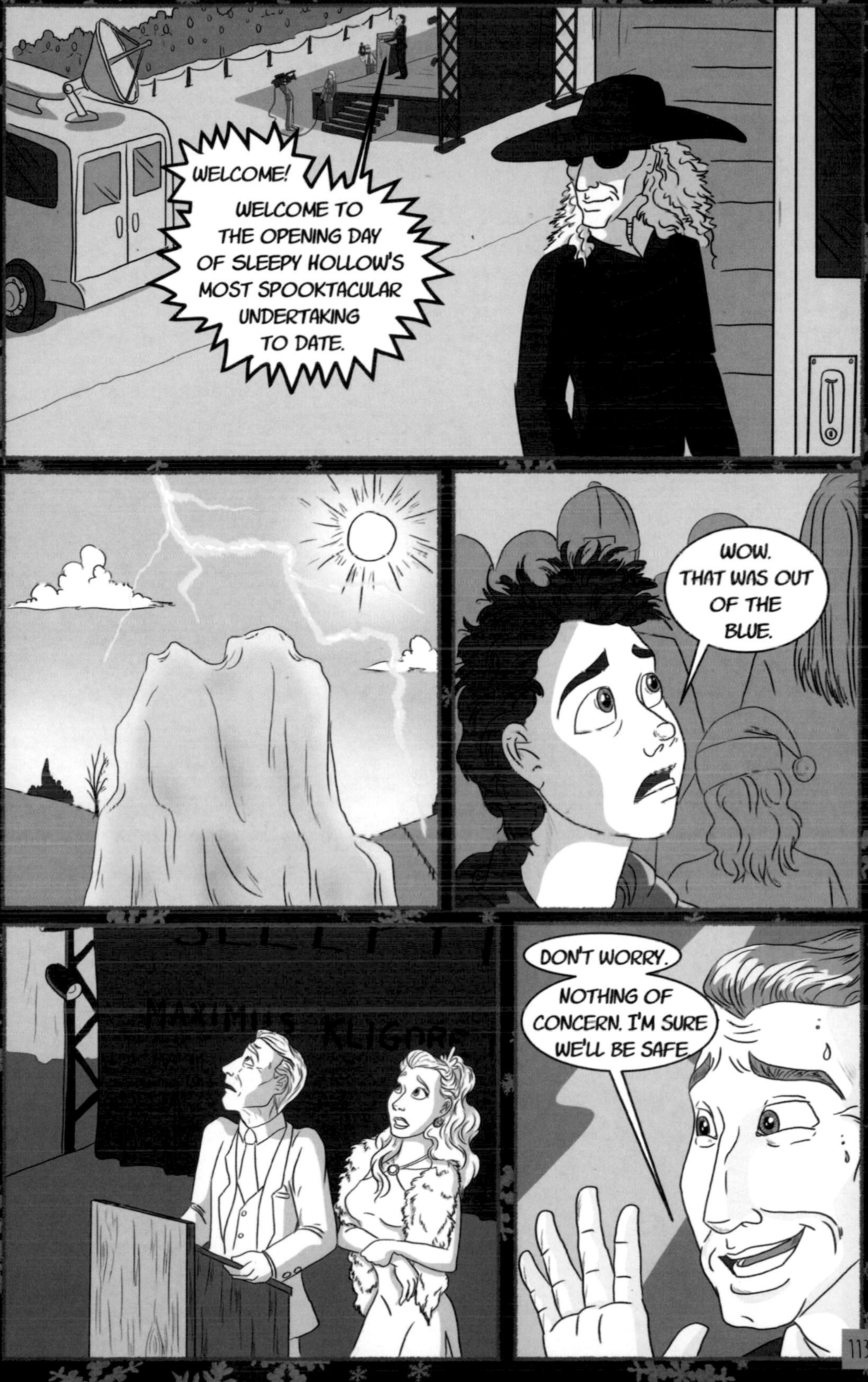
WELCOME!
WELCOME TO THE OPENING DAY OF SLEEPY HOLLOW'S MOST SPOOKTACULAR UNDERTAKING TO DATE.
WOW. THAT WAS OUT OF THE BLUE.
DON'T WORRY.
NOTHING OF CONCERN. I'M SURE WE'LL BE SAFE

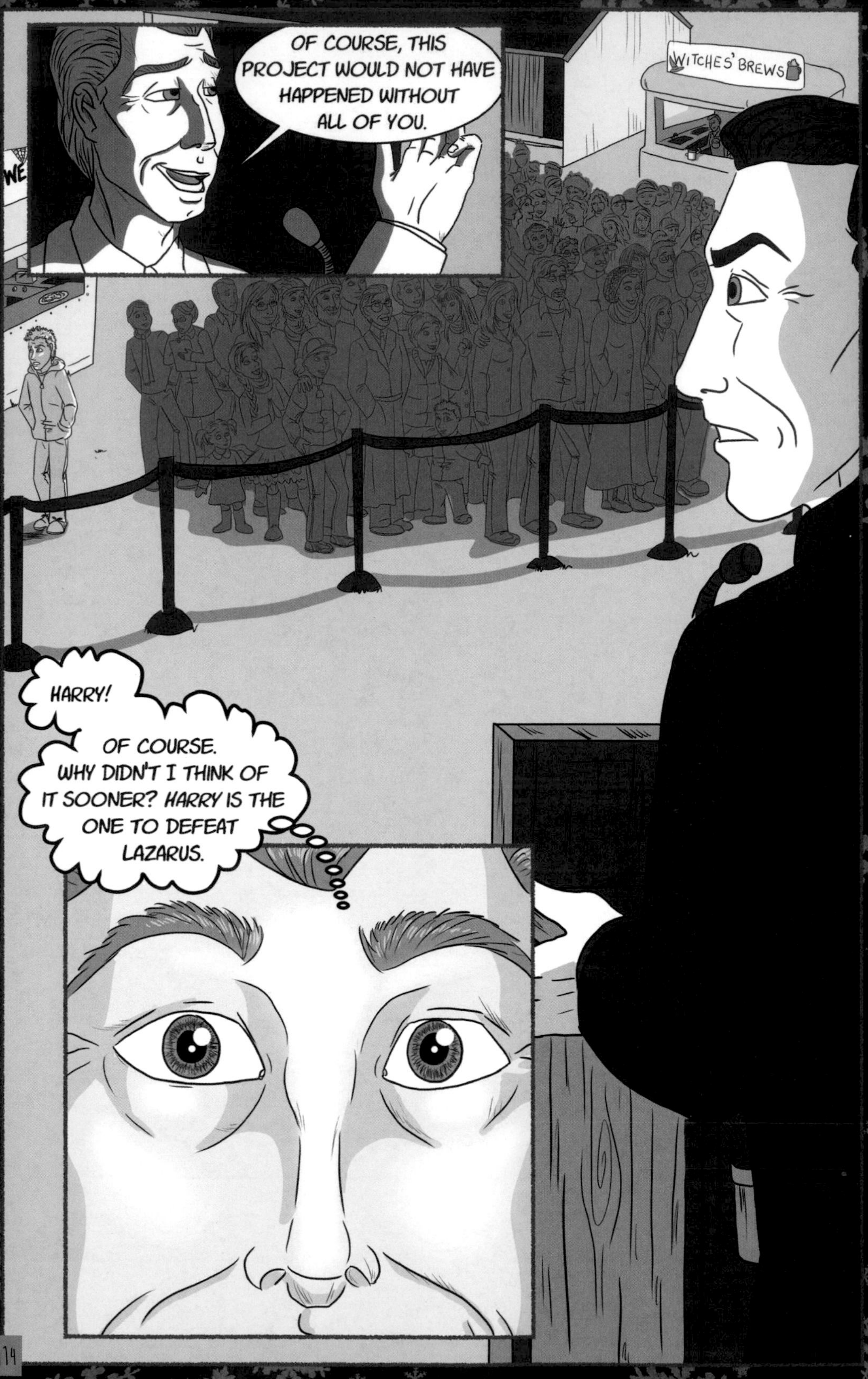
OF COURSE, THIS PROJECT WOULD NOT HAVE HAPPENED WITHOUT ALL OF YOU.
WITCHES' BREWS
HARRY!
OF COURSE. WHY DIDN'T I THINK OF IT SOONER? HARRY IS THE ONE TO DEFEAT LAZARUS.

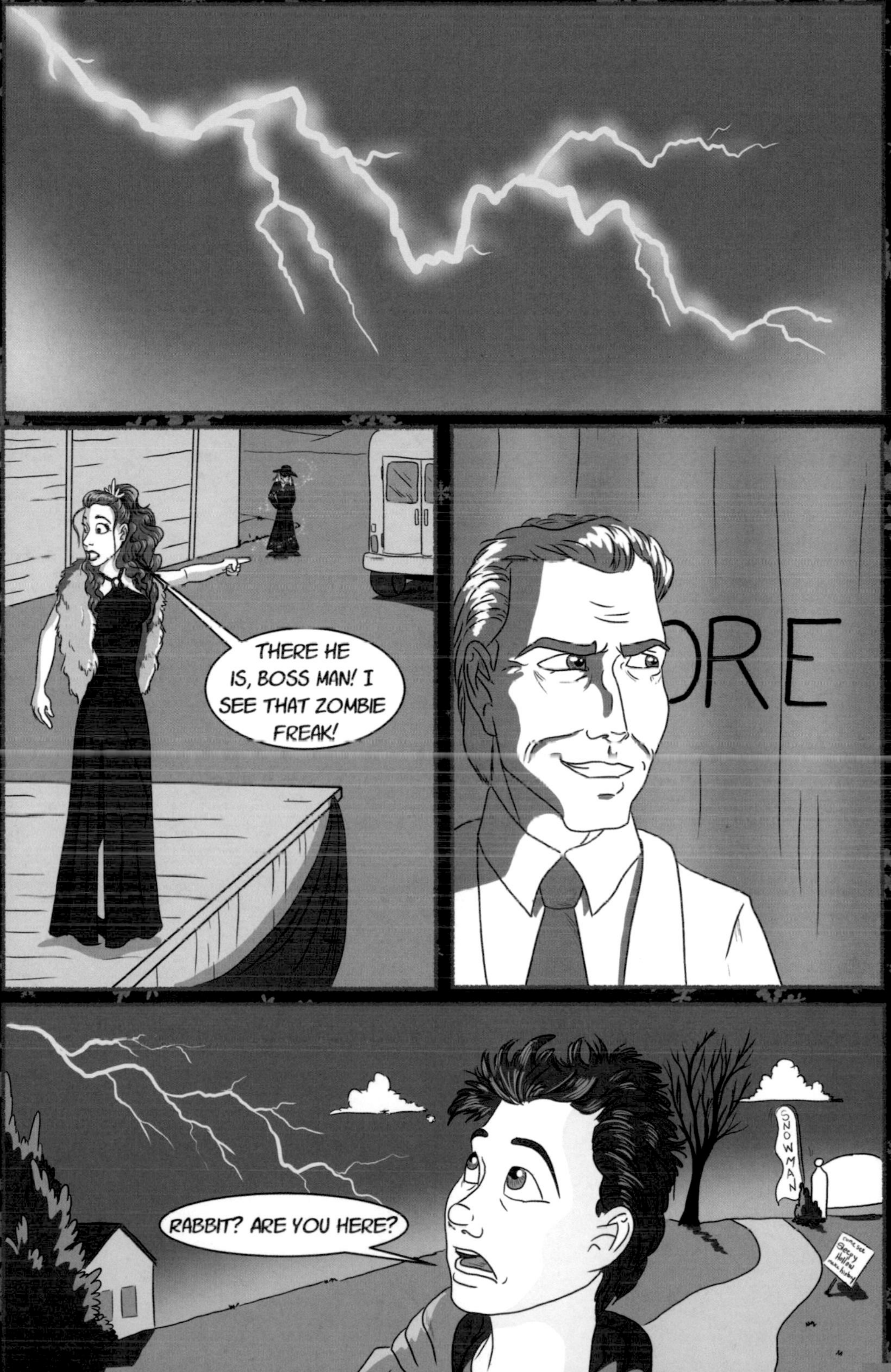
THERE HE IS, BOSS MAN! I SEE THAT ZOMBIE FREAK!
ORE
RABBIT? ARE YOU HERE?
SNOWMAN

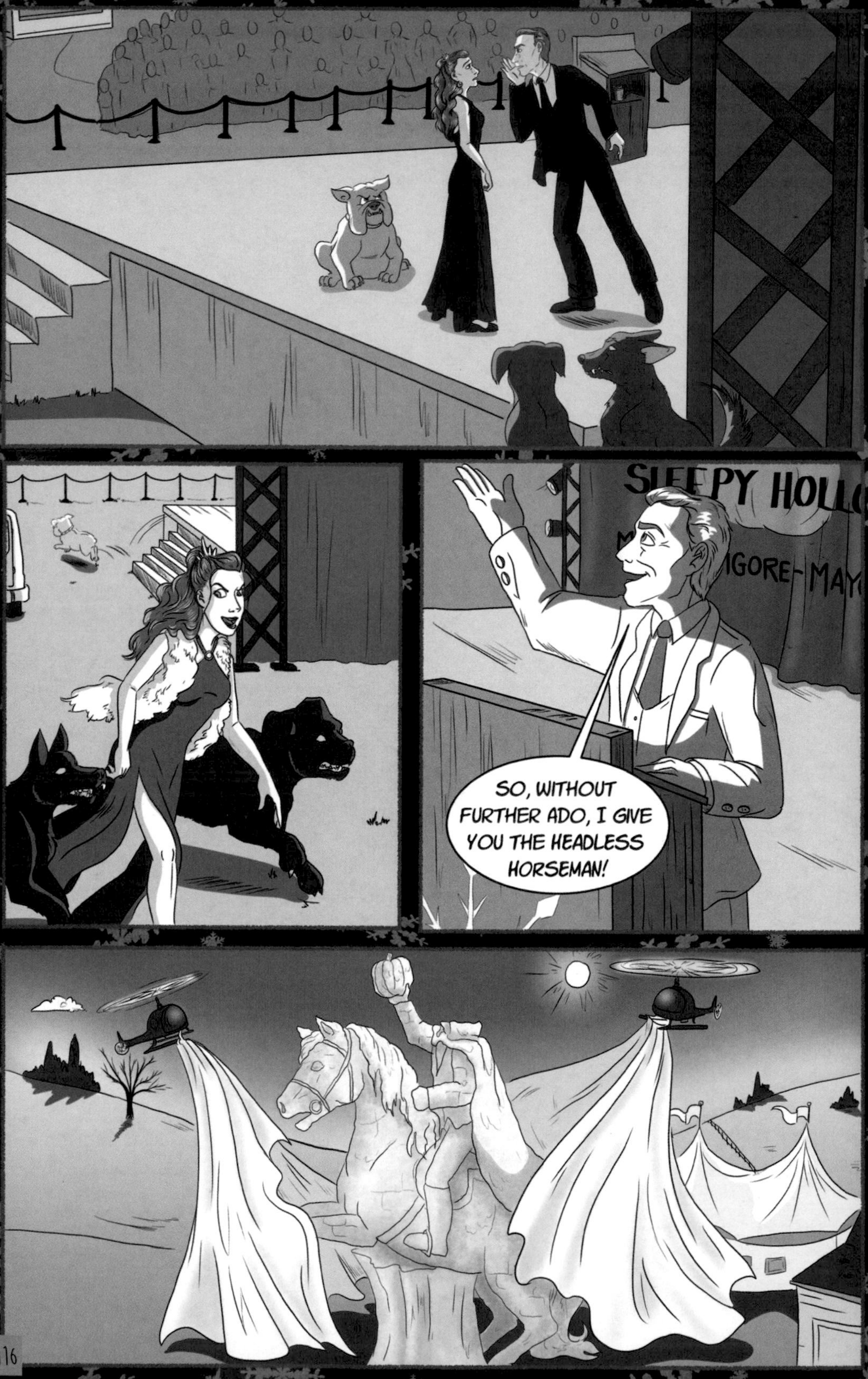
SO, WITHOUT FURTHER ADO, I GIVE YOU THE HEADLESS HORSEMAN!

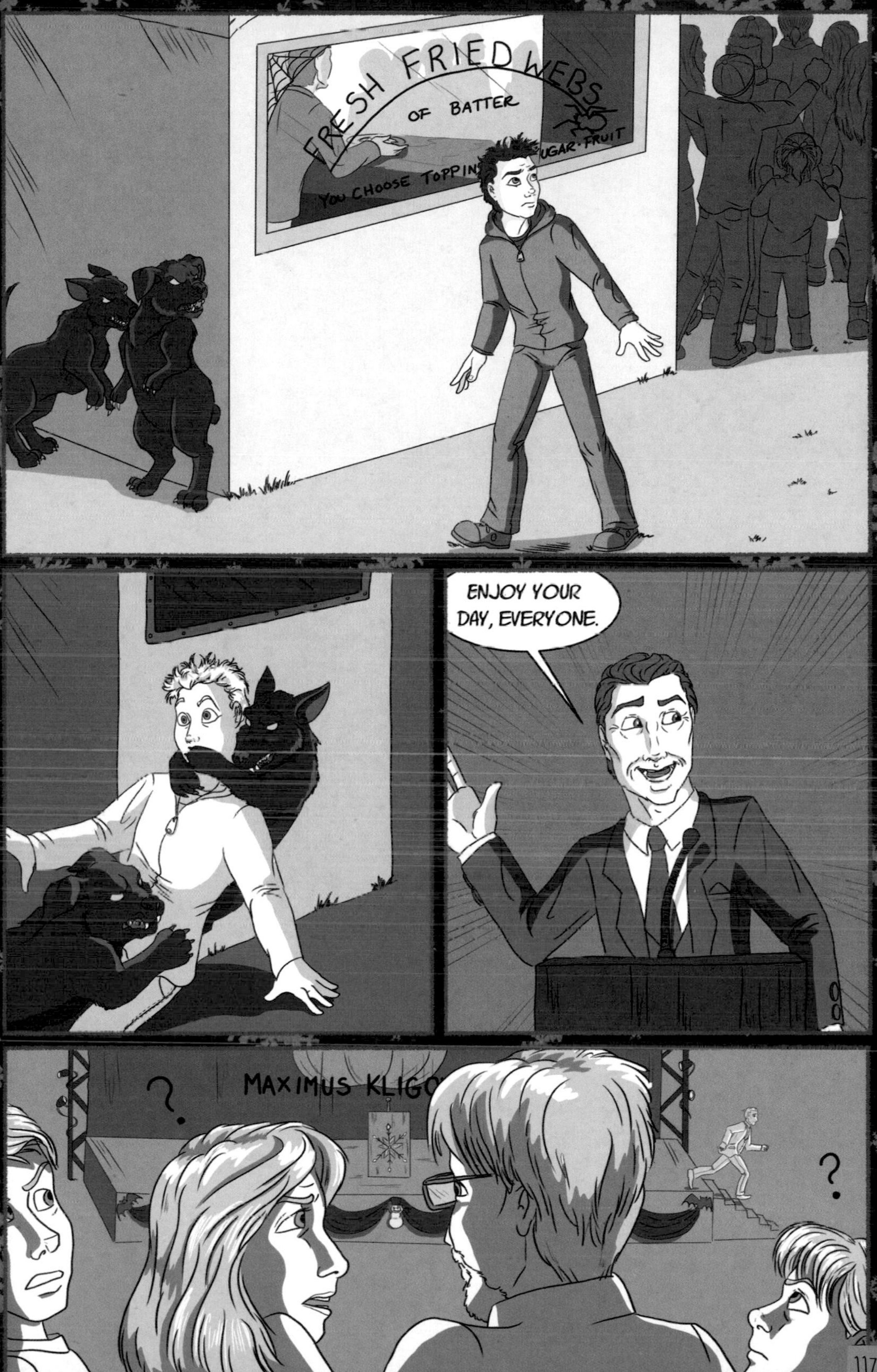
FRESH FRIED WEBS
OF BATTER
ENJOY YOUR DAY, EVERYONE.
?
?

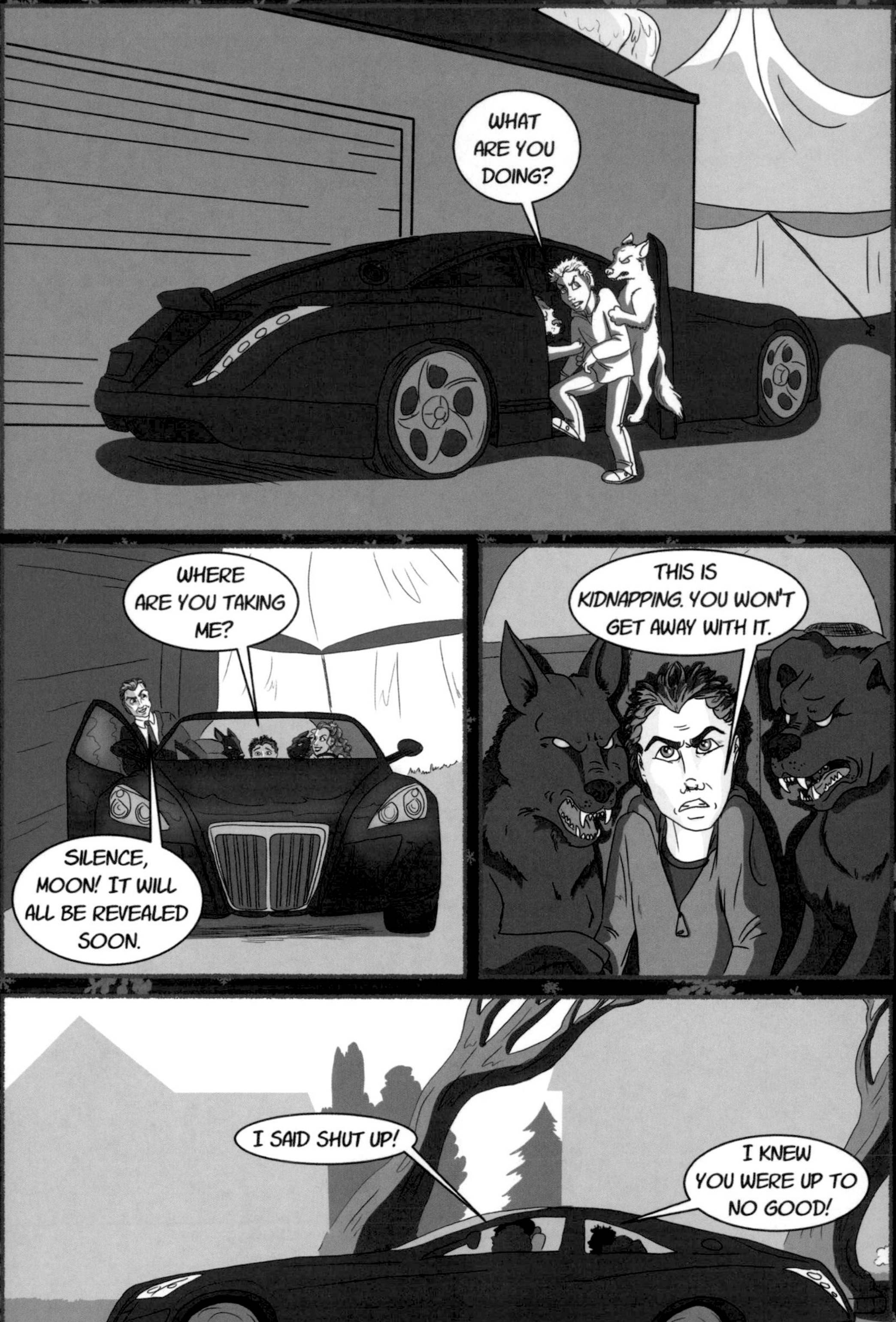
WHAT ARE YOU DOING?
WHERE ARE YOU TAKING ME?
SILENCE, MOON! IT WILL ALL BE REVEALED SOON.
THIS IS KIDNAPPING. YOU WON'T GET AWAY WITH IT.
I SAID SHUT UP!
I KNEW YOU WERE UP TO NO GOOD!

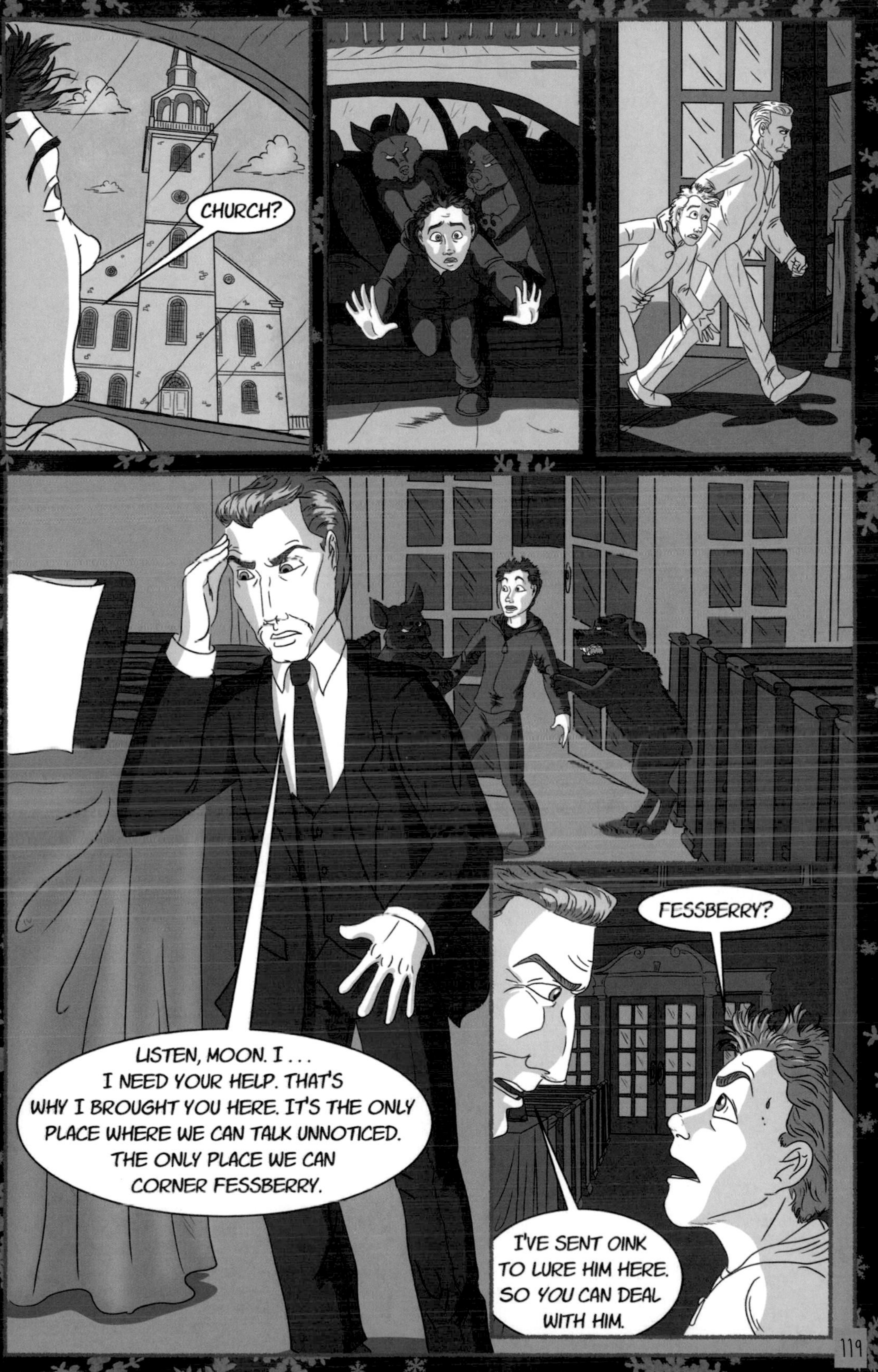
CHURCH?
LISTEN, MOON. I . . . I NEED YOUR HELP. THAT'S WHY I BROUGHT YOU HERE. IT'S THE ONLY PLACE WHERE WE CAN TALK UNNOTICED. THE ONLY PLACE WE CAN CORNER FESSBERRY.
FESSBERRY?
I'VE SENT OINK TO LURE HIM HERE. SO YOU CAN DEAL WITH HIM.

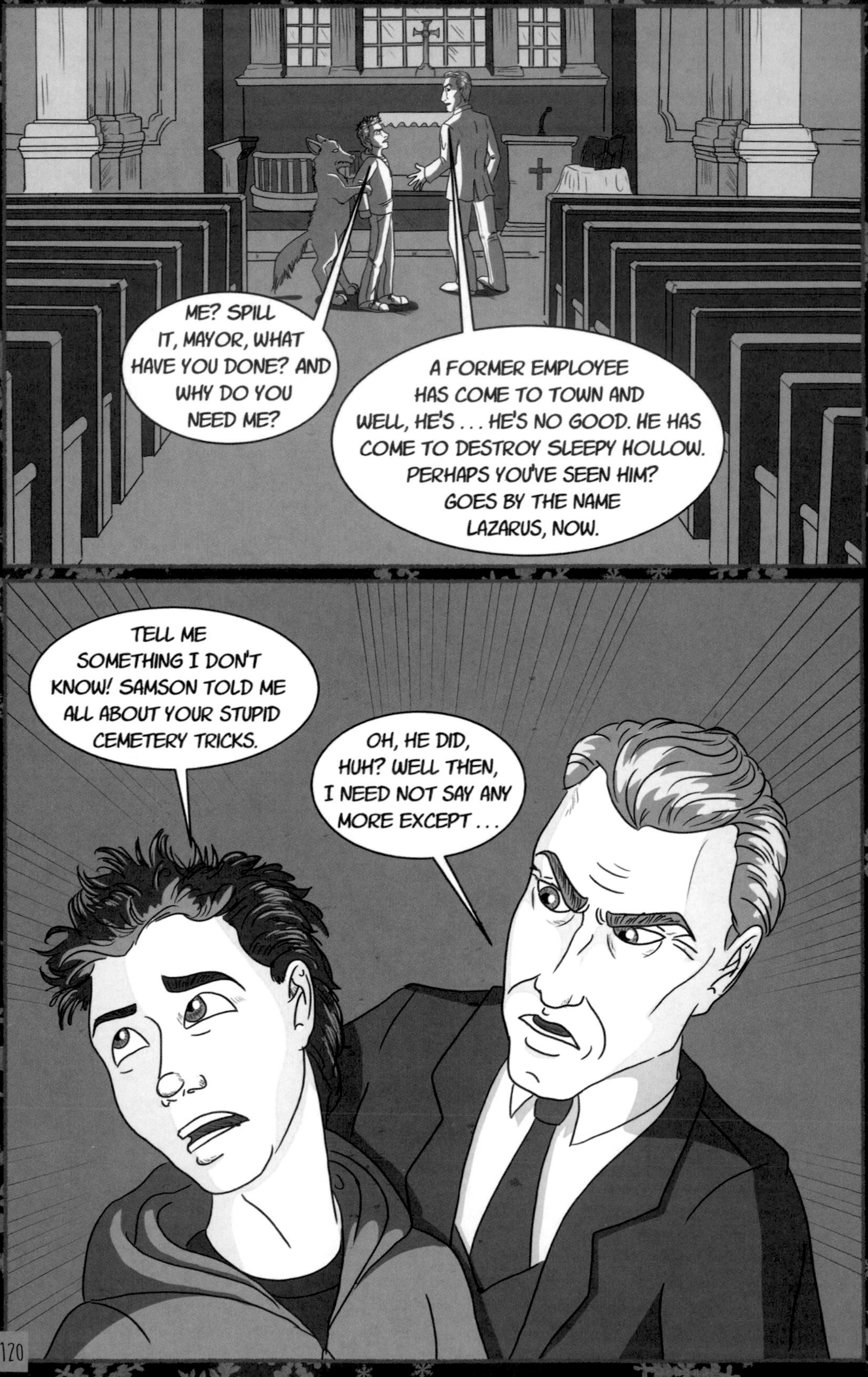
ME? SPILL IT, MAYOR, WHAT HAVE YOU DONE? AND WHY DO YOU NEED ME?
A FORMER EMPLOYEE HAS COME TO TOWN AND WELL, HE'S . . . HE'S NO GOOD. HE HAS COME TO DESTROY SLEEPY HOLLOW. PERHAPS YOU'VE SEEN HIM? GOES BY THE NAME LAZARUS, NOW.
TELL ME SOMETHING I DON'T KNOW! SAMSON TOLD ME ALL ABOUT YOUR STUPID CEMETERY TRICKS.
OH, HE DID, HUH? WELL THEN, I NEED NOT SAY ANY MORE EXCEPT . . .

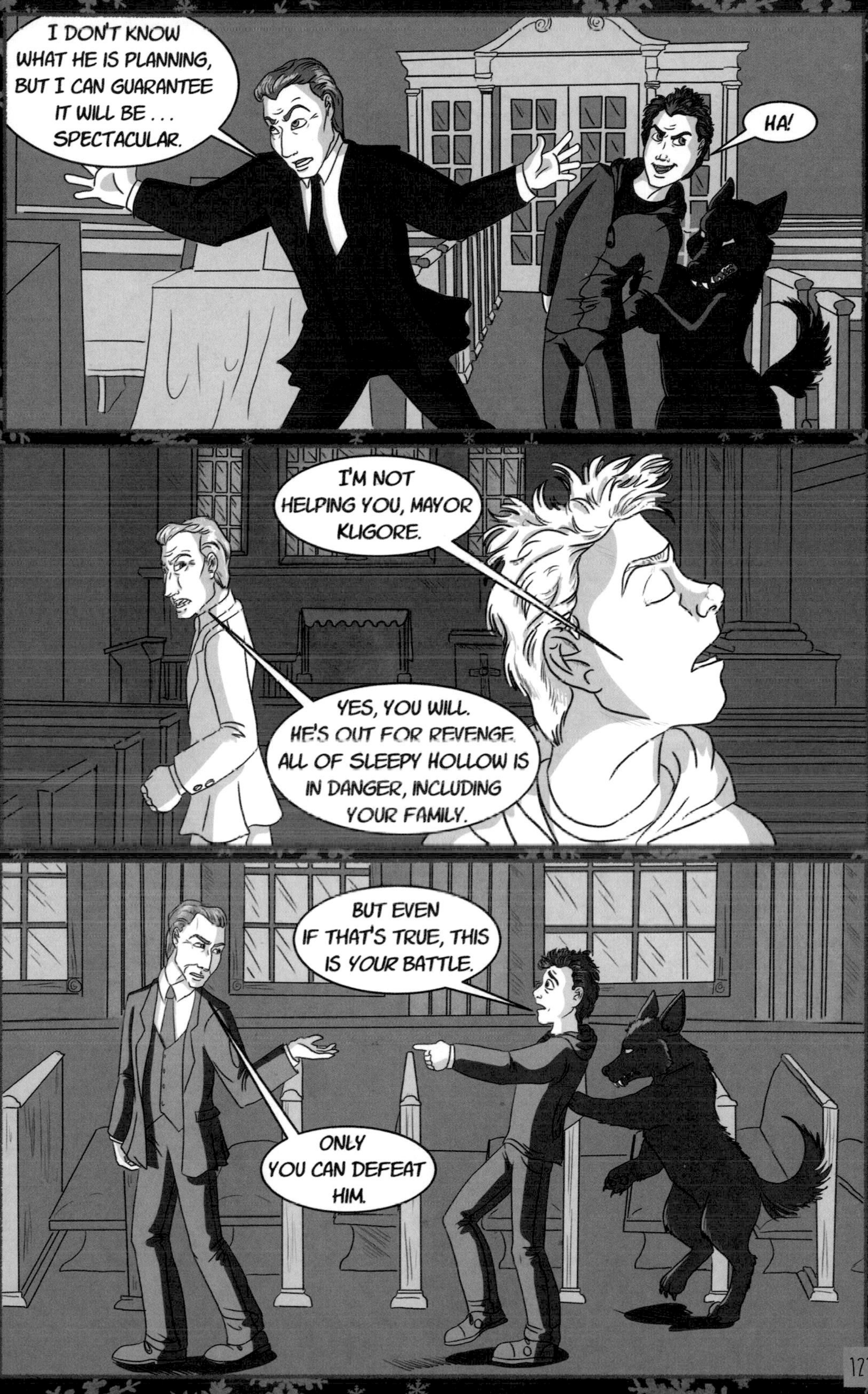
I DON'T KNOW WHAT HE IS PLANNING, BUT I CAN GUARANTEE IT WILL BE . . . SPECTACULAR.
HA!
I'M NOT HELPING YOU, MAYOR KLIGORE.
YES, YOU WILL. HE'S OUT FOR REVENGE. ALL OF SLEEPY HOLLOW IS IN DANGER, INCLUDING YOUR FAMILY.
BUT EVEN IF THAT'S TRUE, THIS IS YOUR BATTLE.
ONLY YOU CAN DEFEAT HIM.

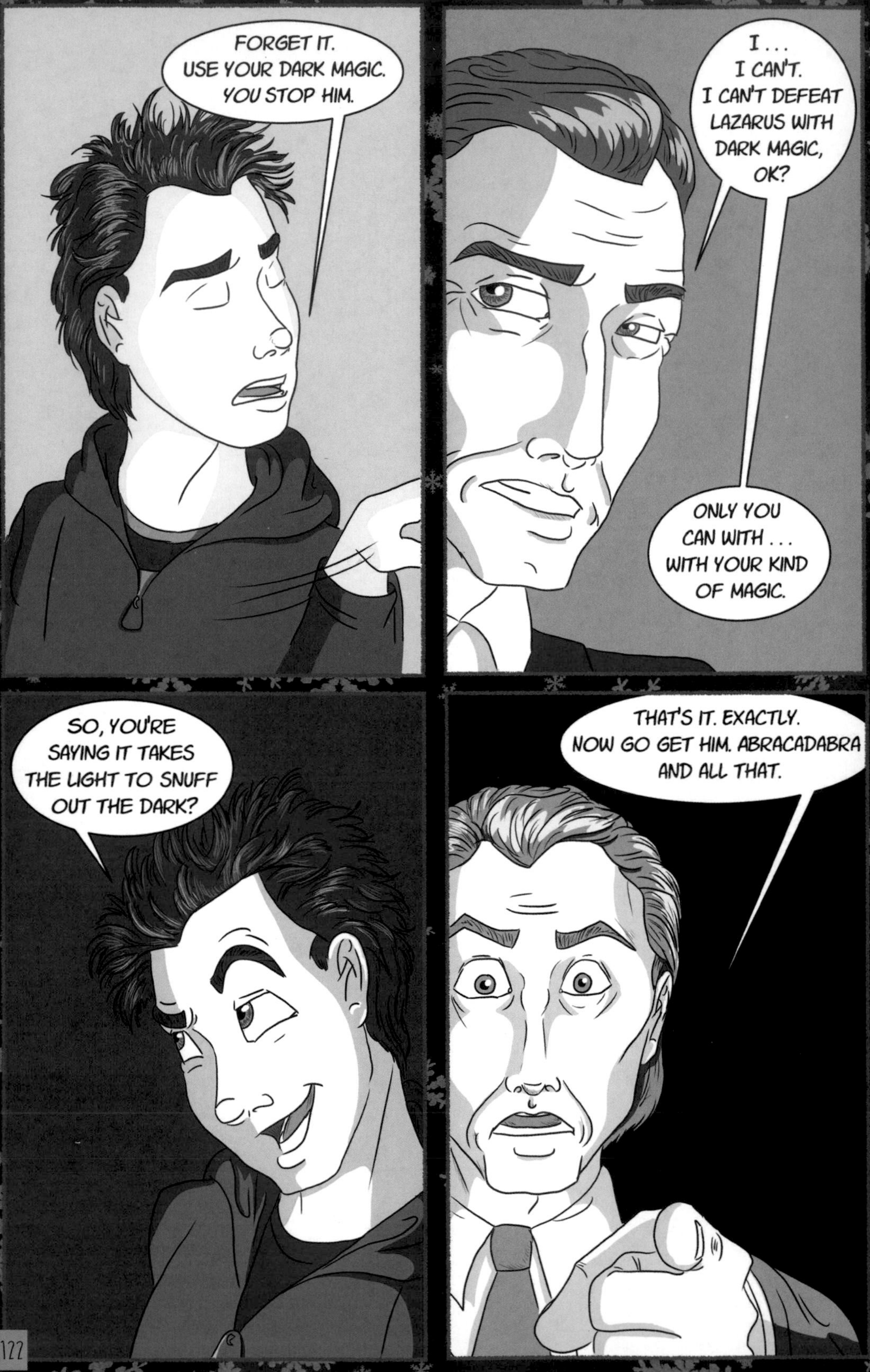
FORGET IT.
USE YOUR DARK MAGIC.
YOU STOP HIM.
I . . .
I CAN'T.
I CAN'T DEFEAT
LAZARUS WITH
DARK MAGIC,
OK?
ONLY YOU
CAN WITH . . .
WITH YOUR KIND
OF MAGIC.
SO, YOU'RE
SAYING IT TAKES
THE LIGHT TO SNUFF
OUT THE DARK?
THAT'S IT. EXACTLY.
NOW GO GET HIM. ABRACADABRA
AND ALL THAT.

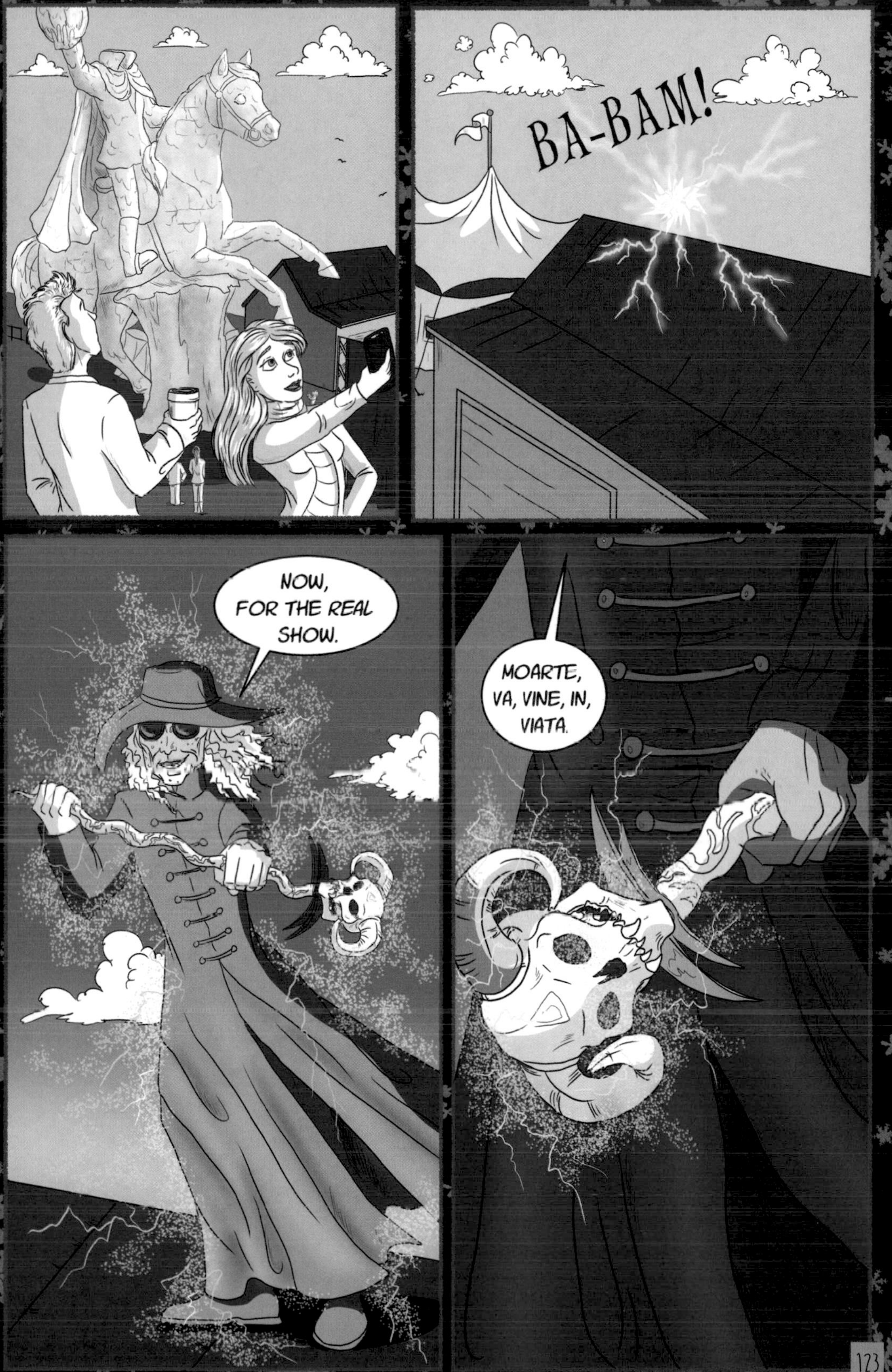
BA-BAM!
NOW, FOR THE REAL SHOW.
MOARTE, VA, VINE, IN, VIATA.

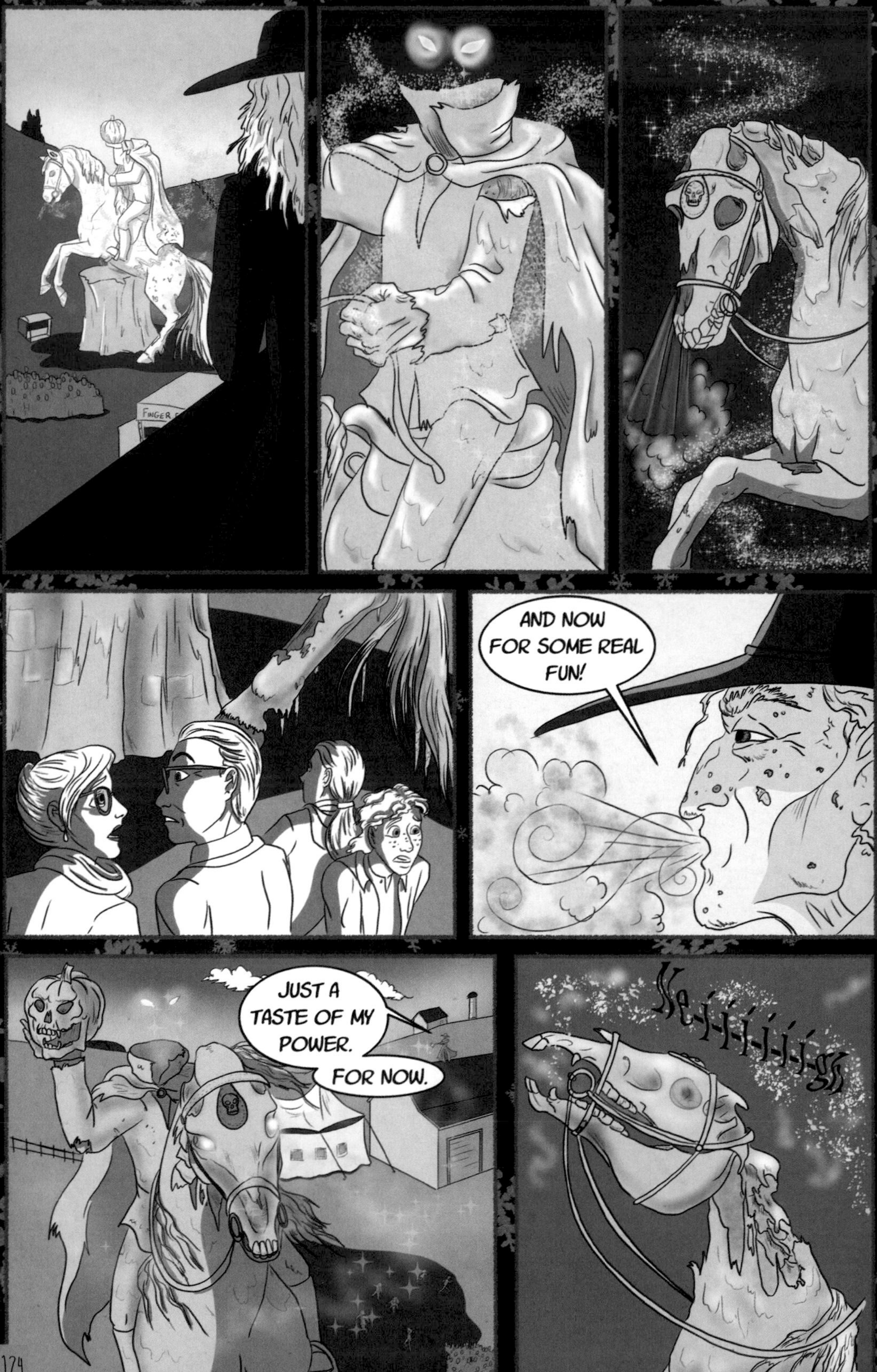
FINGER
AND NOW FOR SOME REAL FUN!
JUST A TASTE OF MY POWER.
FOR NOW.
Ne-i-i-i-i-i-i-gh

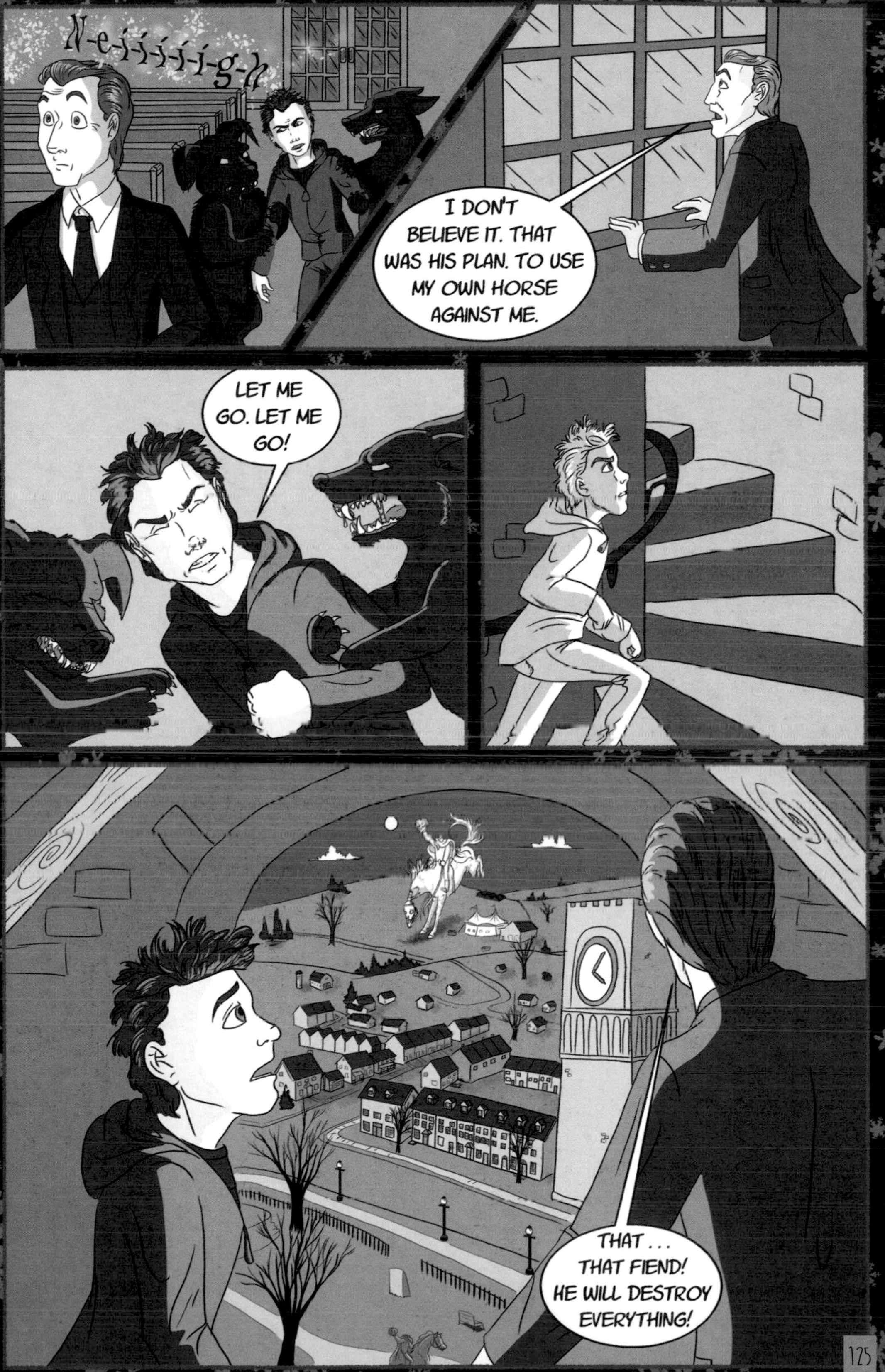
N-e-i-i-i-i-i-g-h
I DON'T BELIEVE IT. THAT WAS HIS PLAN. TO USE MY OWN HORSE AGAINST ME.
LET ME GO. LET ME GO!
THAT . . . THAT FIEND! HE WILL DESTROY EVERYTHING!

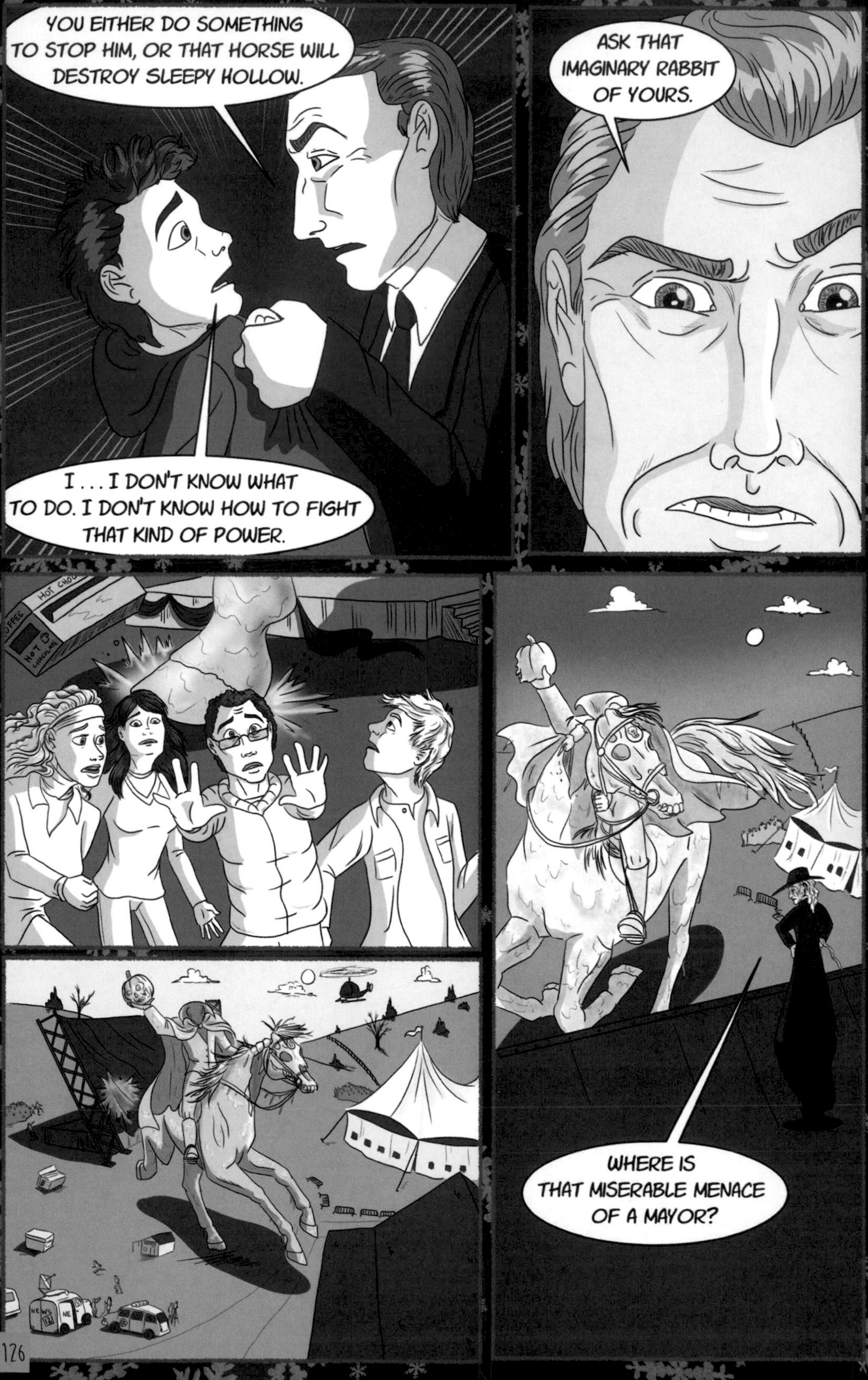
YOU EITHER DO SOMETHING TO STOP HIM, OR THAT HORSE WILL DESTROY SLEEPY HOLLOW.
I . . . I DON'T KNOW WHAT TO DO. I DON'T KNOW HOW TO FIGHT THAT KIND OF POWER.
ASK THAT IMAGINARY RABBIT OF YOURS.
WHERE IS THAT MISERABLE MENACE OF A MAYOR?

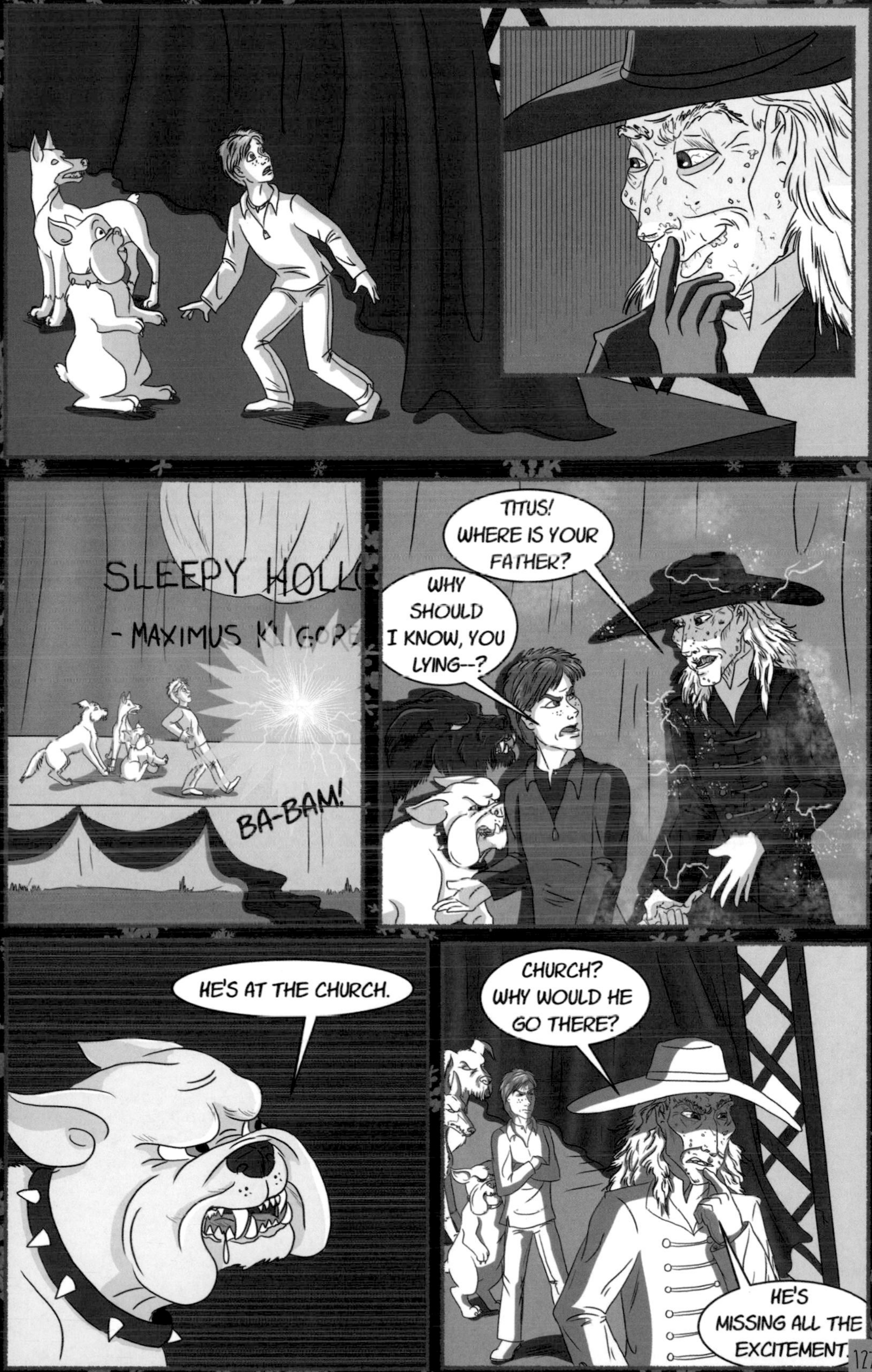
SLEEPY HOLLO
- MAXIMUS KILGORE
BA-BAM!
TITUS! WHERE IS YOUR FATHER?
WHY SHOULD I KNOW, YOU LYING--?
HE'S AT THE CHURCH.
CHURCH? WHY WOULD HE GO THERE?
HE'S MISSING ALL THE EXCITEMENT.

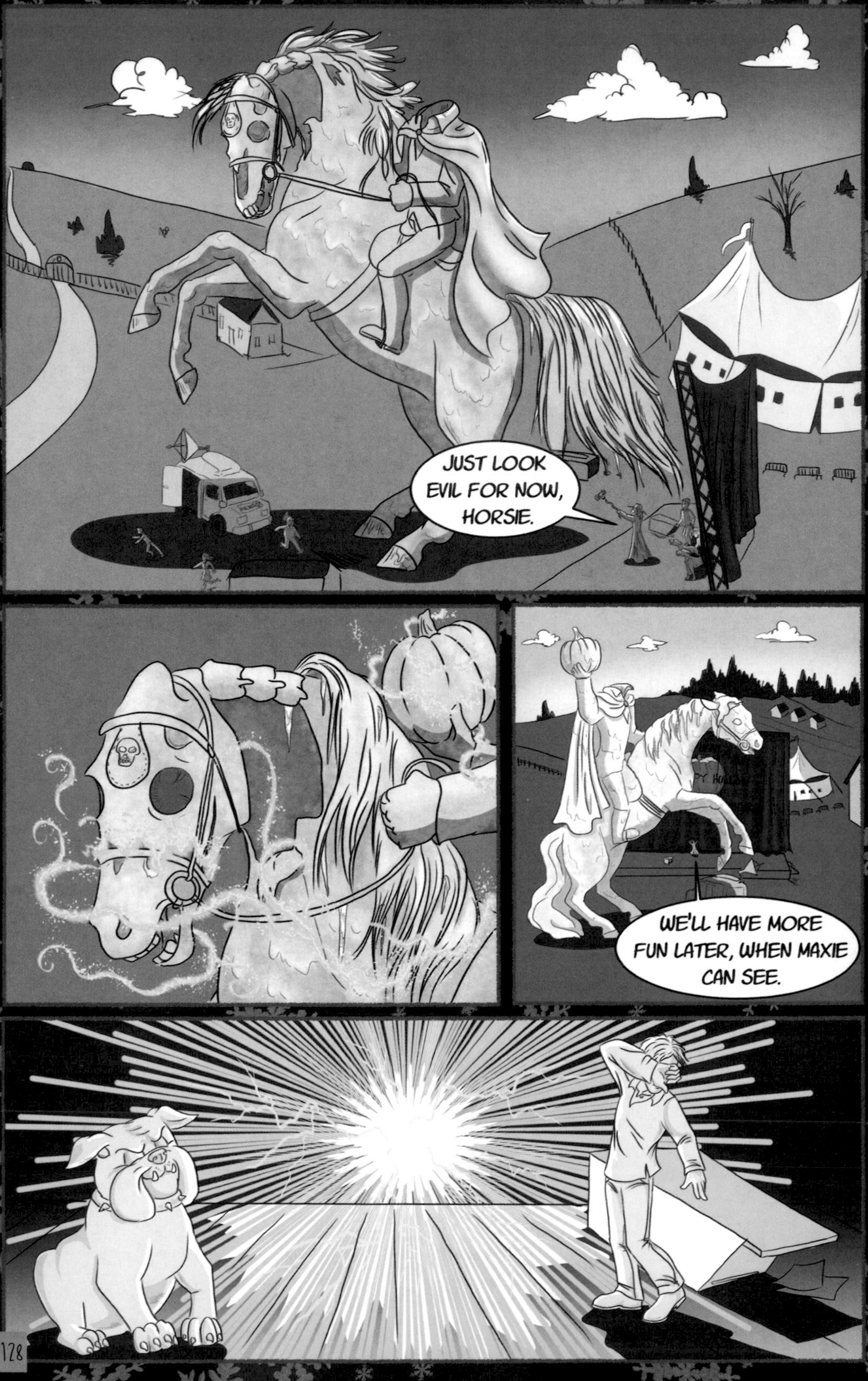
JUST LOOK EVIL FOR NOW, HORSIE.
WE'LL HAVE MORE FUN LATER, WHEN MAXIE CAN SEE.

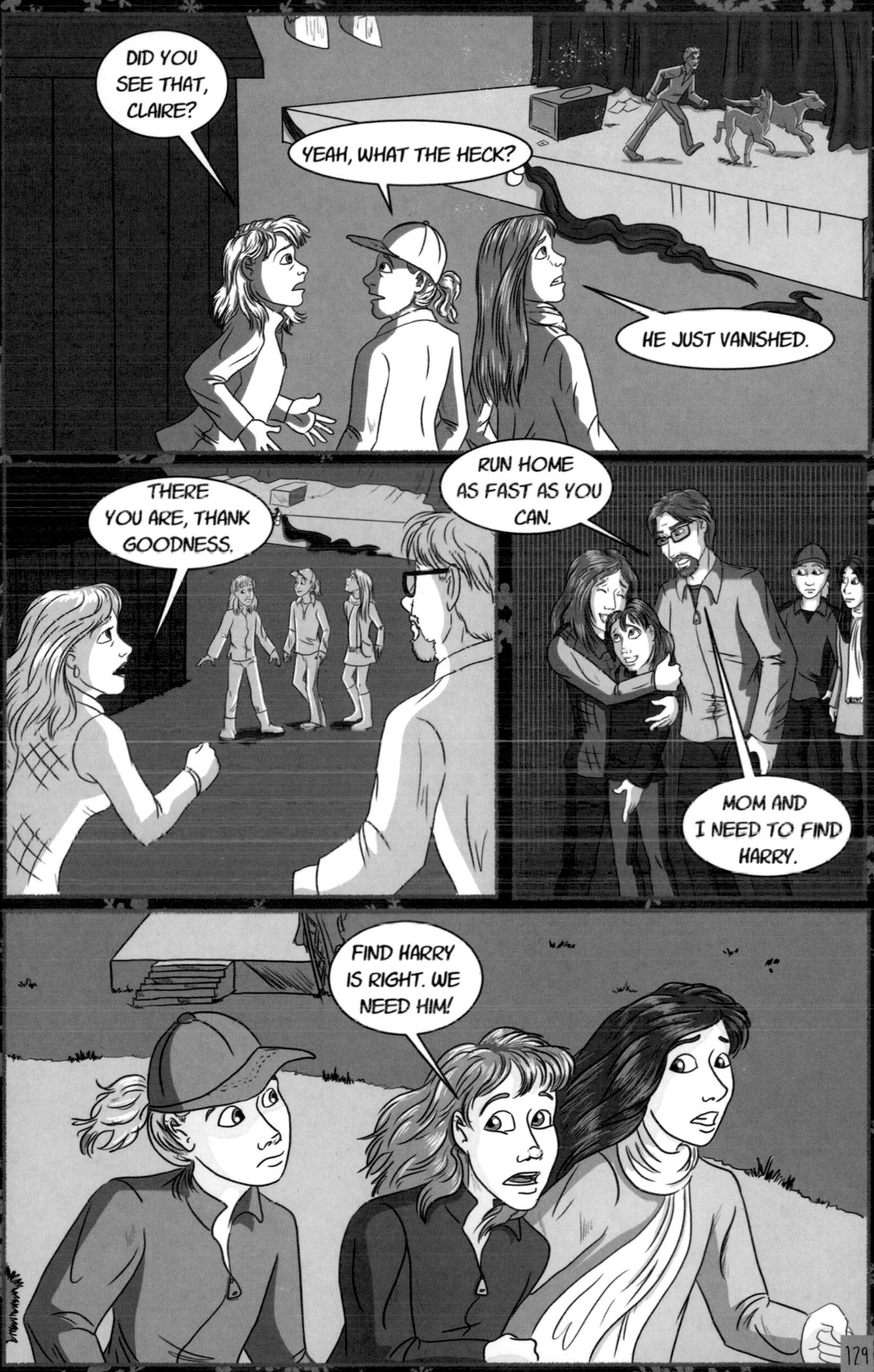
DID YOU SEE THAT, CLAIRE?
YEAH, WHAT THE HECK?
HE JUST VANISHED.
THERE YOU ARE, THANK GOODNESS.
RUN HOME AS FAST AS YOU CAN.
MOM AND I NEED TO FIND HARRY.
FIND HARRY IS RIGHT. WE NEED HIM!

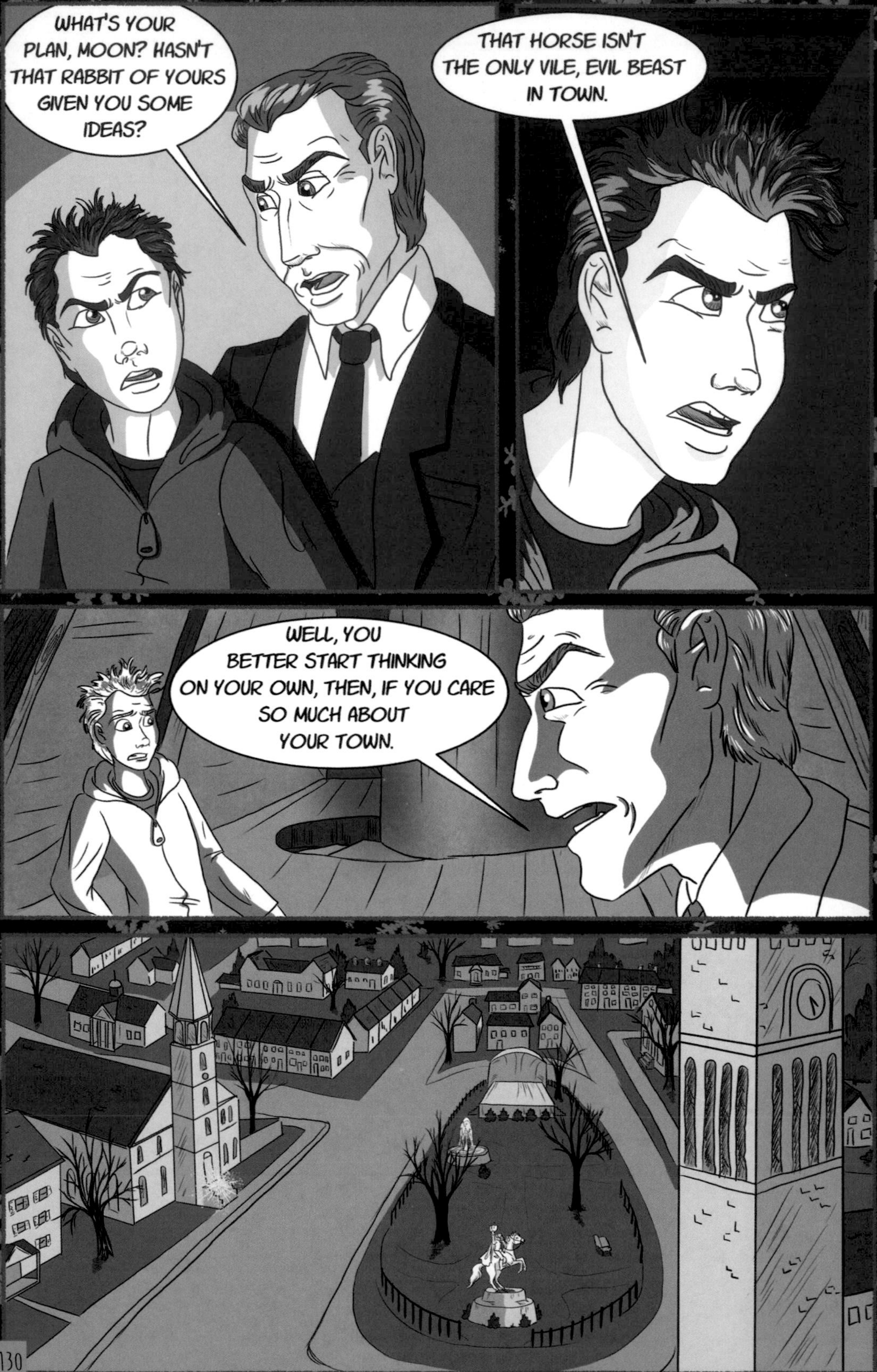
WHAT'S YOUR PLAN, MOON? HASN'T THAT RABBIT OF YOURS GIVEN YOU SOME IDEAS?
THAT HORSE ISN'T THE ONLY VILE, EVIL BEAST IN TOWN.
WELL, YOU BETTER START THINKING ON YOUR OWN, THEN, IF YOU CARE SO MUCH ABOUT YOUR TOWN.

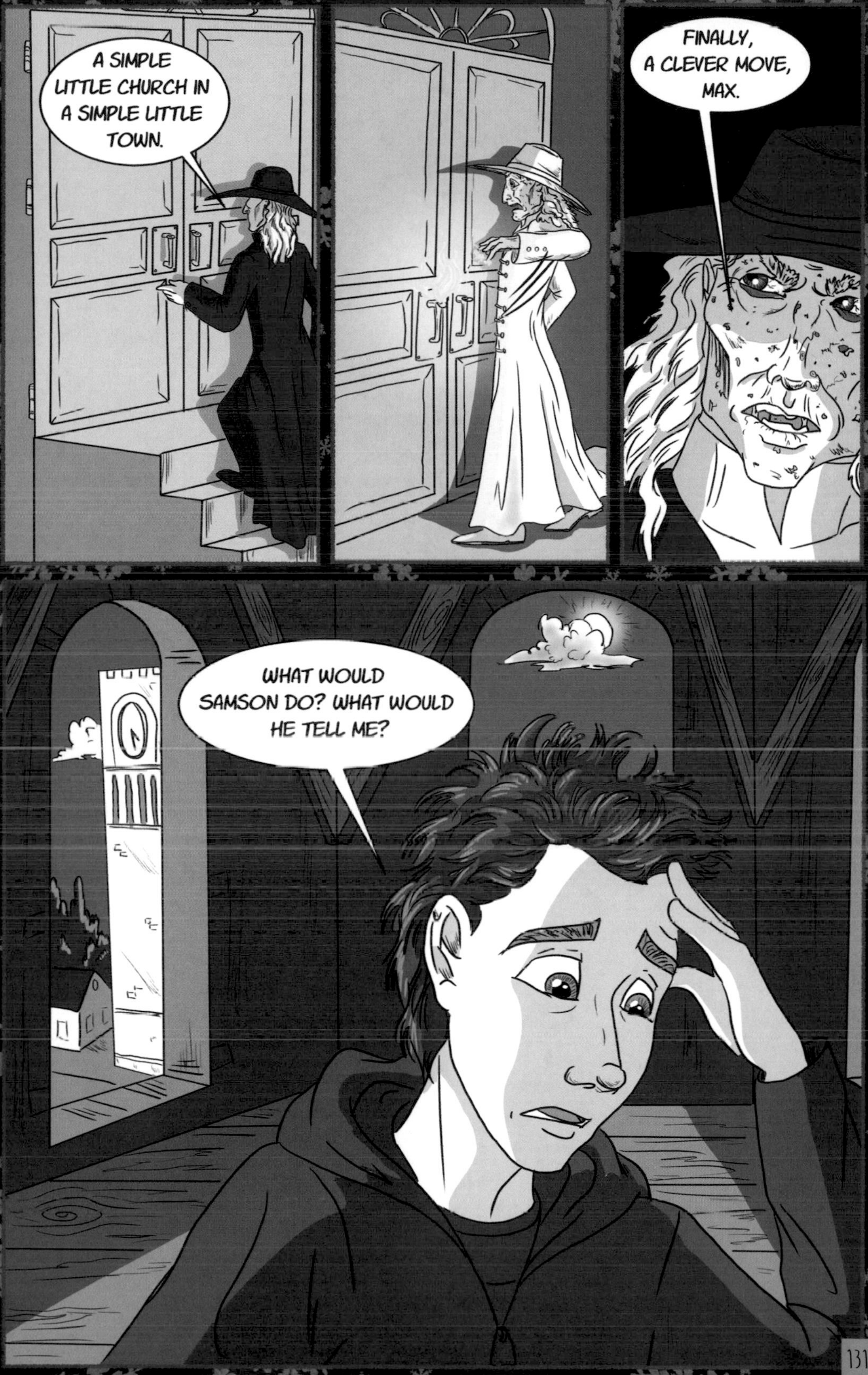
A SIMPLE LITTLE CHURCH IN A SIMPLE LITTLE TOWN.
FINALLY, A CLEVER MOVE, MAX.
WHAT WOULD SAMSON DO? WHAT WOULD HE TELL ME?

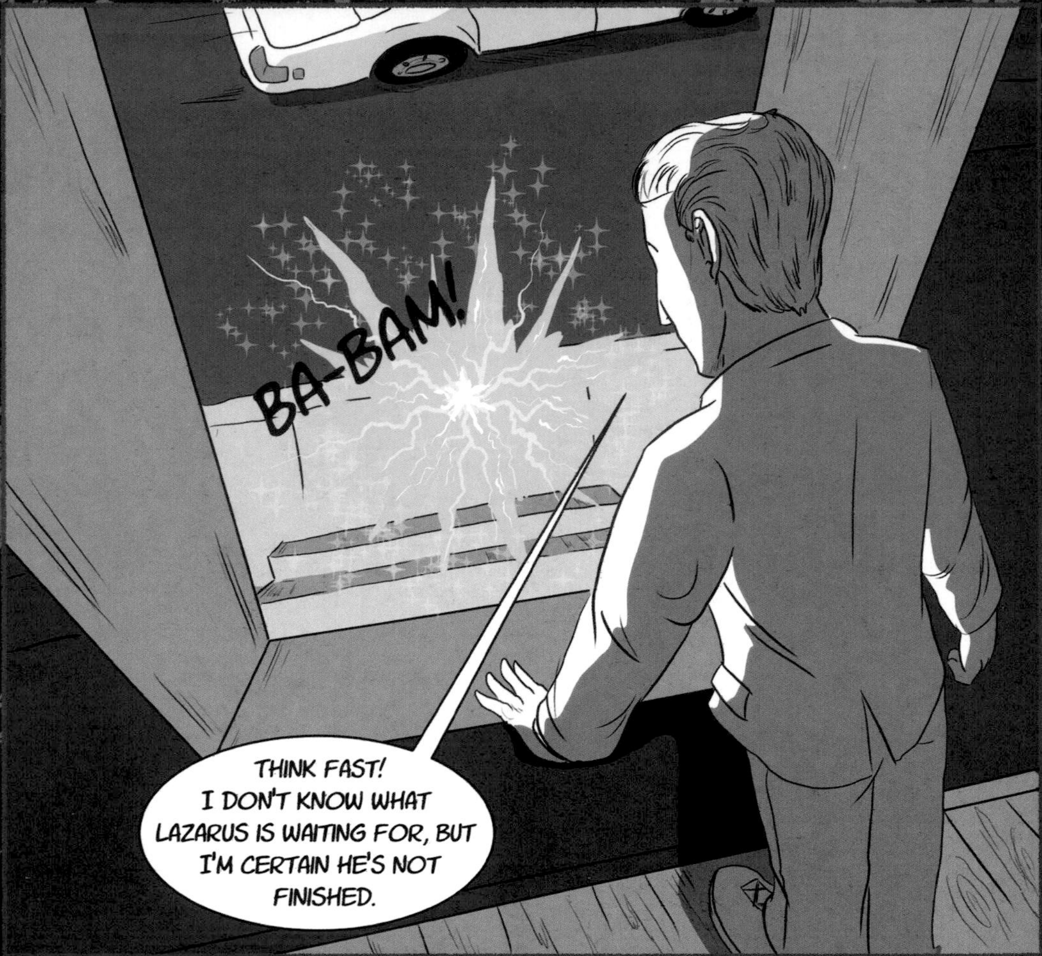
BA-BAM!
THINK FAST! I DON'T KNOW WHAT LAZARUS IS WAITING FOR, BUT I'M CERTAIN HE'S NOT FINISHED.

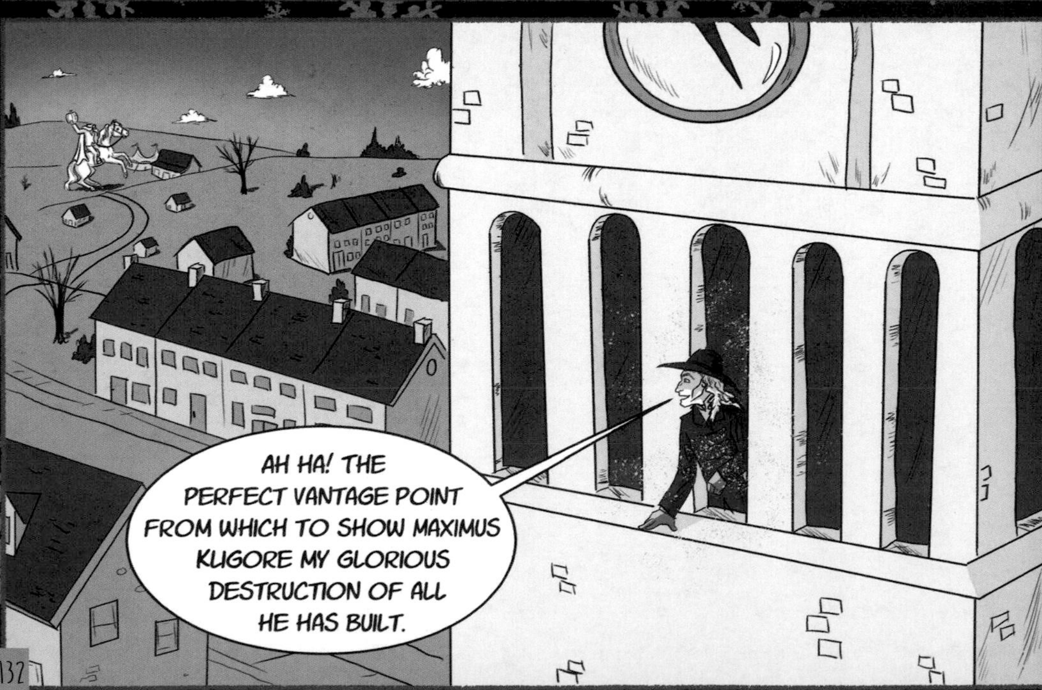
AH HA! THE PERFECT VANTAGE POINT FROM WHICH TO SHOW MAXIMUS KLIGORE MY GLORIOUS DESTRUCTION OF ALL HE HAS BUILT.

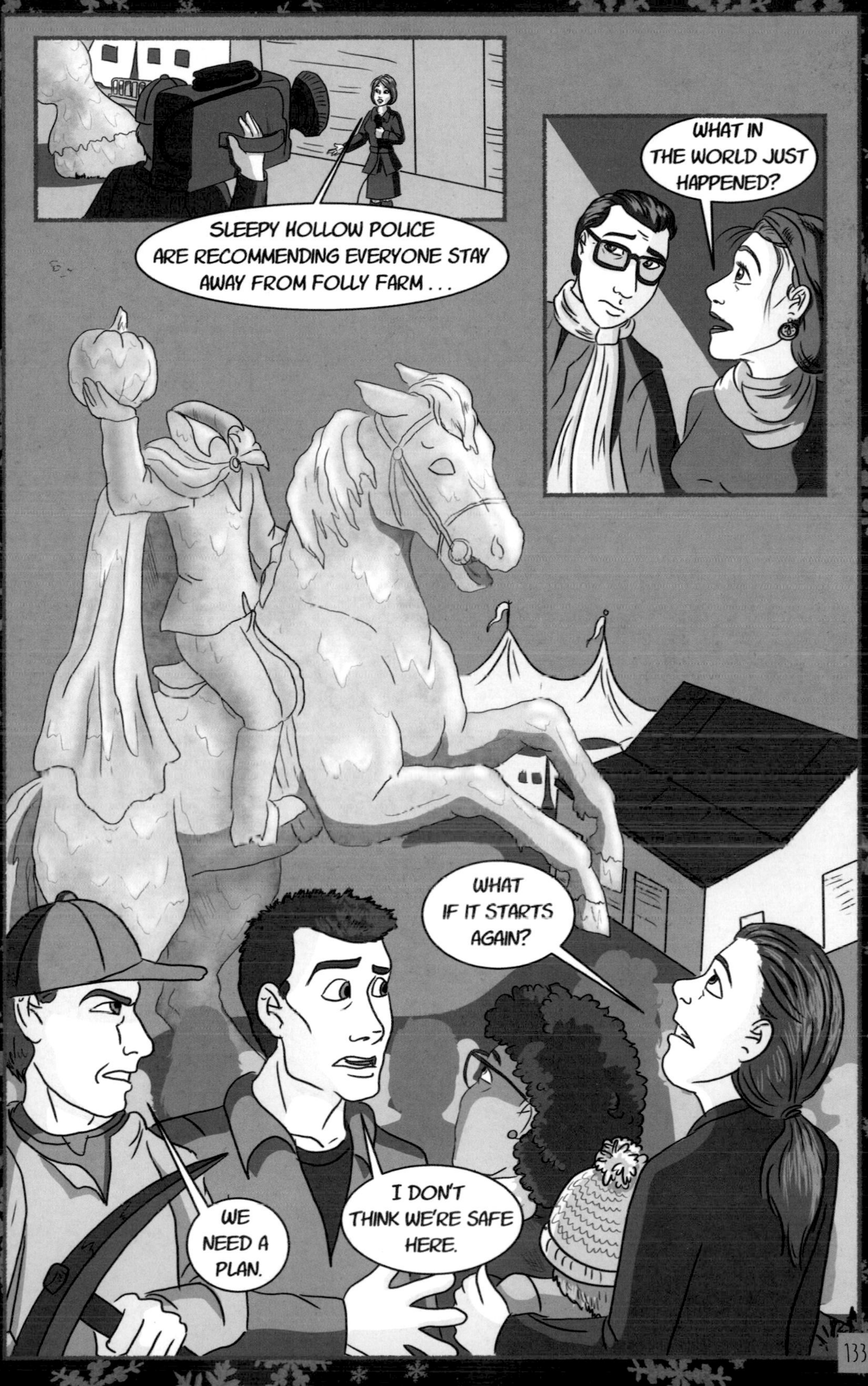
SLEEPY HOLLOW POLICE ARE RECOMMENDING EVERYONE STAY AWAY FROM FOLLY FARM . . .
WHAT IN THE WORLD JUST HAPPENED?
WHAT IF IT STARTS AGAIN?
WE NEED A PLAN.
I DON'T THINK WE'RE SAFE HERE.

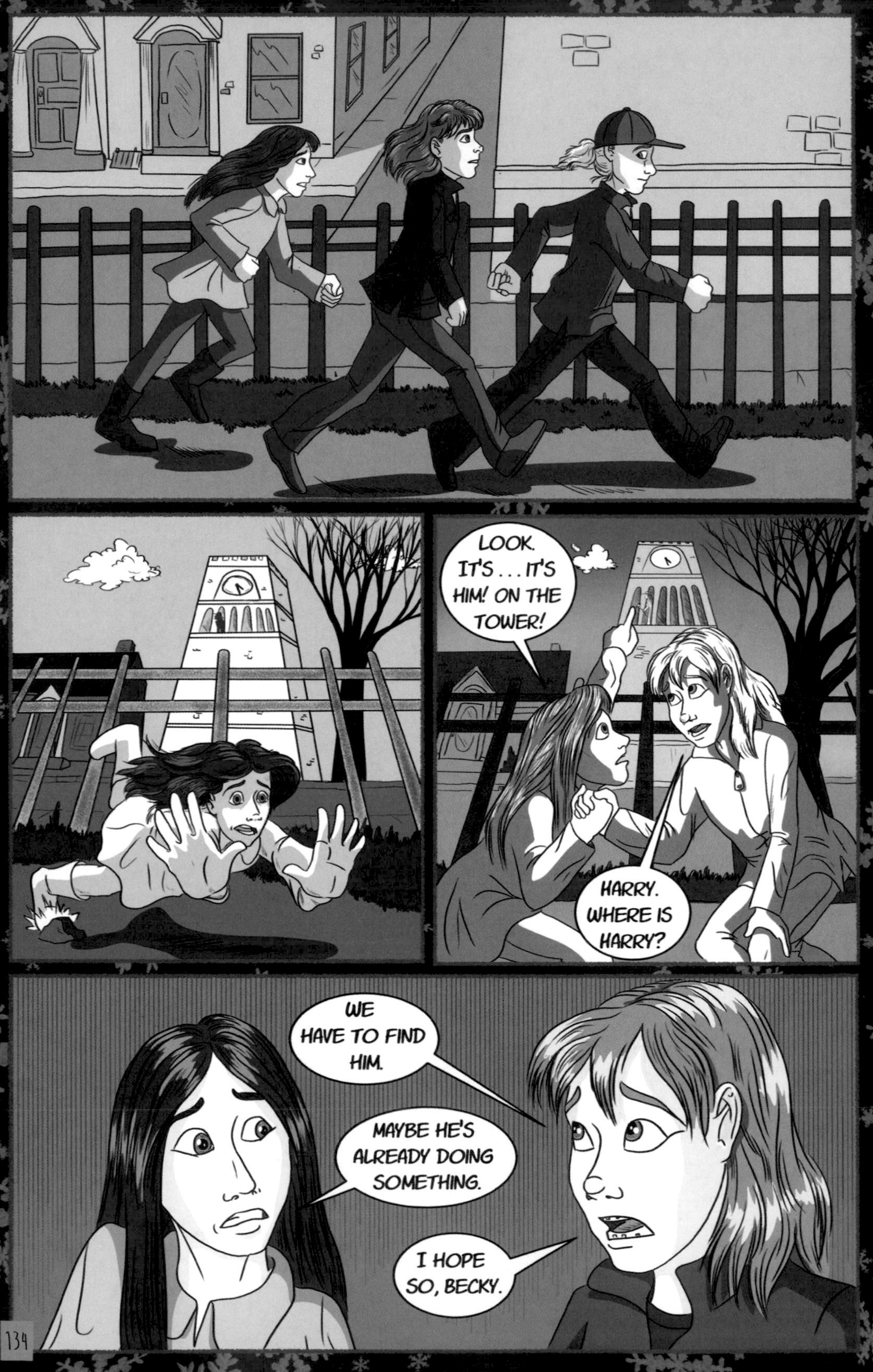

LOOK. IT'S . . . IT'S HIM! ON THE TOWER!
HARRY. WHERE IS HARRY?
WE HAVE TO FIND HIM.
MAYBE HE'S ALREADY DOING SOMETHING.
I HOPE SO, BECKY.

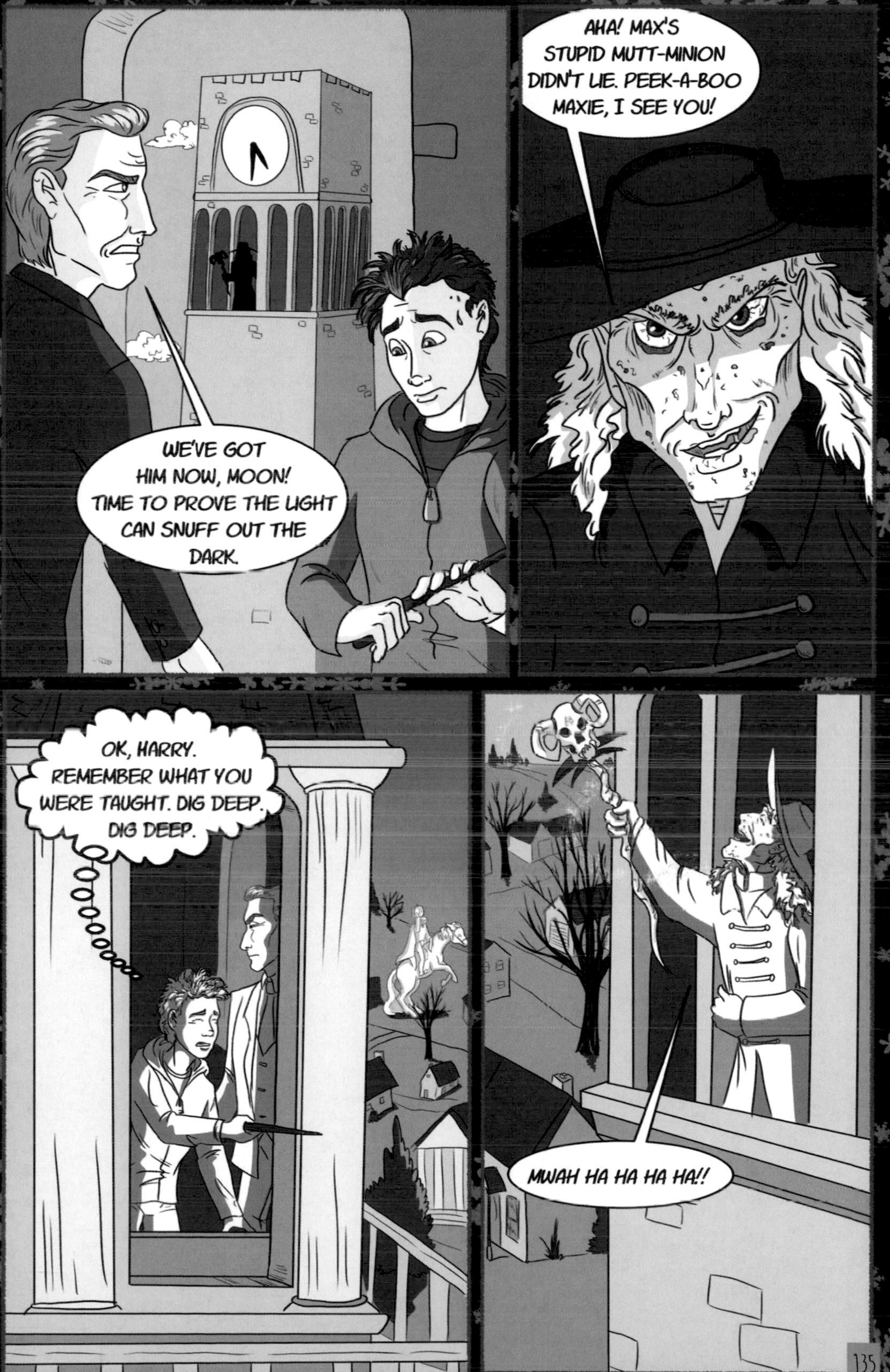
WE'VE GOT HIM NOW, MOON! TIME TO PROVE THE LIGHT CAN SNUFF OUT THE DARK.
AHA! MAX'S STUPID MUTT-MINION DIDN'T LIE. PEEK-A-BOO MAXIE, I SEE YOU!
OK, HARRY. REMEMBER WHAT YOU WERE TAUGHT. DIG DEEP. DIG DEEP.
MWAH HA HA HA HA!!

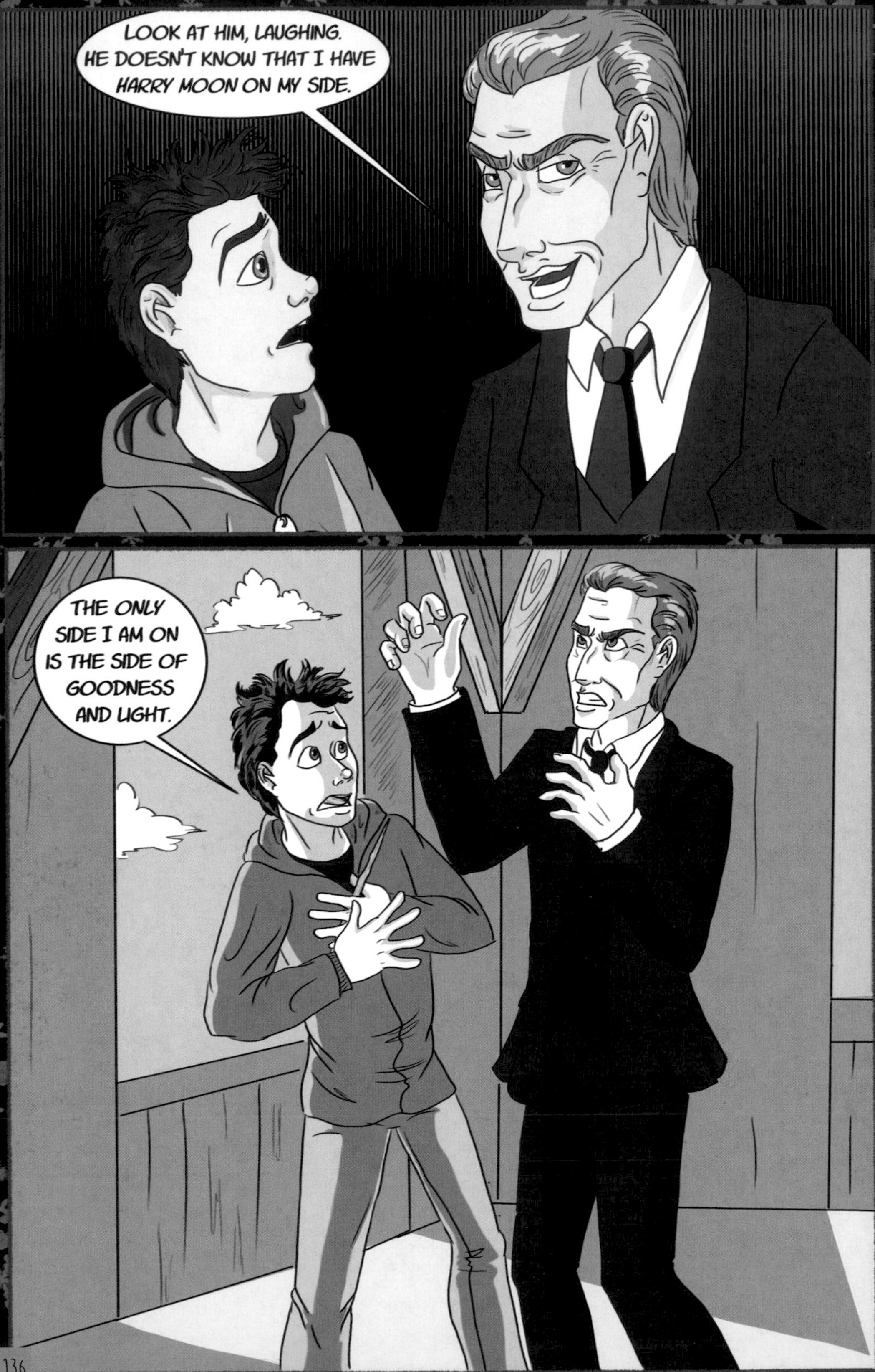
LOOK AT HIM, LAUGHING. HE DOESN'T KNOW THAT I HAVE HARRY MOON ON MY SIDE.
THE ONLY SIDE I AM ON IS THE SIDE OF GOODNESS AND LIGHT.

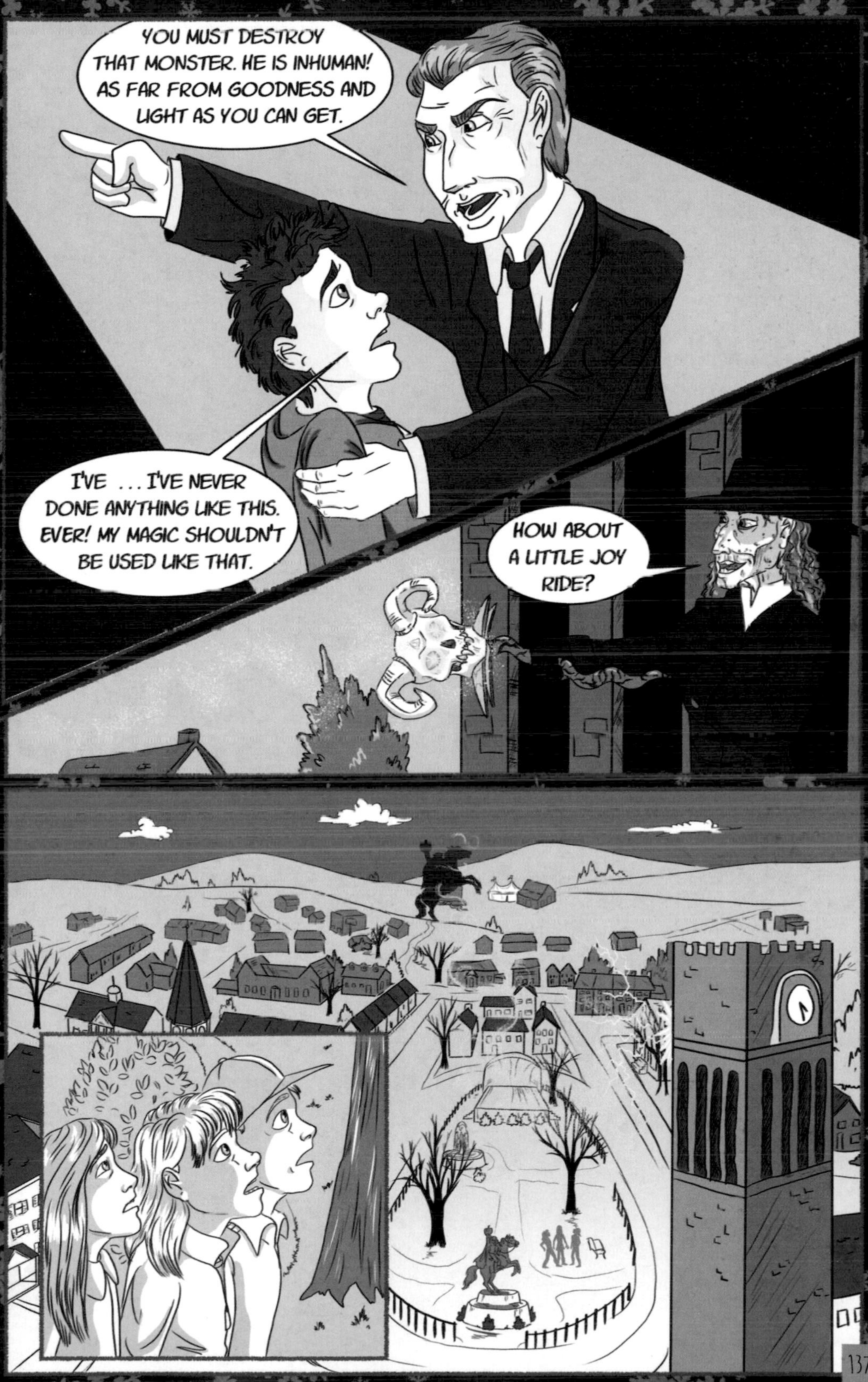
YOU MUST DESTROY THAT MONSTER. HE IS INHUMAN! AS FAR FROM GOODNESS AND LIGHT AS YOU CAN GET.
I'VE . . . I'VE NEVER DONE ANYTHING LIKE THIS. EVER! MY MAGIC SHOULDN'T BE USED LIKE THAT.
HOW ABOUT A LITTLE JOY RIDE?

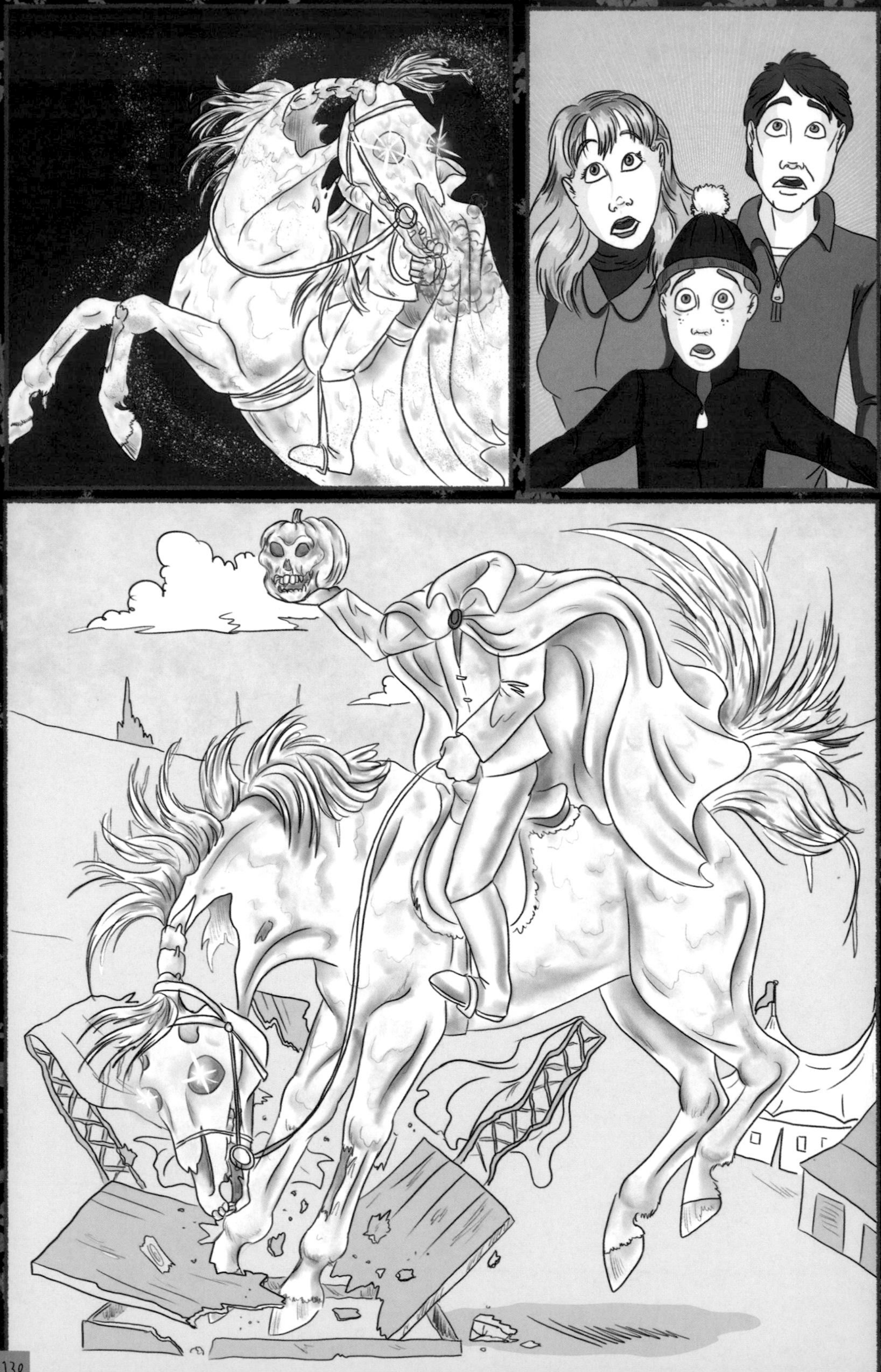

LOOK! ON THE CHURCH TOWER!

IS THAT HARRY?

AND MAYOR KILGORE.

RUN. BOTH OF YOU.

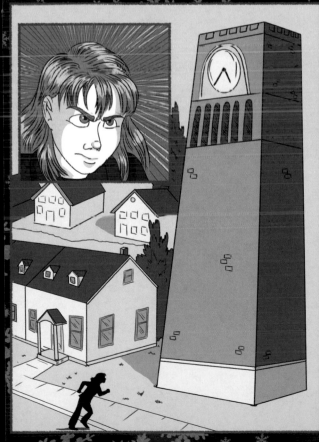

RUN HOME!

WHAT IS SHE DOING???

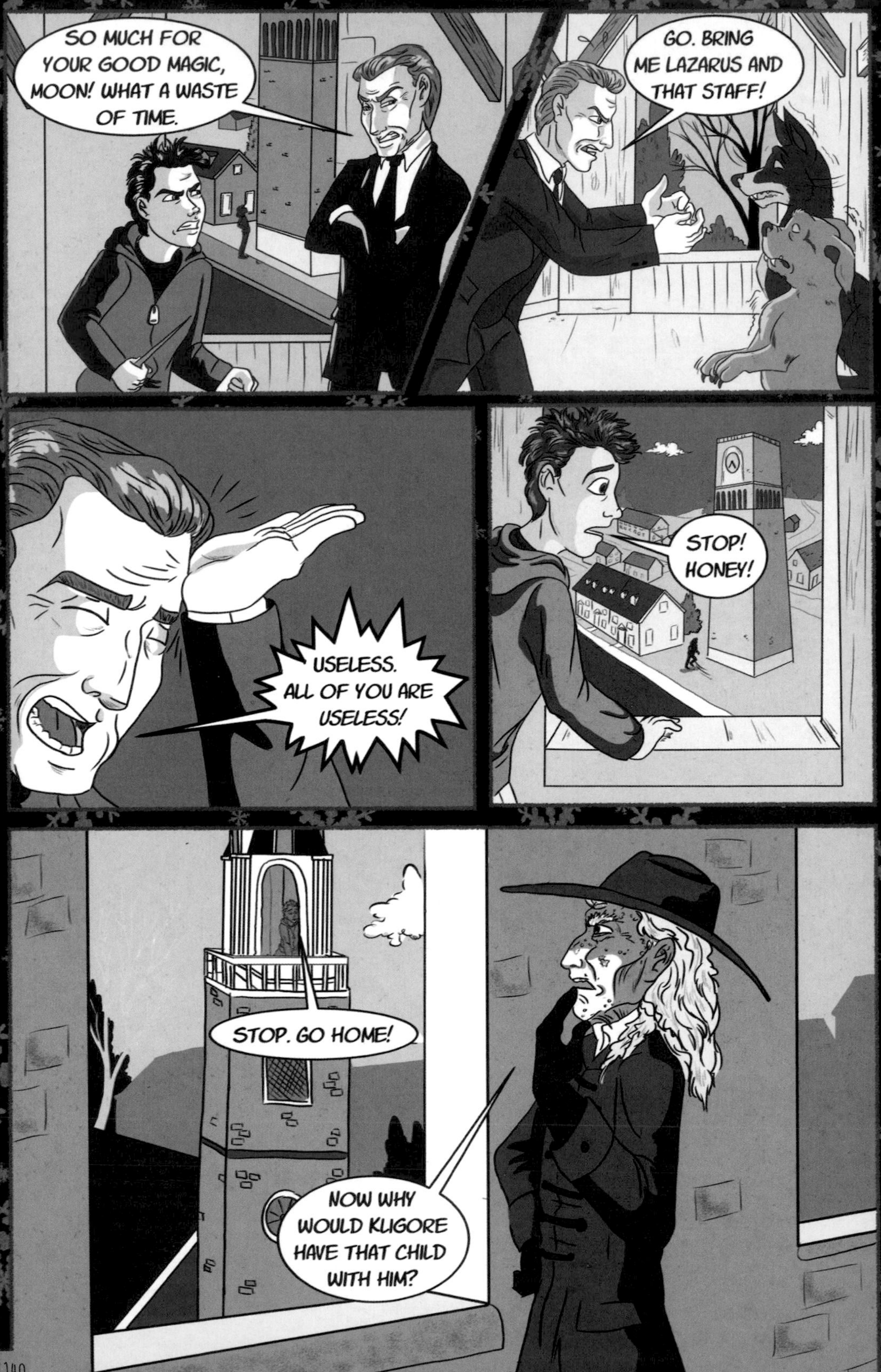
SO MUCH FOR YOUR GOOD MAGIC, MOON! WHAT A WASTE OF TIME.
GO. BRING ME LAZARUS AND THAT STAFF!
USELESS. ALL OF YOU ARE USELESS!
STOP! HONEY!
STOP. GO HOME!
NOW WHY WOULD KLIGORE HAVE THAT CHILD WITH HIM?

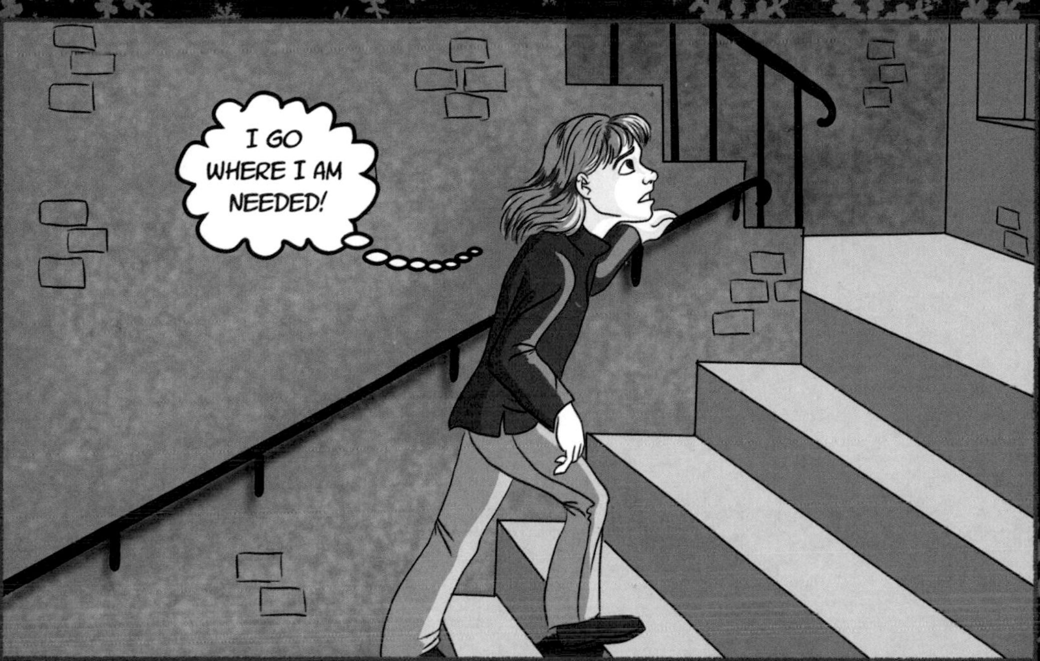
I GO WHERE I AM NEEDED!

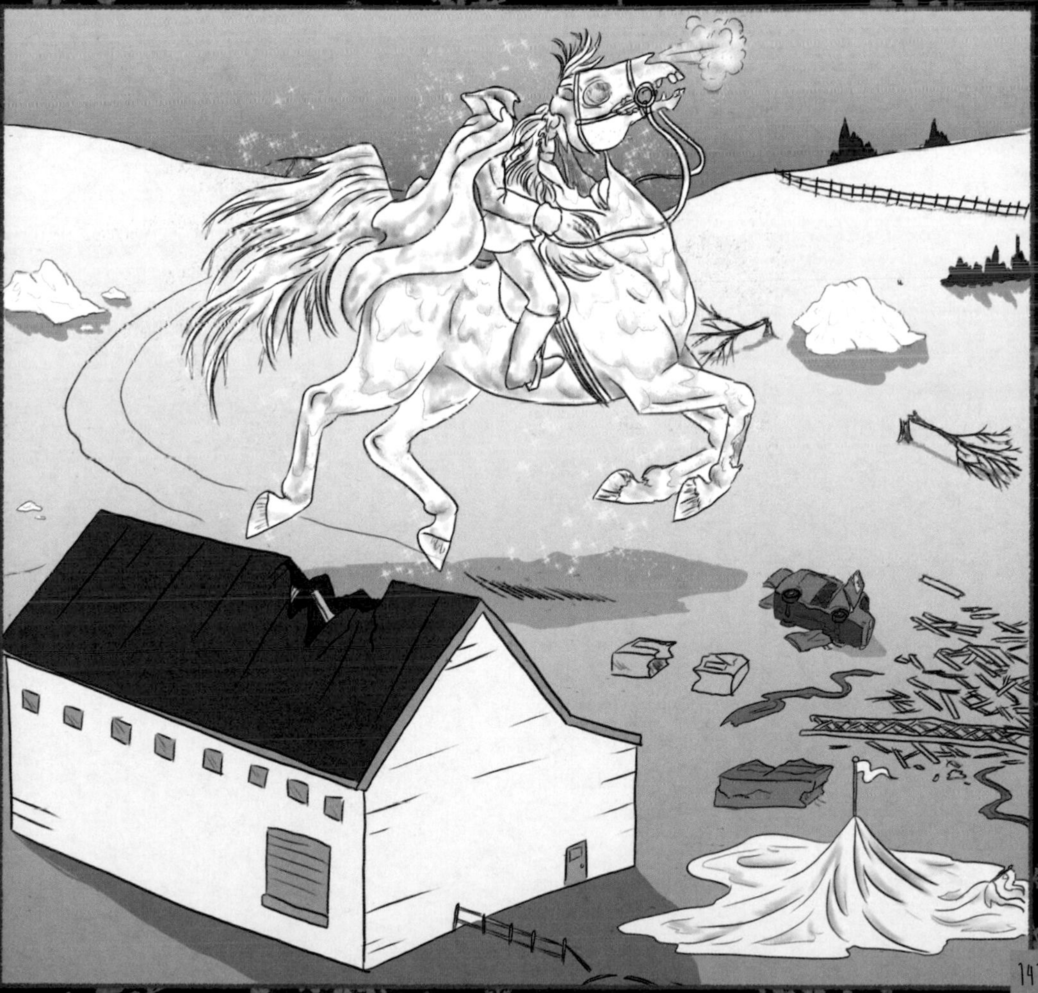

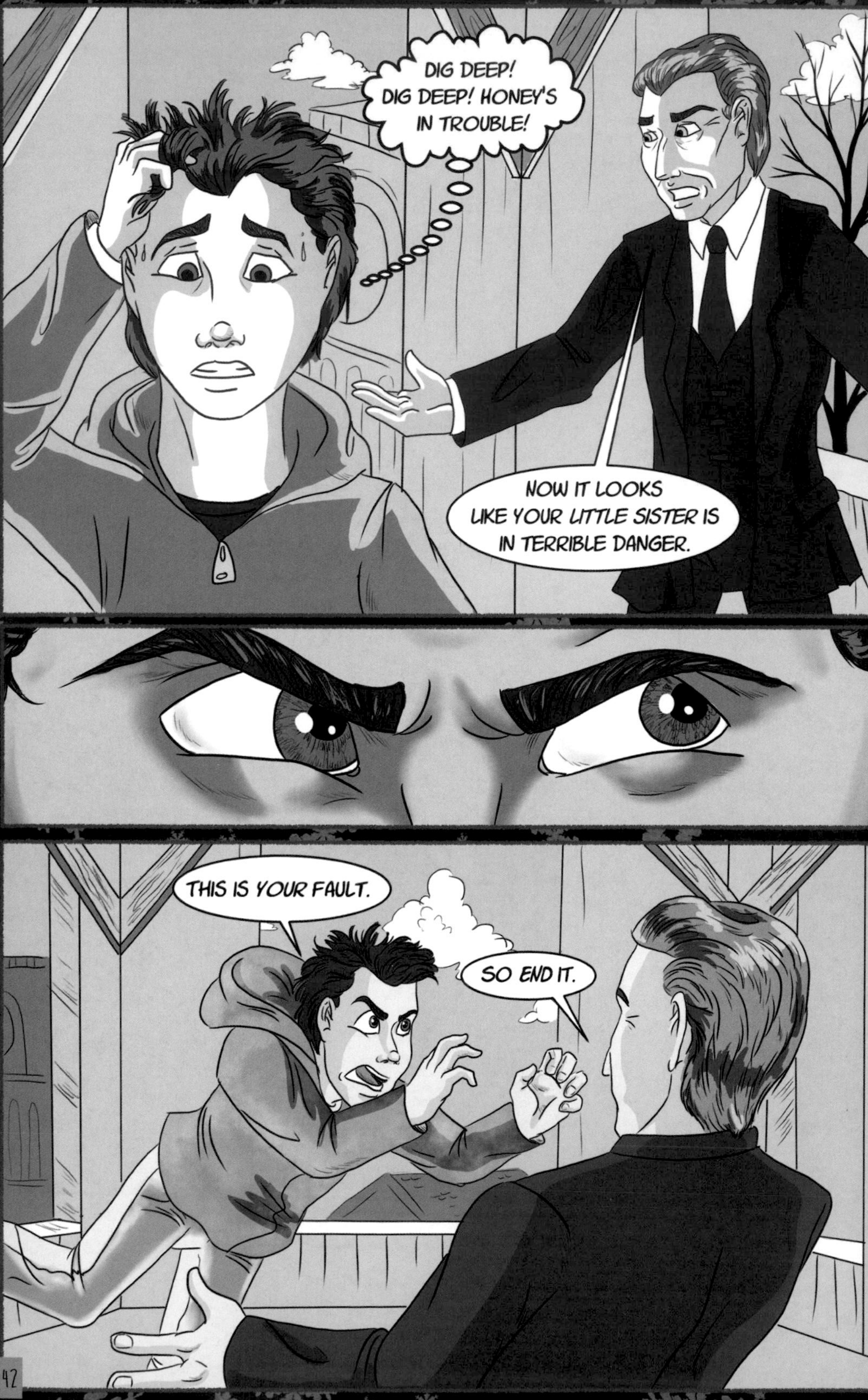
DIG DEEP!
DIG DEEP! HONEY'S IN TROUBLE!
NOW IT LOOKS LIKE YOUR LITTLE SISTER IS IN TERRIBLE DANGER.
THIS IS YOUR FAULT.
SO END IT.

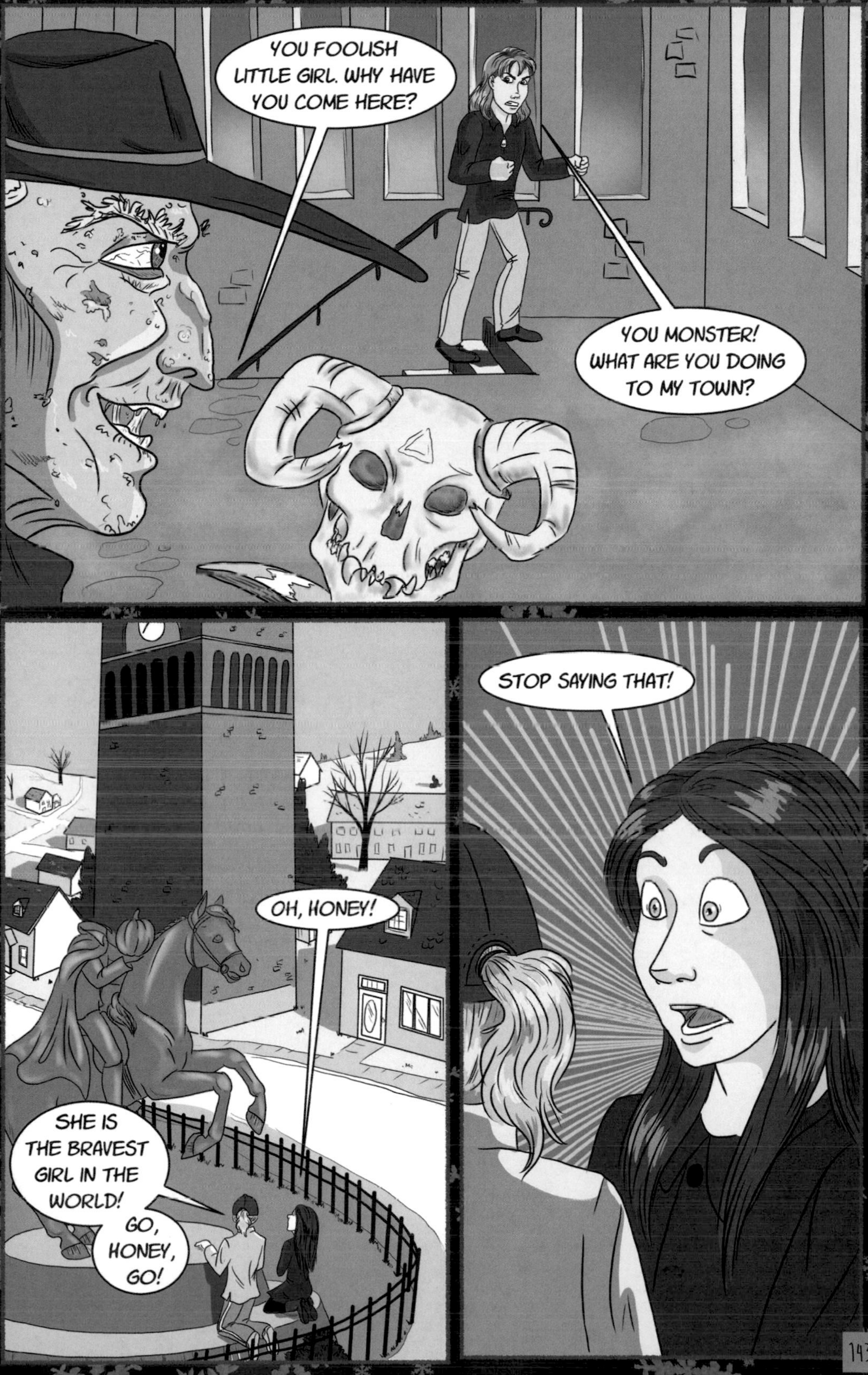
YOU FOOLISH LITTLE GIRL. WHY HAVE YOU COME HERE?
YOU MONSTER! WHAT ARE YOU DOING TO MY TOWN?
OH, HONEY!
SHE IS THE BRAVEST GIRL IN THE WORLD!
GO, HONEY, GO!
STOP SAYING THAT!

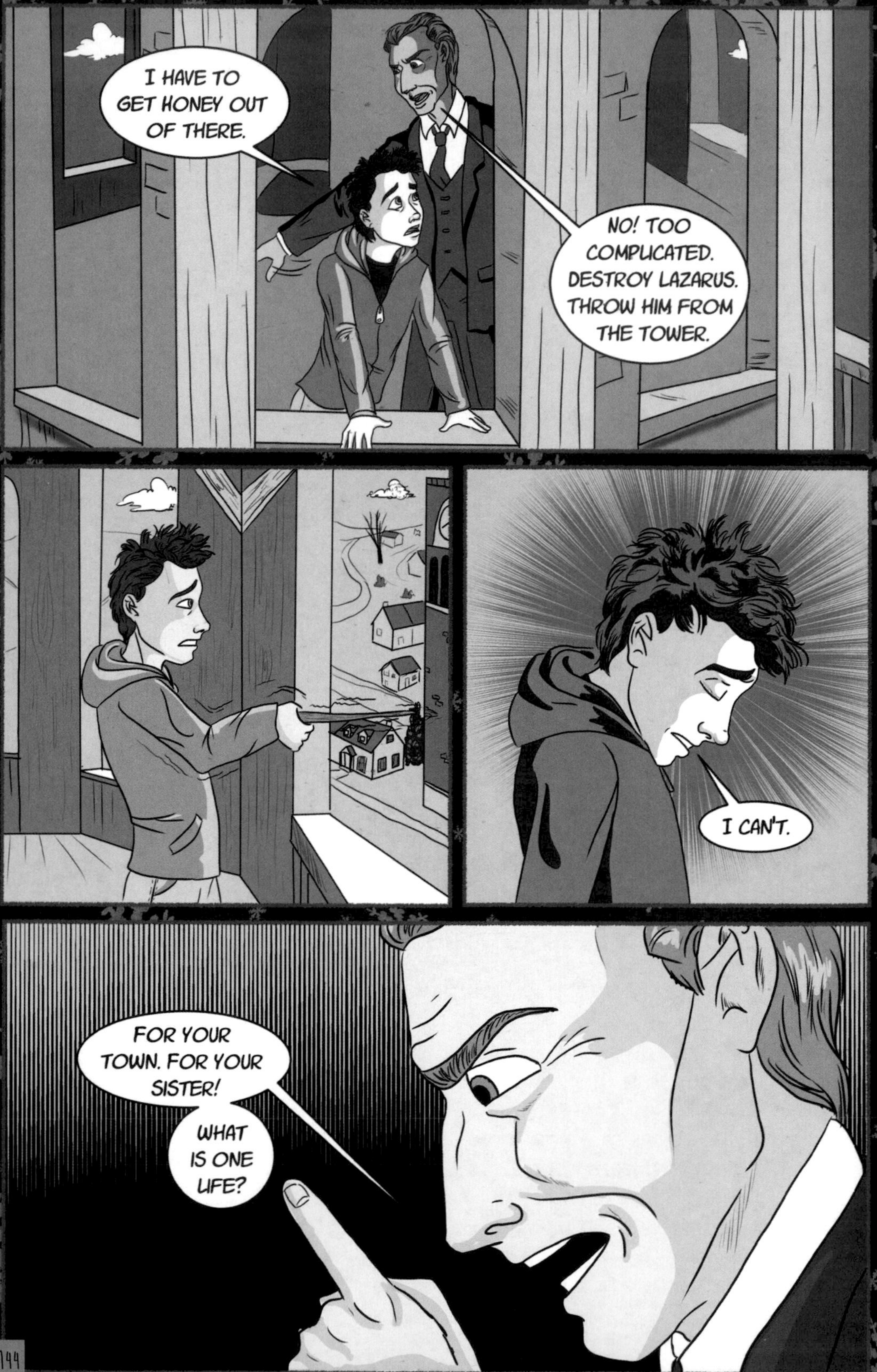
I HAVE TO GET HONEY OUT OF THERE.
NO! TOO COMPLICATED. DESTROY LAZARUS. THROW HIM FROM THE TOWER.
I CAN'T.
FOR YOUR TOWN. FOR YOUR SISTER!
WHAT IS ONE LIFE?

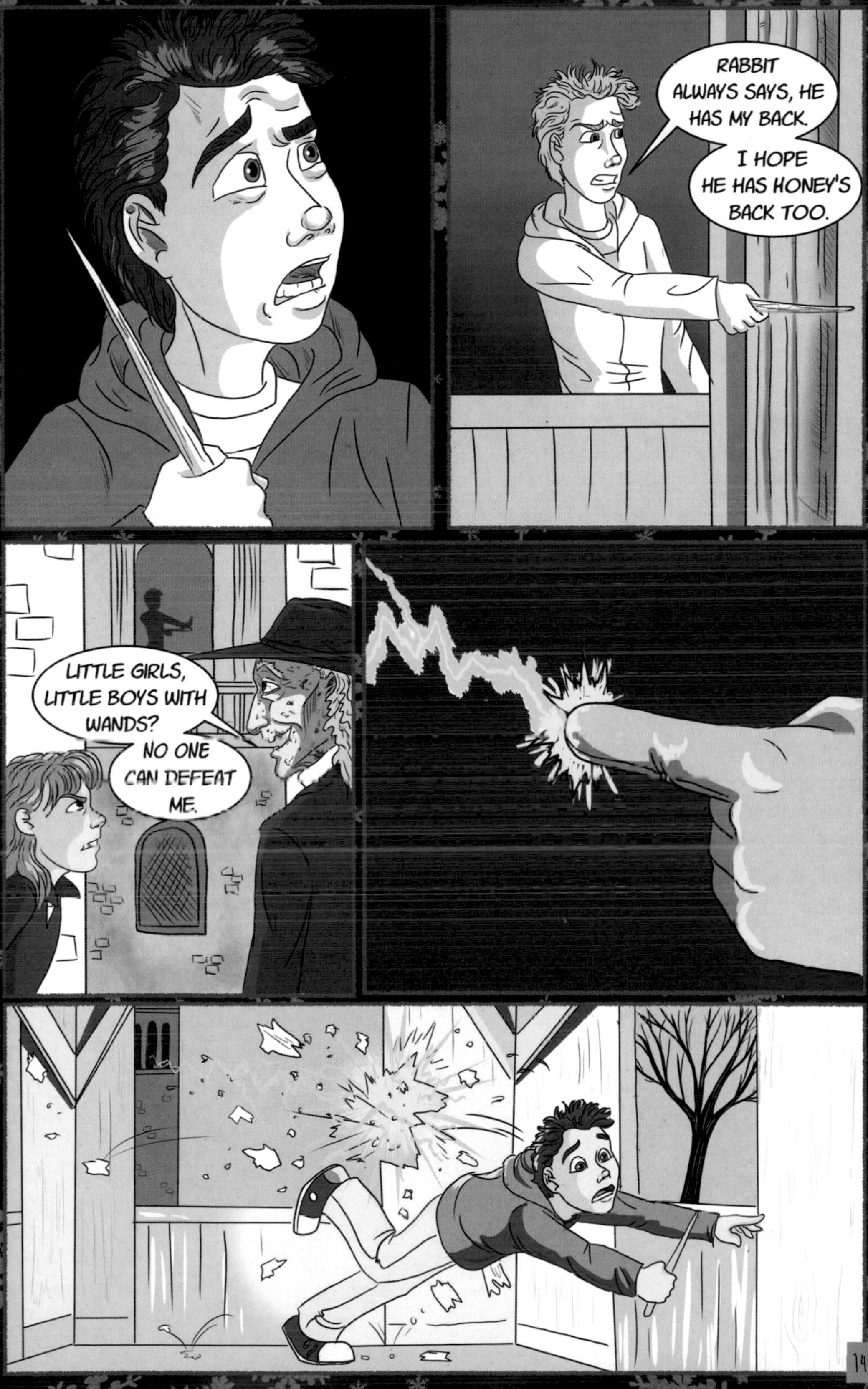
RABBIT ALWAYS SAYS, HE HAS MY BACK.
I HOPE HE HAS HONEY'S BACK TOO.
LITTLE GIRLS, LITTLE BOYS WITH WANDS?
NO ONE CAN DEFEAT ME.

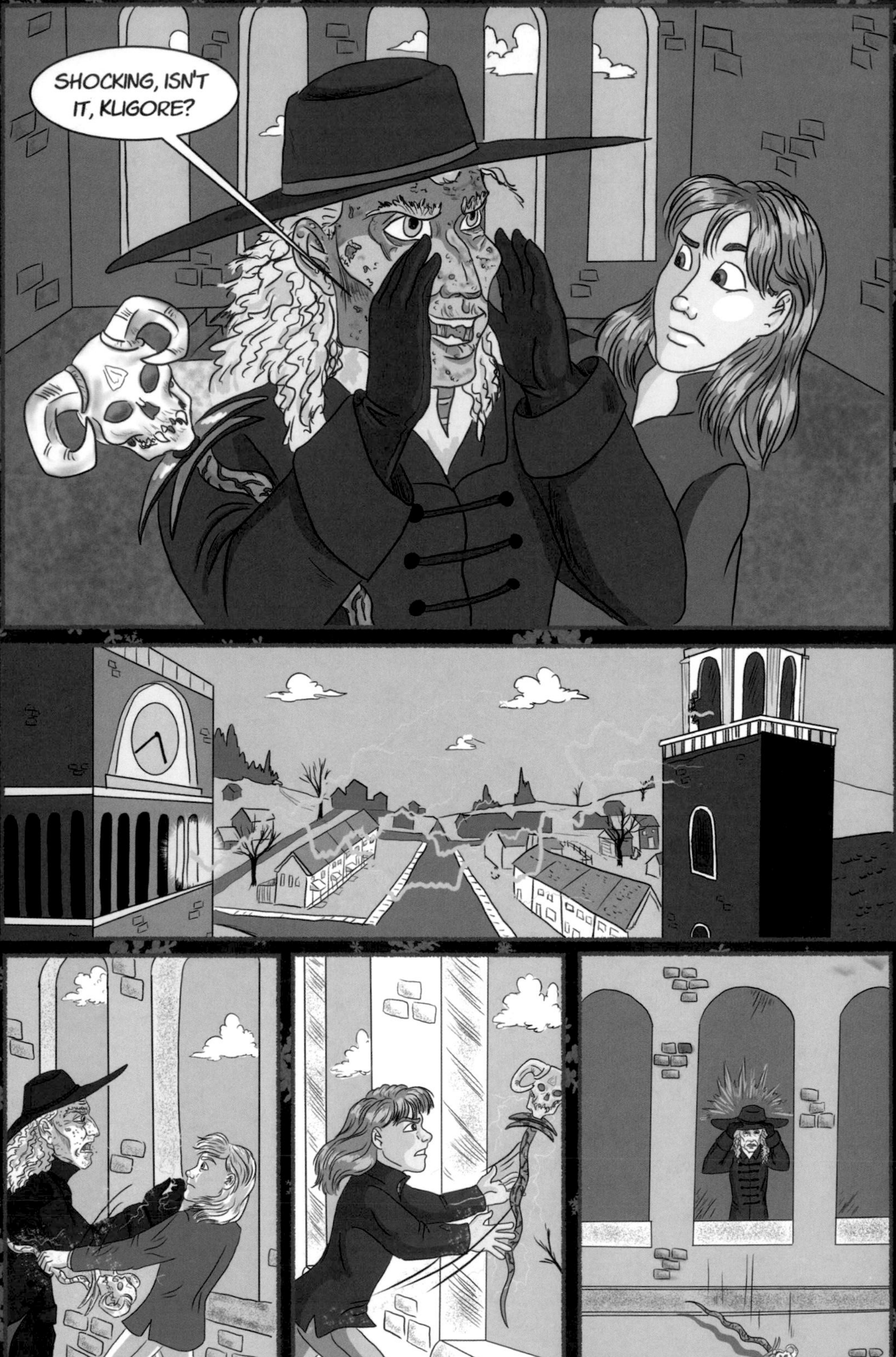
SHOCKING, ISN'T IT, KLIGORE?

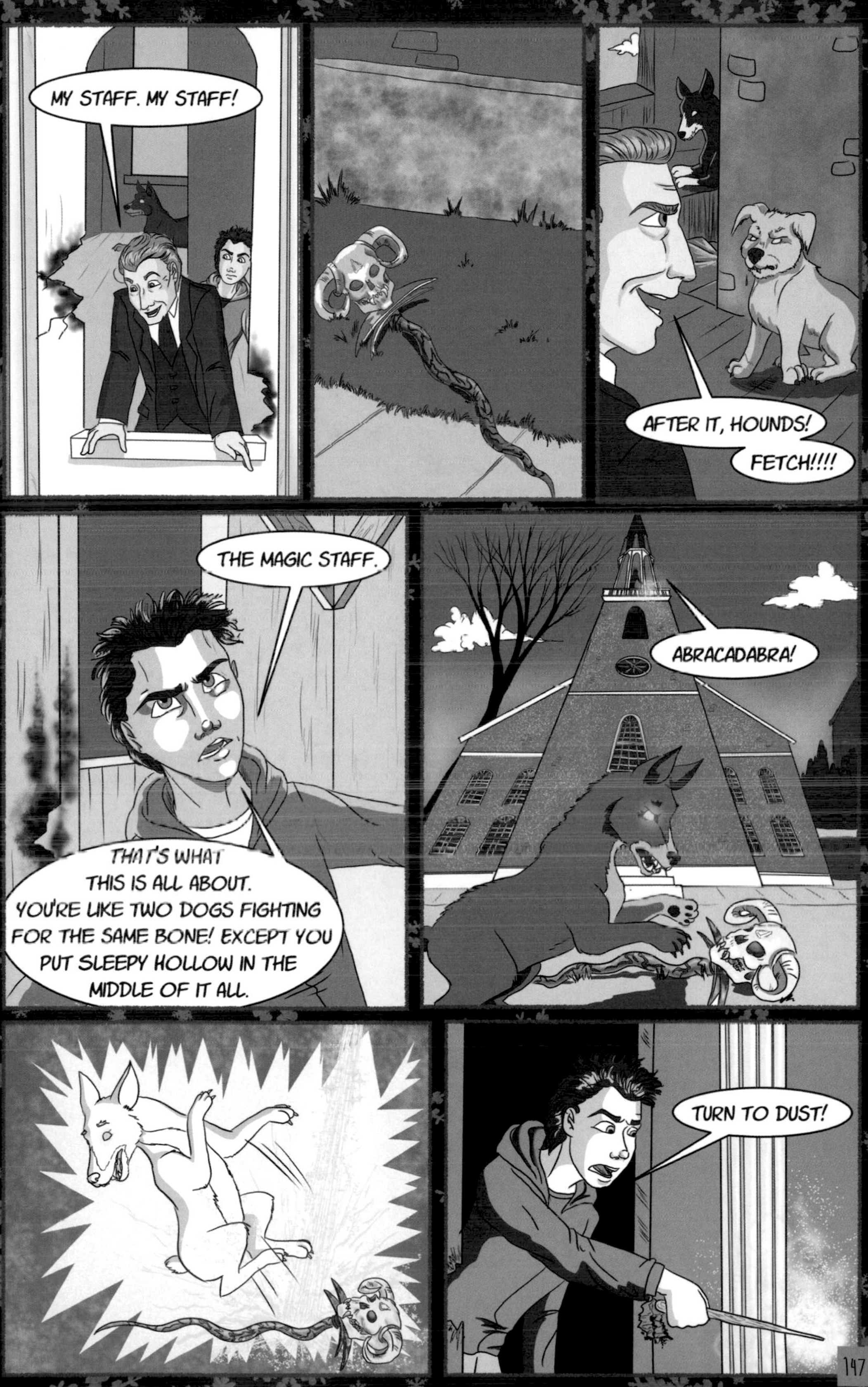
MY STAFF. MY STAFF!
AFTER IT, HOUNDS!
FETCH!!!!
THE MAGIC STAFF.
THAT'S WHAT THIS IS ALL ABOUT. YOU'RE LIKE TWO DOGS FIGHTING FOR THE SAME BONE! EXCEPT YOU PUT SLEEPY HOLLOW IN THE MIDDLE OF IT ALL.
ABRACADABRA!
TURN TO DUST!

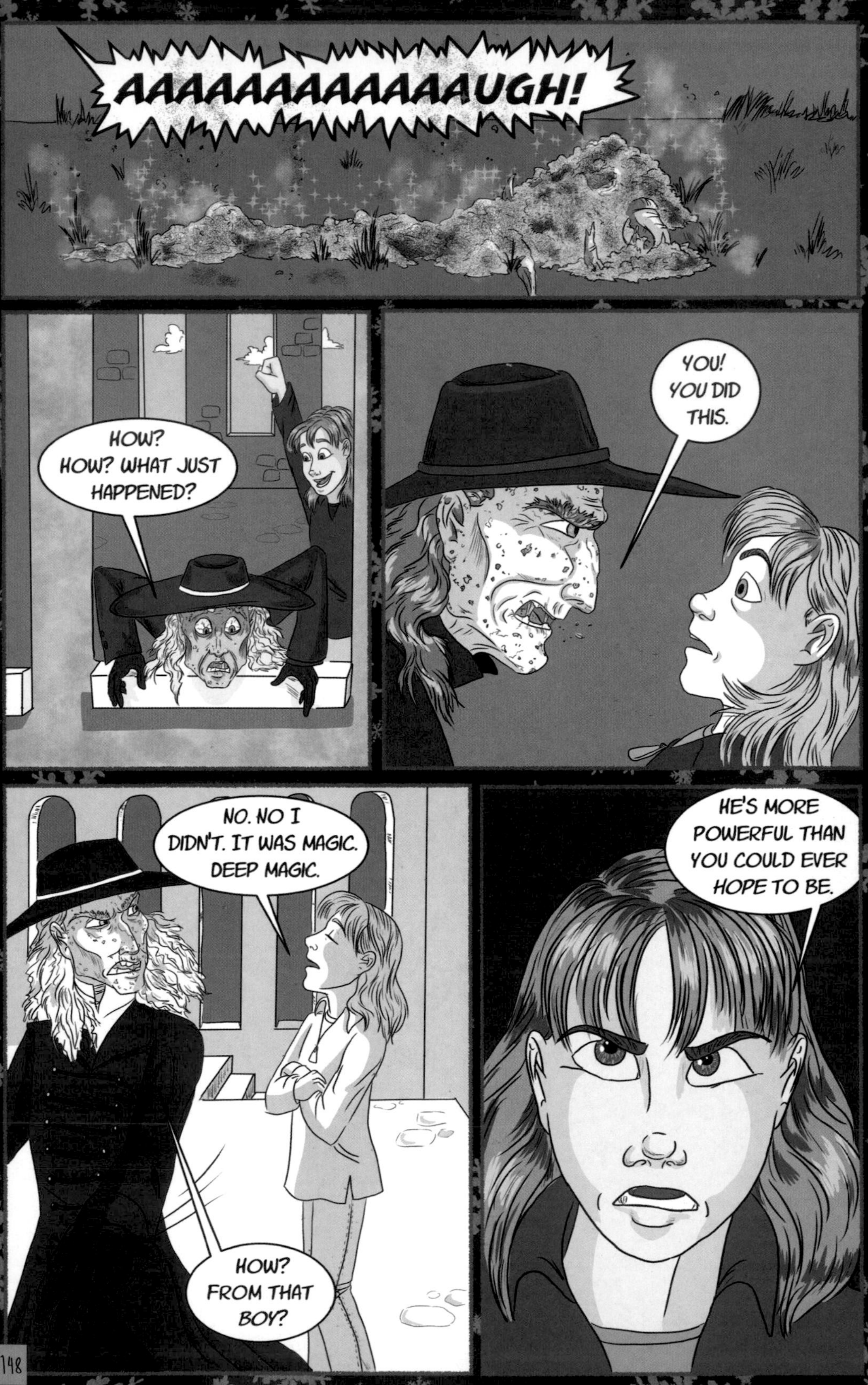
AAAAAAAAAAAAUGH!
HOW? HOW? WHAT JUST HAPPENED?
YOU! YOU DID THIS.
NO. NO I DIDN'T. IT WAS MAGIC. DEEP MAGIC.
HOW? FROM THAT BOY?
HE'S MORE POWERFUL THAN YOU COULD EVER HOPE TO BE.

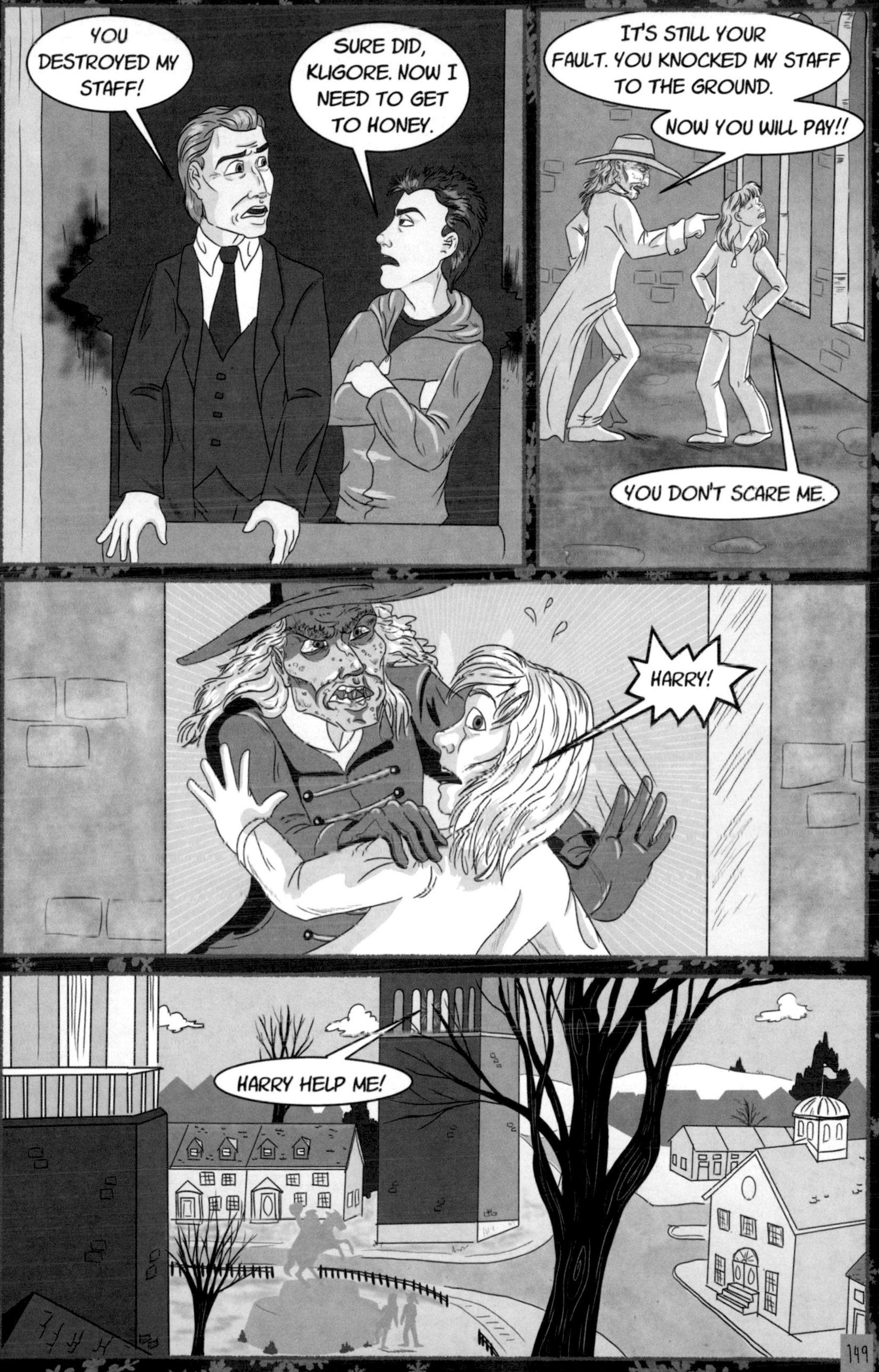
YOU DESTROYED MY STAFF!
SURE DID, KLIGORE. NOW I NEED TO GET TO HONEY.
IT'S STILL YOUR FAULT. YOU KNOCKED MY STAFF TO THE GROUND.
NOW YOU WILL PAY!!
YOU DON'T SCARE ME.
HARRY!
HARRY HELP ME!

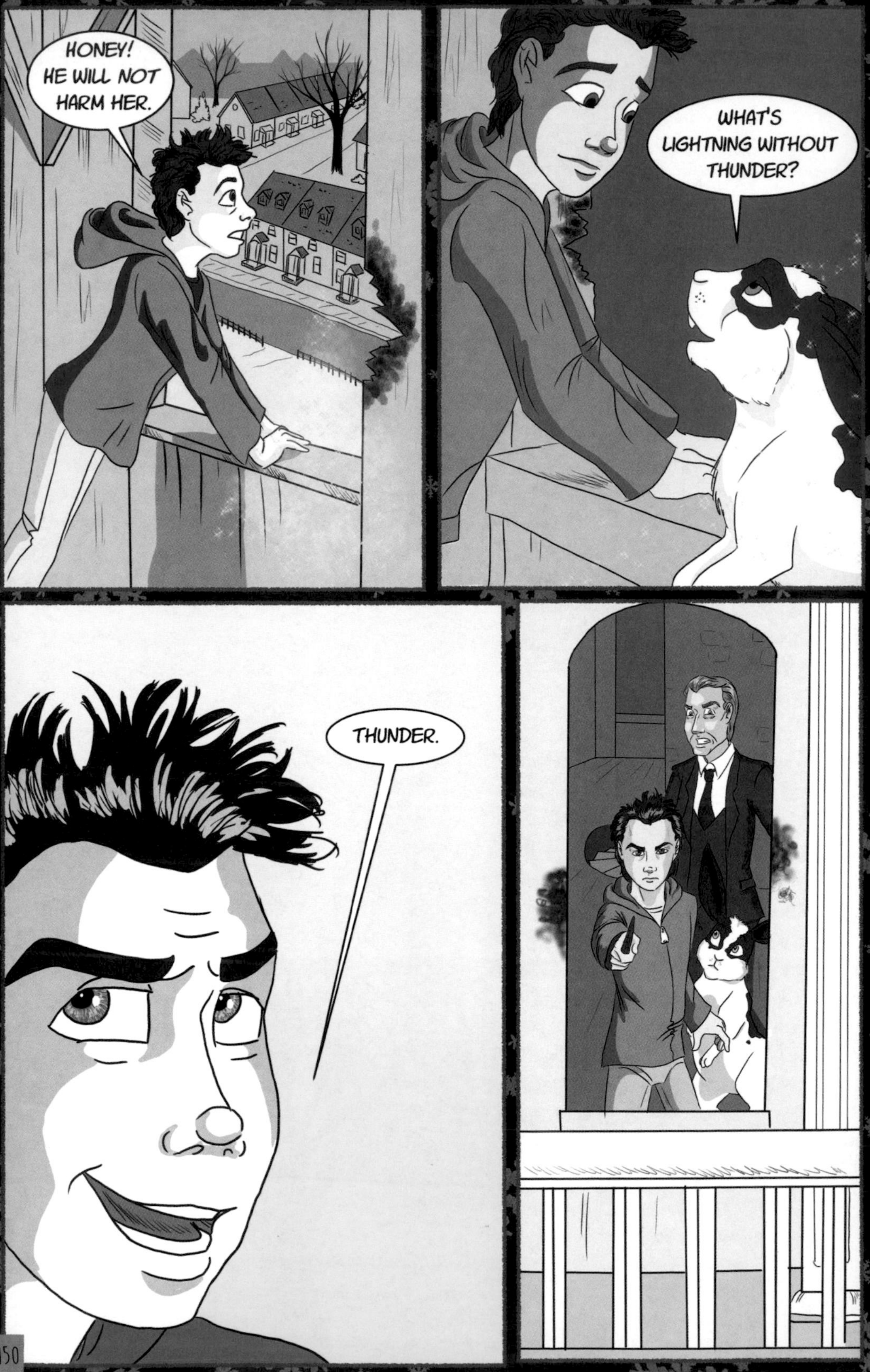
HONEY! HE WILL NOT HARM HER.
WHAT'S LIGHTNING WITHOUT THUNDER?
THUNDER.

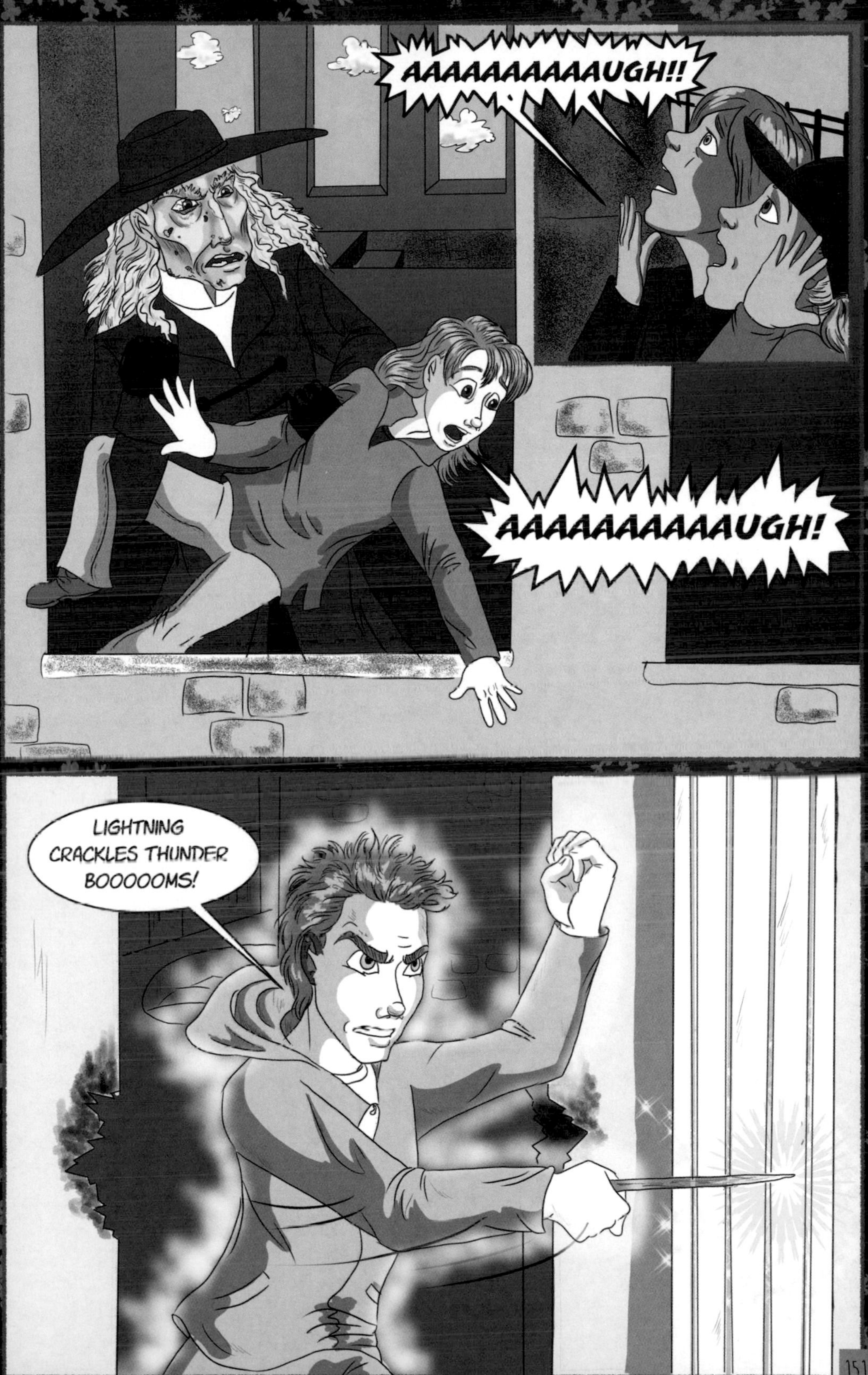
AAAAAAAAAAUGH!!
AAAAAAAAAAAUGH!
LIGHTNING CRACKLES THUNDER BOOOOOMS!

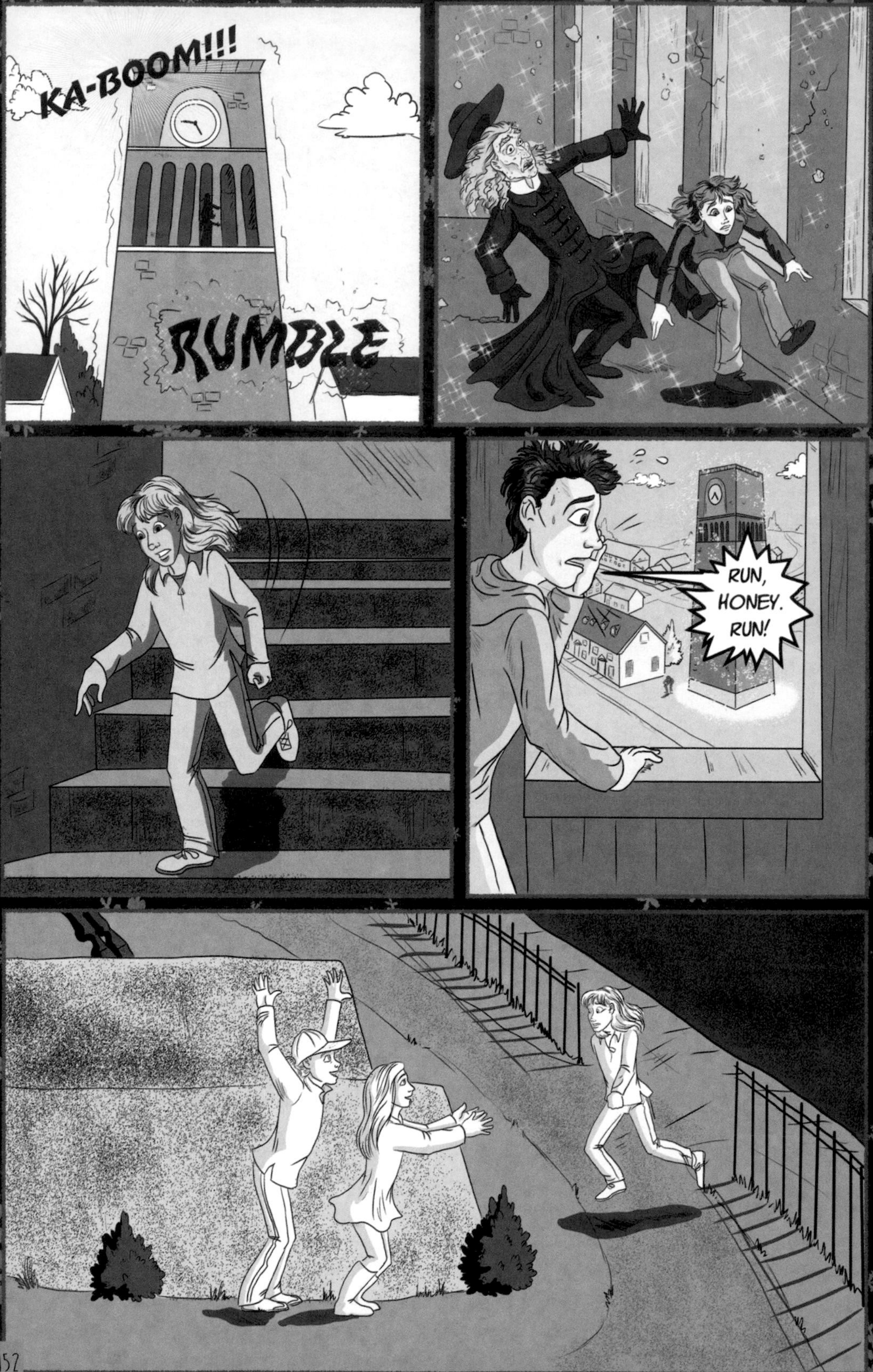
KA-BOOM!!!
RUMBLE
RUN, HONEY. RUN!

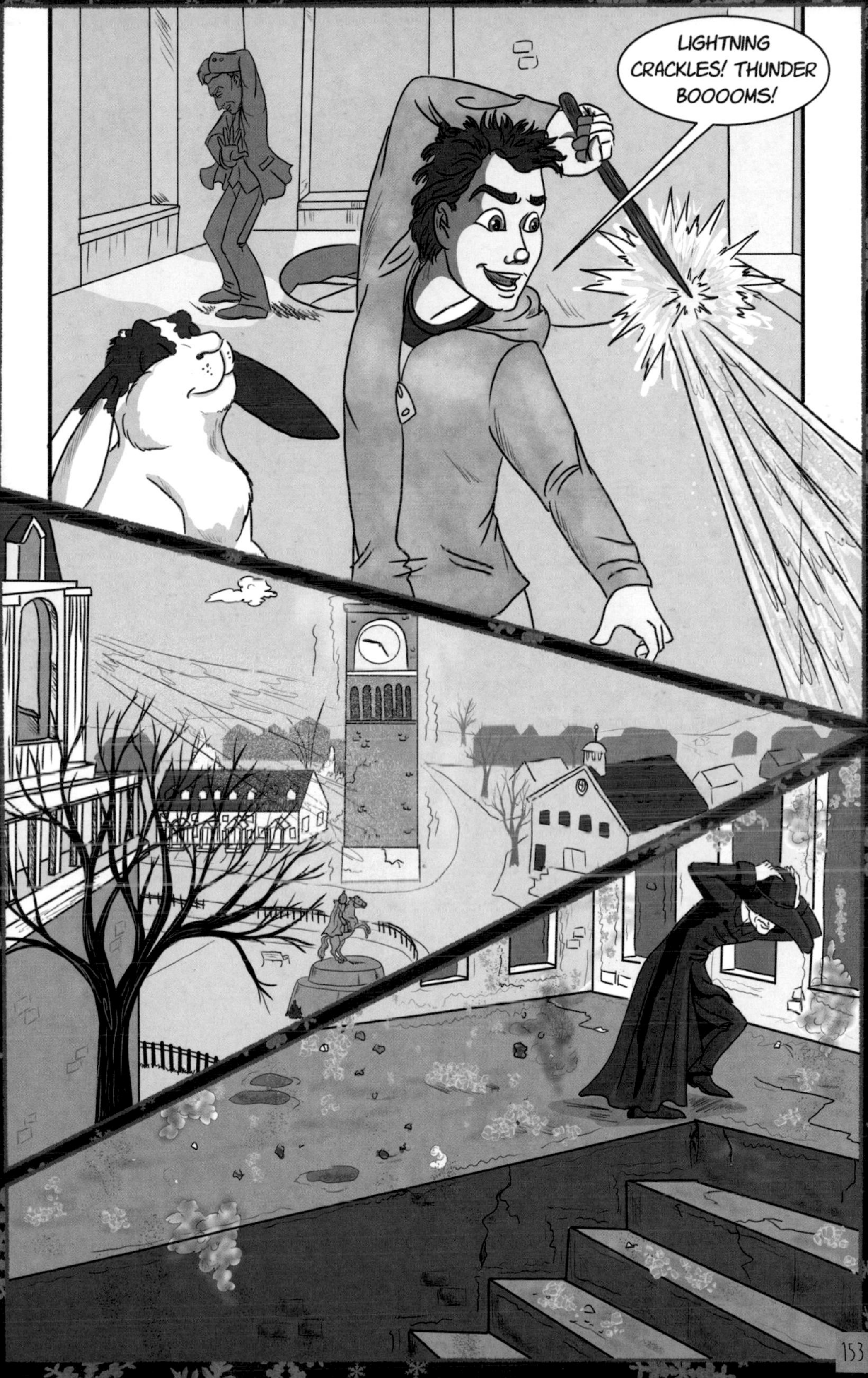
LIGHTNING CRACKLES! THUNDER BOOOOMS!

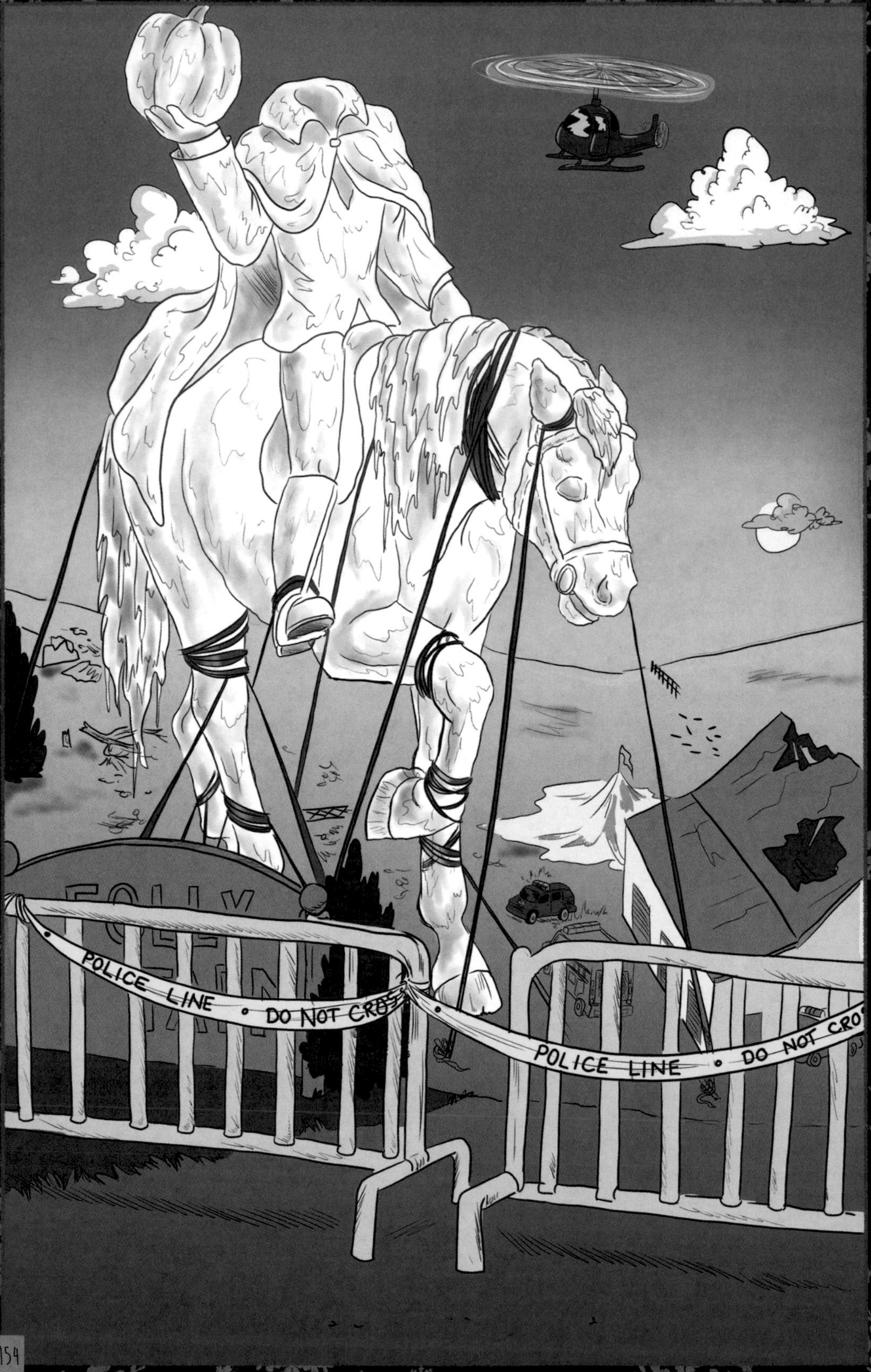
POLICE LINE • DO NOT CROS
POLICE LINE • DO NOT CRO

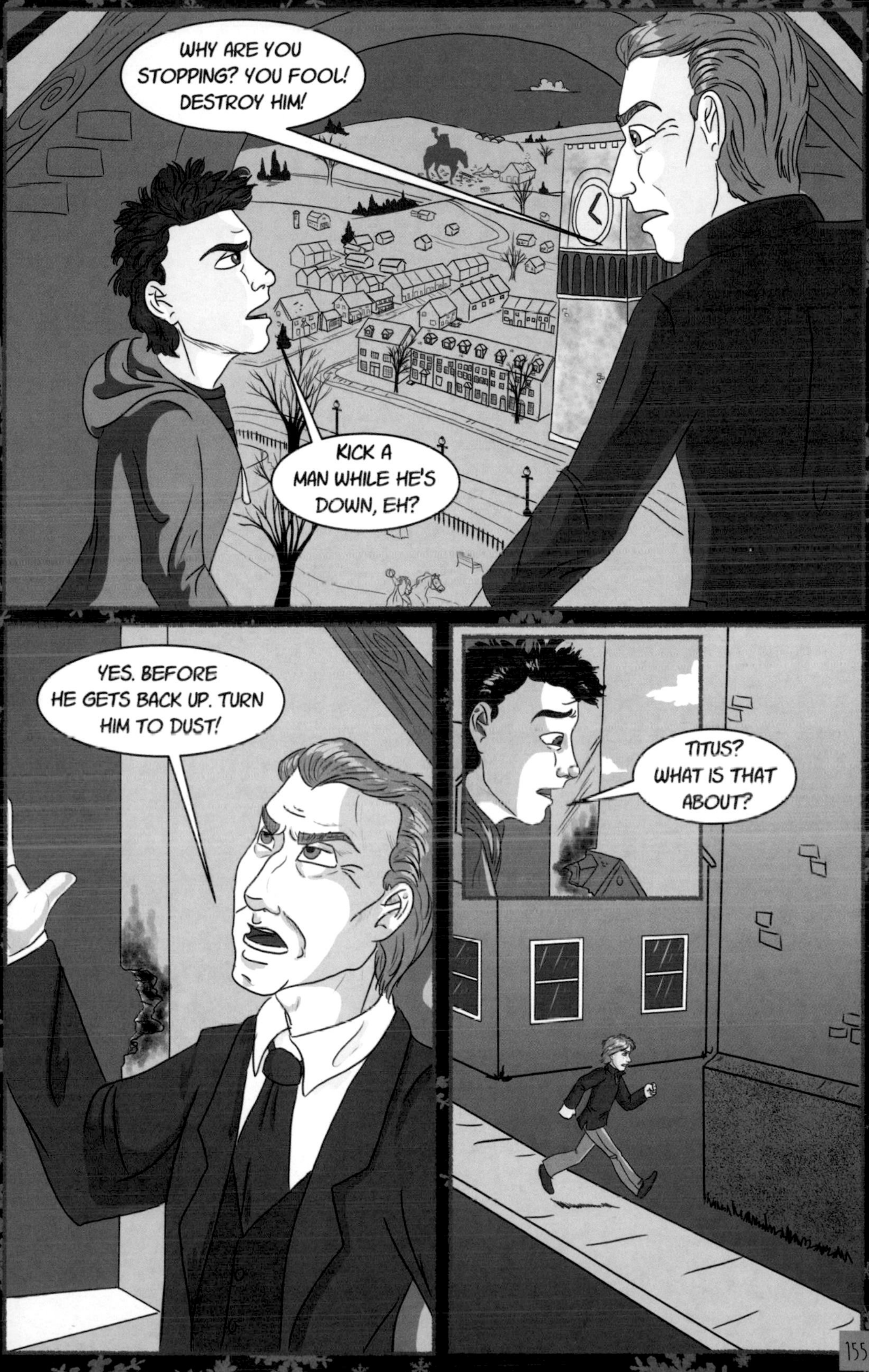
WHY ARE YOU STOPPING? YOU FOOL! DESTROY HIM!
KICK A MAN WHILE HE'S DOWN, EH?
YES. BEFORE HE GETS BACK UP. TURN HIM TO DUST!
TITUS? WHAT IS THAT ABOUT?

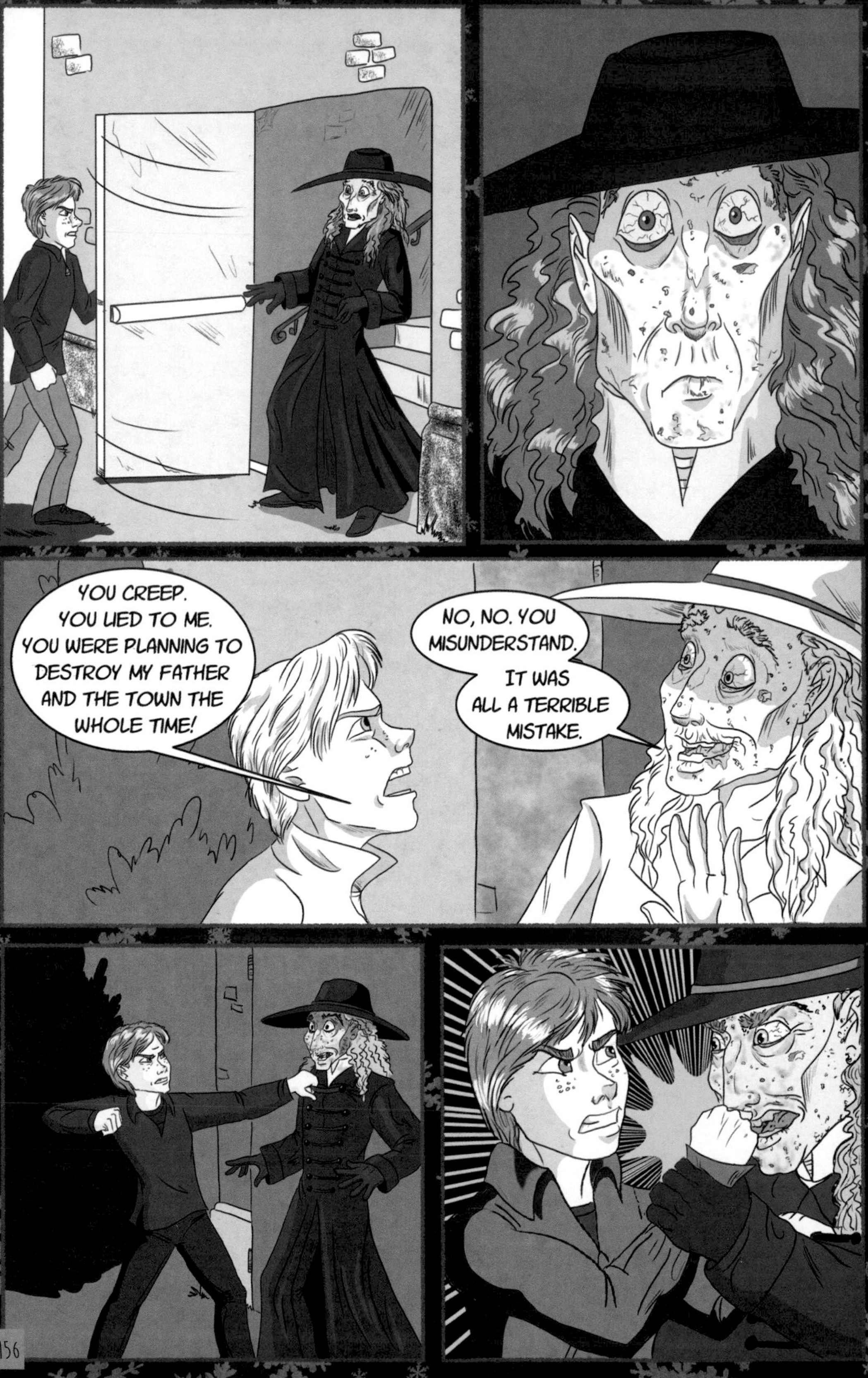
YOU CREEP.
YOU LIED TO ME.
YOU WERE PLANNING TO DESTROY MY FATHER AND THE TOWN THE WHOLE TIME!
NO, NO. YOU MISUNDERSTAND.
IT WAS ALL A TERRIBLE MISTAKE.

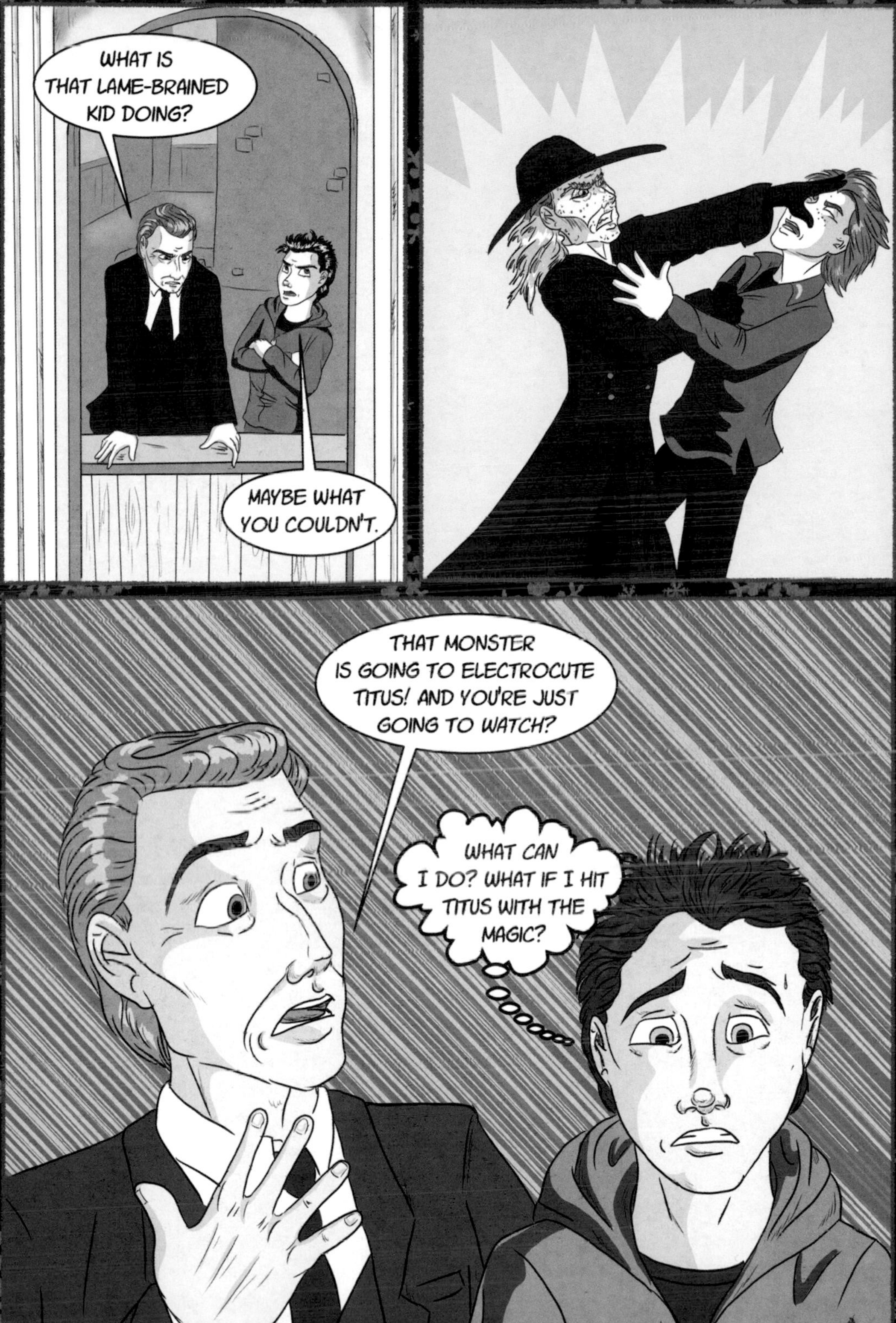
WHAT IS THAT LAME-BRAINED KID DOING?
MAYBE WHAT YOU COULDN'T.
THAT MONSTER IS GOING TO ELECTROCUTE TITUS! AND YOU'RE JUST GOING TO WATCH?
WHAT CAN I DO? WHAT IF I HIT TITUS WITH THE MAGIC?

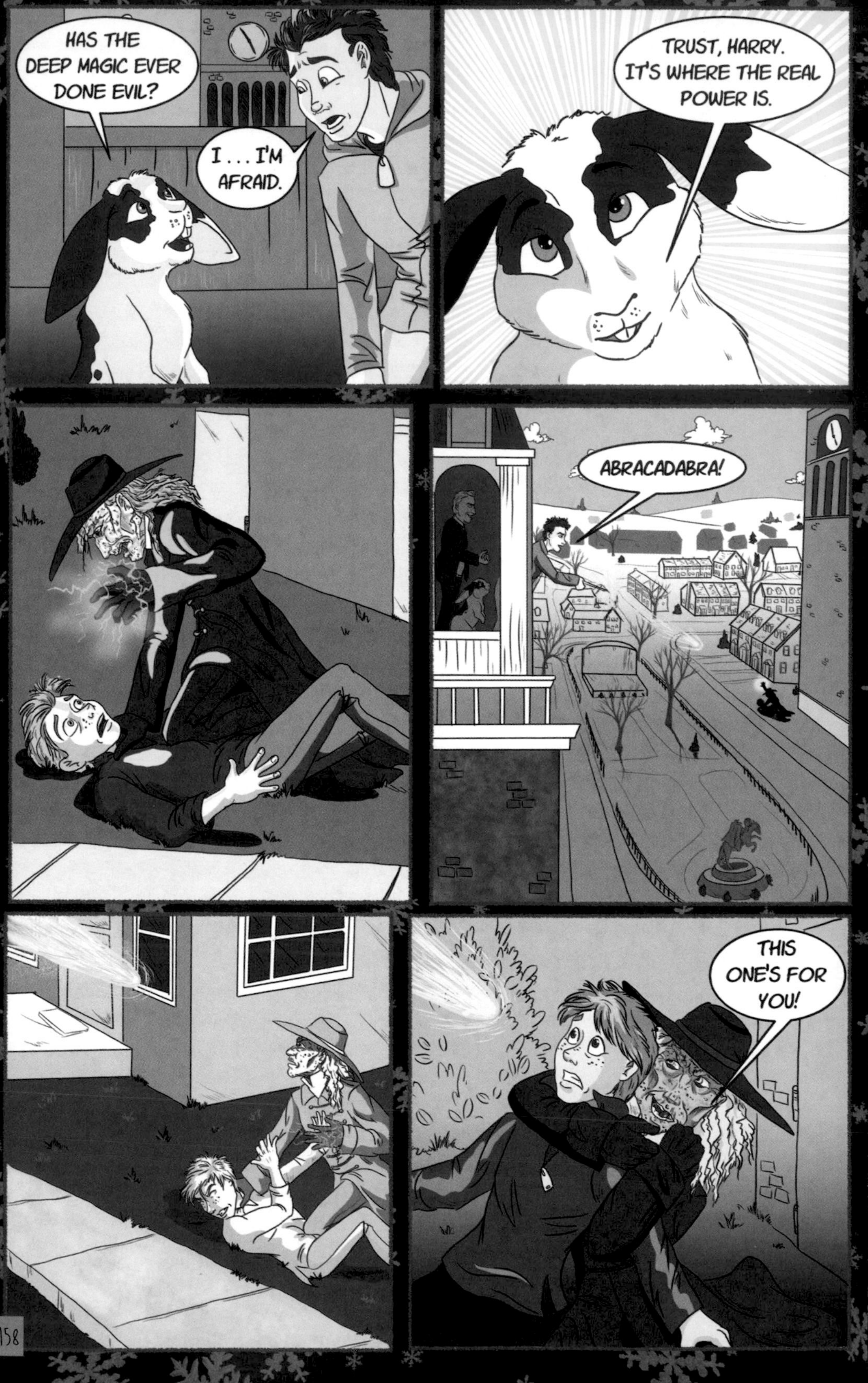
HAS THE DEEP MAGIC EVER DONE EVIL?
I . . . I'M AFRAID.
TRUST, HARRY. IT'S WHERE THE REAL POWER IS.
ABRACADABRA!
THIS ONE'S FOR YOU!

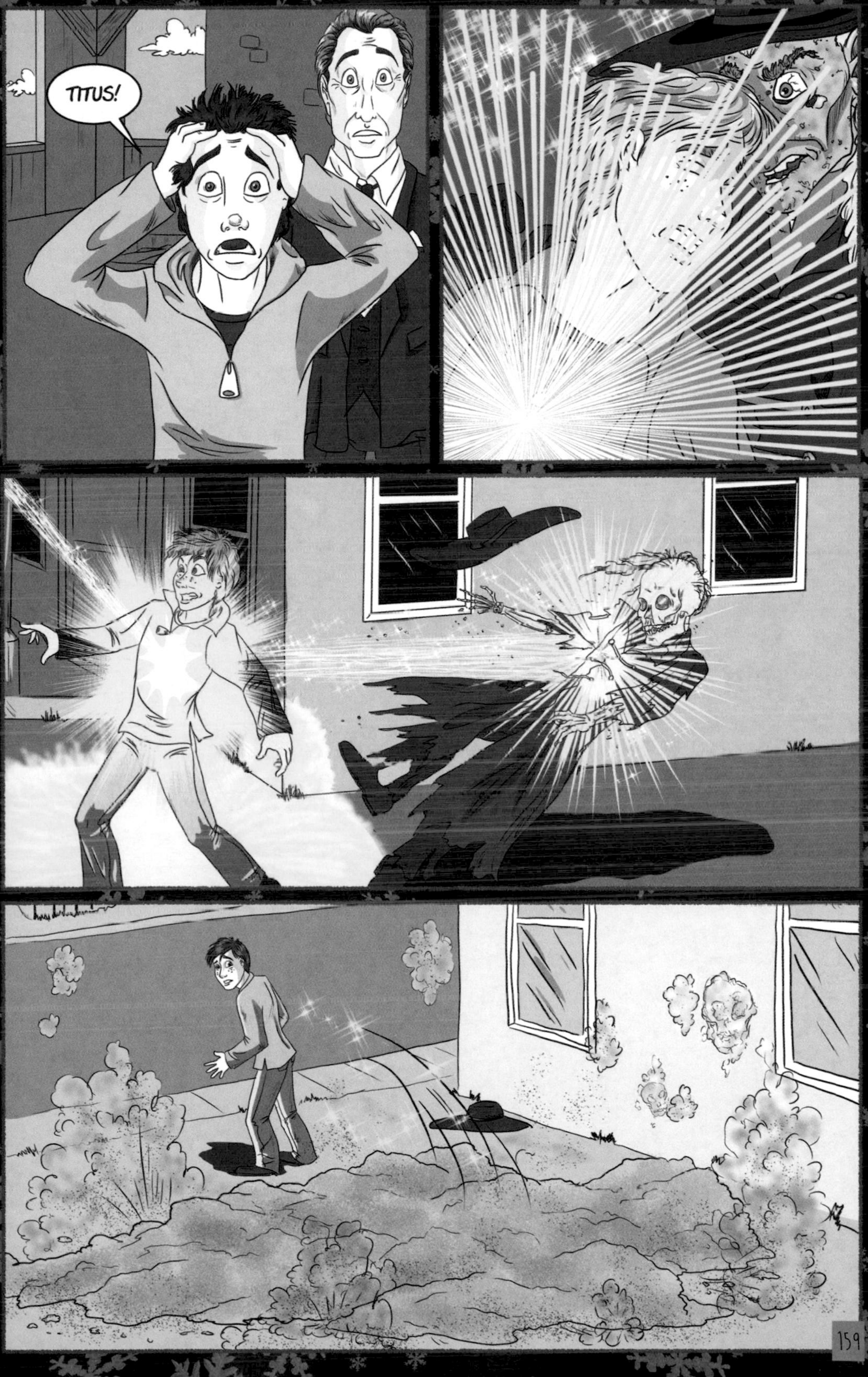
TITUS!

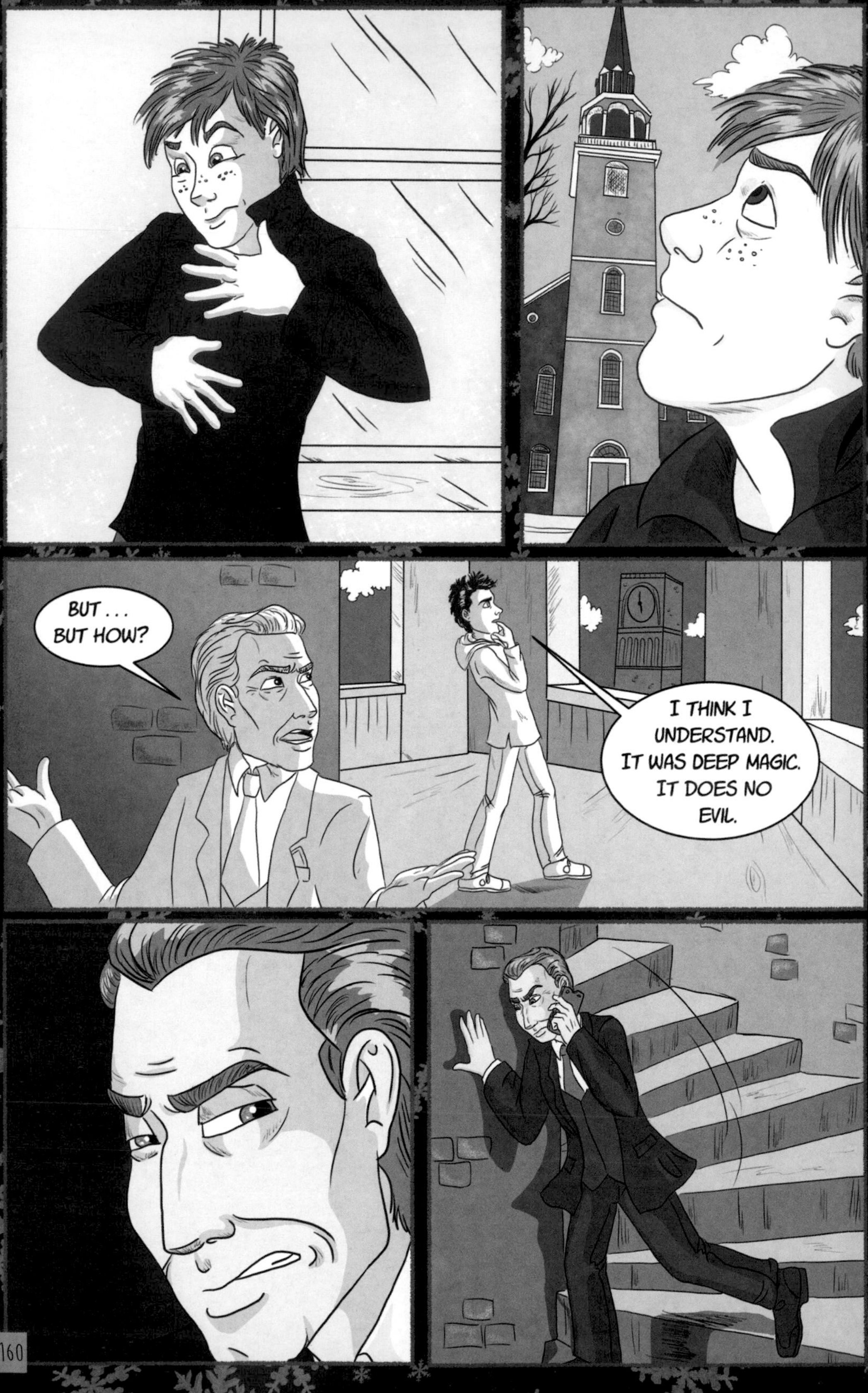
BUT . . .
BUT HOW?
I THINK I UNDERSTAND. IT WAS DEEP MAGIC. IT DOES NO EVIL.

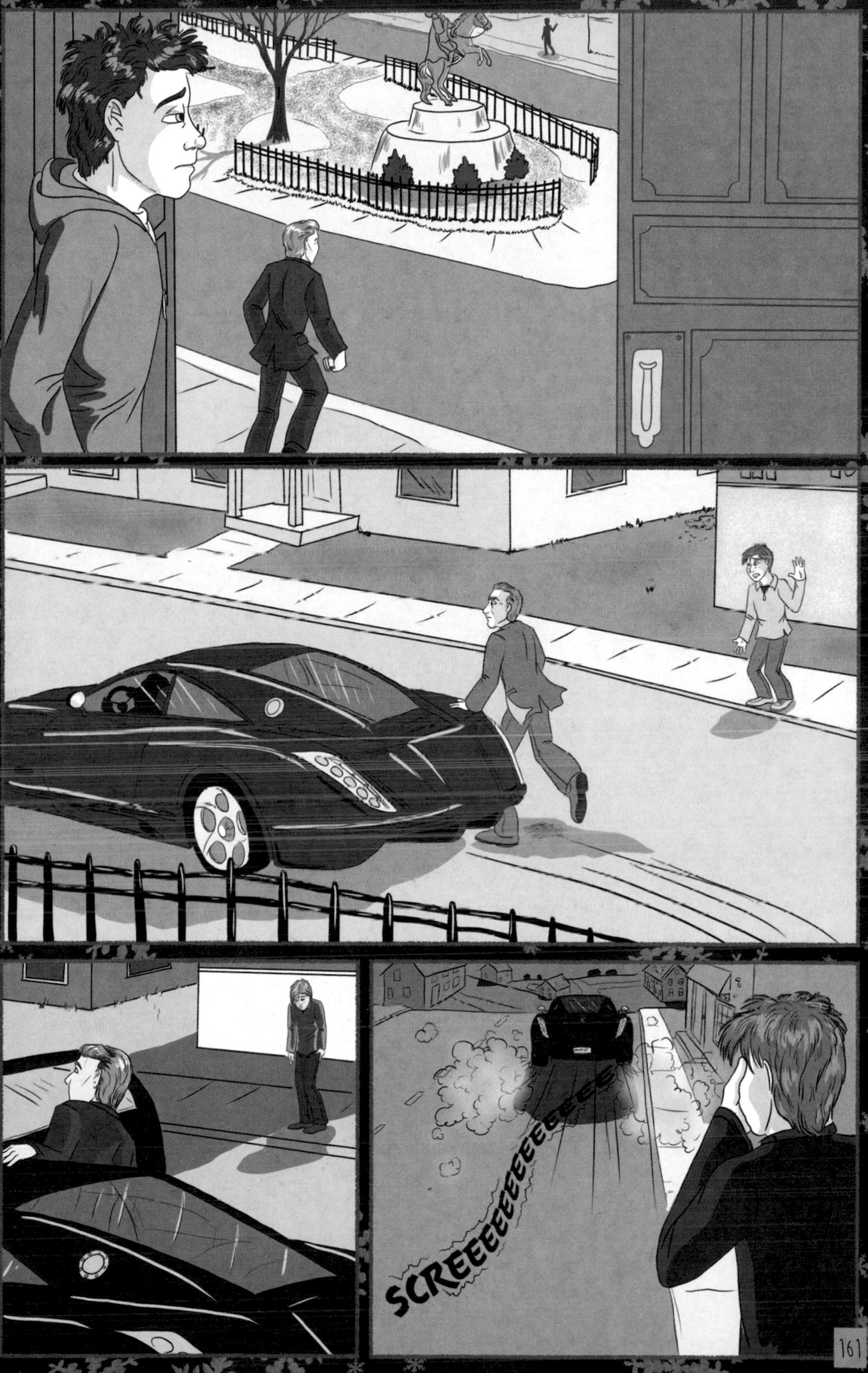
SCREEEEEEEEEEEEEE

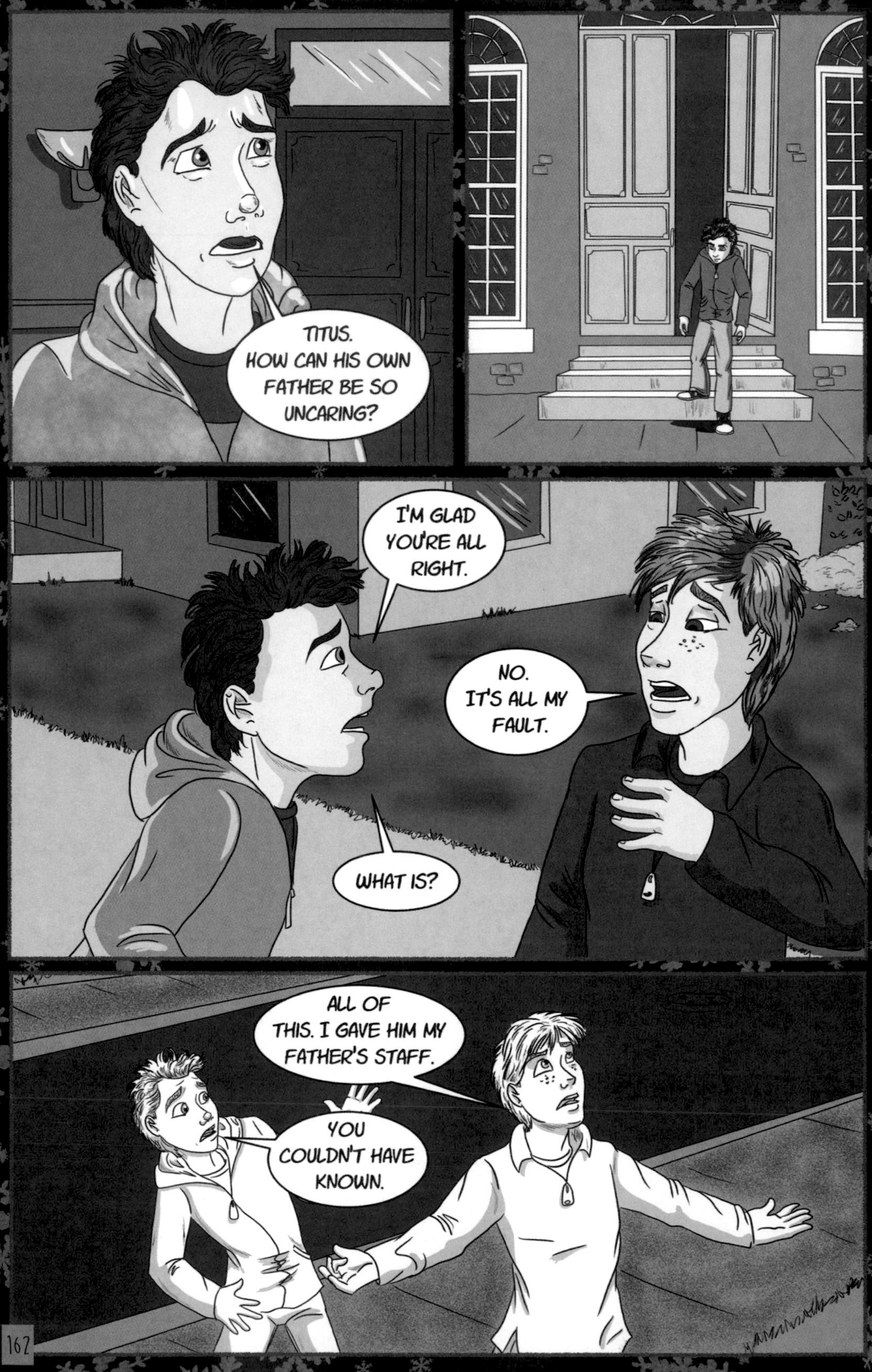
TITUS. HOW CAN HIS OWN FATHER BE SO UNCARING?
I'M GLAD YOU'RE ALL RIGHT.
NO. IT'S ALL MY FAULT.
WHAT IS?
ALL OF THIS. I GAVE HIM MY FATHER'S STAFF.
YOU COULDN'T HAVE KNOWN.

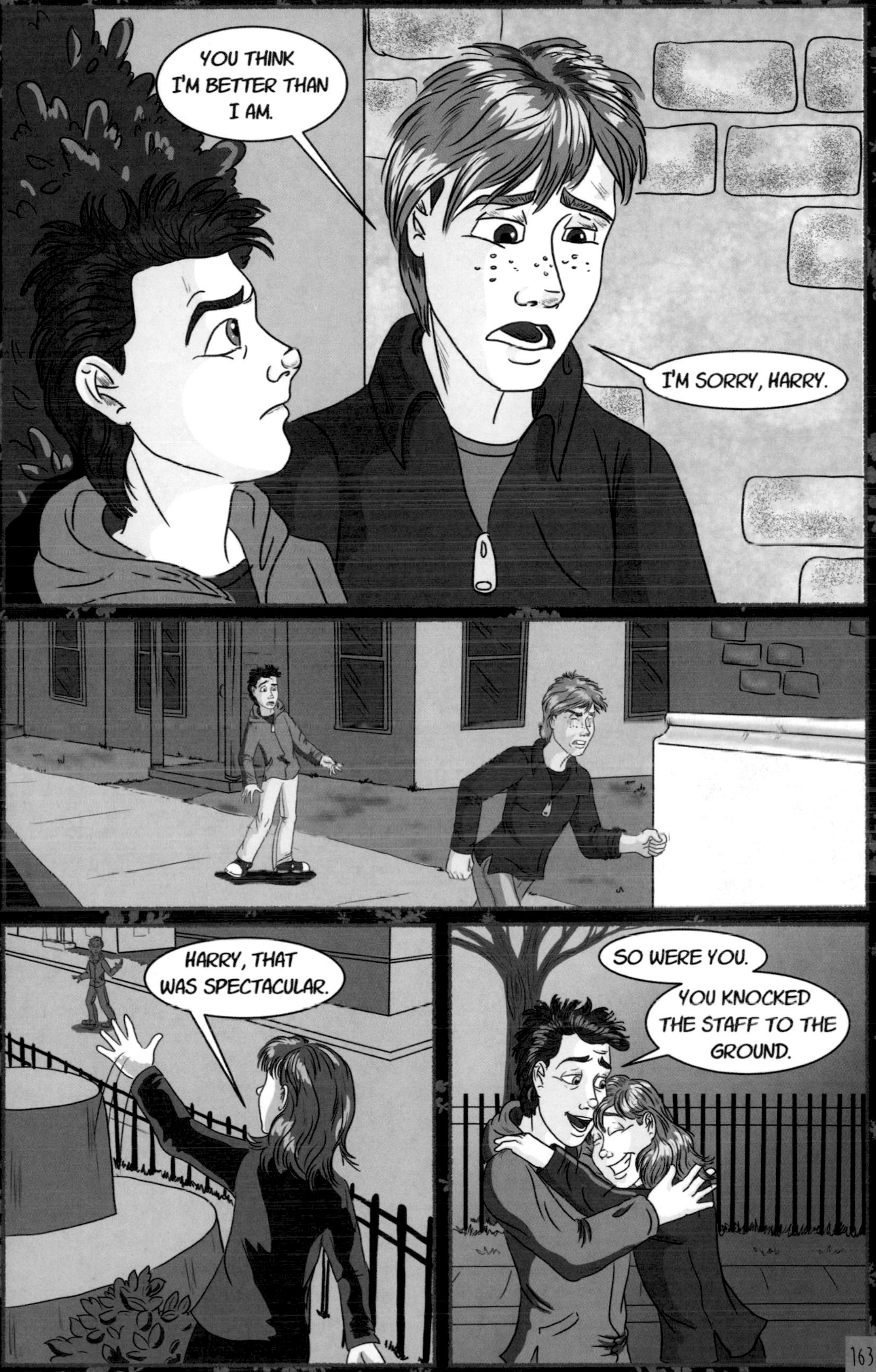
YOU THINK I'M BETTER THAN I AM.
I'M SORRY, HARRY.
HARRY, THAT WAS SPECTACULAR.
SO WERE YOU.
YOU KNOCKED THE STAFF TO THE GROUND.

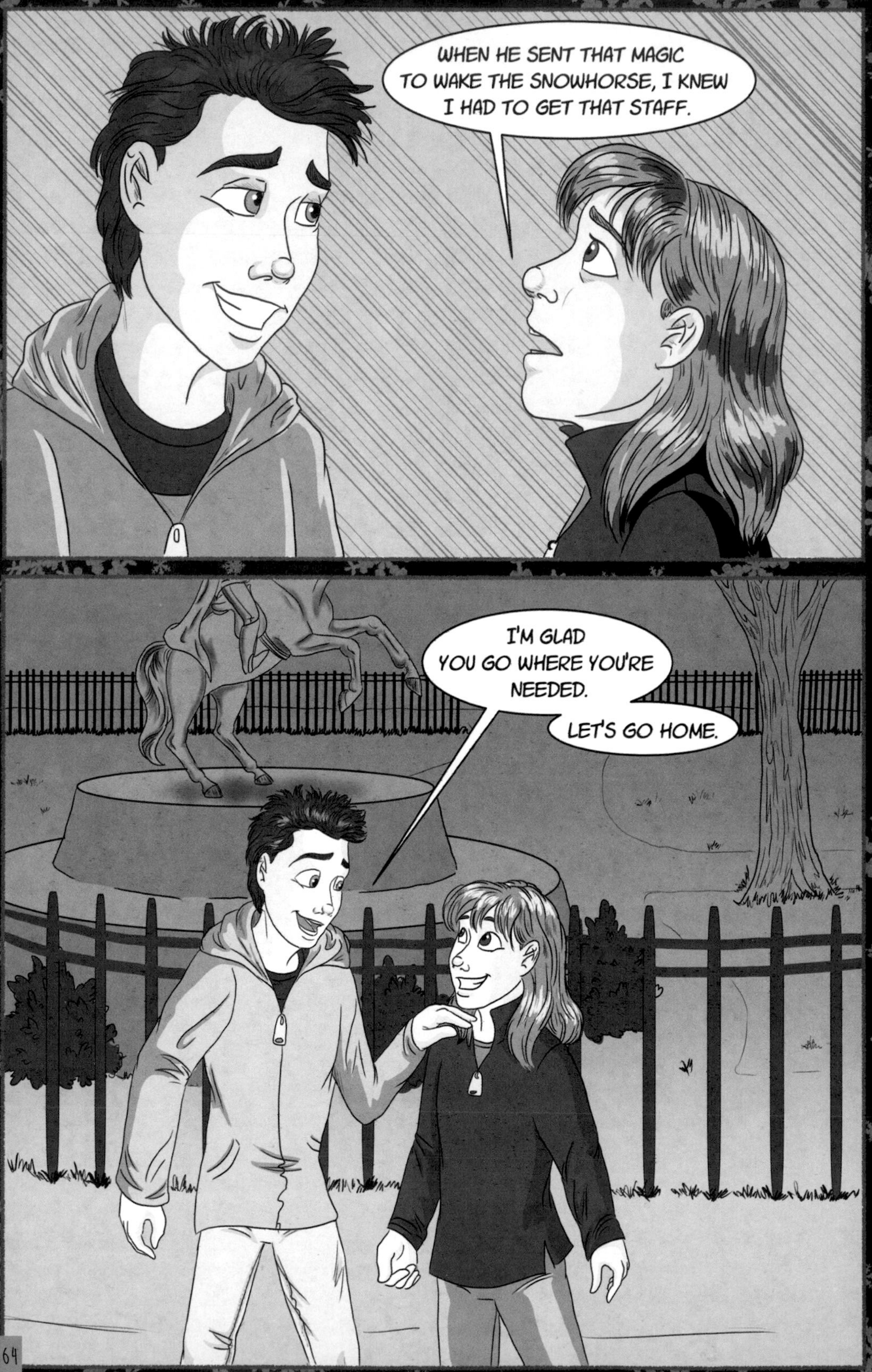
WHEN HE SENT THAT MAGIC TO WAKE THE SNOWHORSE, I KNEW I HAD TO GET THAT STAFF.
I'M GLAD YOU GO WHERE YOU'RE NEEDED.
LET'S GO HOME.

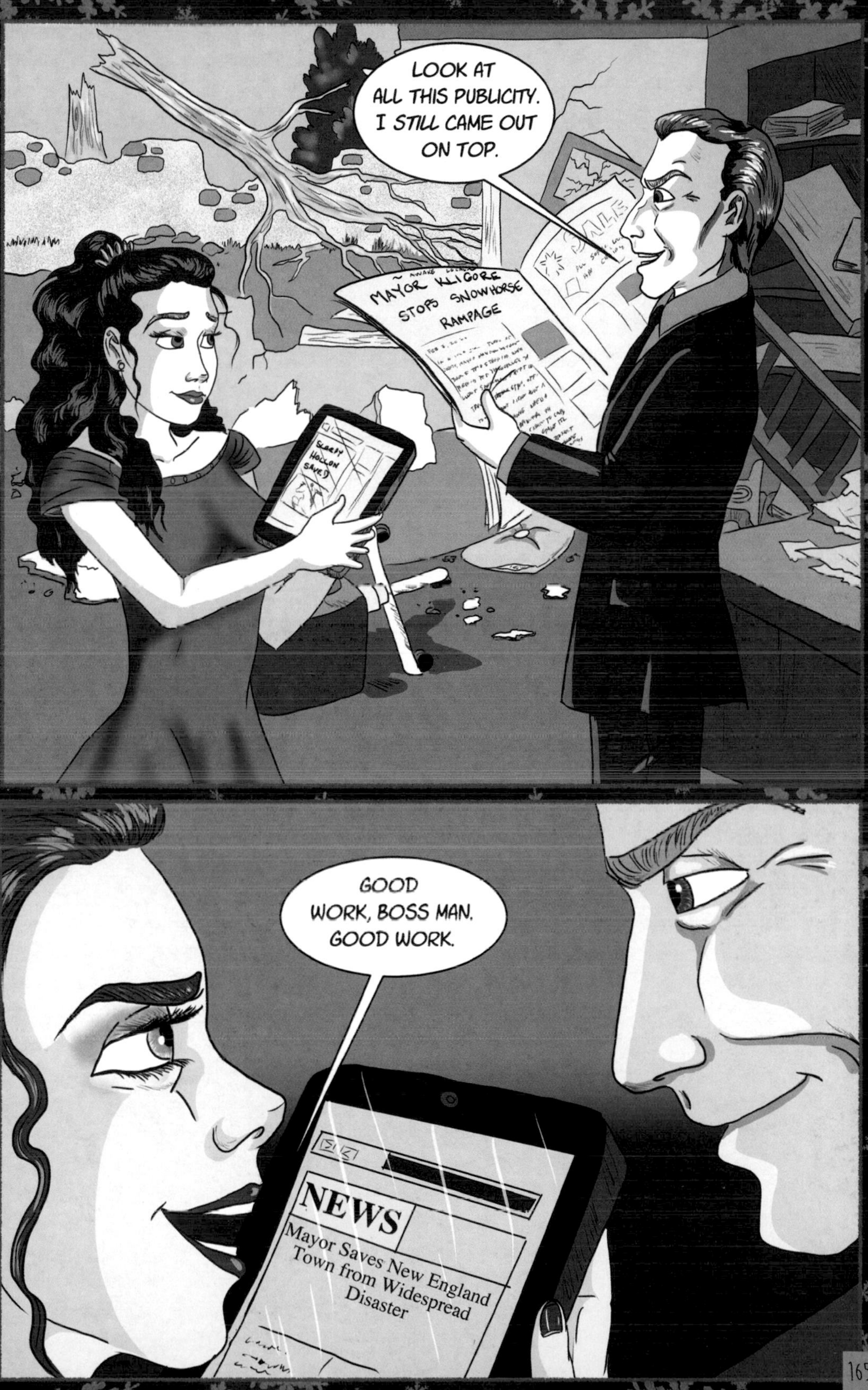
LOOK AT ALL THIS PUBLICITY. I STILL CAME OUT ON TOP.
MAYOR KLIGORE STOPS SNOWHORSE RAMPAGE
SLEEPY HOLLOW SAVED!
GOOD WORK, BOSS MAN. GOOD WORK.
NEWS
Mayor Saves New England Town from Widespread Disaster

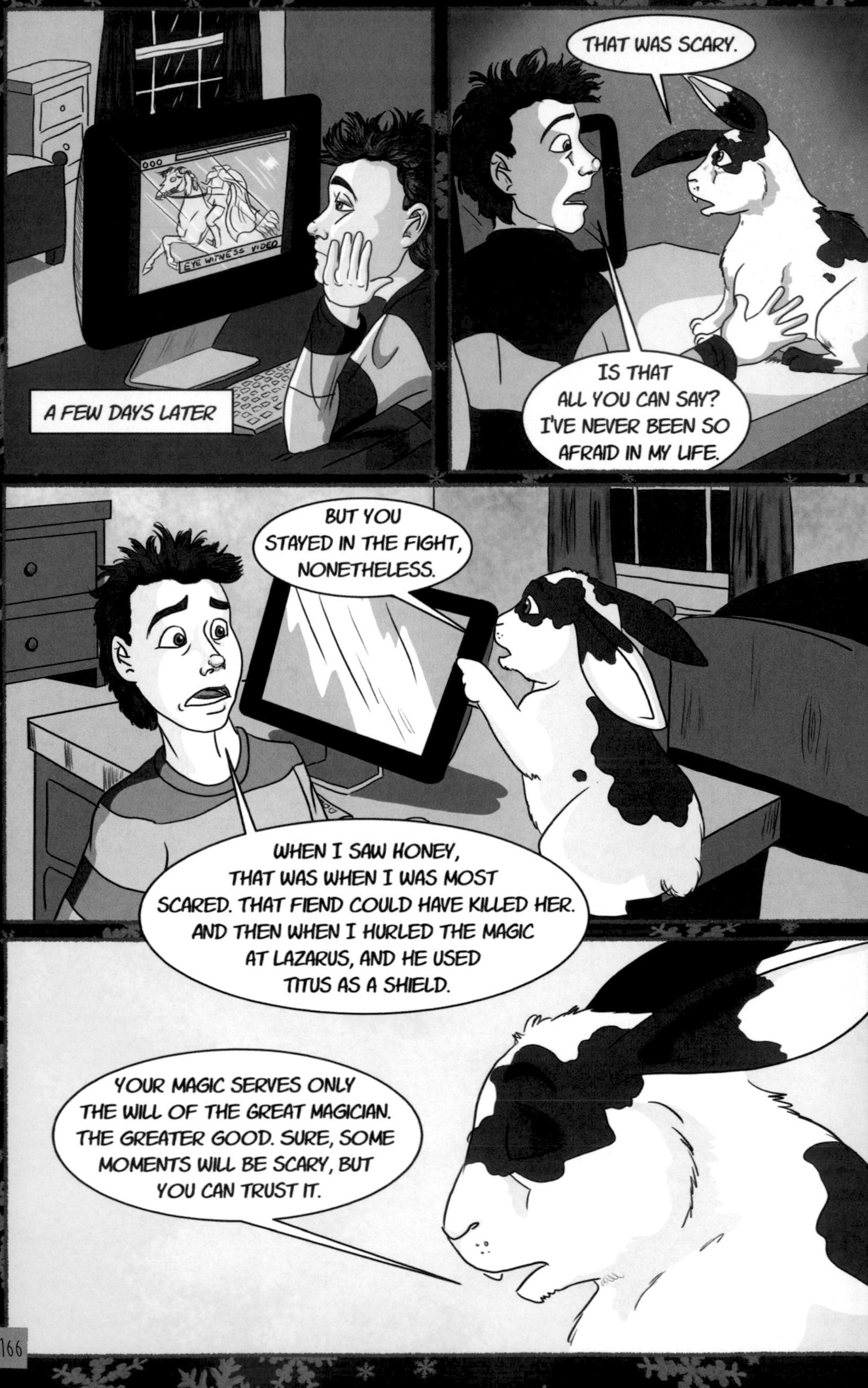
A FEW DAYS LATER
EYE WITNESS VIDEO
THAT WAS SCARY.
IS THAT ALL YOU CAN SAY? I'VE NEVER BEEN SO AFRAID IN MY LIFE.
BUT YOU STAYED IN THE FIGHT, NONETHELESS.
WHEN I SAW HONEY, THAT WAS WHEN I WAS MOST SCARED. THAT FIEND COULD HAVE KILLED HER. AND THEN WHEN I HURLED THE MAGIC AT LAZARUS, AND HE USED TITUS AS A SHIELD.
YOUR MAGIC SERVES ONLY THE WILL OF THE GREAT MAGICIAN. THE GREATER GOOD. SURE, SOME MOMENTS WILL BE SCARY, BUT YOU CAN TRUST IT.

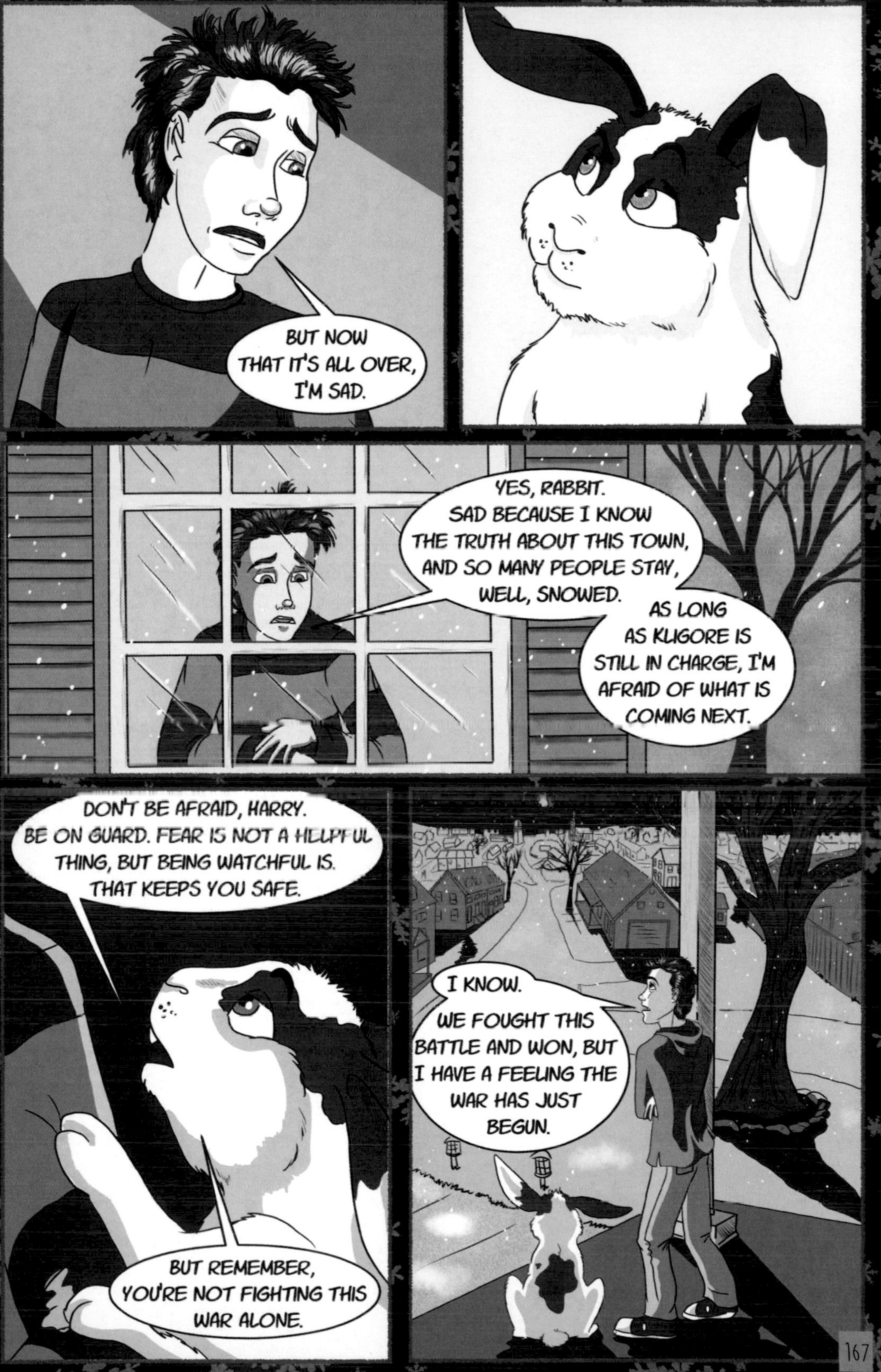
BUT NOW THAT IT'S ALL OVER, I'M SAD.
YES, RABBIT. SAD BECAUSE I KNOW THE TRUTH ABOUT THIS TOWN, AND SO MANY PEOPLE STAY, WELL, SNOWED.
AS LONG AS KLIGORE IS STILL IN CHARGE, I'M AFRAID OF WHAT IS COMING NEXT.
DON'T BE AFRAID, HARRY. BE ON GUARD. FEAR IS NOT A HELPFUL THING, BUT BEING WATCHFUL IS. THAT KEEPS YOU SAFE.
BUT REMEMBER, YOU'RE NOT FIGHTING THIS WAR ALONE.
I KNOW.
WE FOUGHT THIS BATTLE AND WON, BUT I HAVE A FEELING THE WAR HAS JUST BEGUN.

ABOUT THE AUTHOR

Mark Andrew Poe

INKADINK author Mark Andrew Poe never thought about being a children's writer growing up. His dream was to love and care for animals, specifically his friends in the rabbit community.

Along the way, Mark became successful in all sorts of interesting careers. He entered the print and publishing world as a young man, and his company did really, really well.

Mark became a popular and nationally sought-after health care advocate for the care and well-being of rabbits.

Years ago, Mark came up with the idea of a story about a young man with a special connection to a world of magic, all revealed through a remarkable rabbit friend. Mark worked on his idea for several years before building a collaborative creative team to help bring his idea to life. And Harry Moon was born.

In 2014, Mark began a multi-book print series project intended to launch *The Adventures of Harry Moon* into the youth marketplace as a hero defined by a love for a magic where love and 'DO NO EVIL' live. Today, Mark continues to work on the many stories of Harry Moon. He lives in suburban Chicago with his wife and his twenty-five rabbits.

harrymoon.com

DEVELOPING SNOWMAN

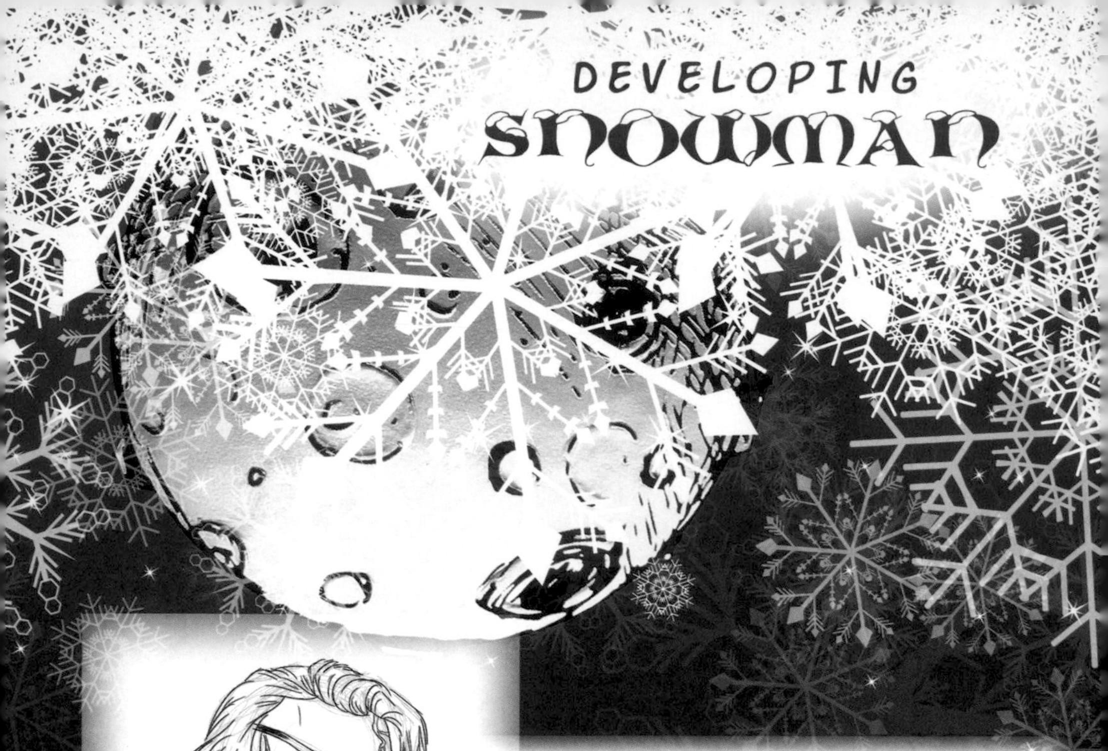

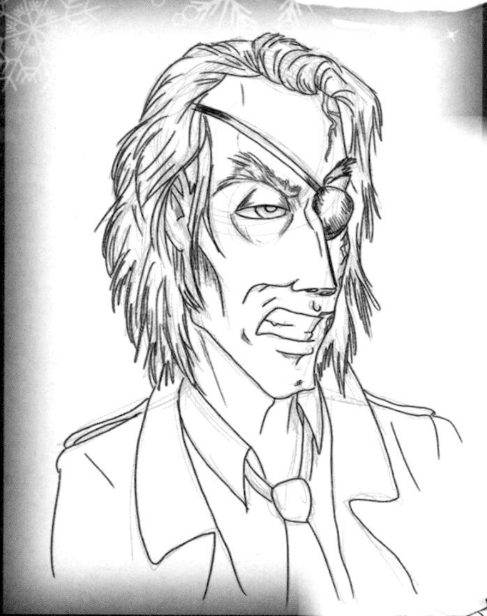

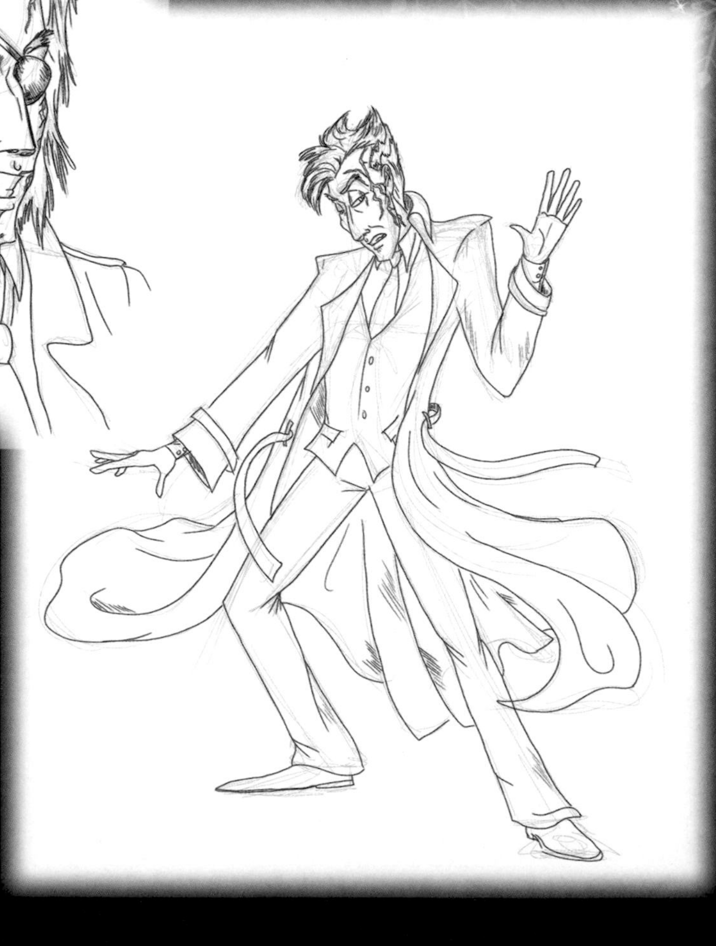

LAZARUS SKETCHES

PAGE STORY DEVELOPMENT

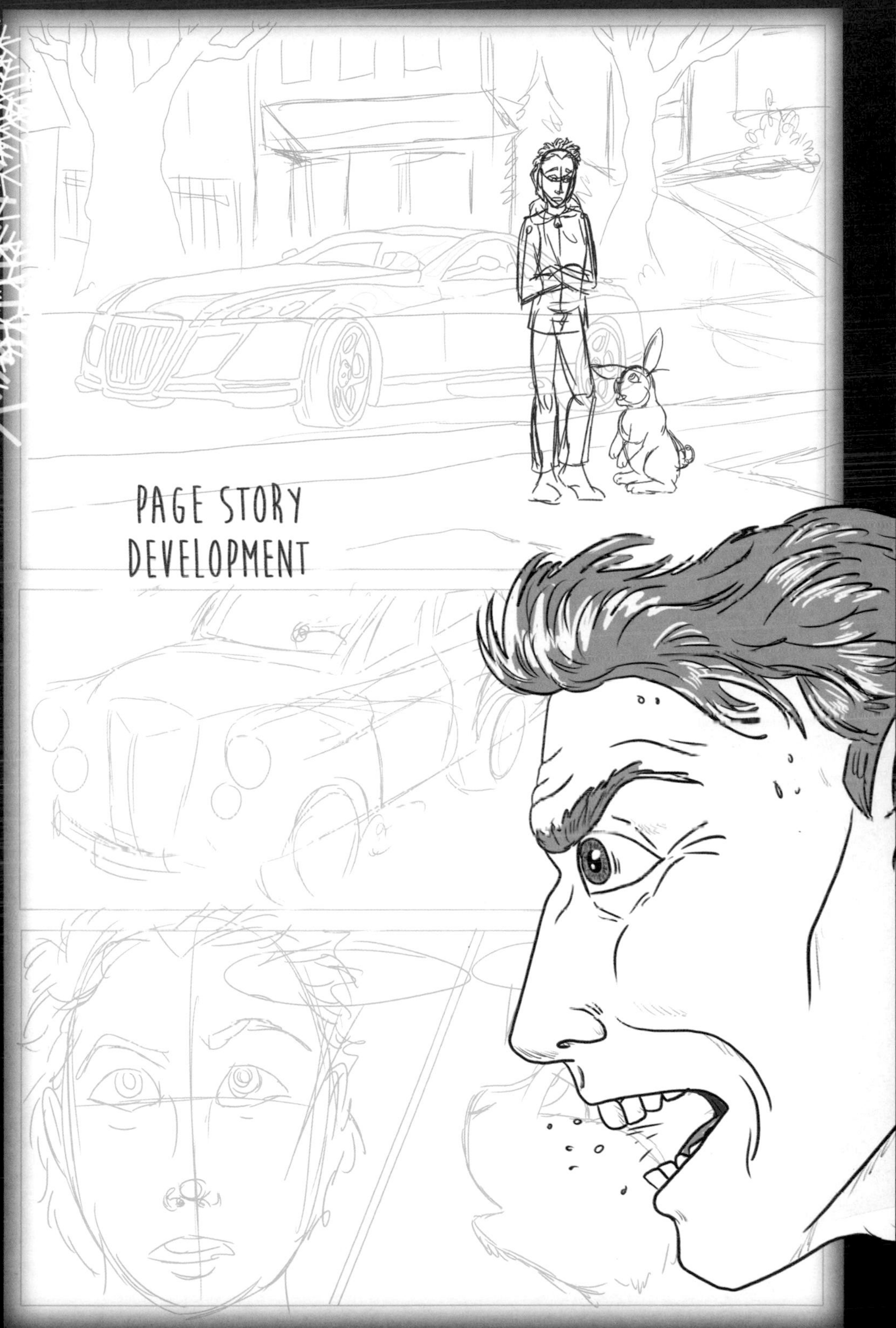

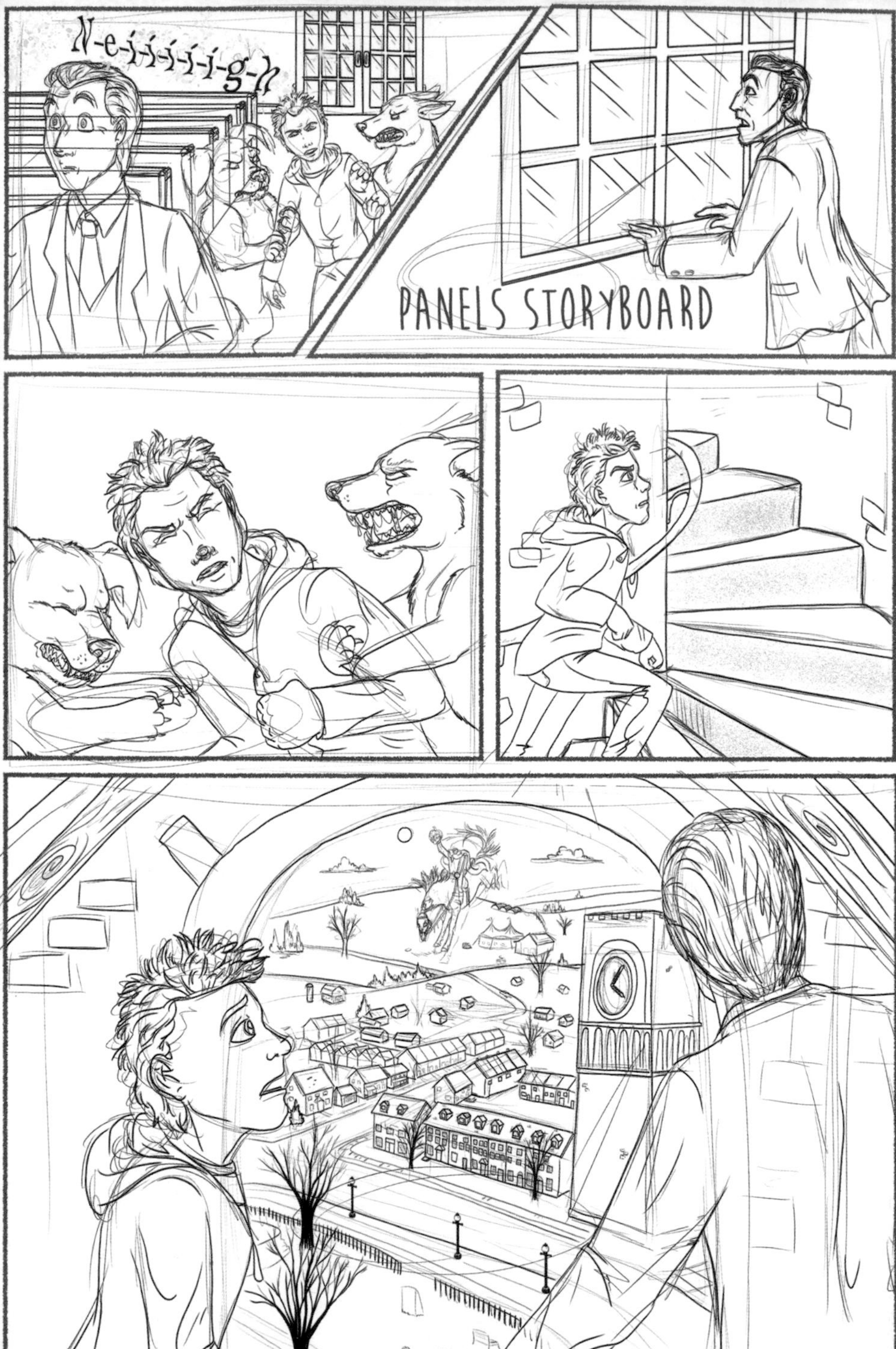
N-e-i-i-i-i-i-g-h
PANELS STORYBOARD

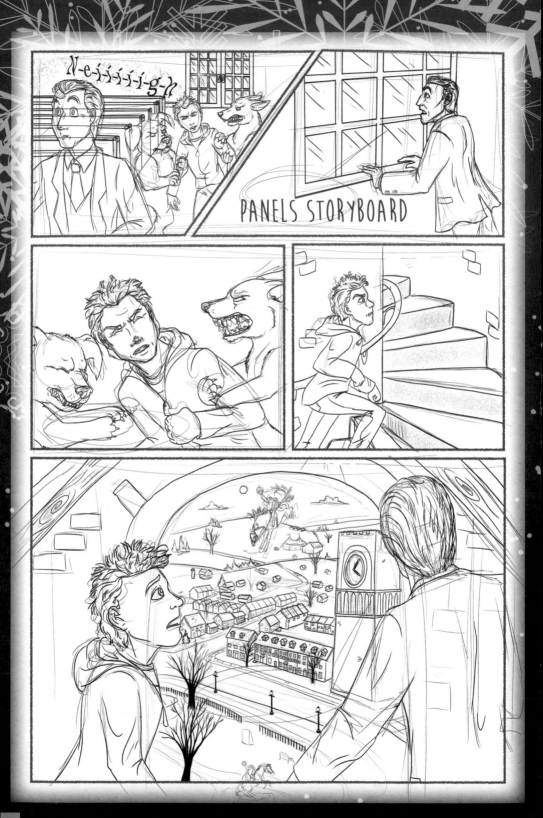

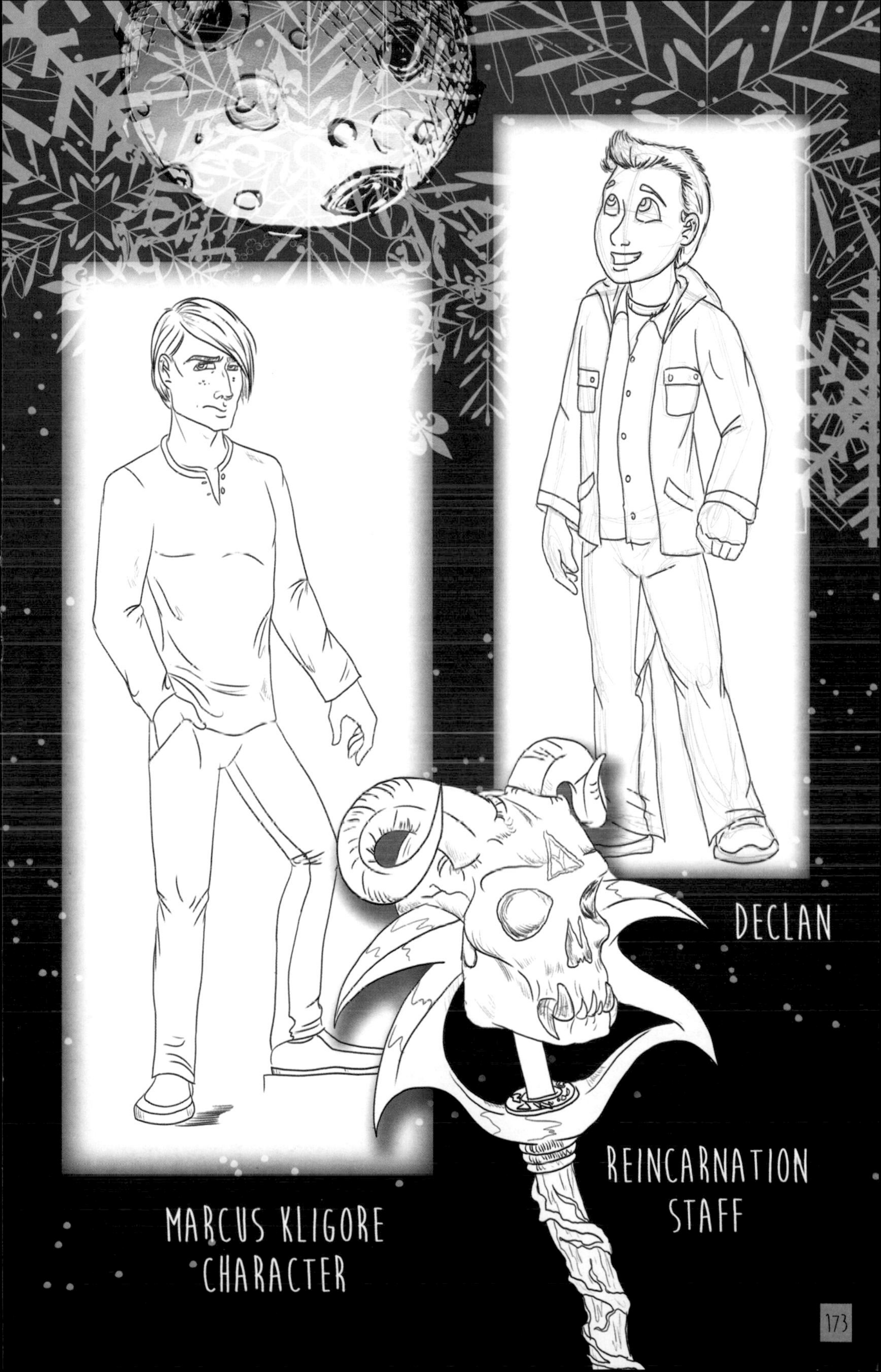
DECLAN
REINCARNATION STAFF
MARCUS KLIGORE CHARACTER

PAGE PLANNING

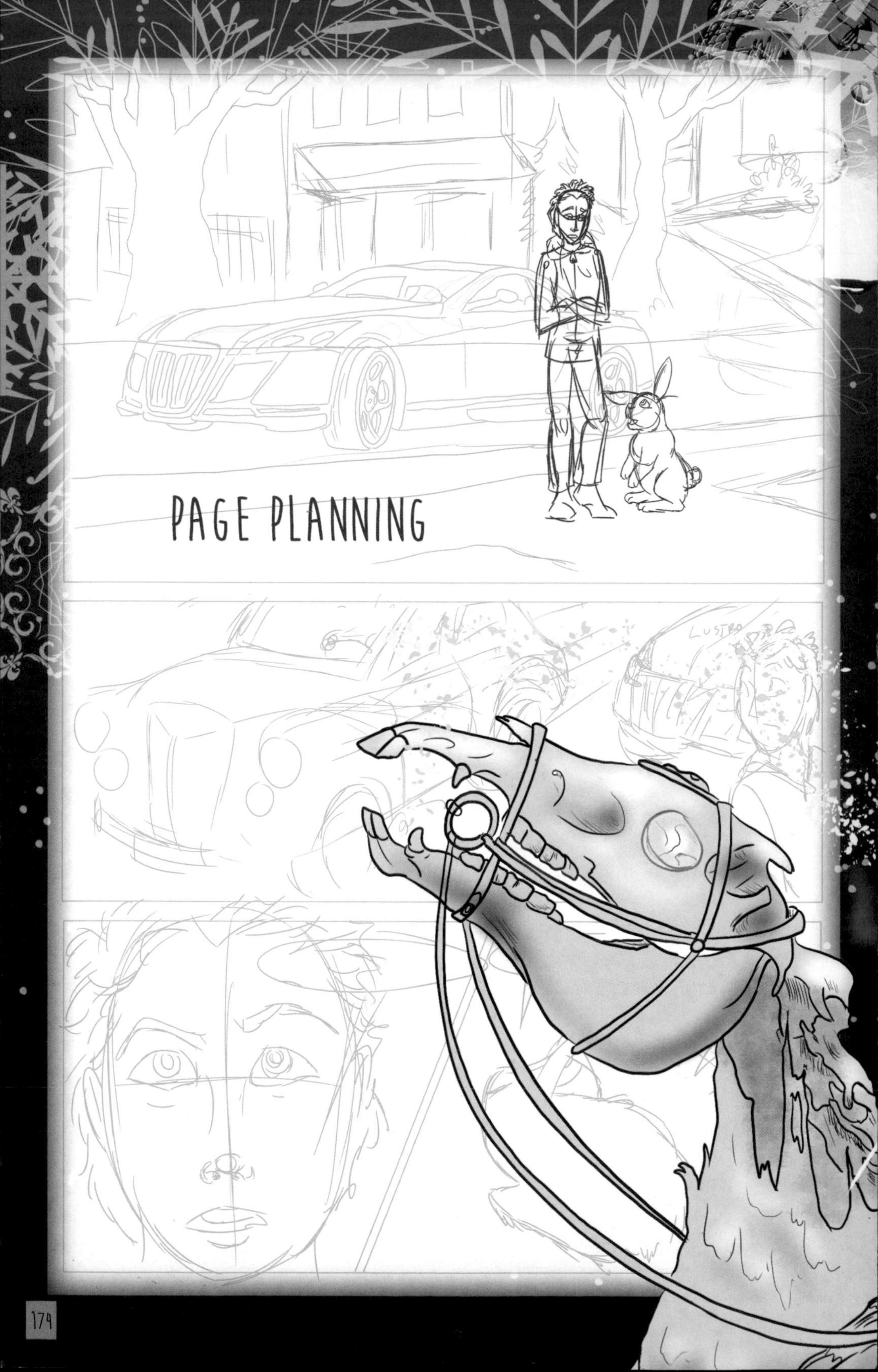
LUSTRO

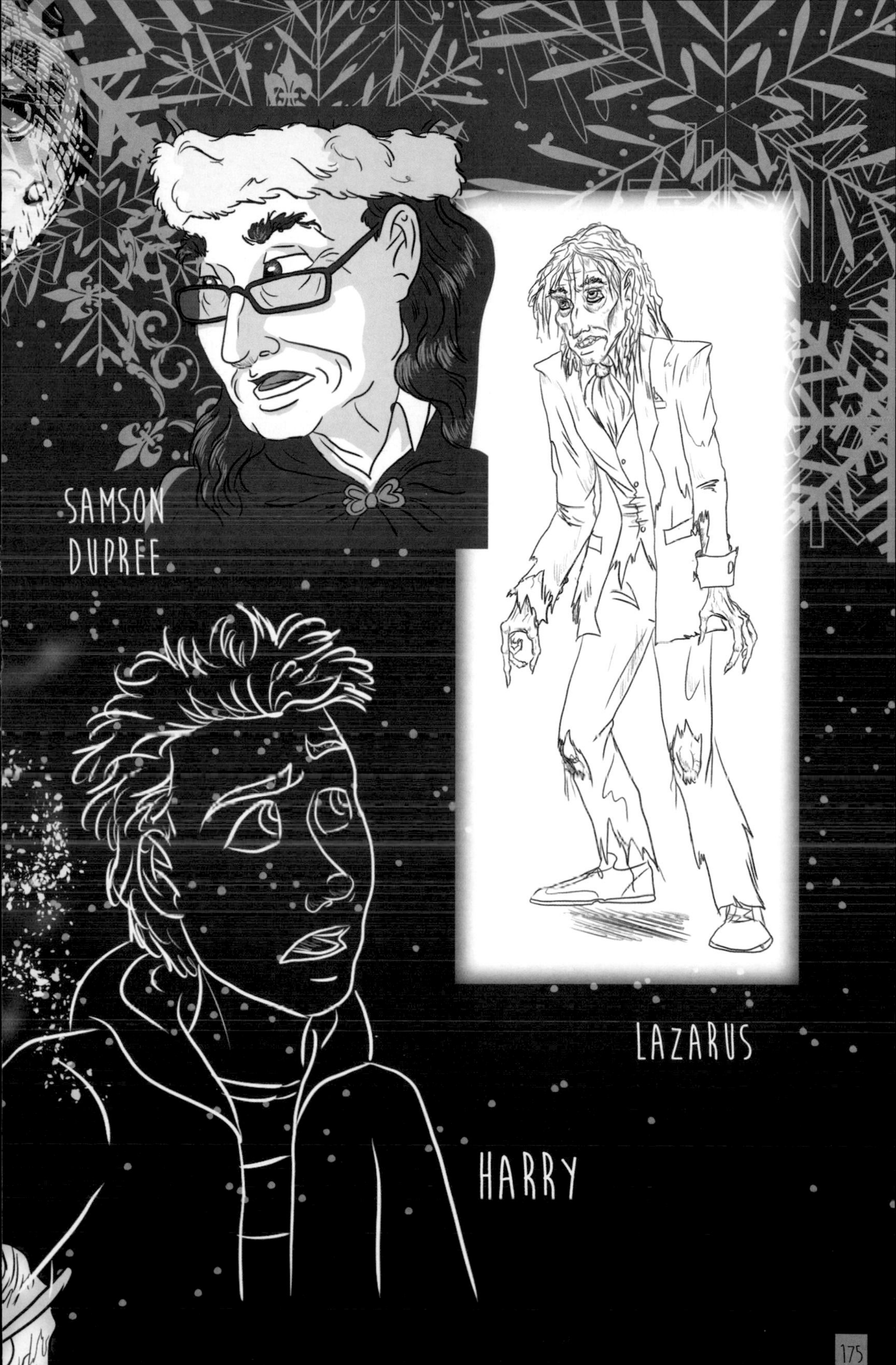
SAMSON
DUPREE
LAZARUS
HARRY

HARRY'S BATTLES CONTINUE . . .

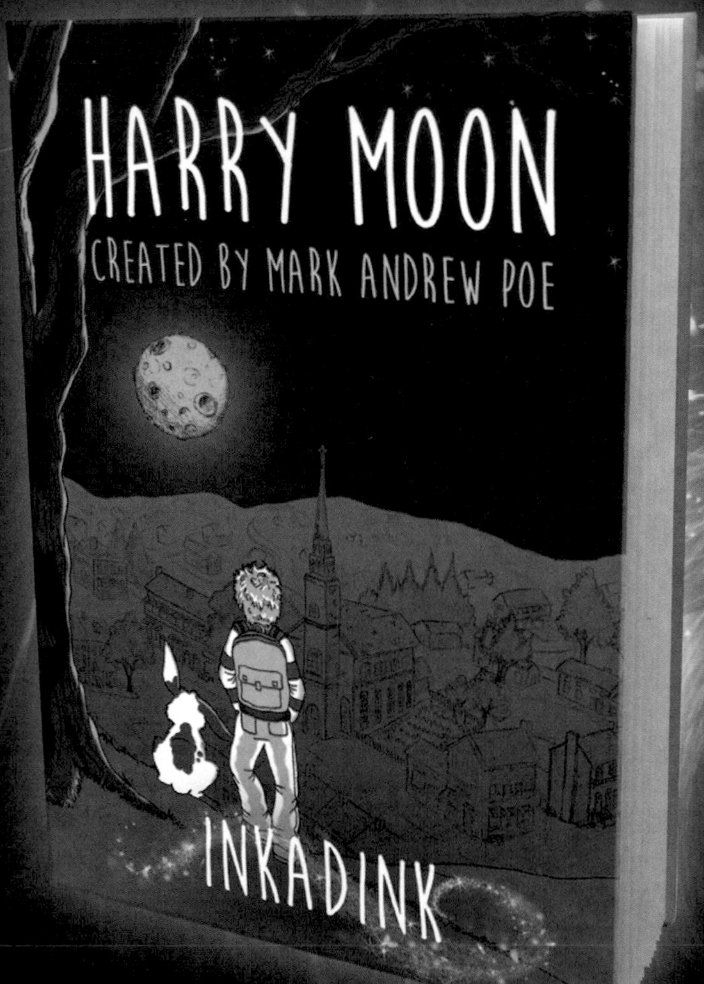
HARRY MOON
CREATED BY MARK ANDREW POE
INKADINK

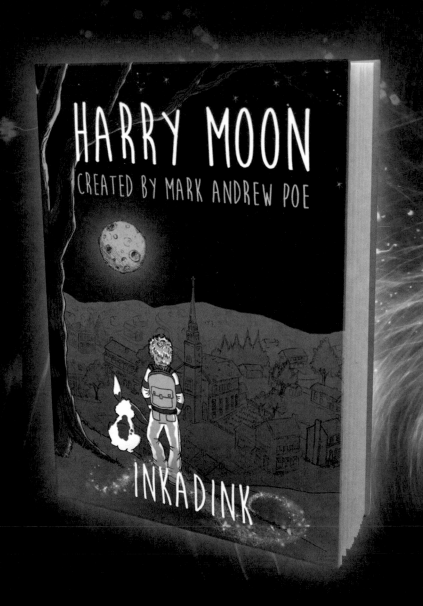

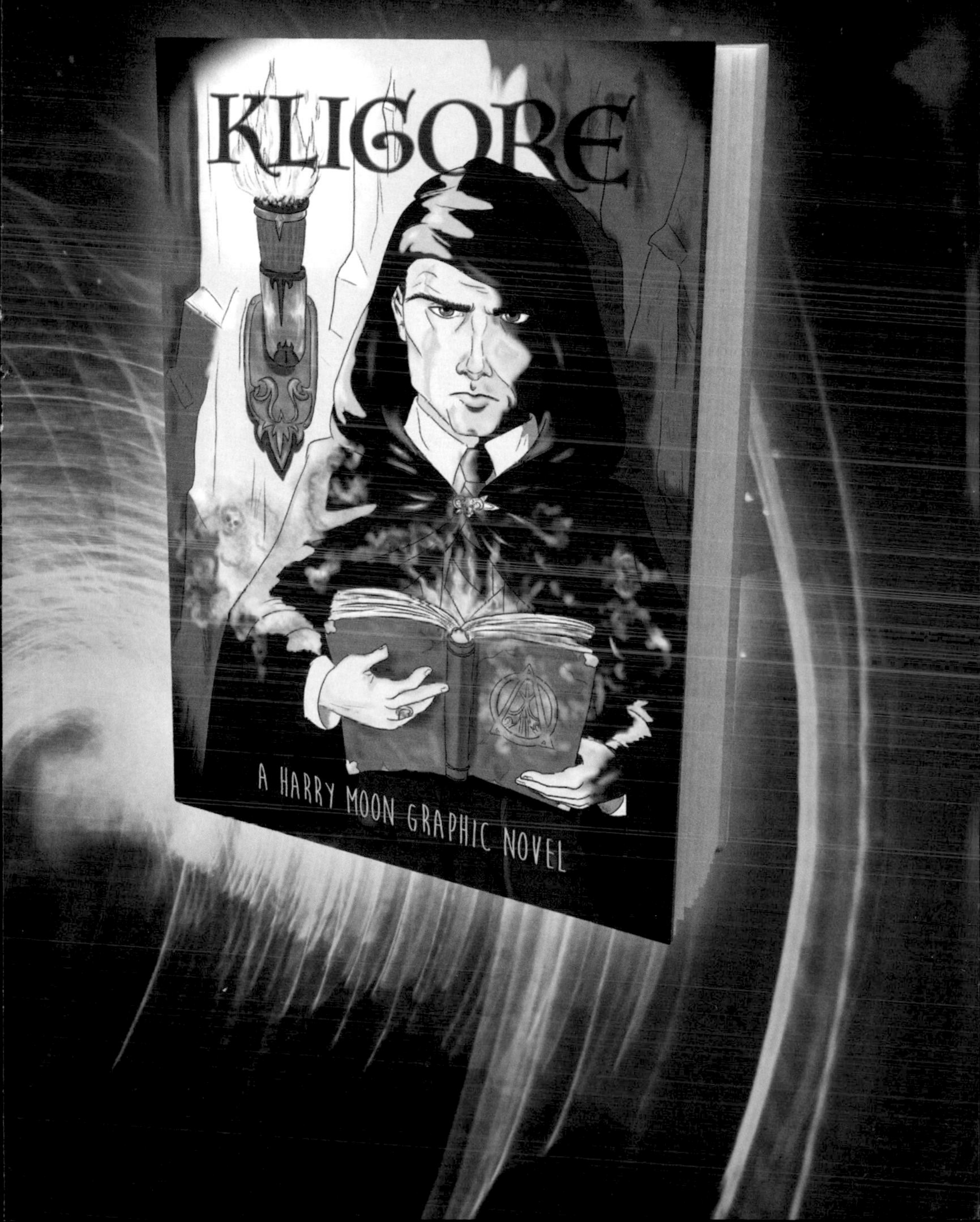
KLIGORE
A HARRY MOON GRAPHIC NOVEL